Navigating Leadership and Policy Management in Education

Bolapeju Mary Agboola
The University of the West Indies, Mona, Jamaica

Canute S. Thompson
The University of the West Indies, Mona, Jamaica

IGI Global
Publishing Tomorrow's Research Today

Published in the United States of America by
IGI Global
701 E. Chocolate Avenue
Hershey PA, USA 17033
Tel: 717-533-8845
Fax: 717-533-8661
E-mail: cust@igi-global.com
Web site: https://www.igi-global.com

Library of Congress Cataloging-in-Publication Data

CIP PENDING

ISBN13: 9798369392157
Isbn13Softcover: 9798369392164
EISBN13: 9798369392171

Vice President of Editorial: Melissa Wagner
Managing Editor of Acquisitions: Mikaela Felty
Managing Editor of Book Development: Jocelynn Hessler
Production Manager: Mike Brehm
Cover Design: Phillip Shickler

British Cataloguing in Publication Data
A Cataloguing in Publication record for this book is available from the British Library.

All work contributed to this book is new, previously-unpublished material.
The views expressed in this book are those of the authors, but not necessarily of the publisher.

To all the Great Leaders, Managers, Educators,
Planners, Policymakers. Practitioners and Students Who Inspire Us to Write
this Book

Editorial Advisory Board

Table of Contents

Detailed Table of Contents

Chapter 1
Ensuring STEM Teacher Quality to Meet the Demands of the Caribbean
Labor Market Beyond the 21st Century 1

Debbie Devonish, University of Technology, Jamaica
Sadpha Bennett, Ministry of Education and Youth, Jamaica
Kavelle Hylton, STEM Builders Learning Hub Limited, Jamaica
Juanita King, Ministry of Education and National Reconciliation, Saint
*   Vincent and the Grenadines*
Donna Barrett, Metropolitan Regional Educational Services Agency,
*   USA*

This chapter examines the evolving STEM (Science, Technology, Engineering, and Mathematics) landscape in the Caribbean, focusing on opportunities, challenges, and strategies for improving teacher quality. It proposes a robust framework for effective STEM teacher training, drawing on case studies from Jamaica, St. Vincent and the Grenadines, and the state of Georgia in the US. It addresses critical areas like future-oriented education, professional development, regional planning, recruitment and retention, diversity, peer teaching, collaboration with Higher Education Institutions (HEIs), and government policy support. The analysis highlights pockets of excellence and innovations but emphasizes the need for a robust framework for effective STEM teacher training. It calls for investment in capital, collaboration with Higher Education Institutions (HEIs), and a unified understanding of STEM. This approach aims to benefit Caribbean students, teachers, and the region while contributing to the achievement of Sustainable Development Goals (SDGs).

Chapter 2

Vikash Singh, Department of Civil Engineering, Integral University,
Lucknow, India
Ashay Devidas Shende, Department of Civil Engineering, K.D.K.
College of Engineering, Nagpur, India
Prakash Dhopte, Department of Mechanical Engineering, Jhulelal
Institute of Technology, Maharashtra, India
Anwar Ahmad, Department of Civil Engineering, Integral University,
Lucknow, India
R. Jeyalakshmi, Department of English, R.M.K. Engineering College,
Kavaraipettai, India
M. Sudhakar, Department of Mechanical Engineering, Sri Sai Ram
Engineering College, Chennai, India

An essential component of engineering education is national board accreditation, which guarantees the caliber and applicability of curricula. It results in better curriculum that meet industry demands and get students ready for careers in engineering. Initiatives aimed at developing faculty members can help accredited programs by resulting in improved instructional strategies and scholarly direction. Infrastructure and educational resource investments are necessary for accreditation in order to create a supportive learning environment for student achievement. Because of their perceived quality and rigor, graduates from certified schools are more employable and competitive in the labor market. Programs that satisfy national board requirements are better accepted by professionals and organizations, which leads to greater industry-academic connections and improved internship chances. Accredited schools also promote easier transfers to postgraduate study.

Chapter 3

Muhammad Usman Tariq, Abu Dhabi University, UAE & University of Glasgow, UK

This chapter seeks to broaden the scope of computational thinking beyond its traditional boundaries within the disciplines of Science, Technology, Engineering, and Mathematics (STEM). It aims to dispel the prevailing misconception that computational thinking is limited to computer science and digital technology and highlights its applicability in non-STEM fields such as literature, history, art, and social sciences. In the current educational climate that emphasises interdisciplinary approaches, this chapter endeavours to demonstrate the relevance of computational thinking in transcending the conventional confines of these disciplines. The importance of elucidating the fundamental principles of computational thinking has become apparent as we explore its intricate facets. It is essential to understand that computational thinking extends beyond coding and programming to encompass a range of skills including logical analysis, pattern recognition, algorithmic reasoning, and reflection.

Chapter 4

Urmila Yadav, Sharda School of Law, Sharda University, Greater Noida, India

R. Pitchai, Department of Computer Science and Engineering, B.V. Raju Institute of Technology, Telangana, India

V. Gopal, Department of Mechanical Engineering, KCG College of Technology, Karappakkam, India

K. R. Senthil Kumar, Department of Mechanical Engineering, R.M.K. College of Engineering and Technology, Puduvoyal, India

Mitali Talukdar, Amity Business School, Amity University, Kolkata, India

Sampath Boopathi, Department of Mechanical Engineering, Muthyammal Engineering College, Namakkal, India

Higher education leadership requires adept navigation of intricate policy and management landscapes to ensure institutional success and sustainability. Academic leaders must balance internal governance with compliance to external regulations while fostering environments conducive to academic excellence, innovation, and inclusivity. This paper explores the pivotal roles and responsibilities of higher education leaders, emphasizing strategic planning, stakeholder engagement, financial management, and policy implementation. Through examining case studies and current trends, the paper provides insights into effective leadership practices that drive institutional growth. It addresses challenges such as funding, regulatory compliance, and evolving educational demands, offering strategies for leaders to manage these complexities. The findings highlight the importance of adaptive leadership, collaborative decision-making, and proactive policy management in navigating the dynamic higher education sector.

This chapter investigated academics' perceptions of migration and attrition rates in Jamaican and Nigerian universities using mixed methods. Data on attrition were generated using a checklist and academics' perceptions data were obtained with an open-ended questionnaire survey while ensuring confidentiality of the participant's identity and information. Data were analysed with inferential statistics and thematic analysis. The results revealed that academic attrition rates of lecturers and below were higher than senior lecturers and professors, with males higher than females. Job status, organizational factors, and weak retention policy statistically significantly influence attrition and migration decisions. In conclusion, differences exist among academic attrition rates, consequently, the researcher's strategic retention management model identifies factors that induce migration/attrition and their implications for leadership reimagination and the development of retention policies and proactive support practices to manage academics.

Chapter 6

This chapter examines the connections between leadership strategies and enhanced student achievement at higher education institutions. As pressures grow around outcomes, affordability and inclusion, effective leadership has become key to accelerating reforms focused on student success, including increased retention, progression, degree completion and career readiness. Theories explored include transformational, distributed and culturally responsive models. Competencies for contemporary contexts cover cultural competence, change leadership, talent development and data literacy. Examples of successful initiatives promoted include predictive analytics, transition programs, pathway redesigns, early intervention systems and student-centric cultures. Vision, community-building, resource optimization and change management provide frameworks to facilitate progress despite complexity. Findings synthesize scholarship and practice into recommendations translating leadership capabilities to institutional environments enabling all students to thrive.

Chapter 7
Athanasios Tsarkos, Aegean University, Greece

This chapter delves into the transformative potential of Servant Leadership in advancing school effectiveness, exploring its theoretical underpinnings and practical implications within educational settings. By prioritizing empathy, inclusivity, and ethical governance, Servant Leadership fosters environments conducive to the holistic development of students and educators alike. Through a nuanced analysis of relational dynamics, professional development, and organizational health, the text offers insights into overcoming implementation challenges and underscores the model's capacity to navigate the complexities of contemporary education. Looking ahead, it posits a future where Servant Leadership principles guide institutions towards societal contributions, highlighting its role in cultivating a generation of ethical, engaged citizens.

Chapter 8
Mandu Umoren, University of Uyo, Nigeria

This paper explored the forms of individual and collective leadership roles in a collaborative network of professional and non-professional co-producers of university brand features. It was discovered that the three identified broad phases in the co-production of brand features (preparation, execution, evaluation/implementation) represent collective activities with implied opportunities for the exercising of collective and individual leadership roles in formal and informal capacities. The paper concluded that the co-production approach to institutional branding can reduce the seeming feeling of marginalisation among university students.

Based on the research that has been employed in Malaysia, caring leadership has proven a significant relationship with attitudes towards the teaching profession. As a result, a model of relationship between caring leadership and attitude towards the teaching profession in higher education settings suggests the implementation of this model for future caring leaders. This chapter has proposed eleven steps taken to enhance the caring leadership capacity of existing and future caring leaders in caring leadership practices. Grounded from the implementation of caring using examples, networking, professional development, advocating leadership policy, and also measurement, this chapter offers insight into improving caring leadership among existing leaders and future generations of leaders. All of these steps are taken to solve the issue of caring leadership and teacher retention. Therefore, this chapter is not only to improve leadership but also to cultivate caring future leaders in facing the challenging educational world.

Chapter 10

It has been highlighted that a lot of our political leaders and various CEO were all a part of some form of student leadership through their sojourn at the U.W.I. This factors has always been an area for higher education institutions, it is also important to determine how students perceive the leadership development programs from which they are meant to benefit. The study is grounded in the Kolbs, 2015 Experimental learning theory. This posits that we all have the ability to become a leader with different experiences and these experiences impact how we deal with challenges and opportunities to become who we are as professionals and leaders. The researchers embarked on an exploratory qualitative assessment where they utilized past students who were once enrolled in the guild to facilitate interviews. The study used a phenomenological methodological approach in assessing the experiences of these students and assessing these various factors with regard to their personal development.

*A. Dinesh, Department of Communication, Siva Sivani Institute of
Management, Hyderabad, India*

*Shantanu Shandilya, Department of Languages, Vellore Institute of
Technology, India*

*Dhara Vinod Parmar, Department of Design and Merchandising, Parul
Institute of Design, Parul University, Waghodia, India*

*P. Sundharesalingam, Department of MBA, Kongu Engineering College,
Perundurai, India*

*Somu Chinnusamy, Research and Development, RSP Science Hub,
Coimbatore, India*

Higher education leadership is confronted with numerous challenges in the contemporary landscape, requiring innovative solutions to ensure institutional effectiveness and student success. This paper explores the multifaceted nature of directing leadership in higher education, examining challenges such as financial pressures, demographic shifts, technological advancements, and the imperative for diversity and inclusion. Solutions encompass strategic approaches to financial sustainability, embracing technological change, promoting diversity and equity, enhancing student success and well-being, and fostering collaborative partnerships. By addressing these challenges and implementing proactive solutions, leaders can navigate the complexities of higher education effectively, driving institutional growth, innovation, and positive outcomes for students, faculty, and stakeholders.

Preface

The intersection of policy, leadership, and management has become increasingly critical in the ever-evolving landscape of global education. As editors of *Navigating Leadership and Policy Management in Education*, Bolapeju Agboola and Canute Thompson are honored to present a compendium that delves into these vital dimensions of educational development. This volume emerges from a pressing need to bridge gaps identified between the United Nations Vision 2030 targets, specifically Goals 4 and 5, and the practical realities of educational planning and management.

Vision 2030, a global initiative launched by the United Nations in 1992, aims to foster sustainable development across all sectors. Notably, it highlights the crucial role of education in this endeavor, emphasizing the necessity for integrated planning, leadership, and management to achieve effective policy outcomes. The recent COVID-19 pandemic has exacerbated challenges, disrupting development plans and shedding light on critical gaps in our educational systems. This disruption has underscored the need for more robust planning tools and strategies to navigate the complexities of policy implementation and educational leadership.

Research and literature have consistently highlighted the difficulties in translating educational policy into effective practice. Scholars such as Caillods (2015), Akpan (2011), and Burns, Fuster & Köster (2016) have linked these challenges to inadequate implementation frameworks, insufficient change processes, and ineffective strategic leadership. Moreover, recent studies by Hassan & Alosani (2022) and Bush (2018) point to the necessity for improved planning tools and strategies to address these weaknesses.

In response to these needs, this book aims to provide a comprehensive resource that bridges theoretical knowledge and practical application. It is designed to assist policymakers, educational planners, administrators, and scholars in understanding and applying planning tools that can effectively shape educational policy and management. The goal is to support better data utilization, promote collaboration, and foster skills development among education professionals.

Our volume offers a wide range of insights and practical tools across several key areas:

1. **Technology and the Educational System**: Exploring the role of digital technology in transforming education, from ICTs and AI to online education and data technology.
2. **Planning and the Education System**: Addressing school mapping, equity, climate change, financial planning, and curriculum development.
3. **Educational Sustainability**: Providing models for efficiency, skills transition, and strategies for sustainability in education.
4. **Policy in the Educational System**: Examining the socio-political dimensions, governance, transparency, and policy development.
5. **Educational Leadership and Management**: Focused on leadership quality, school effectiveness, and capacity building in a global education context.

Each chapter is meticulously crafted to provide a blend of theoretical foundations and practical applications, ensuring that readers can translate concepts into actionable strategies. We have included contributions from a diverse array of experts, drawing from multiple disciplines to offer a holistic perspective on educational planning and management.

We envision this book as a practical manual and a reference guide for a broad audience, including educational leaders, government agencies, planners, and researchers. We hope that it will not only inform but also inspire meaningful improvements in educational systems worldwide.

As you delve into the pages of this book, we invite you to explore the varied perspectives and tools presented and to apply them in your own contexts to drive progress in educational policy, leadership, and management.

Chapter 1 is on ensuring STEM teacher quality meets the demands of the Caribbean labor market beyond the 21st Century with a focus on the evolving STEM (Science, Technology, Engineering, and Mathematics), the opportunities, challenges, and strategies for improving teacher quality in the Caribbean. It proposes a robust framework for effective STEM teacher training, drawing on case studies from Jamaica, St. Vincent and the Grenadines, and the state of Georgia in the US to address critical areas like future-oriented education, professional development, regional planning, recruitment and retention, diversity, peer teaching, collaboration with Higher Education Institutions (HEIs), and government policy support.

Chapter 2 is about national board accreditation as an essential component of engineering education which guarantees the calibre and applicability of curricula that meet industry demands and get students ready for careers in engineering. The initiatives should aimed at developing faculty members who can help accredited programs by resulting in improved instructional strategies and scholarly direction while infrastructure and educational resource investments are necessary for accreditation to create a supportive learning environment for student achievement.

Chapter 3 broadens the scope of computational thinking beyond its traditional boundaries within the disciplines of Science, Technology, Engineering, and Mathematics (STEM) intending to dispel the prevailing misconception that computational thinking is limited to computer science and digital technology and highlights its applicability in non-STEM fields such as literature, history, art, and social sciences. Elucidating the fundamental principles of computational thinking has become apparent when exploring its intricate facets.

Chapter 4 explores the pivotal roles and responsibilities of higher education leaders, emphasizing strategic planning, stakeholder engagement, financial management, and policy implementation. Through examining case studies and current trends, the chapter provides insights into effective leadership practices that drive institutional growth, examining case studies and current trends, the paper provides insights into effective leadership practices that drive institutional growth.

Chapter 5 is about the strategic retention management approach to academic migration and attrition with policy implications and educational leadership reimagined investigating academics' perceptions of migration and attrition rates in Jamaican and Nigerian universities using explanatory and sequential mixed methods. From inferential statistics and thematic analysis, the strategic retention management model was developed to address identifies factors that induce migration/attrition and their implications for leadership reimagination and the development of retention policies and proactive support practices to manage academics.

Chapter 6 examines the connections between leadership strategies and enhanced student achievement at higher education institutions. In the context of pressures growing around outcomes, affordability, and inclusion, effective leadership has become key to accelerating reforms focused on student success, increased retention, progression, degree completion, and career readiness. Theories and models were explored, and competencies for contemporary contexts cover areas to translating leadership capabilities to institutional environments enabling all students to thrive.

Chapter 7 delves into the transformative potential of Servant Leadership in advancing school effectiveness, exploring its theoretical underpinnings and practical implications within educational settings. By prioritizing empathy, inclusivity, and ethical governance, Servant Leadership fosters environments conducive to the holistic development of students and educators alike. Through a nuanced analysis of relational dynamics, professional development, and organizational health, the text offers insights into overcoming implementation challenges and underscores the model's capacity to navigate the complexities of contemporary education

Chapter 8 on leadership's role in students' co-production of university brand features explored the forms of individual and collective leadership roles in a collaborative network of professional and non-professional co-producers of university brand features. Three broad phases in the co-production of brand features (preparation, execution, evaluation/implementation) represent collective activities with implied opportunities for the exercising of collective and individual leadership roles in formal and informal capacities. The co-production approach to institutional branding can reduce the seeming feeling of marginalisation among university students

Chapter 9 proposed several steps to enhance the caring leadership capacity of existing and future caring leaders in caring leadership practices. Using leader capacity improvement, professional training, changing policy assessments, leadership curriculum development, promotion and awareness, and reflection and improvement, this course offers insignia in developing caring leadership. The chapter also proposes steps that can be considered to improve caring leadership and attitude towards the teaching profession, not only for existing leaders but also to cultivate caring future leaders in facing the challenging educational world.

Chapter 10 about Student Involvement in Leadership Programmes at The U.W.I., Mona, and the Impact They Have On Their Personal and Professional Development determines how students perceive the leadership development programs from which they are meant to benefit exploring Kolb's, 2015 experimental learning theory that posited that we all can become a leader with different experiences and these experiences impact how we deal with challenges and opportunities to become who we are as professionals and leaders.

Finally, **chapter 11,** a study on the powers of higher education leadership and solutions for challenges explores the multifaceted nature of directing leadership in higher education, examining challenges such as financial pressures, demographic shifts, technological advancements, and the imperative for diversity and inclusion. Solutions encompass strategic approaches to financial sustainability, embracing technological change, promoting diversity and equity, enhancing student success and well-being, and fostering collaborative partnerships. By addressing these challenges and implementing proactive solutions, leaders can navigate the complexities of higher education effectively, driving institutional growth, innovation, and positive outcomes for students, faculty, and stakeholders.

As we conclude this preface for *Navigating Leadership and Policy Management in Education*, it is clear that the intersection of policy, leadership, and management in education is both intricate and essential for fostering progress. This volume stands as a testament to the collective expertise and innovative thinking of our contributors, each chapter meticulously addressing critical aspects of educational development in response to current challenges and future needs.

The chapters presented offer a rich tapestry of insights and strategies designed to bridge the gap between theoretical frameworks and practical applications. From enhancing STEM teacher quality in the Caribbean to exploring national board accreditation in engineering, and from broadening computational thinking across disciplines to examining strategic retention management, each contribution is crafted to provide actionable tools and relevant perspectives.

In delving into topics such as the transformative potential of Servant Leadership, the role of leadership in co-producing university brand features, and the nurturing of caring leadership practices, we highlight the diverse approaches necessary for effective educational management. The exploration of leadership strategies for student achievement and the impact of student involvement in leadership programs further underscores the multifaceted nature of educational leadership.

As educational leaders, policymakers, and practitioners engaged with this book, we hope they find the guidance and inspiration needed to navigate the complexities of their roles. By integrating the knowledge and tools offered within these pages, stakeholders can better address the evolving demands of the educational landscape, driving meaningful improvements and fostering sustainable development.

We are confident that this volume will serve as both a practical manual and a source of inspiration, guiding readers through the nuances of policy, leadership, and management in education. Our aspiration is that it will not only inform but also empower individuals to lead with vision and purpose, ultimately contributing to the advancement of educational systems worldwide.

Editors:

Bolapeju Mary Agboola

The University of the West Indies, Mona, Jamaica

Canute Thompson

The University of the West Indies, Mona, Jamaica

Acknowledgment

Our heartfelt appreciation goes to the leadership of the University of the West Indies, the Faculty of Humanities and Education, and the School of Education for providing the enabling environment for us to embark on this book project.

We thank our colleagues, and practitioners who have charted a new course in their efforts to make knowledge readily available and accessible through the publication of reading materials.

We acknowledge our esteemed graduate students at the University of the West Indies, Jamaica, and the University of Uyo, Nigeria who inspired us through our interaction.

We appreciate those persons who helped us to disseminate information about this book far and wide.

We sincerely appreciate the support of the esteemed team of IGI Global, and all who have contributed in one way or the other to the completion of this book.

Finally, our thanks go to God Almighty who provided the insight and strength to make the publication of this book to become a reality.

Chapter 1
Ensuring STEM Teacher Quality to Meet the Demands of the Caribbean Labor Market Beyond the 21st Century

Debbie Devonish
University of Technology, Jamaica

Sadpha Bennett
Ministry of Education and Youth, Jamaica

Kavelle Hylton
STEM Builders Learning Hub Limited, Jamaica

Juanita King
Ministry of Education and National Reconciliation, Saint Vincent and the Grenadines

Donna Barrett
https://orcid.org/0000-0003-0763-2599
Metropolitan Regional Educational Services Agency, USA

ABSTRACT

This chapter examines the evolving STEM (Science, Technology, Engineering, and Mathematics) landscape in the Caribbean, focusing on opportunities, challenges, and strategies for improving teacher quality. It proposes a robust framework for

DOI: 10.4018/979-8-3693-9215-7.ch001

effective STEM teacher training, drawing on case studies from Jamaica, St. Vincent and the Grenadines, and the state of Georgia in the US. It addresses critical areas like future-oriented education, professional development, regional planning, recruitment and retention, diversity, peer teaching, collaboration with Higher Education Institutions (HEIs), and government policy support. The analysis highlights pockets of excellence and innovations but emphasizes the need for a robust framework for effective STEM teacher training. It calls for investment in capital, collaboration with Higher Education Institutions (HEIs), and a unified understanding of STEM. This approach aims to benefit Caribbean students, teachers, and the region while contributing to the achievement of Sustainable Development Goals (SDGs).

INTRODUCTION

The Industrial Revolutions have transformed the global labor market, culminating in a technology-driven economy demanding advanced skills (The Future Jobs, 2023). STEM fields are at the epicenter of this change, driving innovation but also creating a skills gap. To bridge this divide, robust K-12 STEM education is essential. This foundation will equip students with the competencies to excel in STEM fields and collaborate across disciplines to tackle complex challenges.

Considering training in the Caribbean, Jamaica's developing STEM framework prioritizes STEM career training, particularly in engineering, IT outsourcing, and knowledge processing (JAMPRO, 2021; Henry, 2020; Thorpe, 2023; McKenzie, 2023). "However, it is crucial to establish a robust and integrated STEM education across disciplines, moving beyond the traditional silos of science education as in the Caribbean. While not everyone in the Caribbean will pursue STEM careers, a strong science and technology foundation equips all graduates with a growth mindset and lifelong learning skills. Ultimately, the success of any nation's STEM efforts relies on the quality of education, for both students and educators. While STEM education is gaining traction, the Caribbean educational system historically focused on science teacher training and their characteristics in single science subjects in the region. Importantly, Integrated STEM matters because STEM education equips students with technological literacy, critical thinking, and problem-solving skills crucial for future careers. Granshaw (2016) suggests that STEM education prepares students for "jobs not yet conceptualized…" (p.3) and this requires well-prepared STEM educators to prepare students to navigate unforeseen labor market needs and to collaborate to solve local and global problem.

BACKGROUND TO THE STUDY

Significant effort has been invested in education research within the Caribbean over the decades. STEM education has primarily been approached in isolation within the Caribbean, focusing on individual science disciplines rather than STEM integrated learning (Brathwaite, 1978; Alexander & Glasgow, 1981; Soyibo, 1998; Miller, 2000; Sweeney, 2003). This siloed approach, while foundational, requires the development towards a holistic STEM education model essential for the 21st century workforce (Sanghoon, 2018; Ghafar, 2020; Kim et al., 2023). To cultivate a future-ready population capable of addressing complex global challenges, a robust Caribbean STEM curriculum (Griffith, 2024) combined with effective teacher training is imperative.

This chapter explores STEM (Science, Technology, Engineering, and Mathematics) from two perspectives: its interdisciplinary nature (Sweeney & George, 2024) and its potential as a single integrated subject- interdisciplinary and integrated STEM (Kurup, Yang, Dong, 2021). By analyzing case studies from different countries, the chapter will unveil the differences in STEM understandings and practices. The cases will start with the US, where the STEM concept and work in STEM education originated. This will provide a useful context for the examination of other cases to show where they fall in the move towards STEM education. The three cases, in order of presentation, are: STEM education in the USA, with a specific focus on the state of Georgia; Jamaica, with its emerging STEM profile; and St. Vincent and the Grenadines, which is making a bold attempt to engage with STEM education. After considering the comparisons, gaps, and best practices across these cases, the chapter will conclude by suggesting a possible STEM teacher training program framework for consideration in the Caribbean context.

PART 1: UNDERSTANDING THE LABOR MARKET IN THE CARIBBEAN AND THE STEM TEACHER NEED ACROSS JURISDICTIONS

Education is Important for National Growth and Development

Education, in its various forms – formal, informal, and nonformal – plays a critical role in fostering growth and development of people. Human Capital Theory suggests that investment in education directly promotes productivity and powering knowledge drive economies (Becker, 2009; Aslam, 2020). Consequently, nations with higher education levels are likely to experience faster economic growth. Regardless of their development status, all nations strive to achieve the Sustainable

Development Goals. SDG 4 emphasizes the importance of quality education in driving better economic and social outcomes (United Nations, 2015). By facilitating the development of a skilled workforce through formal education, encouraging innovation and creativity through informal and non-formal channels, and nurturing an informed citizenry, education empowers nations to achieve stronger economic progress and social well-being.

Higher Education (HE) and the Labor Market Mismatch: A Pressing Challenge

The growing number of graduates entering the workforce has exposed a critical misalignment between Higher Education (HE) and labor market needs. Traditionally, higher education guaranteed better jobs, but this is no longer the case (Anft, 2013). One challenge is an oversupply of graduates in specific fields, leading to competition for jobs traditionally held by those with lower education levels (Lauder & Mayhew, 2020), such as secretarial or desk clerk positions. This mismatch can be observed in countries like Spain and the US, not just the Caribbean and suggests HE may not be equipping graduates with the skills and knowledge demanded by the evolving job market. Another concern is the potential erosion of vocational education. While robust vocational systems offer valuable alternatives (de Bruijn et al., 2017), their appeal may diminish as more pursue HE degrees. Germany's dual system, aiming to bridge vocational and academic tracks, highlights the difficulty in balancing these paths (Fürstenau et al., 2014).

To address this challenge of vocational versus university training and its graduate workforce outcome, a well-functioning HE system requires well-trained faculty to impart relevant skills to future workers. Continuous evaluation and improvement of HE curricula and teacher training pedagogy are crucial for alignment with labor market needs. A key question remains: Are tertiary institutions successfully transforming their systems (JIS, July 31, 2018), and particularly in STEM teacher training? Who will drive effective STEM implementation for students to meet this 21st century labor market if there exists this misalignment?

The Caribbean's Unnoticed Quality Training Strategy: Collaboration and Trainers

Since the 1950's, the Caribbean has fostered a collaborative approach to teacher training, with islands like Barbados supporting neighbors Grenada, St. Lucia, Montserrat, Dominica and Tortola. Despite this collaboration, research suggests a gap between policy and practice. Teacher training often focuses on curriculum guides, neglecting crucial areas like technology and support for struggling learners (Jennings, 2001). This highlights the need for training that addresses practical classroom realities and social-economic factors to which STEM education includes.

An often-overlooked strategy for quality training lies in the trainers themselves (Zacarias, 2021). The Caribbean lacks specialized requirements for teacher educators, leading to professors who may be experts in their fields but not necessarily impactful on future teacher practice (Mark et al., 2005). The mantle of teacher quality may very well lie in how they are trained and by whom (Cohran-Smith, et al., 2020). Focusing on improving teacher education programs is important, but the quality of teacher trainers and the efficacy of the STEM translation from teachers to students when in practice, across the islands deserves greater attention.-

Science and Technology: AI, Block Chain Advancement, Education and the Labor Market

Education 4.0 integrates new technologies (AI, big data, and internet) into learning, aiming to prepare students for the future workforce (Konkol & Dymek, 2023). This requires a significant shift in HE institutions' approach. The Caribbean needs to explore how Education 4.0 technologies can transform HE. Technologies such as Blockchain can support the creation of learning communities for educators to share ideas and track learning experiences across the region. This collaborative approach can be particularly valuable for smaller Caribbean nations with limited resources. To remain relevant and competitive, Caribbean HE institutions must embrace Education 4.0 and leverage its technologies to transform teacher training, curriculum development, and ultimately, prepare graduates for the demands of the evolving job market.

The Alignment and Misalignment with Caribbean Labor Market Needs

The Caribbean's tourism industry, a major employer, prioritizes service skills in training (Peterson, 2020; Walker et al., 2021). Government initiatives like Jamaica's HEART Trust/NSTA Trust subsidize tourism-related training (Salmon, September 1, 2022). However, limited STEM opportunities (e.g., in tech or renewables) and lower salaries compared to developed nations create a situation where skilled STEM graduates often seek opportunities abroad (Gentles, 2020). This brain drain hinders development and across the Caribbean and Latin America, job trends favor STEM skills. Workers with strong cognitive abilities, fostered through STEM education, command higher salaries and are better positioned for the globalized job market (Apella & Zunino, 2022; Xie et al, 2015). This highlights the need for improved STEM education and teacher training in the region.

5

Focusing on HE for the Labor Market and the Dwindling Teacher Interest

HE, Labor Market Mismatch, and Teacher Shortages

While universities are often seen as job tickets, many degrees have limited career relevance and the mismatch between HE and labor market needs can lead to graduate unemployment. Globally, higher education enrollment is projected to increase until 2032 (Smyth, 2024). However, the Caribbean might not see this trend, particularly in STEM teacher training due to a potential teacher shortage which could be exacerbated by capacity constraints in HE institutions, poor teacher working conditions, and low compensation. There have been high perceived levels of teacher attrition from the Caribbean (George, 2020; Gentles, 2020) and in some developed countries. The Caribbean needs to adapt its HE offerings to better align with labor market demands and invest in infrastructure to support quality STEM teacher training (Bowers et al., 2020).

Candidates Pursuing STEM Teacher Training

The preparation of STEM teachers varies globally (further discussed in Section 4 & Table 1). In the Caribbean, teachers hold major-minor science or mostly single option science degrees, limiting their expertise in broader STEM areas. Recent initiatives, like Jamaica's first Master's in STEM Education, aim to address this (Smith, October 25, 2023). However, despite a 100% rate of qualified teachers serving K1-K12/basic –secondary level in, for example Jamaica (UNESCO, Institute of Statistics) with an average of 23,810 educators (STATIN, 2017), attracting educators to STEM fields remains a challenge. This is not unique to the Caribbean (Kennedy et al., 2018), and the lived experiences of science educators in the region deserve exploration (Du Plessis, 2018; Devonish et al., 2018; Hylton, 2022; Soyibo, 1994). Figure 1 highlights these challenges, which can negatively impact both enrollment in STEM programs and the quality of the teaching workforce.

Figure 1. Challenges in STEM Programs

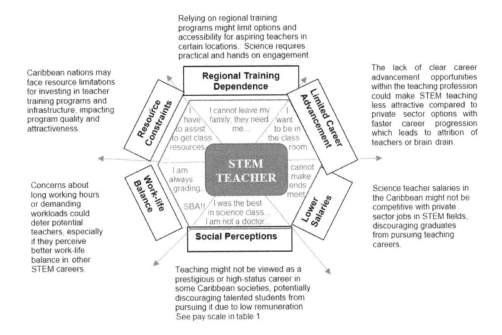

Relying on regional training programs might limit options and accessibility for aspiring teachers in certain locations. Science requires practical and hands on engagement.

The lack of clear career advancement opportunities within the teaching profession could make STEM teaching less attractive compared to private sector options with faster career progression which leads to attrition of teachers or brain drain.

Caribbean nations may face resource limitations for investing in teacher training programs and infrastructure, impacting program quality and attractiveness.

Concerns about long working hours or demanding workloads could deter potential teachers, especially if they perceive better work-life balance in other STEM careers.

Science teacher salaries in the Caribbean might not be competitive with private sector jobs in STEM fields, discouraging graduates from pursuing teaching careers.

Teaching might not be viewed as a prestigious or high-status career in some Caribbean societies, potentially discouraging talented students from pursuing it due to low remuneration See pay scale in table 1.

Regional Training Dependence

Limited Career Advancement

Resource Constraints

Work-life Balance

STEM TEACHER

Lower Salaries

Social Perceptions

I cannot leave my family, they need me...

I have to assist to get class resources

I want to be in the class room.

I am always grading...

cannot make ends meet

SBA!!

I was the best in science class... I am not a doctor.

STEM Frameworks: Guiding Integrated Learning

Frameworks like the Next Generation Science Standards (NGSS) inclusive of STEM, outline learning goals and methods for integrating science, technology, engineering, and mathematics (National Research Council, 2011, 2012). This shift from siloed subjects fosters a more interconnected and real-world learning experience. The concept is evolving, with "convergence education" emerging (A.U.S. Interagency Working Group on Convergence, 2022). This approach emphasizes tackling complex problems by blending knowledge and skills across disciplines; 'transdisciplinary' to create innovative solutions, aligning with the goal of fostering problem-solving skills for real-world challenges through a unified approach (OSTP, 2022).

STEM vs. STEM Education

STEM refers to the scientific and technical knowledge base in Science (Biology, Chemistry, and Physics), Technology, Engineering, and Mathematics, while STEM education focuses on teaching and learning those disciplines (NRC, 2011, 2012). STEM education emphasizes integrated learning approaches to promote interdisciplinary thinking and problem-solving. Frameworks like STEAM or STREAM might add Arts for creativity, or R for religion (Mexico) or Reading, but core scientific content shouldn't be compromised (Clement & Sarama, 2021). In fact, if there is true STEM, the 'A' or 'R' is not necessary. Different regions have their own approaches to STEM education, reflecting efforts to break down educational silos (Kennedy and Odell, 2014). The Caribbean, for example, is reforming its education systems with a focus on integrated STEM education, but the teacher training for STEM as a meta-subject is not currently present. McComas and Burgin (2020) posit a definition for STEM education remains elusive and propose careful consideration when integrating STEM.

STEM-Endorsed Teacher: Growing Recognition

A STEM endorsement is usually an add-on to existing certification. Certification is proof of qualification, while certification is proof of qualification for the employer (Ssebikindu, 2021). The importance of STEM education is prompting organizations to offer training and recognition for STEM teachers. While there's no national certification body in the Caribbean, teachers can seek credentials from private organizations like STEM.org. In the US, there are entities that certify STEM teachers such as Cognia, STEM.org, National Institute for STEM Education (NISE) as well as universities, and state agencies who offer STEM endorsements and certifications.

Methodology

The methodology employed for this research involved a systematic review of academic databases to gather information on effective teacher training and STEM teacher training programs. Recognizing the limited research on science teacher training within the Caribbean's limited STEM ecosystem, we reviewed STEM teacher training in other countries, particularly with the use of case studies. The researchers ask (RQ1) what are the differences in STEM, STEM education, STEM teacher training, the overall STEM Education understandings across jurisdictions and (RQ2) how does it shape our present contexts? Finally, (RQ3) what is the way forward to ensuring teacher quality to meet the demands of the Caribbean labor market beyond the 21st century?

To gain deeper insights, the researchers, STEM educators, trainers, administrators, and Ministry personnel involved in STEM and STEM subject teacher training programs compiled the cases and the comparative table. This comparison helped us unveil STEM contextual and universal understandings and identify gaps in teacher training and potential areas for improvement in Caribbean STEM teacher training programs.

Defining the STEM Educator and Assessing Teacher Quality in STEM Education

Being a STEM teacher is multifaceted, requiring a strong understanding of STEM disciplines, integration skills, and fostering student creativity (Fulton & Britton, 2011). These educators need deep content knowledge, curriculum design, and collaboration skills (Kelley & Knowles, 2016). The ideal profile may vary by region, but effective STEM teachers are adaptable, collaborative, student-centered, and champions of equity (El Nagdi et al., 2018). Their identity is constantly evolving through experiences within the school's STEM environment.

A crucial question in the Caribbean context is the model for STEM teachers. Should it be a single teacher integrating all STEM disciplines, or a team of specialists collaborating on a cohesive curriculum? Both approaches present unique challenges, especially considering the differences between STEM subjects. Current, subject-specific assessments (CSEC and CAPE in the region) hinder STEM integration. Reforming these assessments to promote interdisciplinary learning is necessary (Windschitl, 2009). This would allow Caribbean STEM teachers to explore STEM concepts and activities without the pressure of exam preparation; a characteristic of successful education systems like Finland and New Zealand, where assessments focus on improvement, not high-stakes decisions.

PART 2: CASE STUDIES OF PLANNING FOR STEM TEACHER QUALITY: COMPARING TEACHER TRAINING MODELS AND PERSPECTIVES

STEM education emerged in the mid-20th century to address the growing demand for skilled workers in technical fields. As Xie et al. (2015) highlight, the U.S. economic prowess is closely tied to its scientific and technological advancements. Recognizing the long-term economic benefits of STEM education, policymakers have consistently sought to bolster the field. This culminated in the Obama administration's 'Educate to Innovate' campaign of 2011, which aimed to train 100,000 new STEM teachers. In the United States, a five-year federal strategy for STEM was outlined with three goals: To build strong foundation for STEM literacy; Increase diversity, equity, and inclusion in STEM; and Prepare the STEM workforce for the future. The Committee of STEM Education(CSE, 2018), was an interagency working group including a cross section of both the public and private sector, including members from NASA, Department of Defense, Department of Transportation, NOAA, universities, etc. The strategy set forth continued work in four pathways of cross-cutting approaches for enriching STEM education:

1. Develop and enrich strategic partnerships between "educational institutions, employers, and their communities";
2. Engage students where disciplines converge which includes a focus on "complex real-world problems and challenges that require initiative and creativity";
3. Build computational literacy by "solving complex problems with data";
4. Operate with transparency and accountability.

The U.S. National Science Foundation uses the term, convergence to describe research "solving vexing research problems" that must be solved using a transdisciplinary approach (NSF, nd). A U.S. Interagency Working Group on Convergence (2022) defined convergence education as "driven by compelling or complex socio-scientific problems or topics, where learners apply knowledge and skills using a blended approach across multiple disciplines (i.e. transdisciplinary) to create and innovate new solutions" (OSTP, 2022, p.7). The characteristics include that it is driven by a specific and compelling problem and incorporates significant integration across disciplines.

So initially, there was focus on individual disciplines as in the Caribbean, but STEM has evolved, to an integrated STEM approach, exemplified by robotics and nanotechnologies and engineering disciplines, where students apply knowledge from multiple STEM fields simultaneously. This interdisciplinary approach better reflects real-world problem-solving and encourages creative thinking across traditional subject boundaries. Recognizing the pivotal role of STEM in driving economic growth and global competitiveness, the United States has invested heavily in STEM education. This emphasis stems from the understanding that a robust STEM workforce is essential for maintaining technological leadership and addressing complex societal challenges.

CASE STUDY 1: PLANNING FOR STEM TEACHER QUALITY IN THE STATE OF GEORGIA, USA

The emphasis on STEM across the United States is expansive (Council et al., 2014),ranging from programs that engage students in STEM competencies through courses, competitions, and programs of study, to teacher education programs engaging teachers in ways to enhance their STEM knowledge bases and ability to integrate STEM disciplines through problem based learning and pedagogical content knowledge. Many universities and state agencies offer programs for in-service teachers to get advanced degrees, certifications, or endorsements across the United States.

In considering a model for in-service teacher training, research suggests hallmarks, which include a focus on STEM integration and increasing teacher STEM content and pedagogical content knowledge (constructivist framework) to lead to outcomes for both students and teachers. Desired outcomes for students include 1st century competencies, STEM course taking and persistence, development of a STEM identify, and the ability to make connections among STEM disciplines (Council et al., 2014).

Three main challenges of STEM teacher training include teacher knowledge bases in both their primary subject as well as other STEM disciplines. The needs of teachers vary across different content areas and grade bands. Teachers need time to collaborate with colleagues and support of their administration through planning time (Margot & Kettler, 2019).

In the state of Georgia, in-service teachers have the option of adding a STEM field to existing professional teaching certificates through endorsement programs and advanced degrees to address these needs and challenges. The Georgia Professional Standards Commission (PSC) has a set of standards that universities, school districts, and state agencies may use to propose a STEM endorsement program for approval[1]. One such program that was approved is currently being implemented at a state agency, Metropolitan Regional Services Agency[2]. Because the goals of the STEM Endorsement are authentic interdisciplinary STEM, the STEM endorsement is open to any educator with a professional renewable teaching certificate[3].

The cost of STEM endorsement programs varies across the state, and while some programs lead to an endorsement which adds the STEM field to existing certification, others lead to an advanced degree. Teachers earning an advanced degree receive an increase in salary based on the state salary scale. Teachers receiving a STEM endorsement do not receive a salary increase. Sometimes the STEM degree or endorsement may lead to teachers seeking leadership positions in their school and district.

The Georgia Department of Education also has various STEM initiatives including the opportunity for schools to become STEM certified[4]. Schools may encourage teachers to become STEM endorsed as a way to help refine the school vision of STEM. STEM certified schools go through a set of rigorous standards and must demonstrate the implementation of a STEM vision and culture through the school, identifying real-world problems in their communities, and working with parents and STEM partners such as local businesses or universities in the community. The process of a school becoming STEM certified takes between 2-5 years and during that time the school gets support from state and district STEM leaders as they work towards implementation[5]. Schools in Georgia may also consider STEM certification through Cognia, a national non-profit accreditation agency in the United States[6].

The Metro RESA STEM endorsement is an online course, PSC approved endorsement for K-12 in-service teachers that takes about one year to complete. The assignments completed during this endorsement support STEM instruction, critical STEM skills, and include developing PBL STEM integrated lessons and units for the students in their classrooms. Other assignments include writing a grant, developing a professional resource collection, visiting a STEM certified school, having collaborative discussions with STEM colleagues, and collaborating with STEM partners. Synchronous instruction includes various integrated STEM tasks and asynchronous instruction includes a deep dive into STEM practices and resources. For example, the first synchronous class begins with the global issue of water scarcity and leads to experiences addressing standards linked to the water cycle (science), analyzing data (mathematics), developing solutions (engineering design challenge or EDC), and interactive maps depicting water scarcity (technology). To deepen the interdisciplinary connections, social sciences (SS) and language arts are addressed. This lesson connects to the UN 17 Sustainability Goal 6 Clean Water and Sanitation. During asynchronous classes, STEM candidates explore resources on engaging students in the various STEM disciplines, strategies and resources for implementing local and global phenomena, and support to develop lessons and units. These are outlined in Figure 2.

Figure 2. Water Scarcity

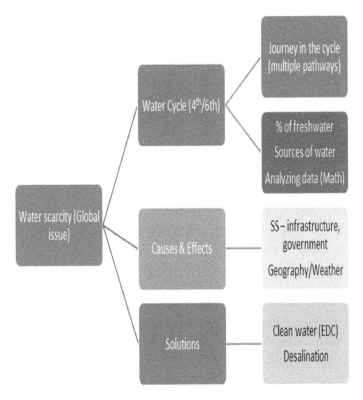

The impact of Colonialism on education and implications for Teacher Training in the Caribbean

The education system in the Caribbean is fundamentally shaped by its British colonial heritage (Brissett, 2021). This historical context has profoundly influenced teaching and learning experiences of HE educators, which remain deeply rooted in colonial educational practices (Colket et al., 2021, Part III) and this also impacts teacher training. It is often thought that teachers teach how they are taught and form a teaching philosophy which then drives their behaviour, there are many factors that influence their teaching philosophy (Olesen & Hora, 2013). Windschitl (2009) admonishes that we must consider what research tells us about how teachers learn to teach science; arguably because we must aim in new training not to tailor what science teachers know, but what they know about teaching to advance continuous discovery. While colonialism introduced formal education, literacy, and exposure to Western knowledge, these benefits were largely confined to elite strata, exacerbating

13

pre-existing social inequalities. The core of the colonial educational project was to produce subjects loyal to the empire, rather than critical citizens. Consequently, the curriculum was eurocentric, privileging British history, literature, and values while marginalizing Caribbean contributions.

These structures and practices often emphasize Science individual subjects, faculties and Science divisions' academic leadership. There is rote learning, teacher-centered instruction, and high-stakes examinations - all hallmarks of the British colonial education model (Boisselle, 2016). Brisset (2018) affirms that the legacies of colonialism not only affected education, but highlights the never-ending loop, arguing that colonialism allows exacerbation of current neoliberal globalization forces. The political-economic frailties in the Caribbean, social challenges, violence and crime rates all negatively impact education. "Post-colonial education inequities, characterized by limited access and a pedagogy akin to master-slave relationships that are utilitarian and acritical, have also had deleterious consequences on Caribbean societies" (Brisset, 2018,p.197).

Despite the diversity among Caribbean nations and their individual contexts, a common thread unites their educational systems: all Caribbean students must complete five years of secondary education and demonstrate competence in the Caribbean Secondary Education Certificate (CSEC) examinations. These examinations, administered by the Caribbean Examinations Council (CXC), are a direct legacy of the colonial system and continue to significantly influence curriculum and instruction across the region. Also, this shared examination requirement necessitates that teachers across the Caribbean collectively prepare students for success in these examinations, often at the expense of more progressive or locally-relevant educational approaches. Teachers are trained to teach this common curriculum and unfortunately concentrate on having students master content of the syllabi for high stake exams and thus do not engage in utilizing pedagogical strategies taught during their training (Devonish, 2018), but fall into a unbecoming culture of didactic and teacher-centered modalities (Sweeney & George, 2024).

It is important to note that while this existing system provides a standardized measure of academic achievement, it also presents challenges in addressing local needs and fostering innovation in education. This is because teachers have unlikely been exposed to this type of teaching and learning, resulting in limited contextual science cases or phenomenon for students to relate to. Unfortunately, as the teacher is taught so too shall the student teacher teach, and so the states of mind (efficacy, interdependence, consciousness and craftsmanship) have to be addressed through professional development programs (Mweeba et al., 2021). These programs can intervene to develop these necessary mindsets as outlined by Costa & Garmston (2002). This will help teachers embrace the philosophical and pedagogical shift towards a more flexible and student-centered approach advocated by STEM education

(Devonish, 2016). To truly address the challenges facing Caribbean education, a deep-seated decolonization process is required even at the teacher education stage. This involves not only reforming curricula to incorporate Caribbean history, culture, and perspectives. It also involves transforming pedagogical approaches to foster creativity, inquiry, and agency among students. By critically examining the colonial legacy and embracing indigenous knowledge systems, the Caribbean can build education systems that are truly responsive to the needs and aspirations of its people.

Figure 3. The Caribbean; St. Vincent and the Grenadines

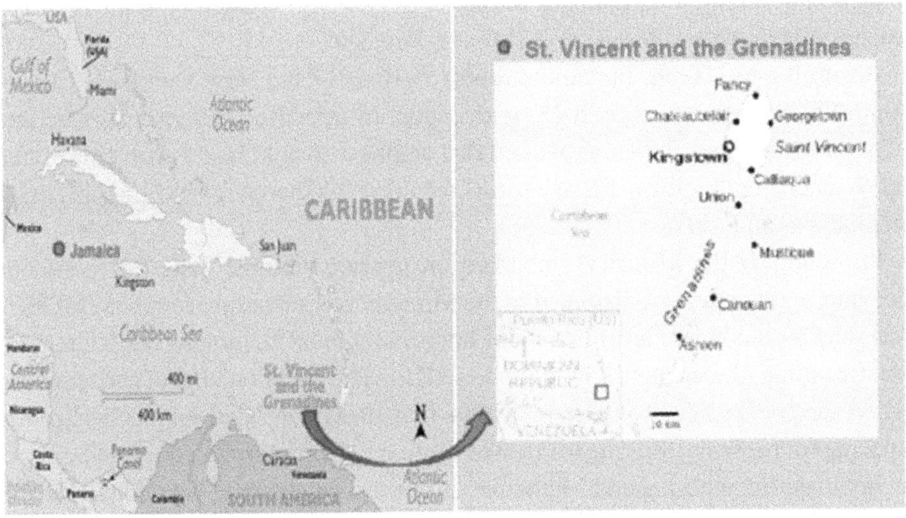

CASE STUDY 2: STEM TEACHER TRAINING IN JAMAICA

Historically, the greatest HE teacher training impetus was in response to the provision of a Negro Education Grant by the British government to assist missionary societies in the education of newly freed slaves. This was the founding of teacher training colleges in the latter half of the nineteenth century—The Mico, whose status upgraded to the Mico University College (2006), Bethlehem, Shortwood, and Moneague Teachers Colleges (Chevannes, 2005). It was in the Asquith report of 1945 via colonial policy, through the commission on higher education in the colonies that became the blueprint for the establishment of University colleges in Africa and the West Indies. The University College of the West Indies (UCWI) was opened in 1948, as a college of London. The federation collapsed but the federal status was maintained. University of the West Indies (UWI) was born and in Trinidad, the Imperial College of agriculture became the faculty of Agriculture of UWI. The third campus was opened in Barbados, 1963 and between 1962 and 1967 centres were established in non-campus countries. Countries in the Organisation of Eastern Caribbean States (OECS) commenced HEI development in the 1970s, with St Vincent and the Grenadines in 1992. The UWI five island was established in Antigua and Barbuda, September 2019.

Jamaica serves as a prime example of teacher training practices in the Caribbean, notably because the University of the West Indies has franchised its Bachelor in Education programme to colleges in the region and the regulatory Joint Board of Teacher Education resides at UWI (Mona), Jamaica.

According to UTech, Ja. annual report 2016-2017 the New Standards Curriculum (NSC) commenced in 2013, with a goal to improve academic attitude and behavior for students. It was explained that emphasis would be on problem solving and Science, Technology, Engineering, Arts and Mathematics (STEM/STEAM) integrated at all levels.[7]

In alignment the Ministry embarked on teacher training, June 2016. At one occasion, six lecturers participated in the Ministry of Education, Jamaica (MOEY) workshop for secondary level Trainer of Trainers for the NSC, among other interventions spanning grades one (K1) to grade 9 (K9). The envisioned goal for Jamaican STEM subject teachers was to demonstrate how ideas transcend subject disciplines exposing connections fostering a full understanding of the interrelatedness of Science, Technology, Engineering and Mathematics in everyday life and beyond (Breiner et al.,2012; Deming & Noray, 2020; McGunagle & Zizka,2020). The overall intent was to foster a student-centered teaching and learning environment with an emphasis on problem solving and real-world solutions.

However, there have been challenges with the teacher training and the translation of STEM education ethos, even though the implementation of the NSC into schools by the nation's teachers (Mayne & Dixon, 2020). Mayne and Dixon (2020) though not addressing STEM, gives insight to the challenges faced by student teachers in Jamaica as they transition to a new curriculum that emphasizes project-based STEM learning and student-centered instruction. Student teachers reported a lack of resources and resistance from cooperating teachers accustomed to older teaching styles creating uncertainty and difficulty in implementing the new curriculum effectively. Supporting this sentiment, Yee-Han et al. (2020), also states, "some teachers are struggling with transitioning" (p.157) and Caribbean studies highlight that the lack of resources affects teacher training (Williams & Staulters, 2014; Lashley (2019); Tsang et.al (2002) and De Lisle (2009). Schweisfurth (2011) emphasized that the lack of materials, human resources and interactions of divergent cultures can hinder quality education implementation.

Arguably, with new insight, the current expectations for training of STEM teachers in Jamaica is far more demanding than the training of science teachers (Chemistry, Physics, Biology) or mathematics teachers (MoEY-core curriculum-interview, January 2024). Historically, traditional teaching methodologies and philosophies centered on the content of the discipline, and the teacher, as is still the case 2024. The student and their learning realities were then not considered, outside of assessment for scores. This challenge is not unique to Jamaica but is echoed across the Caribbean, including Trinidad and Tobago and Guyana (Yee-Han et. al; 2020) where an examination driven approach has foiled efforts to transform teaching practices to student centered learning. Livingstone et al (2017) argues that examination and lack of policy alignment confuses teachers and fail to address their more intentional concern of student performance on exit examinations.

There are many collaborations that allow professional development of mathematics and science teachers through government funded teacher training institutions (BOOST, June 22, 2022; JIS 2001; SRC Summer Attachment Workshop) and the MOEY continues to embark on mathematics and science teacher training through the core curriculum unit and the Jamaica Teaching Council (JTC). The Jamaica Teaching Council (JTC) was established in 2004 as part of the Task Force on Educational Reform Report. Its primary goals are to improve the quality of education in Jamaica and to professionalize the teaching profession. Key initiatives of the JTC include:

1. Master Teacher Programme: Master Teacher Programme: Initiated in 1998, this program certifies exemplary teachers as master teachers. Its overall aim is to retain national science teacher talent and promote teaching excellence for better student outcomes.
2. Lead Teacher Programme: This program trains certified master teachers to support their peers through organized sessions and within their schools. The training focuses on science subject content and, more recently, STEM education principles for pedagogy.
3. National Forum for Innovations in Teaching (FIT): The JTC hosts this annual event to promote innovation in education. The 2024 event will be the third staging, themed "Celebrating Achievements and Re-imagining Education for the 21st Society and Labour Force."

Despite these efforts, the JTC faces several challenges of limited resources and understaffing of the team; lack of support from the Jamaica Teachers' Association (JTA) and incomplete legislative status (still a draft paper in the Gazette) (Dr.

Thomas, personal communication, April, 2023; JTC, 2023; Reynolds, February 2014; Small, November 18, 2023).

Other initiatives offer support to lecturers of government funded teacher training institutions (Hunter, October 30, 2020) or science teachers which is sometimes extended across the Caribbean with organizations collaborating Association of Science Teachers in Jamaica (ASTJ), (UNESCO, CSF, OAS, ITEN) to address professional development (Devonish, 2021). However, mainstream training under the Joint Board of Teacher Education under the University of the West Indies and the Teacher Training Colleges currently offer bachelor's degrees in the teaching of mathematics, biology, chemistry, physics, or a combination of these. Although the University of the West Indies also offers degrees in education with similar subject specializations none of the teacher training programs currently offer teacher training as STEM educators to meet the needs as described above (MoEY, core curriculum, interview January 2024). This is worth further introspection as well as the unveiling that for the sciences, there is no equivalent STEM content syllabi used for teacher training either. Training is needed to alter cultural norms, attitudes and behavior to influence implementation of teacher best practices; teacher reflexivity and an overall appreciation of their teacher role in facilitating STEM practices and philosophy in a convergent, transdisciplinary modality (Interagency Working Group on Convergence 2022, November). The lack of training STEM teachers in this fashion may hurt students' survival in the technological 21st century global economy (Parris, 2002).

CASE STUDY 3: STEM TEACHER TRAINING IN ST. VINCENT AND THE GRENADINES (SVG)

The multi-island nation of St. Vincent and the Grenadines as shown in Figure 3 occupies a strategic position within the Eastern Caribbean, forming the southernmost tip of the Windward Islands chain. This archipelago comprises the larger island of Saint Vincent, surrounded by a constellation of smaller islands including Bequia, Mustique, Canouan, Mayreau, Union Island, Palm Island, Petit Saint Vincent, and numerous islets (gov.vc., 2023). According to the 2022 data from the Statistical Office within the Ministry of Finance, Economic Planning, and Information Technology, the total population of SVG is approximately 110,418 individuals (https://stats.gov.vc/reference/).

In SVG, as of 2022, primary education involves 67 primary schools: 3 special needs schools and 29 secondary schools. The teacher workforce has 972 primary school teachers of which 768 (79%) were trained in teaching science. However, untrained teachers who teach science at the primary level are required to have completed science courses at the secondary level at minimum. Of the 870 secondary school teachers, UNESCO suggests that in 2020 only 62% were qualified (UNES-CO Institute of Statistics, 2024). According to Ministry of Education and National Reconciliation, while SVG lacks a formal STEM teacher certification program, the country actively promotes STEM integration through various initiatives.

Teacher training prioritizes general science certifications, but the Ministry of Education and private groups like STEMSVG offer workshops to equip teachers with STEM knowledge.

These workshops are facilitated by trained science teachers, not necessarily those with dedicated STEM certification. The annual National Science & Technology Fair plays a crucial role in teacher development. By showcasing student projects and fostering collaboration, the fair exposes teachers to current trends and inspires them to incorporate more engaging STEM-based methods into their lessons.

Additionally, a new science curriculum with integrated STEM activities is under development, the Harmonized Primary Curriculum (OHPC) for science which is inspired by the Next Generation Science Standards (NGSS) and includes several activities designed for teachers to introduce STEM in their classrooms. Once completed OHPC will require that teachers receive professional development in how to deliver these STEM-based components.

Evidently, SVG has been considering the professional development of its science teachers to incorporate and become STEM aware teachers. These efforts highlight SVG's commitment to STEM education, despite challenges like limited funding and high teacher attrition. Despite the challenges, SVG envisions a brighter future with an increased number of STEM-trained teachers. These educators will integrate STEM principles into their lessons, fostering a vibrant learning environment for the nation's students.

To achieve this, SVG considers pursuing several avenues that address funding, professional development and overall policy adjustments. By acknowledging these challenges and implementing targeted solutions, SVG can effectively cultivate a generation of passionate and skilled STEM educators, ultimately empowering its students to thrive in the future (Ministry of Education and National Reconciliation, Science Coordinator Interview, January 2024).

Table 1. STEM and STEM Education Teacher Training Comparisons

	Jamaica	St. Vincent & Grenadines	Other Caribbean Regions with differing contexts	USA (State of Georgia)	Comments
Who does training?	MoEY Joint Board of Teacher Education- Teacher Colleges University of Technology, Jamaica (Faculty of Science & Sport) Northern Caribbean University, Jamaica	Division of Teacher Education (DTE) at the St. Vincent and the Grenadines' Community College (SVCC).	In the OECS countries, the Teachers' College has been incorporated into the Community Colleges (Mark et al 2005). Table 3. *Main teacher training institutions per country* (Dominica, Grenada, Guyana, Haiti, Honduras, Nicaragua,, St. Lucia and St. Vincent & Grenadines In Zacarias (2021, p.12).	There is a state department of education that provide educational resources. Public or private Universities, School Districts, Private companies e.g. STEM. org and NISE and state agencies offer STEM certification post baccalaureate. In Georgia, 7 universities, 2 school districts, and 6 state agencies offer PSC state approved STEM endorsements.	Training is done by accredited national bodies. For Jamaica institutions and courses of study are accredited by the University Council of Jamaica. Tertiary Commission (J-TEC), the University Council of Jamaica (UCJ) and the Jamaica Teaching Council.
Profile of the facilitators	Universities are classified as HEI but not colleges. Ideally, HEI have facilitators with terminal degrees qualified within their specific field.	Colleges are not considered HEI and the hiring of teacher trainers hired is the choice of the College based on its governance structure.			There is no enforced standard across the region, as to the profile of the STEM teacher trainer, nor the competencies for STEM education pedagogy and there is no data on the existing effectiveness.

continued on following page

Table 1. Continued

	Jamaica	St. Vincent & Grenadines	Other Caribbean Regions with differing contexts	USA (State of Georgia)	Comments
Training funding and stakeholder expectations	The Teachers' colleges are Ministry funded and receive a subvention for overall student support. Student loan bureau and bonding.	Students self-fund their tuition fees. They are also assisted by various funding agencies e.g. Mustique Charitable Foundation and the Taiwanese Embassy.	Barbadian nationals are government funded at Erdiston Teachers' Training College. In 2018 Government of Barbados articulated a policy that reintroduced the payment where they give back a set number of hours in approved community service per year. (https://unesdoc.unesco.org/ark:/48223/pf0000135341) Ministry of Education, Technical and vocational training, https://www.mes.gov.bb/GiveBack/	Teachers or their school districts may pay for STEM training.	In Jamaica there is limited funding toward STEM. STEM education is however being supported haphazardly through varied inputs and intervention. (1) STEM scholarships (STEM career perspective-HEI) (2) STEM-K12-sixth form programme. (3) STEM institutions (STEM training perspective-Secondary level K3-K10) (4) STEM national awareness (collaboration with industry) STEM education and the ethos of integration is being incorporated through the education system via the MoEY, National Standards Curriculum (K1-K9) (limited compliance) Notice only #1 deals with teacher training.
Training Levels for Science teachers & STEM teachers	Baccalaureate Post – Baccalaureate	Baccalaureate		Post Baccalaureate	

continued on following page

Table 1. Continued

	Jamaica	St. Vincent & Grenadines	Other Caribbean Regions with differing contexts	USA (State of Georgia)	Comments
Profile of the preservice teacher candidate/ teacher trainee (to get B.Ed. in Teaching) To acquire Teacher Training (PgDip.)	Candidates with CSEC qualifications. 5 CSEC with proficiency in their science subject preference/s. Postgraduates with Science degree (BSc) or MSc train to gain the pedagogy-'how to teach training' –the STEM education.			Post Baccalaureate STEM endorsements in Georgia are different from STEM degrees earned during undergraduate programs. Teachers must have a clear renewable certificate to add a STEM field. This is similar to other endorsements such as Gifted, Reading, Online Learning, and Dyslexia. Many schools in Georgia seek STEM or STEAM certification.	
Training and credit hours	Standard across all institutions 135 credits As a discipline teacher education has four stages 1. Pre-service (2) preparation/ initial formation (3)In-service (4) Retirement (Mark et al., 2005).			Estimated 100-200 contact hours of coursework In Georgia, state approved STEM endorsements take about a year to complete.	Number of credits within the existing training model is standard across institutions in the Caribbean.
Training Components and Characteristics STEM Education	Present and improving but not measured for graduate teacher output. Not monitored for inclusion nor maintenance within the colleges during teacher training.	Present and improving.		STEM Education is used for instruction.	STEM education which focuses on PBL and emphasis for hands-on learning, problem-solving, and critical thinking skills through the pedagogical practices and skillsets is incorporated in all subject areas not only the Sciences in the Jamaican school system. It has been introduced right across the teaching arena as a best practice for teaching delivery.

continued on following page

Table 1. Continued

	Jamaica	St. Vincent & Grenadines	Other Caribbean Regions with differing contexts	USA (State of Georgia)	Comments
Training Components and Characteristics	Pure Science subjects (Math, Biology, Chemistry and Physics) X-credit hours/ one term of school observation *(pair engagement with peer assistance)* Two terms of teaching practicum *(with sustained coaching)* Developing a teacher portfolio of lessons taught for grading	Subject specific emphasis. STEM taught as discrete subjects		Developing and implementing STEM PBL lessons and units Writing a grant to help with STEM implementation, Visiting a STEM certified school Having collaborative discussions with STEM colleagues Collaborating with STEM partners. https://www.gapsc.com/Rules/Current/EducatorPreparation/505-3-.94.pdf?dt=636295079754667208	To gain teacher certification teachers produce a portfolio of work that demonstrates proficiency across 15 STEM teacher actions (NISE).

continued on following page

Table 1. Continued

	Jamaica	St. Vincent & Grenadines	Other Caribbean Regions with differing contexts	USA (State of Georgia)	Comments
Curriculum	Subject specific emphasis (STEM taught as discrete subjects) The education component may or may not include: PBL problem-based learning EDP engineering design processing Subject integration			The curriculum includes a focus on STEM integration. The standards and rules for STEM endorsement has differing features to that of the Caribbean: S1: rigorous content integration across STEM and STEM related disciplines S3: PBL, partnership projects, STEM school visits S4: PBL, EP, interdisciplinary STEM focus S5: STEM careers https://www.gapsc.com/Rules/Current/EducatorPreparation/505-3-.01.pdf?dt=%3C%25#Eval('strTimeStamp')%20%%3E	There is no STEM curriculum for STEM teacher training and or STEM endorsement in the Caribbean. STEM has a multitude of topic areas and each jurisdiction tailors the teacher training syllabi to incorporate these creatively into modules: 1. aerospace engineering 2. astrophysics 3. astronomy 4. biochemistry 5. biomechanics 6. chemical engineering 7. chemistry 8. civil engineering 9. computer science 10. mathematical biology 11. nanotechnology 12. neurobiology 13. nuclear physics 14. physics 15. Robotics e.g. STEM.org has modules or teaching tracks with titles such as Drones & 21st Century Technology/Sports Science/Zombie Apocalypse/Building a better Mouse Trap" A fully immersed STEM integration.

	Jamaica	St. Vincent & Grenadines	Other Caribbean Regions with differing contexts	USA (State of Georgia)	Comments
Quality Assurance Mechanism	Licensing (JTC) X Certification✓ Professional registration (JTC)……..X Professional certification X Accreditation *Jamaica has one known certified STEM teacher and accredited STEM institution (via STEM.org)* *The status of JTC is still wavering, no complete enforcement…(Smith, September 29, 2023)*https://www.jamaicaobserver.com/2023/09/29/legislators-question-proposal-in-jtc-bill-for-protection-against-legal-action-20231018-1403-333014/			Licensing ✓ Certification✓ Professional registration✓ Professional certification✓ Accreditation✓	State accountability measures are discussed at every instance of educational reform and the positing of a report. Jamaica Teaching Council is the arm of the MOE, Jamaica that will monitor, assess, track, register and certify all subject teachers. However, he JTC, standards will focus on the process of teaching, rather than the outcome. (Gulpers, 2013).
Academic Qualification	1. Graduate untrained – unqualified (GUU) 2. Graduate untrained (GU) 3. Graduate trained (GT) 4. Nongraduate trained (NT) Reference for abbreviation				
Certification and option for upward training.	On graduation teachers get a BEd Postgrad. Dip to teach single Science subjects. They also have major and minor options. To upgrade 1. GUU needs to enroll in a BEd programme 2. GU -Postgrad. Dip Ed. 3. GT-M.Ed. NT-BEd. (Zacarias, 2021; Mark et al. 2005)		The Eastern Caribbean Joint Board of Teacher Education (JBTE) – certifies teachers in Early to Secondary and TVET Education in Anguilla, Antigua and Barbuda, Barbados, British Virgin Islands, Dominica, Grenada, Montserrat, St Kitts & Nevis, St Lucia, St Vincent and the Grenadines	Schools can be certified as STEM schools Teachers may become STEM certified (endorsed) Master in Education with a concentration in STEM	

	Jamaica	St. Vincent & Grenadines	Other Caribbean Regions with differing contexts	USA (State of Georgia)	Comments
Employment	MoEY First degree (GT-BEd. Science) candidate to teach up to K9 (grade 9/third form) BSc. and Postgraduate diploma – to teach K10-K12		NT only has a teaching diploma or certificate. GUU does not have any teacher certification and may be a high school graduate teaching.	STEM Endorsed teachers in Georgia may seek a leadership and/or a STEM position in schools and districts. For example, elementary schools may have a STEM teacher position. Districts may have STEM a leadership position.	In the Caribbean examples the hiring of teachers and the grade level, or subjects they are certified to teach is not enforced. A Caribbean STEM subject teacher could be hired in the state of Georgia. This teacher would be hired to teach the STEM subject they are certified to teach, but they would not be called a STEM endorsed teacher. E.g. A physics teacher would teach physics and is called a science teacher.
Post Employment Professional Development and maintenance of standard	Jamaica lacks an overall comprehensive PD framework. Partnerships with institutions and cooperative entities provide avenues for professional development activities. Presently PD is the onus of the individual Science teacher. Jamaica Teacher Council (JTC) is still not yet established to enforce teacher certification.			The state of Georgia offers a framework STEM certification for schools and opportunities for STEM endorsements based on state standards (Post Baccalaureate). https://stemsteamgeorgia.com/	
Numbers Employed		972 primary school teachers of which 768 are trained to teach science (i.e. 79%).			

	Jamaica	St. Vincent & Grenadines	Other Caribbean Regions with differing contexts	USA (State of Georgia)	Comments
STEM Support	MoE (core curriculum) Association of Science Teachers of Jamaica Universities Colleges Industry partners			STEM Candidates seek partnerships with STEM professionals to gain perspective of what it is to work in a STEM or STEM related field There is also the expectation that they will collaborate with colleagues to plan interdisciplinary STEM PBLs.	
Remuneration ($US)	NT, Trained teacher with Diploma $14,299.74-$18,304.87 GU, Graduate Pre-trained $14,299.74-$18,304.87 GT, Trained Graduate MEd, MSc, PgDip $19,108.33-$2447.47 Jamaica pay scales can be found: https://www.mof.gov .jm/wp-content/uploads/ Teachers-salary-2022-2025 -1-1.pdf	Teacher I: $6822.22-$9222.22 Teacher II: $8493.33-$11480.00 Teacher III: $13057.78-$17,031.11 Teacher IV: $15635.56 -$20,195.56 Teacher V (Year 1&2): $18,173.33 -$23,586.67 Teacher V: $20724.44 -$26,435.56		The State of Georgia pay scale can be found at https://www.gadoe.org/ Finance-and-Business -Operations/Budget -Services/Documents/ FY24%20State%20Salary %20Schedule.pdf The pay structure is by years of service and the level attained. 0-2 years (Entry) $42,458.08-$60857.33 9-10 years (7) $$50,508.25-$56,254.67 11-12 years (Level 1) $51,796.33-$57697.67 21+years (Level 6) $58,838.00-$8728.35	Exchange rate used XCD=$2.70 US Jam=$157 US There is no additional compensation for a STEM endorsement, but a Master degree in STEM would lead to a salary increase as would a Master's degree in any field. Compensation varies depending on the counties they work. Higher remuneration in metro Atlanta.

Part 3: What Stem Education and Stem Teacher Training Should Look Like Beyond 21ST Century

Do not fix what is broken, improve what is done well, fill gaps and improve incrementally with data driven research.

How exciting, Jamaica's team of high school students 2023 won a gold medal in the Katherine Johnson Award category for engineering documentation at the FIRST Global Challenge Robotics competition in Singapore. Grenada's team won the Rajaa Cherkaoui El Moursli Award for Courageous Achievement, while St Lucia's team won the Temasek Women in STEM Award[8] and the year before 2022, Jamaica also won two other awards. These feats showcase the potential of STEM and STEM education in the Caribbean. Yet, the reality often falls short. In Jamaica, while there are nine pilot STEM schools, they remain underfunded and in mid-transition, struggling to deliver their full potential.

However, dedicated science teachers across the Caribbean strive to incorporate STEM principles into their lessons, achieving impressive results. Students consistently participate in regional and international STEM competitions, delivering innovative presentations and displays.

However, significant challenges persist, including low national literacy (Jamaica 87%) and science literacy levels even lower, poor academic performance in regional CSEC exam results, and the low ranking of Jamaica in the Program for International Student Assessment (PISA), paint a worrying picture. These challenges underscore the urgent need for teacher support and training to enhance student engagement with STEM subjects and better prepare them for the demands of the 21st-century workforce.

Addressing these barriers requires more than just dedicated teachers; it necessitates providing them with the necessary support, resources, and training to become even more effective educators. Renewed focus on teacher quality is essential to overcome these obstacles and ensure the success of STEM education in the Caribbean.

Let us not be inhibited by Reality (What STEM-STEM education should be?)

It is clear that if the region is not inhibited by political perspectives, funding or any other conceived challenge then this is what STEM teacher training would entail, see the following:

The best students would be recruited for STEM teacher training (Darling-Hammond et al, 2019). A robust content for the pure sciences would be translated from secondary school into science subject majors for teacher training. The teaching of STEM requires teachers to have a strong foundation in each relevant subject, deep knowledge, in order to make meaningful connections between concepts across disciplines (Council et al., 2014; Ntemngwa & Oliver, 2018; Radloff & Guzey, 2016). A robust STEM foundation will include scientific knowledge and process skills not just a superficial knowledge of STEM disciplines. If STEM teacher training in the Caribbean is to be as an advanced postgraduate training, then candidates must have a robust science background in their Bachelor's degree before seeking an advanced degree or STEM endorsement status. If we want all science teachers going through teacher training in the Caribbean to be STEM teachers, then the existing curriculum would have to navigate an additional STEM training component.

Notably, the science teacher training programs have seen a worrying decline in the numbers in the last 10 years in Jamaica. Numbers have decreased to single digit enrollment for Physics, Chemistry, Biology and Mathematics majors. Subject teacher training has been stopped for lack of uptake into the teacher training program (Science education Lecturer, Jamaica, interview January 2024). This is due primarily to poor teachers' pay, fueling attrition, and low CSEC level proficiency attainment. Ideally broadening the candidate pool to consider STEM preservice candidates of diverse experiences and perspectives could be beneficial.

A STEM teacher training curriculum with modules depicting the true integration of the four strands of STEM according to International Technological Engineering Educators Association (ITEEA) would be available. The STEM curriculum integration requires prerequisite knowledge of many science subject areas and topics. (Granshaw 2016). There is limited to zero research which illustrates what an ideal or acceptable STEM integrated curricula is for the Caribbean, with its unique context. However, there are increasing modules being advanced such as Kim et al. (2023) which shows a model for levels of integrating STEM on a continuum moving towards convergence on subjects. Diversity would be addressed for the Caribbean teaching workforce because there are differences in the language, culture, and experience. The training would include establishing a student-centered environment.

The STEM teacher embracing technology, in a future-oriented approach to teacher education (Technology Education) would be included. Teachers teach how they have been taught (Cox, 2014). Technology has the potential to significantly improve teacher preparation. Personalized learning experiences, increased resource accessibility, and improved teacher collaboration are all made possible by technology. In order to adequately educate educators for the challenges of the globalized economy of the twenty-first century, teacher education must be progressive. This entails giving educators the know-how to instruct in a technologically advanced classroom, encouraging students to think critically and solve problems.

Participating STEM teacher training institutions would be resourced to deliver this STEM curricula to preservice or in service teachers.

Participating in STEM teacher training institutions would meet the accreditation standards for STEM teacher training delivery at international standards. **STEM teachers would have set tailored professional development (PD) activities.** Continuous professional development for STEM teachers is the only way to remain current with the most recent pedagogical approaches, topic knowledge, and technological breakthroughs. Unfortunately, in Jamaica, there is no structured framework for continuous professional development. This results in an ad-hoc system where training is offered by various stakeholders, including the Ministry of Education. Teacher participation in these PD activities is either voluntary or mandated, lacking a consistent approach to improving educator skills and knowledge.

Promotion of STEM teacher leadership, according to the three leadership strands (Instructional, Policy and Association Leadership) of the STEM Leadership framework (AAPT, n.d.). STEM teachers must maintain a community of practice, with adequate coaching facility. The importance of peer teaching and mentorship dictates that the STEM Teacher education should not be conducted in isolation from the communities it serves.

There needs to be a regional approach to teacher quality planning, especially since many Caribbean nationals go to regional universities such as the University of the West Indies for training. Given the interconnectedness of the Caribbean region, a collaborative approach to planning for teacher quality is essential. This could involve sharing best practices, developing regional teacher standards, and conducting joint research on teacher effectiveness.

STEM teachers would be adequately compensated. Emphasizing fair compensation and valuing teachers is essential for job satisfaction and retention (Worth, et al., 2022; LiVecchi, 2017). The Caribbean region faces challenges in attracting and retaining qualified teachers. However, premium quality teachers with a higher degree in STEM qualification should be duly acknowledged for their contribution to nation building.

STEM teachers would be STEM certified and their professional journey and output would be effectively monitored. The certification would identify a science subject teacher (e.g. BEd, BSc, PgDip etc., a STEM teacher (higher degree-MEd-STEM) and a STEM endorsed (BSc-STEM) qualified individual. This would eventually prevent incidents of non-qualification alignment among the employed Science teacher workforce.

The educational and national policies would be ready to support the new STEM evolution for teachers, students and stakeholders. Higher Education Institutions academics have to collaborate and lead a charge to have ongoing research which is essential to improve teacher education and ensure that teachers are well-equipped to meet the needs of their students. Data driven research can help identify effective STEM teaching practices, develop new pedagogical approaches, and assess the impact of STEM teacher education programs on student learning. Similarly, Governments hold a crucial responsibility in ensuring that teachers in the Caribbean receive high-quality education and training. Through investments in teacher education programs, adequate funding for schools, and clear standards for teacher certification, governments can empower teachers to meet the needs of their students and prepare them for success in the 21st century.

The national K1-K12 curriculum, the regional examinations would be ready, revised to facilitate the emersion of STEM in the curriculum, for STEM teachers to teach STEM via STEM education.

The Global Push for STEM Education: Navigating Cultural and Economic Constraints in the Caribbean

Though cultures and economies will dictate reality, we reiterate that national development and realization of the SDGs is hinged on education (Bergman et al., 2018). Globally, education systems are evolving towards integrated STEM curricula (K1-K12), requiring teachers with new skills and knowledge. However, a formal framework for training such "STEM educators" is often lacking (National Academies of Sciences, Engineering, and Medicine, 2018). While this trend holds promise, applying it, STEM, directly to the Caribbean presents challenges. Limited finances, infrastructure, and existing policies may render full-fledged STEM implementation unfeasible. Additionally, achieving effective curriculum implementation relies heavily on educator buy-in, and navigating cultural and institutional inertia in education is notoriously complex (Fullan, 2014).

This chapter argues that imposing a one-size-fits-all approach to STEM education in the Caribbean is not sustainable and instead proposes a flexible framework that considers cultural and economic realities while promoting STEM integration within existing capacities. Until Ministries of Education reach a consensus on a unified STEM path, it is suggested to continue full-fledged Science education, gradually implementing intentional STEM teacher training to transform science classrooms and align with specific career and institutional paths.

In conclusion, we suggest that the existing science teacher training in Jamaica and the Caribbean be maintained but with specified STEM implementation for standardized teacher training, robust curriculum development, and strong connections between education, industry, and community training programs:

1. Training—integration towards convergence in the course of study for all teachers.
2. STEM content be added for science teachers in training.
3. Professional development for in-service Science teachers
4. Professional engagement for Trainers of Trainers of STEM teachers
5. STEM endorsement for teachers who will be placed in STEM academies
6. Incorporate STEM emphasis training and support endorsement via the Master teacher Programme (JTC) and Training institutions. Endorse Science Master Teachers for coordinating STEM in the Secondary schools.

Through this approach, teachers can be equipped with the necessary skills and knowledge to prepare Caribbean students for the demands of the 21st century workforce, regardless of gaping resource constraints.

ACKNOWLEDGEMENTS

We would like to acknowledge the following for their contributions to the paper: Kavelle Hylton is a STEM Endorsed Teacher through STEM.org. In initial meetings she provided insights on STEM Educator training. We also thank Sadpha Bennett, from the Jamaican Ministry of Education (Core Curriculum unit), for sharing perspective and information on international STEM initiatives, which aided our study.

REFERENCES

Alexander, G., & Glasgow, J. (1981). UNICEF regional primary school project: Report on teacher training and curriculum development activities, 1978–1980. *Caribbean Journal of Education*, 8(1), 75–101.

American Association of Physics Teachers (AAPT). (n.d.). STEM Leadership Framework. Retrieved from https://www.aapt.org/aboutaapt/organization/contactus.cfm

Anft, M. (2013). The STEM crisis: Reality or myth. *The Chronicle of Higher Education*, 58(12), 1–14.

Apella, I., & Gonzalo, Z. (2022). Technological change and labour market trends in Latin America and the Caribbean: A task content approach. *CEPAL Review*, 2022(136), 63–85. DOI: 10.18356/16840348-2022-136-4

Aslam, A. (2020). The hotly debated topic of human capital and economic growth: Why institutions may matter? *Quality & Quantity*, 54(4), 1351–1362. DOI: 10.1007/s11135-020-00989-5

Becker, G. S. (2009). *Human Capital*. University of Chicago Press.

Bergman, Z., Bergman, M., Fernandes, K., Grossrieder, D., & Schneider, L. (2018, November 28). The contribution of UNESCO chairs toward achieving the UN Sustainable

Boisselle, L. N. (2016). Decolonizing science and science education in a postcolonial space (Trinidad, a developing Caribbean nation, illustrates). *SAGE Open*, 6(1), 2158244016635257. DOI: 10.1177/2158244016635257

BOOST. (2022). Building out our STEM Teacher-A well needed boost for the education sector. *The Jamaica Gleaner*. Retrieved on March 14, 2024 from https://jamaica-gleaner.com/article/news/20220622/building-out-our-stem-teachers-well-needed-boost-education-sector

Bowers, S. W., Williams Jr, T. O., & Ernst, J. V. (2020). Profile of an elementary STEM educator.

Brathwaite, W. E. (1978). *In-service strategies for improving teacher abilities in science education*. In the proceedings of the regional primary science conference, (pp. 156-160). University of the West Indies, Cave Hill, Barbados: Caribbean Regional Science Project.

Breiner, J. M., Harkness, S. S., Johnson, C. C., & Koehler, C. M. (2012). What is STEM? A discussion about conceptions of STEM in education and partnerships. *School Science and Mathematics*, 112(1), 3–11. DOI: 10.1111/j.1949-8594.2011.00109.x

Brissett, N. (2021). *A critical appraisal of education in the Caribbean and its evolution from colonial origins to twenty-first century responses*. Oxford Research Encyclopedia of Education., DOI: 10.1093/acrefore/9780190264093.013.1650

Brissett, N. O. M. (2018). Education for Social Transformation (EST) in the Caribbean: A Postcolonial Perspective. Mathematics (2227-7390), 6(12), 197. DOI: 10.3390/educsci8040197

Chevannes, B. (2005). Legislation of tertiary education in the Caribbean.

Clements, D. H., Sarama, J., Baroody, A. J., Kutaka, T. S., Chernyavskiy, P., Joswick, C., & Joseph, E. (2021). Comparing the efficacy of early arithmetic instruction based on a learning trajectory and teaching-to-a-target. *Journal of Educational Psychology*, 113(7), 1323–1337. DOI: 10.1037/edu0000633

Colket, L., Carswell, A., & Light, T. P. (2021). *Becoming*. Dio Press Incorporated.

Costa, A. L., & Garmston, R. J. (2002). *Cognitive coaching: A foundation for Renaissance Schools* (2nd ed.). Christopher-Gordon Publishers.

Council, N. R., Education, D. O. B. A. S. S. A., Education, B. O. S., & Standards, C. O. A. C. F. F. N. K. S. E. (2012). *A Framework for K-12 Science Education*. National Academies Press.

Council, N. R., Engineering, N. A. O., & Education, C. O. I. S. (2014, February 28). *STEM Integration in K-12 Education*. National Academies Press.

Cox, S. E. *"Perceptions and Influences Behind Teaching Practices: Do Teachers Teach as They Were Taught?"* (2014). Theses and Dissertations. 5301. https://scholarsarchive.byu.edu/etd/5301

Darling-Hammond, L., Saunders, R., Podolsky, A., Kini, T., Espinoza, D., Hyler, M., & Carver-Thomas, D. (2019). *Best practices to recruit and retain well-prepared teachers in all classrooms*. Learning Policy Institute.

de Bruijn, E., Billett, S., & Onstenk, J. (Eds.). (2017). *Enhancing teaching and learning in the Dutch vocational education system*. Professional and Practice-Based Learning., DOI: 10.1007/978-3-319-50734-7

De Lisle, J. (Ed.). External examinations beyond national borders: Trinidad and Tobago and the Caribbean Examination Council. In B. Vlaardingerbroek & N. Taylor (Eds.), Secondary School External Examination Systems: Reliability, Robustness and Resilience (pp. 265-290). New York: Cambria Press, 2009.

Deming, D., & Noray, K. (2019). STEM careers and the changing skill requirements of work. In *National Bureau of Economic Research, Inc.* EconPapers. Retrieved January 5, 2024, from https://econpapers.repec.org/paper/nbrnberwo/25065.htm

Development Goals. (●●●)...*Sustainability*, 10(12), 4471. DOI: 10.3390/su10124471

Devonish, D. (2021). The role of professional organizations in education: The COVID-19 response in Jamaica by science teachers. *Revista Conexiones: Una Experiencia Más Allá Del Aula, 13*(2), 42–55. https://www.mep.go.cr/sites/defaultfiles/2revistaconexion es2021_a4.pdf

Devonish, D. D. (2016). The cognitive coaching approach: A professional Development model for science educators and for students' academic achievement. (Unpublished doctoral dissertation). Northern Caribbean University, Manchester, Jamaica

Devonish, D. D., Lawrence, P. S., & Zamore, C. (2018). A case study on the challenges of implementing diverse instructional strategies into the science lesson post university. *Journal of Arts Science and Technology.*, 11(1), 55–71.

Du Plessis, A. E. (2018). The lived experience of out-of-field STEM teachers: A quandary for strategizing quality teaching in STEM? *Research in Science Education*, 50(4), 1465–1499. DOI: 10.1007/s11165-018-9740-9

El Nagdi, M., Leammukda, F., & Roehrig, G. (2018). Developing identities of STEM teachers at emerging STEM schools. *International Journal of STEM Education*, 5(1), 36. Advance online publication. DOI: 10.1186/s40594-018-0136-1 PMID: 30631726

Fullan, M. (2014). *Teacher development and educational change*. Routledge. DOI: 10.4324/9781315870700

Fulton, K., & Britton, T. (2011). STEM Teachers in professional learning communities: From good teachers to great teaching. In *ERIC*. National Commission on Teaching and America's Future. Retrieved March 12, 2024, from https://eric.ed.gov/?id=ED521328

Fürstenau, B., Pilz, M., & Gonon, P. (2014). The dual system of vocational education and training in Germany – What can be learnt about education for (other) professions. *International Handbook of Research in Professional and Practice-Based Learning*, 427–460. https://doi.org/DOI: 10.1007/978-94-017-8902-8_16

Gentles, C. H. (2020). Stemming the tide: A critical examination of issues, challenges and solutions to Jamaican teacher migration. In *Exploring Teacher Recruitment and Retention* (pp. 197–209). Routledge. DOI: 10.4324/9780429021824-18

George, L. (2020). Exploring the M in STEM: Post-secondary participation, performance and attrition in mathematics. *Canadian Journal of Science, Mathematics and Technology Education = Revue Canadienne de l'Enseignement des Sciences, des Mathématiques et de la Technologie*, 20(3), 441–461. DOI: 10.1007/s42330-020-00095-6

Ghafar, A. (2020). Convergence between 21st century skills and entrepreneurship education in higher education institutes. *International Journal of Higher Education*, 9(1), 218. DOI: 10.5430/ijhe.v9n1p218

Government of Saint Vincent and the Grenadines. (n.d.). Retrieved on March 5, 2024 from https://www.gov.vc/

Granshaw, B. (2016). STEM education for the twenty-first century: A New Zealand perspective. *Australasian Journal of Technology Education*, 3(1). Advance online publication. DOI: 10.15663/ajte.v3i1.43

Griffith, S. (2024). The Future of Research in the Caribbean: The Roles and Responsibilities of Caribbean Scholars in Producing Knowledge for the Region. *Caribbean Journal of Education and Development*, 1(1), 51–56. DOI: 10.46425/cjed601018736

Henry, C. (2020). *GSAJ Assisting Technology Focused MSMEs To Grow*. Retrieved January 24, 2024, from https://jis.gov.jm/gsaj-assisting-technology-focused-msmes-to-grow/

Hunter, J. (2020). *High Possibility STEM Classrooms*. Routledge.

Hunter, J. (October 30, 2020). Support for teacher training institutions. *JIS*. Retrieved on February 5, 2024 from https://jis.gov.jm/support-for-teacher-training-institutions/

Hylton, K. (2022). STEM education in Jamaica: A case of practitioners. *International Studies in Educational Administration (Commonwealth Council for Educational Administration & Management, 50*(2), 46.

JAMPRO. (2021). *Outsourcing*. Retrieved February 24, 2024, from https://dobusinessjamaica.com/wp-content/uploads/2021/11/Sector-E-book-Outsourcing.pdf

Jennings, Z. (2001). Teacher education in selected countries in the Commonwealth Caribbean: The ideal of policy versus the reality of practice. *Comparative Education*, 37(1), 107–134. DOI: 10.1080/03050060020020453

JIS. (2018, May 14). Gov't looking to create integrated higher education system. *JIS*. Retrieved January 5, 2024, from https://moey.gov.jm/govt-looking-to-create-integrated-higher-education-system/

Kelley, T. R., & Knowles, J. G. (2016). A conceptual framework for integrated STEM education. *International Journal of STEM Education*, 3(1), 11. Advance online publication. DOI: 10.1186/s40594-016-0046-z

Kennedy, B., Hefferon, M., & Funk, C. (2018). Half of Americans think young people don't pursue STEM because it is too hard. *Pew Research Centre*. Retrieved January 25, 2024, from http://pewrsr.ch/2Dr2RxJ

Kennedy, T. J., & Odell, M. R. L. (2014). Engaging students in STEM Education. *International Council of Associations for Science Education, 25*(3), 246–258. https://eric.ed.gov/?id=EJ1044508

Kim, K., Bae, E., & Lee, M. (2023). Developing a Model for Sustainable Development in Education Based on Convergence Education. *International Journal of Educational Methodology*, 9(1), 249–259. DOI: 10.12973/ijem.9.1.249

Konkol, P., & Dymek, D. (2023). *Supporting Higher Education 4.0 Challenges and Opportunities* (1st ed.). Routledge.

Kurup, P. M., Yang, Y., Li, X., & Dong, Y. (2021). Interdisciplinary and integrated STEM. *Encyclopedia*, 1(4), 1192–1199. DOI: 10.3390/encyclopedia1040090

Lashley, L. (2019). A reflective analysis of the selection and production of instructional material for curriculum delivery at the primary level in postcolonial Guyana. *SAGE Open*, 9(2), 215824401985844. DOI: 10.1177/2158244019858445

Lauder, H., & Mayhew, K. (2020). Higher education and the labour market: An introduction. *Oxford Review of Education*, 46(1), 1–9. DOI: 10.1080/03054985.2019.1699714

LiVecchi. A. J. (2017). *The opportunity cost of teaching for secondary STEM instructors*. [Doctoral dissertation, University of Houston]. https://www.proquest.com/docview/2187144226

Livingstone, S., Ólafsson, K., Helsper, E. J., Lupiáñez-Villanueva, F., Veltri, G. A., & Folkvord, F. (2017). Maximizing opportunities and minimizing risks for children online: The role of digital skills in emerging strategies of parental mediation. *Journal of Communication*, 67(1), 82–105. DOI: 10.1111/jcom.12277

Margot, K. C., & Kettler, T. (2019). Teachers' perception of STEM integration and education: A systematic literature review. *International Journal of STEM Education*, 6(1), 2. Advance online publication. DOI: 10.1186/s40594-018-0151-2

Mark, P., Joseph, R., & Remy, C. (2005). A harmonized policy framework for teacher education in the Caribbean. Trinidad and Tobago: Retrieved from http://webcache. googleusercontent. com/search

Mayne, H., & Dixon, R. A. (2020). The epistemological dilemma: Student teachers shared experiences of Jamaica's National Standards Curriculum (NSC). *Journal of Curriculum and Teaching*, 9(4), 29. DOI: 10.5430/jct.v9n4p29

McComas, W. F., & Burgin, S. (2020). A Critique of "STEM" Education: Revolution-in-the-Making, Passing Fad, or Instructional Imperative? *Science & Education*, 29(4), 805–829. Advance online publication. DOI: 10.1007/s11191-020-00138-2

McGunagle, D., & Zizka, L. (2020). Employability skills for 21st-century STEM students: The employers' perspective. *Higher Education. Skills and Work-Based Learning*, 10(3), 591–606. DOI: 10.1108/HESWBL-10-2019-0148

McKenzie, V. (2023, September 18). Jamaica needs more engineers to meet its developmental needs – Clarke. *Our Today*. Retrieved March 24, 2024, from https:// our.today/jamaica-needs-more-engineers-to-meet-its-developmental-needs-clarke

Miller, E. (2000). *Education For All in the Caribbean in the 1990s: Retrospect and prospect*. UNESCO., Available online https://www.unesco.org/ext/field/carneid/ monograph.pdf

Mweemba, A. H., McClain, J.Jr, Harris, B., & Newell-McLymont, E. F. (2021). Improving Teaching Practices and Repertoire using the Cognitive Coaching Approach for 21st Century Teachers: A Call for Action. *East African Journal of Education and Social Sciences*, 2(2), 17–33.

National Academies of Sciences, Engineering, and Medicine. (2018). *Graduate STEM education for the 21st century*. National Academies Press.

National Research Council. (2011, 2012). Retrieved February 3, 2024 from https:// www.nationalacademies.org/

Ntemngwa, C., & Oliver, J. S. (2018). The implementation of Integrated Science Technology, Engineering and Mathematics (STEM) Instruction using robotics in the middle school science classroom. *International Journal of Education in Mathematics, Science and Technology*, 12–40. DOI: 10.18404/ijemst.380617

Olesen, A., & Hora, M. T. (2013). Teaching the way they were taught? Revisiting the sources of teaching knowledge and the role of prior experience in shaping faculty teaching practices. *Higher Education*. Advance online publication. DOI: 10.1007/s10734-013-9678-9

Peterson, R. R. (2020). Over the Caribbean top: Community well-being and over-tourism in small island tourism economies. *International Journal of Community Well-being*, 6(2), 89–126. DOI: 10.1007/s42413-020-00094-3 PMID: 34723109

Quinn, C. M., Reid, J. W., & Gardner, G. E. (2020). S+ T+ M= E as a convergent model for the nature of STEM. *Science & Education*, 29(4), 881–898. DOI: 10.1007/s11191-020-00130-w

Radloff, J., & Guzey, S. (2016). Investigating preservice STEM teacher conceptions of STEM education. *Journal of Science Education and Technology*, 25(5), 759–774. DOI: 10.1007/s10956-016-9633-5

Reynolds, J. (February 1, 2014. Ripped to Shreds-JTA says it could trigger legal action. Retrieved on July 30, 2024 from https://jamaica-gleaner.com/gleaner/20140201/lead/lead1.html

Salmon. S. (September 1, 2022). Tourism Workers Receive Training and Certification Through HEART/NSTA Trust. *JIS*. Retrieved on January 30, 2024 from https://jis.gov.jm/tourism-workers-receive-training-and-certification-through-heart-nsta-trust/

Sanghoon, B. (2018). Doing 'convergence education' properly in college. *Happy Education*, 5, 59–61. https://url.kr/7ctzf3

Schweisfurth, M. (2011). Learner-centred education in developing country contexts: From solution to problem? *International Journal of Educational Development*, 31(5), 425–432. https://www.researchgate.net/publication/232398671_Learner-centred_education_in_developing_country_contexts_From_solution_to_problem. DOI: 10.1016/j.ijedudev.2011.03.005

Small, S. (2023, November 18). Mixed views on sanctions against unlicensed teachers: Committee reviewing JTC bill debates whether principals should also be sanctioned. Jamaica Gleaner. Retrieved on July 30, 2024, from https://jamaica-gleaner.com/article/news/20231118/mixed-views-sanctions-against-unlicensed-teachers#google_vignette

Smith, R. (2023, October 25). *Master of Science in STEM Education*. Shortwood Teachers College. Retrieved January 18, 2024, from https://shortwood.edu.jm/master -of-science-in-stem-education/

Smyth, E. (2024). "Education." T*he national development plan in 2023: Priorities and capacity* (2024): 66.

Soyibo, K. (1994). Occupational stress factors and coping strategies among Jamaican high school science teachers. *Research in Science & Technological Education*, 12(2), 187–192. DOI: 10.1080/0263514940120207

Soyibo, K. (1998). An Assessment of Caribbean integrated science textbooks' practical tasks. *Research in Science & Technological Education*, 16(1), 31–41. DOI: 10.1080/0263514980160103

Ssebikindu, L. (2021). Certificate vs. endorsement: what's the difference? *Graduate Programs for Educators*. Retrieved January 18, 2024, from https://www .graduateprogram.org/2021/10/certificate-vs-endorsements-whats-the-difference/

STATIN. (2017). Retrieved on March 8, 2024 from https://statinja.gov.jm/Demo _SocialStats/Education.aspx

Sweeney, A. E. (2003). An overview of science education in the Caribbean: Research, policy and practice.

Sweeney, A. E., & George, L. (2024). STEM Education in the Caribbean: Challenges, Goals, and Possibilities. *Caribbean Journal of Education and Development*, 1(1), 103–110. DOI: 10.46425/cjed1101019192

The Future of Jobs Report. 2023. (2023, April 30). In https://www.weforum.org/ publications/the-future-of-jobs-report-2023/in-full/. World Economic Forum.

The White House Office of Science and Technology Policy. (2022, November). Convergence education: A guide to transdisciplinary STEM learning and teaching. Retrieved February 27, 2024, from https://www.whitehouse.gov/ostp/news-updates/ 2022/11/30/nstc-convergence-education-a-guide-to-transdisciplinary-stem-learning -and-teaching/

Thorpe, S. (2023). A vision for STEM education at the University of Technology, Jamaica. *In SoutheastCon 2023 (Pp. 793-797)*, 793–797.

Tsang, M. C., Fryer, M., & Gregorio, G. (2002). *Access, equity and performance: Education in Barbados, Guyana, Jamaica, and Trinidad and Tobago*. Inter-American Development Bank. https://publications.iadb.org/en/access-equity-and-performance -education-barbados-guyana-jamaica-and-trinidad-and-tobago

United Nations. (2015). *Transforming our World: The 2030 Agenda for Sustainable Development*. Retrieved June 18, 2023, from https://sdgs.un.org/publications/transforming-our-world-2030-agenda-sustainable-development-17981Vasquez, J. A., Sneider, C., & Comer, M. (2013). STEM Lesson Essentials. Heinemann Educational Books.

Walker, B. T., Lee, T. J., & Li, X. (2021). Sustainable development for small island tourism: Developing slow tourism in the Caribbean. *Journal of Travel & Tourism Marketing*, 38(1), 1–15. DOI: 10.1080/10548408.2020.1842289

Williams, S. A. S., & Staulters, M. L. (2014). Instructional collaboration with rural educators in Jamaica: Lessons learned from an international interdisciplinary consultation project. *Journal of Educational & Psychological Consultation*, 24(4), 307–329. DOI: 10.1080/10474412.2014.929968

Windschitl, M. (2009, February). Cultivating 21st century skills in science learners: How systems of teacher preparation and professional development will have to evolve. In Presentation given at the National Academies of Science Workshop on 21st Century Skills, Washington, DC (Vol. 15).

Worth, J., Tang, S., & Galvis, M. A. (2022). Assessing the Impact of Pay and Financial Incentives in Improving Shortage Subject Teacher Supply. Report. *National Foundation for Educational Research*.

Xie, Y., Fang, M., & Shauman, K. (2015, August 1). STEM Education. *Annual Review of Sociology*, 41(1), 331–357. DOI: 10.1146/annurev-soc-071312-145659 PMID: 26778893

Yee Han, P., Joong, N., Ramsawak-Jodha, P., Anderson, S., & Hutton, S. (2020). Understanding the ecologies of education reforms: Comparing the perceptions of secondary teachers and students in Jamaica, Guyana, and Trinidad and Tobago. *Caribbean. Journal of Mixed Methods Research*, 1(1). Advance online publication. DOI: 10.37234/CJMMR

Zacarias. (2021). Teaching under construction. Challenges in teacher professional development in Central America and the Caribbean. *SUMMA*.

ENDNOTES

[1]   https://www.gapsc.com/

[2]   Metro RESA https://www.mresa.org/

3   https://www.mresa.org/endorsements/stem-endorsement

4   https://www.gadoe.org/Curriculum-Instruction-and-Assessment/CTAE/Pages/
     STEM.aspx

5   https://www.gadoe.org/Curriculum-Instruction-and-Assessment/CTAE/Pages/
     STEM.aspx

6   https://www.cognia.org/services/accreditation-certification/

7   https://www.utech.edu.jm/publications/AnnualReport2016-17/69/#zoom=z;
     p.69

8   reference, February 14=https://jamaica.loopnews.com/content/jamaicans
     -including-pm-hail-gold-medal-team-robotics-competition-678704

Chapter 2
Impacts of National Board Accreditation (NBA) on Engineering Disciplines in India

Vikash Singh
Department of Civil Engineering, Integral University, Lucknow, India

Anwar Ahmad
Department of Civil Engineering, Integral University, Lucknow, India

Ashay Devidas Shende
https://orcid.org/0000-0002-2082 -1311
Department of Civil Engineering, K.D.K. College of Engineering, Nagpur, India

R. Jeyalakshmi
https://orcid.org/0000-0003-1651 -4949
Department of English, R.M.K. Engineering College, Kavaraipettai, India

Prakash Dhopte
Department of Mechanical Engineering, Jhulelal Institute of Technology, Maharashtra, India

M. Sudhakar
Department of Mechanical Engineering, Sri Sai Ram Engineering College, Chennai, India

ABSTRACT

An essential component of engineering education is national board accreditation, which guarantees the caliber and applicability of curricula. It results in better curriculum that meet industry demands and get students ready for careers in engineering. Initiatives aimed at developing faculty members can help accredited programs by resulting in improved instructional strategies and scholarly direction. Infrastructure and educational resource investments are necessary for accreditation in order to create a supportive learning environment for student achievement.

DOI: 10.4018/979-8-3693-9215-7.ch002

Because of their perceived quality and rigor, graduates from certified schools are more employable and competitive in the labor market. Programs that satisfy national board requirements are better accepted by professionals and organizations, which leads to greater industry-academic connections and improved internship chances. Accredited schools also promote easier transfers to postgraduate study.

INTRODUCTION

A vital component of engineering education is national board accreditation, which guarantees institutional integrity and academic performance. It is an official acknowledgement that an engineering curriculum satisfies particular requirements, guaranteeing graduates are competent in their chosen sector. Evaluations and cycles of continuous improvement are part of accreditation, and they cover curriculum design, faculty credentials, infrastructure, and student results. Its noteworthy effects encompass improving the caliber of education, increasing the employability of students, cultivating industry recognition, and advancing worldwide competitiveness(Venkatasubramanian et al., 2024).

The goal of national board certification is to standardize engineering curricula so that they satisfy industry standards and advances in technology. Basic engineering concepts, sophisticated technical know-how, and critical soft skills like communication and cooperation must all be included in accredited programs. Students who complete this demanding curriculum development process will be prepared for careers in engineering. In order to maintain relevance and quality, accredited programs are required to periodically evaluate and update their curricula to reflect new developments and trends(Zhen et al., 2023).

In engineering programs, national board accreditation has a big impact on faculty development. To deliver top-notch education and mentorship, accredited bodies expect their faculty members to be highly educated and experienced with both academic qualifications and professional experience. In order to improve teaching efficacy and subject area competence, accredited programs also provide chances for professional development, including conferences, workshops, and research funding. Students benefit from an enhanced learning experience as a result of this focus on teacher development(Sudhakar & Tamilselvi, 2023).

The infrastructure and educational materials used in engineering programs are greatly impacted by the accreditation process. In order to facilitate students' learning and research endeavors, accredited programs are required to furnish sufficient facilities, labs, and technical resources. This provides access to academic databases and libraries as well as cutting edge hardware and software. Investing in state-of-the-art infrastructure helps students learn via doing and gets them ready for industry-specific technologies. Comprehensive support services that promote student achievement and well-being include career counseling and mental health resources(Pare, 2023).

The career pathways and employability of engineering graduates are greatly impacted by national board accreditation. Employers like graduates from approved schools because they may be certain of their rigor and quality. Being accredited denotes quality and dependability and points to an extensive and uniform training program. This gives graduates a competitive edge in the labor market and increases their employability. Since many graduate programs require applicants to have completed their undergraduate degree from recognized schools, accreditation also makes advanced study easier(Komunjeru & Roberts, 2023).

By forming cooperative links with organizations and leaders in the industry, accredited engineering programs enhance industry awareness and cooperation. Internships, industry-sponsored initiatives, guest lecturers, and job placement services are a few examples of these connections. Through these encounters, students are able to bridge the gap between academic learning and professional practice by gaining real-world engineering difficulties and practical experience(Yenugu, 2022). Accreditation by national boards is essential to keeping engineering programs competitive throughout the world. International recognition of accredited programs enables graduates to pursue further education and job options. This draws instructors and students from throughout the world, creating a varied learning environment. Additionally, accreditation fosters information sharing, which advances innovation and international engineering standards.

Engineering disciplines benefit greatly from national board accreditation, which raises standards of instruction, student performance, industry recognition, and competitiveness in the global market. Ensuring quality in engineering education by maintaining high standards and constant development is its main function. This chapter explores the critical role that accreditation will have in determining the direction that engineering specialties will go(Moharir et al., 2022). Engineering programs undergo a methodical accreditation procedure administered by accredited organizations to guarantee they adhere to high standards. It entails a thorough examination of the teaching staff, curriculum, facilities, academic performance, and institutional support. The objective is to give students a top-notch education that will equip them for careers in engineering.

An institution self-evaluation, which looks at its advantages, disadvantages, compliance with accrediting standards, and opportunities for development, is the first step in the accreditation process. Subsequently, the organization provides the accrediting authority with a self-study report detailing its compliance with standards and future improvement plans. An accrediting team made up of seasoned educators and business people reviews the self-study report after inspecting the program's facilities, speaking with instructors and students, and going over paperwork and procedures. This in-depth visit confirms the data in the self-study report and offers a thorough understanding of the program's functioning(Thiruvengadam et al., 2022).

The self-study reports and on-site visits are used by the accrediting organization to establish the accreditation status of a program. Programs that comply with criteria receive accreditation, frequently for a certain length of time; those that don't may receive provisional accreditation, which requires them to fix certain issues before receiving full certification. Accreditation is an ongoing process that requires periodic reviews to maintain accreditation status, ensuring that accredited programs stay current with industry standards and educational best practices, ensuring continuous improvement(Vasudevan & SudalaiMuthu, 2020).

In engineering education, accreditation is essential because it guarantees program quality and rigor and gives employers, parents, students, and other stakeholders confidence in the worth and legitimacy of the education received. This guarantee is essential in a time when educational quality might differ greatly between schools. Employers value accredited engineering graduates' broad and industry-relevant education, which opens up a wide range of prospects. Graduating students who receive this designation will have an advantage over other candidates in the job market. In many engineering specialties, accreditation is a requirement for certification and license and is crucial for professional activity(Helm & Huber, 2022).

Because it mandates that programs be reviewed and improved on a regular basis to remain competitive and in line with industry standards, accreditation encourages accountability and continual development in educational institutions. This benefits students and boosts the institution's standing in the marketplace. Engineering schools that are accredited serve society and industry alike, creating graduates who are capable of taking on challenging tasks and advancing technology. This guarantees a consistent stream of knowledgeable engineers for advancement and financial expansion. Graduates with accreditation are frequently accepted abroad, opening doors to further education and employment prospects. The engineering profession advances globally as a result of this widespread recognition, which encourages international collaboration and information sharing(Dwijayani, 2019; Poornima, 2019).

The significance of accreditation in engineering education cannot be overstated. It guarantees that programs are delivered to the highest standards, enhances graduates' employability and professional preparedness, promotes institutional improvement, and benefits industry and society by producing competent and skilled engineers.

Scope

This chapter examines how national board accreditation affects engineering education, with particular attention to infrastructure, student outcomes, industry recognition, curriculum design, faculty development, and global competitiveness.

It offers a thorough grasp of how engineering programs are shaped and improved by accrediting requirements. In order to show how accreditation affects engineering institutions and stakeholders in the actual world, case studies that highlight various accrediting organizations, their standards, and procedures are included in the study.

Background

Global engineering education is guaranteed to be of high quality and uniformity through national board accreditation. It came about as a result of the demand for uniformity in professional practice and education. Unrestricted engineering education in the early 20th century resulted in differences in graduate competency and program quality. In order to design and implement basic criteria, professional associations and educational institutions worked together to create accrediting agencies. Engineering education must meet strict standards set by accrediting organizations such as ABET in the US and NBA in India. These standards include curriculum content, delivery strategies, faculty credentials, and student results. The certification procedure has changed throughout time in response to input from professional groups, academia, and industry in order to be current and useful in a quickly changing technological environment.

Objectives

- to investigate the effects of certification on graduates' capacity to satisfy industry needs and their level of professional preparation.
- to investigate the advantages of industry-academic partnerships—such as internships, research collaborations, and job placements—that result from certification.
- to evaluate the degree to which graduates of certified engineering programs are recognized internationally.
- to make suggestions for new accrediting paths that prioritize diversity, creativity, and technological progression adaptability.

ENHANCING EDUCATIONAL QUALITY

By setting strict criteria, national board certification dramatically raises the caliber of engineering programs, as seen in Figure 1. These organizations guarantee thorough, up-to-date, and pertinent education for the public and business sectors. Improvements in curriculum are fueled by accreditation, which benefits students' educational results(Baashar et al., 2022; Moharir et al., 2022).

Figure 1. Enhancing Educational Quality

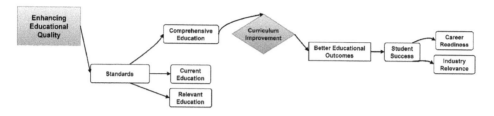

Alignment with Industry Standards

By bringing courses into line with industry norms, accreditation improves them. Accredited programs cover advanced technical skills, new technologies, and fundamental engineering concepts. They frequently collaborate with academic leaders and industry specialists. This raises the standard of education by guaranteeing that students have the skills necessary to succeed in their jobs(Mane, 2015; Viswanadhan & Rao, 2005).

- Emphasis on Core skills: According to accreditation criteria, engineering graduates must be proficient in core skills such ethical behavior, effective communication, problem-solving, and critical thinking. Programs need to create classes and exercises that develop these abilities so that graduates may work in professional settings and be technically competent. This all-encompassing method equips students to take on challenging technical problems.
- continual Curriculum Review and Improvement: Maintaining accreditation requires constant curriculum review and improvement because it's a continual process. Programs that seek accreditation are required to update their curriculum on a regular basis in order to meet market demands and technological improvements. In order to improve educational quality, feedback from stakeholders like as students, professors, industry partners, and alumni is helpful in identifying areas that need improvement and putting the required adjustments into place.
- Integration of Theoretical and Practical Knowledge: The integration of theoretical and practical knowledge through classroom instruction, laboratory work, project-based learning, and internships is emphasized by accreditation criteria. These practical experiences bridge the gap between academic learning and industry expectations by assisting students in applying theoretical

concepts to real-world issues, improving their problem-solving skills, and gaining significant exposure to professional practice.

- Integration of Emerging Technologies: Engineering schools need to keep up with the rapid advancement of technology, and accrediting agencies are pushing for the integration of modern subjects and emerging technologies into their curricula. This guarantees that pupils are up to date on the newest instruments, methods, and fashions in the industry. In order to prepare students to be leaders and innovators in their respective professions, accredited programs are increasingly including subjects like cybersecurity, advanced manufacturing, renewable energy, and artificial intelligence.

- Improved Teaching Strategies and Materials: Accreditation promotes creative teaching strategies and materials including blended and online learning, flipped classrooms, online and online learning, and simulation tools. To give students a rich and encouraging learning environment, it also necessitates investments in contemporary infrastructure and learning materials, such as cutting-edge laboratories, software, and access to academic databases.

By aligning curricula with industry standards, emphasizing core competencies, guaranteeing ongoing review and improvement, combining theoretical and practical knowledge, embracing emerging technologies, and improving teaching strategies and resources, national board accreditation considerably raises the caliber of engineering programs. Students gain from this ongoing improvement, which also advances the engineering discipline.

Faculty Development

Faculty development plays a major role in the quality of engineering programs; national board accreditation organizations place a high value on credentials, professional growth, and good teaching. Programs must hire instructors with advanced degrees and a wealth of industry experience in order to maintain accreditation, guaranteeing that theoretical understanding and practical understanding are crucial components of an all-encompassing engineering education(Pradhan, 2021; Shah & Kolhekar, 2021).

Opportunities for ongoing professional development, such as attending conferences, workshops, and seminars on the most recent developments in engineering technology and pedagogy, should be provided by accredited programs to their faculty members. This guarantees that faculty members remain up to date on new tools, software, and techniques and assists educators in incorporating contemporary industrial practices into their instruction. It also bridges the gap between theoretical understanding and practical application.

Faculty participation in academic work and research is required by accreditation, which improves student learning while also advancing knowledge. In the classroom, active researchers introduce cutting-edge discoveries that promote critical thinking. Institutions may help with this by providing access to cutting-edge labs and technology, research funds, and sabbatical opportunities.

Peer reviews and student feedback systems are frequently included in accredited programs in order to evaluate and improve the quality of their instruction. This supports educators in honing their teaching techniques and building a solid, cohesive team dedicated to high standards in education. More junior colleagues are frequently mentored by senior faculty members, who help them with curriculum creation, research methodology, and successful teaching techniques.

Infrastructure and Learning Resources

In order to guarantee that students have access to contemporary, well-equipped facilities that support both theoretical learning and practical application—including classrooms, laboratories, workshops, and computing resources that satisfy industry standards—accreditation bodies assess the quality of infrastructure and learning resources in engineering education(Venkatesh & King, 2021).

For practical experimentation, testing, and prototyping in engineering education, state-of-the-art laboratories are essential. These labs are furnished with the newest tools and technology thanks to accreditation authorities, which enables students to work on actual projects and obtain real-world experience. Electrical engineering schools may include circuit design and microcontroller technology, while mechanical engineering programs could include sophisticated machining tools and materials testing equipment.

In order for students to become proficient in tools like CAD, CAE, and various simulation software—which are widely used in the industry and highlight the significance of computing resources in modern engineering—accredited programs must provide them with access to high-performance computing facilities and modern software suites.

Institutions must maintain well-stocked libraries and online resources, including industry periodicals, academic journals, reference books, and textbooks, in order to meet accreditation criteria. These libraries facilitate academic study and research activities by giving faculty and students access to the most recent findings and innovations.

The importance of support services in the educational process—such as career counseling, academic advising, and mental health resources—is emphasized by accreditation. Academic advising helps students choose their classes, become ready for the workforce, and find their way through the educational system. Career counseling provides advice on internships, professional development opportunities, and job placements. Resources for mental health offer assistance with stress management and overall wellbeing.

In order to ensure that students in approved engineering programs obtain a thorough, industry-relevant education that equips them for successful engineering jobs, faculty development and a strong infrastructure are essential.

IMPACT ON STUDENT OUTCOMES AND EMPLOYABILITY

Higher Employability Rates

Engineering graduates' employability is greatly increased by accreditation because companies value the stringent standards and theoretical underpinnings of these programs. A thorough curriculum including advanced technical abilities, foundational engineering concepts, and critical soft skills like problem-solving, teamwork, and communication is offered by accredited institutions(Das et al., 2024; Durairaj et al., 2023; Prabhuswamy et al., 2024).

Figure 2. Impacts on Student Outcomes and Employability

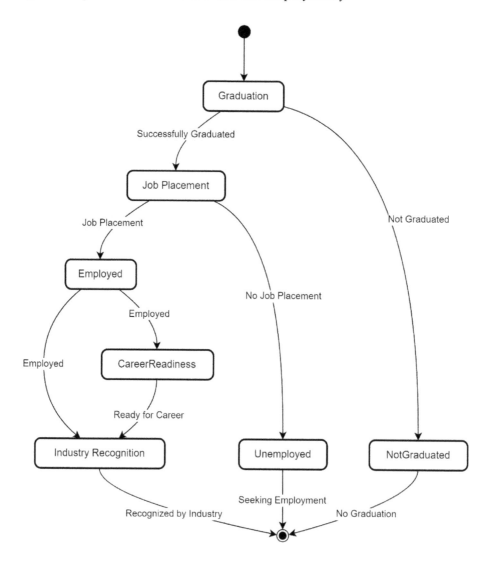

Figure 2 shows how many different factors have a substantial influence on employability and student performance. Having completed a recognized degree, one's prospects of finding work right away after graduation are increased. Employers like graduates from recognized programs because they guarantee quality and consistency. recognized programs follow stringent criteria and implement ongoing quality improvement procedures, which guarantee that the curriculum is up to date and meets the demands of the industry.

Internships, cooperative education, and industrial projects are frequently incorporated into the curricula of accredited schools to provide students with hands-on experience in real-world engineering difficulties. Employers find this more enticing because it shows that students can apply what they have learned in the classroom to real-world scenarios, which is a critical component of employability.

Accreditation promotes long-term professional progression in addition to improving employment opportunities. Because of their competence and extensive education, graduates from approved schools are frequently chosen for leadership and specialized jobs. Higher beginning wages and quicker job advancement are the outcomes of this choice. Due to adherence to its criteria by licensing authorities and employers, accreditation also promotes mobility between nations and regions.

Preparation for Professional Practice

Accredited engineering programs provide students with a thorough understanding of both the fundamentals and advanced engineering concepts, preparing them for professional practice. The courses in these programs are carefully designed to reflect the complexity of contemporary engineering challenges. They include both core disciplines and multidisciplinary areas, ensuring that students get the technical expertise required for success in their chosen sector(Das et al., 2024; Prabhuswamy et al., 2024; Sharma et al., 2024).

A focus on hands-on and experiential learning is placed on accredited programs, which include lab sessions, design projects, and fieldwork to help students apply abstract ideas to real-world issues. This practical method develops critical thinking and problem-solving abilities, which are essential for practicing professional engineering. Capstone projects that mimic real-world engineering activities are frequently included in accredited programs. These projects force students to work with peers, integrate knowledge from several subject areas, and develop, implement, and test engineering solutions. Professionals from the business and academic communities assess these initiatives and offer their practical insights.

Students enrolled in accredited engineering schools graduate with a thorough awareness of professional responsibility, engineering ethics, and the larger effects that engineering solutions have on the environment and society. Students who have this ethical grounding will be better able to handle difficult moral and ethical decisions in the workplace. Accreditation in education focuses on developing essential soft skills, particularly communication skills, which are highly valued in the workplace. Students are required to present their work, write technical reports, and collaborate in teams, enhancing their ability to convey complex technical information effectively.

Graduates from accredited programs are guaranteed to be knowledgeable about current industry standards and best practices, enabling them to make valuable contributions in their professional responsibilities. This keeps their curriculum up to date with the most recent developments in technology, guaranteeing that graduates have access to the instruments, methods, and approaches that are now employed in the engineering industry. Continuous improvement is frequently necessary for accreditation, requiring that programs be updated on a regular basis to take into account the newest developments in technology and business processes. Graduates are well-prepared for upcoming problems thanks to this dynamic approach, which also prepares them for changes in the sector in the future and present professional practice.

Accreditation provides a demanding education that equips graduates for professional engineering practice, which enhances student outcomes and employability. Comprehensive curriculum, real-world experience, ethical instruction, and industry standards are all provided by accredited schools, guaranteeing that graduates are prepared to excel in the workplace and make significant contributions to the engineering community.

Pathways to Advanced Studies

Through the provision of paths to higher study, national board accreditation in engineering has a substantial influence on student outcomes and employability. Graduates of accredited programs are in great demand for graduate study due to their demanding curricula, excellent academic standards, and industry alignment(Agrawal et al., 2023; Durairaj et al., 2023; Venkatasubramanian et al., 2024).

Because it guarantees the caliber and rigor of undergraduate education, accreditation plays a critical role in opening doors to graduate study. Both domestic and foreign graduate programs encourage or require applicants to have completed their undergraduate studies at recognized universities. Graduate admissions committees are aware that individuals who have completed approved programs have a thorough education and are ready for the difficulties of further study. Additionally, accreditation guarantees that students have gained the fundamental information and abilities needed to thrive in graduate-level courses. Students enrolled in certified engineering programs have a solid academic foundation in their field of study because to the programs' standardized curriculum and demanding academic criteria. In order to address the more complex and specialized subjects taught in graduate-level courses, this foundation is necessary.

Engineering program accreditation fosters academic performance and research by enabling undergraduate students to work with faculty on research projects, take part in conferences and competitions, and cooperate on these activities. Their abilities are improved, and it also gets them ready for thesis and research at the graduate level. Since graduates with advanced engineering degrees are widely sought after in a variety of industries like technology, manufacturing, energy, and healthcare, accreditation increases students' employability and competitiveness in the labor market. Students can specialize in particular fields through further study, which increases their employment options and earning potential.

Students pursuing graduate engineering degrees can gain practical experience through corporate partnerships, co-ops, and internships. This enables people to create professional networks, acquire practical skills, and apply theoretical knowledge to real-world problems. Employability is improved by accredited undergraduate programs that prioritize experiential learning. Engineering students with accreditation have a better chance of going on to PhD programs and landing research jobs in universities, government organizations, and corporate laboratories. Because they have had extensive research experience and intense academic preparation, graduates with advanced degrees are well-prepared for these competitive contexts.

The engineering national board accreditation facilitates students' access to postgraduate education, improving their performance and employment. In order to prepare students for graduate school and professions, accredited programs provide a solid academic basis, chances for research, and industry experiences. Engineering leaders and innovators of the future are shaped by the culture of academic achievement that is fostered by accreditation.

INDUSTRY RECOGNITION AND PARTNERSHIPS

Figure 3. Industry Recognition and Partnerships

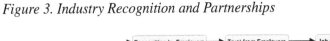

Value of Accreditation in the Industry

The engineering business places a great value on national board certification because of its strict requirements, extensive curriculum, and dedication to producing graduates of the highest caliber. Employers and professionals give preference to recruiting graduates of certified schools since they have the information, abilities, and competences required for the job(Gift et al., 2024; Pasumarthy et al., 2024; Puranik et al., 2024).

In the sector, accreditation is essential for guaranteeing consistency and quality. Reputable organizations subject accredited schools to a thorough review process that looks at student results, faculty qualifications, infrastructure, and curriculum design. This guarantees that graduates obtain a thorough education that satisfies industry requirements and equips them to handle the rigors of the workplace. Figure 3 shows collaborations and industry recognition. In engineering programs, accreditation denotes legitimacy and dependability as well as a dedication to best practices and ongoing development in the field. Graduates are of higher caliber as a result of this recognition, which increases their attractiveness as job prospects.

Because engineering programs involve extensive preparation, businesses respect graduates from accredited programs, which enhances their reputation and competitiveness. Due to this acknowledgment, there is an increased need for graduates, which raises beginning earnings, placement rates, and job options. Strong industry ties, the development of talent pipelines, research collaborations, and tackling business difficulties are all advantageous to accredited programs. Through these collaborations, students may take advantage of industry-sponsored projects, co-ops, internships, and mentorship from professionals in the field, all of which help them become more employable and get real-world experience in engineering methods.

In the engineering sector, accreditation fosters a culture of continuous learning and professional growth, enabling professionals to pursue additional education and remain abreast of industry developments. Companies understand how crucial it is to make ongoing educational investments in order to maintain their competitiveness in a fast changing technological environment. For engineering professionals, accredited programs also provide worldwide recognition and mobility, opening doors to employment prospects and postgraduate study abroad. This international recognition promotes knowledge sharing and cross-cultural collaboration while increasing the variety and competitiveness of the engineering workforce. For engineering work to be high-quality, credible, and relevant to industry demands, accreditation is essential. It boosts industry relationships, raises the demand for graduates, and offers chances for professional growth and career success. Accreditation shapes the future of engineering by promoting collaboration between academics and industry and conforming to industry standards.

Strengthening Industry-Academic Collaboration

The engineering national board accreditation enhances the caliber of instruction and cultivates solid industry-academia collaborations. Through these partnerships, engineering schools are kept current, attentive to industry demands, and generate graduates who are ready for the workforce. Through internships and co-ops, accredited schools frequently work with industry partners to give students real-world experience and exposure to a range of engineering-related topics. These internships combine classroom instruction with practical experience, improving students' employability and offering insightful knowledge of standards and procedures in the business. All things considered, certification guarantees that engineering schools stay current and workforce-ready(Prabhuswamy et al., 2024; Venkatasubramanian et al., 2024).

Professionals from the industry are invited to speak as guest lecturers, adjunct professors, or advisers in accredited engineering programs, contributing their practical experience and industry insights to the classroom. These programs include industry seminars, panel discussions, and guest lectures to present a variety of viewpoints and career paths in the engineering sector. Collaborative research and development initiatives are another example of how industry and academics may work together to address complicated problems, provide novel solutions, and push technology boundaries. These projects involve industry stakeholders. These partnerships frequently lead to sponsored studies, cooperative research projects, and technology transfer agreements that are advantageous to both business and academics.

Engineering schools that seek accreditation are encouraged to form advisory boards composed of alumni and executives in the field who can offer insightful feedback on programmatic improvements, curriculum development, and market trends. These boards make sure that curricula are in line with the demands of the business and new technology; they also help students find jobs and mentorship opportunities in the industry, thereby fostering a stronger connection between academia and the workforce. Encouraging collaboration between students, professors, and industry representatives, accredited engineering programs take part in conferences, trade exhibitions, and networking activities. These gatherings result in money for research, partnerships, and employment possibilities. Accreditation by national boards in engineering is essential for enhancing industry-academic cooperation. Through networking events, guest lecturers, advisory boards, cooperative projects, internships, and cooperative projects, accredited programs interact with business partners. These partnerships improve students' educational experiences, increase their employability, and promote engineering knowledge. Engineering schools that are accredited are guaranteed to be responsive to industry demands and to provide graduates who are prepared for the workforce(Das et al., 2024; Durairaj et al., 2023).

Internship and Job Placement Opportunities

Engineering national board accreditation raises academic standards, promotes industry recognition, and opens up beneficial internship and employment prospects. Professionals and businesses hold accredited programs in high regard because of their strict criteria and conformity with industry requirements. Accreditation is seen by employers as a symbol of quality, demonstrating to graduates that they have undergone adequate job preparation. Strong ties are frequently maintained between accredited programs and business partners, who actively seek cooperation on a range of projects(Abd Latiff et al., 2022; R. Bhat et al., 2022).

With the help of industry partners, accreditation gives students access to internship opportunities that give them real-world experience and transferable skills. Through these internships, students may create professional networks, gain practical skills, and apply academic knowledge to real-world tasks. They also give students the chance to learn about many industries, study different technical specialties, and define their future objectives. Employers frequently employ internships as a pipeline for hiring, providing successful interns with full-time job prospects when they graduate. This smooth transition from internship to full-time job is evidence of the high caliber of instruction offered by recognized schools.

When it comes to engineering graduates finding employment, accreditation plays a major role. Employers like graduates from recognized institutions because of their professionalism, technical proficiency, and work readiness. Aside from resume writing seminars, practice interviews, career fairs, networking events, and alumni links, accredited institutions also provide career placement services. Career counselors collaborate extensively with students to determine their objectives, interests, and abilities. They then offer help and advice during the job search process. Engineering programs that are accredited provide students with access to cutting-edge technology, real-world problems, and opportunities to engage with professionals in the field. Additionally, it guarantees that curriculum reflect the demands and tendencies of the sector today. Programs with accreditation participate in joint research collaborations, industry-sponsored projects, guest lectures, and seminars for professional development. Industry partners and advisers offer insightful commentary and advice on curriculum development, helping to create programs that generate graduates who are ready for the needs of the job market.

The engineering national board accreditation promotes industry collaborations and recognition, giving students access to worthwhile internship and employment possibilities. Strong ties with business partners enable accredited schools to provide students with practical experience, help with career placement, and exposure to real-world engineering challenges—all of which improve their preparedness for the workforce.

GLOBAL COMPETITIVENESS

International Recognition of Accredited Programs

By guaranteeing worldwide recognition and legitimacy, national board accreditation in engineering boosts competitiveness on the global stage. It acts as a tool for quality control, certifying that an engineering program satisfies exacting requirements of excellence. Graduates are highly valued in the international economy because of this recognition, which transcends national boundaries. Accreditation is often regarded by employers as a symbol of excellence and dependability, signifying that graduates have the essential knowledge, abilities, and competences to thrive in the engineering field(R. Bhat et al., 2022; Sengupta & Das, 2023).

Figure 4. International Recognition of Accredited Programs

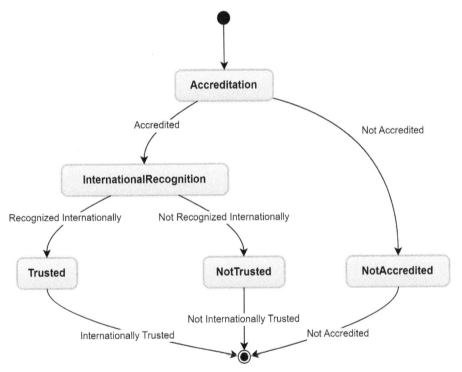

International accrediting agencies and professional associations accept accredited engineering schools, which makes it easier for credits and certificates to be transferred between nations. This removes obstacles and doubts regarding the caliber of the graduates' education, enabling them to pursue work or more study. The ability of engineering professionals to work abroad, acquire a variety of experiences, collaborate on foreign projects, and support innovation and development on a worldwide scale is another benefit of accredited schools. The international recognition of recognized programs is shown in figure 4.

Because of their acknowledgment by academic institutions and industry as well as their reputation for excellence, accredited engineering programs draw a broad student base. By exposing students to a variety of viewpoints, cultures, and ideas, diversity enhances the learning process and equips them for cross-cultural cooperation and teamwork. Additionally, accredited programs encourage alliances and worldwide engagement amongst engineering schools through faculty collaborations, student exchange programs, and cooperative research initiatives. These collaborations offer chances for cross-cultural learning, teamwork on cutting-edge research, and exposure to global best practices in engineering research and teaching.

Globally harmonizing engineering standards and procedures is another benefit of accreditation. Together with their worldwide counterparts, accrediting agencies create uniform standards and evaluation criteria for engineering schools. By ensuring uniformity and comparability across various certification systems, this partnership facilitates the international recognition of engineering programs and the global acceptance of graduates' credentials.

By guaranteeing worldwide recognition and credibility, national board accreditation in engineering increases competitiveness on the global stage. Employers, accrediting agencies, and professional associations appreciate graduates from accredited schools highly. Professional mobility is made easier by accreditation, which also draws in a varied student body, encourages cross-border cooperation, and unifies worldwide engineering standards. It maintains high standards of quality and performance, equipping engineers for success in a world that is changing quickly and becoming more interconnected.

Attracting International Students and Faculty

International professors and students are drawn to engineering programs with national board accreditation, which increases global competitiveness. International students feel more confident since accredited programs are acknowledged for their quality and excellence on a worldwide scale. The demand for engineering degrees overseas has increased as a result of this guarantee of high-quality education that satisfies worldwide standards. Programs with accreditation have a big role in drawing in overseas students(Dwijayani, 2019; Pare, 2023).

Engineering programs that have earned accreditation are highly valued for their dedication to innovation, academic achievement, and ongoing development. These universities draw world-class academics because they provide chances for career advancement, expert cooperation, and access to cutting-edge resources. Engineering degrees from accredited universities are also recognized internationally, enabling graduates to seek professional certification and license in a number of nations. As a result, graduates are more equipped to take advantage of global employment prospects, and an engineering degree gains value and becomes a sought-after qualification for companies throughout the globe.

Through outreach activities, marketing campaigns, and collaborations with foreign organizations, accredited engineering schools actively seek out and enrol overseas faculty members and students. They offer support services such as academic guidance, language aid, cultural orientation programs, and visa assistance. The academic atmosphere is enhanced and cross-cultural exchange is encouraged by the presence of foreign teachers and students. While international faculty members add knowledge, research interests, and worldwide networks, they also enhance the academic prestige and research output of authorized programs. They bring a diversity of viewpoints, experiences, and ideas to the classroom.

By drawing in foreign instructors and students, accreditation in engineering raises the programs' competitiveness on a worldwide scale. Accredited schools are known for their inventiveness, dedication to ongoing development, and high caliber of instruction. These institutions frequently collaborate with universities and research institutes throughout the world on collaborative research initiatives, student exchange programs, dual degree programs, and faculty exchanges. This offers chances for multidisciplinary cooperation, cross-cultural learning, and exposure to international best practices in engineering education and research. International students contribute to the worldwide growth of engineering education and research by enriching the academic environment, fostering cooperation and collaborations, and promoting cultural interchange.

Contributions to Global Engineering Standards

By encouraging the creation and upkeep of international engineering standards, national board accreditation in engineering dramatically increases competitiveness on the world stage(Goyal et al., 2022a, 2022b).

- Alignment with Global Best Practices: To be accredited, engineering programs must adhere to globally accepted norms for the design of the curriculum, the credentials of the faculty, the performance of the students, and institutional support. By guaranteeing that their graduates satisfy the highest standards in the area, these criteria guarantee that their graduates meet worldwide expectations for engineering proficiency and professionalism.

- Promotion of creativity and Excellence: Engineering programs that are accredited are more likely to exhibit creativity and excellence, which in turn leads to breakthroughs in research and technology as well as multidisciplinary partnerships. This dynamic approach helps engineers become more competitive in the global marketplace and fosters the creation of novel solutions to pressing global issues.

- Accredited engineering program graduates have international recognition and mobility because of their high caliber and reputation, which are highly valued by businesses, associations of professionals, and educational institutions. They can pursue higher education, research partnerships, and employment possibilities in many countries and areas because to their mobility.

- Contribution to Global Engineering Standards: To provide uniform standards and guidelines for engineering education, accrediting organizations such as ABET and ENAEE work with academic institutions and professional groups around the globe. This partnership promotes mutual recognition, guarantees uniformity and comparability in international engineering programs, and eases the international movement of engineering professionals. Global engineering standards are closely maintained by organizations such as ABET and ENAEE.

- Improvement of Cross-Cultural competency: Accredited engineering programs place a high priority on students' global views and cross-cultural competency. They do this by providing exposure to a variety of contexts, international exchange programs, and intercultural collaborative projects. These courses give graduates the abilities and know-how required to prosper in the globalized world of today and to function well in intercultural settings.

Through the development of global engineering standards, the promotion of innovation, the facilitation of international mobility, the alignment of programs with worldwide best practices, and the improvement of cross-cultural competency, national board certification in engineering dramatically increases global competitiveness. Graduates from accredited programs are ready for success in an increasingly globalized and fast changing environment.

CHALLENGES AND CONSIDERATIONS

Maintaining Accreditation Standards

Ensuring engineering programs meet the demanding criteria imposed by accrediting agencies is a problem. These requirements include student results, instructor credentials, program design, and institutional support. While achieving first accreditation is a noteworthy accomplishment, it takes time and consistent effort to maintain compliance. Engineering accreditation standards must be continuously adjusted to reflect changing industry trends and best practices in education. Because of social issues, industrial demands, and technology breakthroughs, engineering specialties are always changing. Curricula, teaching strategies, and learning materials must be reviewed and updated on a regular basis for accredited programs. This requires faculty members to engage in resource-intensive research, professional development, and curriculum enhancement(Cheng et al., 2019; Dwijayani, 2019; Poornima, 2019).

Programs must adhere to rigorous assessment and evaluation procedures in order to meet accreditation criteria. Data collection and analysis on student outcomes, teacher credentials, and program success are mandated by accrediting agencies. But putting in place thorough evaluation procedures and guaranteeing data integrity may be difficult and time-consuming, particularly for organizations with little funding and administrative assistance.

Transparency and accountability are required by accreditation criteria at every level of the institution. Regular reviews, self-evaluations, and site inspections are required of accredited programs in order to show compliance and ongoing development. Faculty, staff, administrators, and stakeholders must collaborate, communicate, and coordinate effectively. It also need a culture of openness to criticism and innovation and adaptation.

Resource Allocation and Funding

Allocating funds and resources effectively to sustain accreditation criteria presents issues for engineering programs. Faculty development, infrastructural improvements, evaluation tools, and administrative assistance are all associated with the cost of accreditation. Programs that seek accreditation must be able to draw in and keep faculty members who possess advanced degrees, work experience, and a dedication to quality. Nonetheless, there is fierce rivalry for the best employees since the sector pays well and provides excellent benefits. Academic institutions find it difficult to attract and maintain faculty members who fulfill accreditation standards in the absence of sufficient financing and incentives.(Babu et al., 2022; Pasumarthy et al., 2024)

Infrastructure and educational materials must be extensively invested in to meet accreditation criteria. In order to facilitate student learning and research, accredited programs must include state-of-the-art facilities, labs, and computer resources. These investments, however, can be expensive and frequently call for a little amount of financial backing. Due of the significant paperwork, reporting, and compliance activities required by certification procedures, accreditation-related administrative expenditures can put a burden on budgets. Funds may need to be set aside by institutions for site visits, external consultants, and accreditation costs. Timelines for accreditation may also call for hiring temporary workers or adding more personnel to satisfy criteria, which would increase costs. It is difficult to maintain accreditation requirements for engineering programs because of changes in the industry, thorough evaluation procedures, accountability, openness, and resource allocation. Strong leadership, strategic planning, stakeholder participation, and ongoing improvement are needed to address them. Engineering programs can preserve quality, enhance student results, and promote the engineering profession by overcoming these obstacles.

Adapting to Technological and Industry Changes

In order to stay relevant and competitive in the quickly changing field of engineering education, accredited engineering programs must constantly update their curriculum, teaching strategies, and infrastructure in response to industry changes and technological advancements(Puranik et al., 2024; Sharma et al., 2024; Venkatasubramanian et al., 2024).

- Curriculum Evolution: Through frequent review and update cycles, engineering curriculum must adjust to new technology, industry trends, and social demands. In order to guarantee that curriculum adhere to industry standards and best practices, accredited programs should strike a balance between fundamental engineering concepts and cutting-edge innovations. They should also work in conjunction with academic experts, industry partners, and professional groups.
- Integration of Emerging Technologies: Curriculum and research activities for accredited programs must take into account cutting-edge technologies including blockchain, artificial intelligence, Internet of Things, and renewable energy. This calls for expenditures on instructional resources, laboratory facilities, and faculty development. Programs also need to prepare students for future technology developments and provide them with the skills they need to innovate and adapt in quickly changing surroundings.

- Industry Engagement and Partnerships: In order to keep current with labor demands and industry advances, accredited programs must uphold industry partnerships through advisory boards, industry-sponsored projects, internships, and co-ops. This calls for constant coordination, input from the industry, and adaptability to the demands of a changing market.
- Faculty Development and Training: By upgrading their knowledge and pedagogical approaches, faculty members play a critical role in helping the classroom adjust to changes in technology and business. To keep abreast of current technology and industry trends, as well as to attract qualified staff for curriculum that are always evolving, accredited programs should make investments in faculty development initiatives such as workshops, seminars, and professional development opportunities.
- Resource Allocation and Funding: To keep up with technical and industry developments, accredited programs need to make investments in infrastructure, hardware, software licensing, and teaching materials. They must use external grants, industry collaborations, alumni donations, and institutional resources to deploy resources and get financing for technology improvements, faculty development, and curriculum revisions.

It is difficult for accredited engineering schools to keep up with developments in the industry and in technology. Through a commitment to innovation, the cultivation of industry relationships, faculty development investments, and judicious resource allocation, they may rise to the forefront of equipping students for success in the quickly changing engineering field.

BEST PRACTICES

Successful Accredited Engineering Programs

Accredited engineering programs that are successful exhibit industry relevance, academic quality, student success, and innovation via the use of best practices in program conception, execution, and ongoing improvement(Mahrishi & Abbas, 2023; Mishra & Aithal, 2023).

- Industry-Relevant Curriculum: Programs that are successful keep their curriculum updated to reflect current trends and industry demands. They update and assess their course offerings frequently to make sure they remain relevant and take into account new multidisciplinary viewpoints, technology, and methods. This guarantees that graduates can successfully contribute to industrial innovation and are well-prepared for the needs of the workforce.

- Possibilities for Hands-On Experience: Promising programs provide their students opportunities for experiential learning that go beyond the classroom theory. Lab trials, design projects, co-ops, internships, industry-sponsored initiatives, and research experiences are a few examples of these. Through experiential learning, students may build practical skills, obtain significant industrial experience, and apply academic concepts in real-world contexts.

- Good Faculty Leadership and Development: Promising programs are characterized by a faculty team of seasoned instructors and business experts who are dedicated to the success of their students and ongoing development. To remain up to date with changes in the market, pedagogical breakthroughs, and research advancements, faculty members regularly participate in professional development programs. They provide a positive learning environment by acting as mentors, counselors, and role models for the kids.

- Sturdy Evaluation and Ongoing Improvement Procedures: Robust assessment procedures are employed by successful programs to gauge stakeholder satisfaction, program efficacy, and student learning results. They gather and examine information from several sources, including as job reviews, alumni surveys, student performance evaluations, and course assessments. Programs use this data to pinpoint areas that need improvement and put evidence-based tactics into practice in order to raise program standards and boost student achievement.

- Commitment to Diversity, Equity, and Inclusion: To provide a friendly and inclusive learning environment for all students, successful programs give priority to diversity, equity, and inclusion efforts. They actively seek out and assist underrepresented groups in engineering, offer tools and services to help students succeed, and cultivate an environment that values mutual respect, acceptance, and understanding.

- Robust Industry ties and Engagement: Employers, professional groups, government agencies, and research institutions are just a few of the industry stakeholders that successful programs foster strong ties with. Through these agreements, students may have access to cutting-edge resources and facilities, network with professionals in the field, and acquire experience in the workplace. Industry relationships also help to ensure that programs are relevant and responsive to industry demands by providing information on workforce requirements, research objectives, and curriculum development.

- Global Perspective and Internationalization: To prepare students for success in a globalized society, successful programs embrace a global perspective and give internationalization projects top priority. They include study abroad options, chances for international engagement, and worldwide research partnerships that introduce students to a variety of engineering techniques, languages, and cultures. In order to increase program awareness and reputation, successful programs may also pursue international accreditation or take part in worldwide engineering networks.

Engineering programs that are accredited and adhere to best practices in curriculum design, experiential learning, faculty development, assessment, diversity, equity, and inclusion, as well as industry engagement and global perspective, can become leaders in engineering education by improving program quality, student success, and industry relevance.

Table 1. *Comparative Analysis of Accredited vs. Non-Accredited Engineering Programs*

Aspect	Accredited Programs	Non-Accredited Programs
Curriculum Design	Aligned with industry standards and evolving technological trends.	Lack standardized curriculum and may not meet industry requirements.
Faculty Qualifications	Faculty possess advanced degrees and industry experience.	Faculty qualifications may vary, leading to inconsistency.
Infrastructure and Resources	Well-equipped labs, modern facilities, and access to resources.	Limited resources, outdated facilities, and inadequate equipment.
Student Outcomes	High graduation rates, improved employability, and career readiness.	Lower graduation rates, limited job prospects, and skills gaps.
Industry Recognition	Recognized by employers and industry professionals.	Lack recognition and credibility, may face skepticism from employers.
Continuous Improvement	Regularly reviewed and updated to meet accreditation standards.	Lack formal assessment processes and mechanisms for improvement.
Global Competitiveness	Attract international students and faculty, recognized globally.	Limited visibility and recognition on the global stage.
Alumni Success	Graduates have higher chances of success and career advancement.	Alumni may face challenges in job search and career progression.

The distinctions between accredited and non-accredited engineering programs are shown in Table 1. Higher quality standards, more qualified instructors, better facilities, and better student results are all features of accredited programs. Additionally, accreditation improves alumni achievement, industry visibility, and competitiveness worldwide, giving graduates a number of benefits.

FUTURE DIRECTIONS AND TRENDS

Figure 5. Future Directions and Trends

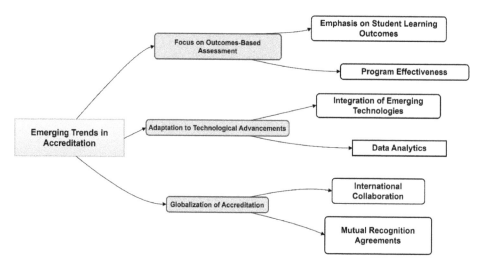

Emerging Trends in Accreditation

The figure 5 depicts the future direction and trends in various industries. Adopting these suggestions and keeping abreast of trends in engineering education and certification will enable programs to continually improve and adjust to the ever-changing demands of society, industry, and students(A. Bhat et al., 2023; Senapati & Singh, 2023).

- Instead of focusing on inputs or procedures, accrediting agencies are moving toward outcomes-based evaluation, which evaluates program efficacy and student learning outcomes. This change is indicative of a trend toward assessing how education affects students' achievement in school and preparation for the workforce. Accreditation standards are also evolving to include new technologies into engineering education, such virtual reality, data analytics, and artificial intelligence. As organizations strive toward mutual recognition agreements and harmonized standards to enable international movement of engineering professionals and guarantee uniform program quality globally, the globalization of accreditation is also gaining traction.
- It is probable that engineering education in the future will adopt an interdisciplinary approach, including ideas from other disciplines such as computer

science, biology, and sustainability. This highlights interdisciplinary cooperation and reflects the complexity of engineering problems. As technology advances and businesses change, lifelong learning and skill development will become increasingly important. For engineering schools to remain competitive in the workforce, professional development and upskilling opportunities will be necessary. Engineering education will continue to heavily rely on experiential learning, which includes co-ops, internships, project-based learning, and industry partnerships.

Recommendations for Continuous Improvement

- Adaptation to Industry requirements: To guarantee alignment with current industry practices, engineering schools should periodically assess industry trends and requirements. They should also update their curriculum and resources through collaborations with the sector, advisory boards, and program evaluations.
- Enhancement of Diversity and Inclusion: Engineering programs should prioritize diversity, equity, and inclusion; they should also recruit and support underrepresented groups; promote cultural competence; and help students feel like they belong. All of these actions will help to create a warm and inclusive learning environment.
- Integration of Emerging Technologies: Programs should work with industry partners, invest in faculty development, update lab facilities, and integrate cutting-edge technologies like renewable energy, artificial intelligence, and machine learning into their research activities and curricula.
- Continuous Assessment and Improvement: To gauge stakeholder satisfaction, program efficacy, and student learning outcomes, engineering programs should have strong assessment procedures in place. Programs may find areas for improvement and apply evidence-based tactics to increase program quality and student achievement by using this data-driven approach.
- Global Engagement and Collaboration: To increase visibility, encourage cross-cultural exchange, and foster collaboration, engineering programs should interact with global networks and international partners. Possible avenues for this include study abroad initiatives, cooperative research projects, and applying for accreditation from other countries.

CONCLUSION

Engineering education is greatly influenced by national board accreditation, which guarantees excellence, applicability, and ongoing development. It affects student performance, industry recognition, global competitiveness, and the quality of education. Programs that have earned accreditation adhere to strict criteria and give students a thorough education for prosperous professions. These programs improve employability and professional preparation by incorporating emerging technology, supporting experiential learning, and aligning with industry demands. These efforts also support industry innovation and economic growth.

Engineering program accreditation fosters international cooperation, industrial ties, and ongoing development. It guarantees that graduates have the know-how and abilities required for a world that is changing quickly. Technology integration, lifelong learning, and multidisciplinary methods will shape engineering education in the future. Programs must embrace diversity, equality, inclusion, global involvement, and ongoing assessment in order to be competitive. This will enable them to better serve the demands of society, business, and students while guaranteeing that graduates have the know-how needed for a world that is changing quickly.

The maintenance and improvement of engineering education standards, the encouragement of innovation, and the training of future engineers for difficult problems all depend on national board accreditation. Engineering programs may make sure they remain relevant and have an influence in a world that is always changing by following the guidelines of accreditation and implementing forward-thinking tactics.

REFERENCES

Abd Latiff, Z. I., Sidik, N., Zin, N. A. M., & Zainuddin, A. (2022). Implementation of Electrical Engineering Laboratory Course for Diploma Studies in Electrical Engineering during [*Pandemic Phase.*]. *COVID*, 19.

Agrawal, A. V., Pitchai, R., Senthamaraikannan, C., Balaji, N. A., Sajithra, S., & Boopathi, S. (2023). Digital Education System During the COVID-19 Pandemic. In *Using Assistive Technology for Inclusive Learning in K-12 Classrooms* (pp. 104–126). IGI Global. DOI: 10.4018/978-1-6684-6424-3.ch005

Baashar, Y., Alkawsi, G., Mustafa, A., Alkahtani, A. A., Alsariera, Y. A., Ali, A. Q., Hashim, W., & Tiong, S. K. (2022). Toward predicting student's academic performance using artificial neural networks (ANNs). *Applied Sciences (Basel, Switzerland)*, 12(3), 1289. DOI: 10.3390/app12031289

Babu, B. S., Kamalakannan, J., Meenatchi, N., Karthik, S., & Boopathi, S. (2022). Economic impacts and reliability evaluation of battery by adopting Electric Vehicle. *IEEE Explore*, 1–6.

Bhat, A., Ahmad, F., Jain, D., Hussain, A., & Ahmad, S. (2023). Numerical Techniques for Calculating Attainment of Course Outcome and Programme Outcome under NEP-2020: Numerical technique for CO and PO under NEP-2020. *International Journal of Information Technology. Research and Applications*, 2(2), 65–72.

Bhat, R., Kamath, C. R., Mathias, K. A., & Mulimani, P. (2022). Practical Implementation of Outcome-Based Education Practices in the Indian Engineering Institutes–Approach An Objective Based Investigation. *Journal of Engineering Education Transformations*, 36(1). Advance online publication. DOI: 10.16920/jeet/2022/v36i1/22133

Cheng, L., Ritzhaupt, A. D., & Antonenko, P. (2019). Effects of the flipped classroom instructional strategy on students' learning outcomes: A meta-analysis. *Educational Technology Research and Development*, 67(4), 793–824. DOI: 10.1007/s11423-018-9633-7

Das, S., Lekhya, G., Shreya, K., Shekinah, K. L., Babu, K. K., & Boopathi, S. (2024). Fostering Sustainability Education Through Cross-Disciplinary Collaborations and Research Partnerships: Interdisciplinary Synergy. In *Facilitating Global Collaboration and Knowledge Sharing in Higher Education With Generative AI* (pp. 60–88). IGI Global.

Durairaj, M., Jayakumar, S., Karpagavalli, V., Maheswari, B. U., & Boopathi, S. (2023). Utilization of Digital Tools in the Indian Higher Education System During Health Crises. In *Multidisciplinary Approaches to Organizational Governance During Health Crises* (pp. 1–21). IGI Global. DOI: 10.4018/978-1-7998-9213-7.ch001

Dwijayani, N. M. (2019). Development of circle learning media to improve student learning outcomes. *Journal of Physics: Conference Series*, 1321(2), 022099. DOI: 10.1088/1742-6596/1321/2/022099

Gift, M. D. M., Senthil, T. S., Hasan, D. S., Alagarraja, K., Jayaseelan, P., & Boopathi, S. (2024). Additive Manufacturing and 3D Printing Innovations: Revolutionizing Industry 5.0. In *Technological Advancements in Data Processing for Next Generation Intelligent Systems* (pp. 255–287). IGI Global. DOI: 10.4018/979-8-3693-0968-1.ch010

Goyal, M., Gupta, C., & Gupta, V. (2022a). A meta-analysis approach to measure the impact of project-based learning outcome with program attainment on student learning using fuzzy inference systems. *Heliyon*, 8(8), e10248. DOI: 10.1016/j.heliyon.2022.e10248 PMID: 36042720

Goyal, M., Gupta, C., & Gupta, V. (2022b). A meta-analysis approach to measure the impact of project-based learning outcome with program attainment on student learning using fuzzy inference systems. *Heliyon*, 8(8), e10248. DOI: 10.1016/j.heliyon.2022.e10248 PMID: 36042720

Helm, C., & Huber, S. G. (2022). Predictors of central student learning outcomes in times of COVID-19: Students', parents', and teachers' perspectives during school closure in 2020—A multiple informant relative weight analysis. *Frontiers in Education*, 7, 7. DOI: 10.3389/feduc.2022.743770

Komunjeru, B., & Roberts, R. (2023). Navigating a culture of evidence: The lived experiences of college of agriculture faculty regarding the academic assessment of students. *Journal of Agricultural Education*, 64(2), 56–70. DOI: 10.5032/jae.v64i2.109

Mahrishi, M., & Abbas, A. (2023). Assessment of Knowledge Gaps in Outcome-Based Education (OBE) Among Engineering Faculty Members: An Empirical Study. *2023 IEEE International Conference on Engineering Veracruz (ICEV)*, 1–6. DOI: 10.1109/ICEV59168.2023.10329631

Mane, S. D. (2015). NBA and NAAC Accreditation of UG Engineering Programmes/Colleges in India: A Review. *International Journal of Scientific Engineering and Applied Science*, 1(6), 2395–3470.

Mishra, N., & Aithal, P. (2023). Academic Leadership in Higher Education. [IJPL]. *International Journal of Philosophy and Languages*, 2(2), 85–97.

Moharir, M., Agavekar, R., Bhore, P., Kadam, H., & Bewoor, A. (2022). Effective Implementation of Peer Review as an Active Learning Technique to Attain Course Outcome: A Case Study. *Journal of Engineering Education Transformations*, 36(Special Issue 1).

Pare, S. K. (2023). Outcome-based Education: Calculating Attainment of Programme Outcome through Course Outcome. *UNIVERSITIES HANDBOOK–34th EDITION (2018), 61*, 60.

Pasumarthy, R., Mohammed, S., Laxman, V., Krishnamoorthy, V., Durga, S., & Boopathi, S. (2024). Digital Transformation in Developing Economies: Forecasting Trends, Impact, and Challenges in Industry 5.0. In *Convergence of Human Resources Technologies and Industry 5.0* (pp. 47–68). IGI Global. DOI: 10.4018/979-8-3693-1343-5.ch003

Poornima, S. N. (2019). Outcome based education, need for the hour-NBA. *Int. J. Adv. Res. Ideas Innov. Technol*, 5(2), 1030–1033.

Prabhuswamy, M., Tripathi, R., Vijayakumar, M., Thulasimani, T., Sundharesal-ingam, P., & Sampath, B. (2024). A Study on the Complex Nature of Higher Education Leadership: An Innovative Approach. In *Challenges of Globalization and Inclusivity in Academic Research* (pp. 202–223). IGI Global. DOI: 10.4018/979-8-3693-1371-8.ch013

Pradhan, D. (2021). Effectiveness of outcome based education (OBE) toward empowering the students performance in an engineering course. *Journal of Advances in Education and Philosophy*, 5(2), 58–65. DOI: 10.36348/jaep.2021.v05i02.003

Puranik, T. A., Shaik, N., Vankudoth, R., Kolhe, M. R., Yadav, N., & Boopathi, S. (2024). Study on Harmonizing Human-Robot (Drone) Collaboration: Navigating Seamless Interactions in Collaborative Environments. In *Cybersecurity Issues and Challenges in the Drone Industry* (pp. 1–26). IGI Global.

Senapati, R., & Singh, S. K. (2023). National Education Policy—2020 and Evaluation Reforms in Higher Education: Envisioning Transformation for 21st Century India. *Special Issue of 'University News,' 61*, 21.

Sengupta, S., & Das, A. K. (2023). Automated Mapping of Course Outcomes to Program Outcomes using Natural Language Processing and Machine Learning. *2023 IEEE 3rd Applied Signal Processing Conference (ASPCON)*, 44–48.

Shah, M., & Kolhekar, M. (2021). A Case-Study on Leveraging the Policies on Outcome-Based Education. *Journal of Engineering Education Transformations*, 35(2), 126–139. DOI: 10.16920/jeet/2021/v35i2/22080

Sharma, D. M., Ramana, K. V., Jothilakshmi, R., Verma, R., Maheswari, B. U., & Boopathi, S. (2024). Integrating Generative AI Into K-12 Curriculums and Pedagogies in India: Opportunities and Challenges. *Facilitating Global Collaboration and Knowledge Sharing in Higher Education With Generative AI*, 133–161.

Sudhakar, V., & Tamilselvi, T. (2023). Analysis of Student's Performance in Engineering Courses Based on Outcome Based Education. *J Adv Educ Philos*, 7(9), 372–375. DOI: 10.36348/jaep.2023.v07i09.006

Thiruvengadam, S., Baskar, S., Jeyamala, C., & Abirami, A. (2022). Systematic Approach in Assessment of Course Outcomes/Program Outcomes for Undergraduate Engineering Programs–A Case Study. *Journal of Engineering Education Transformations, 35*.

Vasudevan, N. (2020). Development of a common framework for outcome based accreditation and rankings. *Procedia Computer Science*, 172, 270–276. DOI: 10.1016/j.procs.2020.05.043

Venkatasubramanian, V., Chitra, M., Sudha, R., Singh, V. P., Jefferson, K., & Boopathi, S. (2024). Examining the Impacts of Course Outcome Analysis in Indian Higher Education: Enhancing Educational Quality. In *Challenges of Globalization and Inclusivity in Academic Research* (pp. 124–145). IGI Global.

Venkatesh, K., & King, C. S. (2021). Challenges and Issues in Implementation of OBE. *Assessment Tools for Mapping Learning Outcomes With Learning Objectives*, 83–96.

Viswanadhan, K., & Rao, N. (2005). Effectiveness of NBA accreditation processes. *National Symposium on Engineering Education (NSEE05)*, 100–108.

Yenugu, S. (2022). The new National Education Policy (NEP) of India: Will it be a paradigm shift in Indian higher education? *Perspectives: Policy and Practice in Higher Education*, 26(4), 121–129.

Zhen, Y., Luo, J.-D., & Chen, H. (2023). Prediction of Academic Performance of Students in Online Live Classroom Interactions—An Analysis Using Natural Language Processing and Deep Learning Methods. *Journal of Social Computing*, 4(1), 12–29. DOI: 10.23919/JSC.2023.0007

KEY TERMS

- **ABET:** Accreditation Board for Engineering and Technology (US)
- **NBA:** National Board of Accreditation (India)
- **CAD:** Council for Accreditation of Educators (International)
- **CAE:** Council for the Accreditation of Educator Preparation (US)
- **ENAEE:** European Network for Accreditation of Engineering Education (Europe)

Chapter 3
Computational Thinking in Educational Policy and Leadership Management

Muhammad Usman Tariq
https://orcid.org/0000-0002-7605-3040
Abu Dhabi University, UAE & University of Glasgow, UK

ABSTRACT

This chapter seeks to broaden the scope of computational thinking beyond its traditional boundaries within the disciplines of Science, Technology, Engineering, and Mathematics (STEM). It aims to dispel the prevailing misconception that computational thinking is limited to computer science and digital technology and highlights its applicability in non-STEM fields such as literature, history, art, and social sciences. In the current educational climate that emphasises interdisciplinary approaches, this chapter endeavours to demonstrate the relevance of computational thinking in transcending the conventional confines of these disciplines. The importance of elucidating the fundamental principles of computational thinking has become apparent as we explore its intricate facets. It is essential to understand that computational thinking extends beyond coding and programming to encompass a range of skills including logical analysis, pattern recognition, algorithmic reasoning, and reflection.

INTRODUCTION

This chapter seeks to broaden the scope of computational thinking beyond its traditional boundaries within the disciplines of Science, Technology, Engineering, and Mathematics (STEM). It aims to dispel the prevailing misconception that computational thinking is limited to computer science and digital technology, and

DOI: 10.4018/979-8-3693-9215-7.ch003

highlights its applicability in non-STEM fields such as literature, history, art, and social sciences. In the current educational climate that emphasises interdisciplinary approaches, this chapter endeavours to demonstrate the relevance of computational thinking in transcending the conventional confines of these disciplines (Tariq, 2024).

The importance of elucidating the fundamental principles of computational thinking has become apparent as we explore its intricate facets. It is essential to understand that computational thinking extends beyond coding and programming to encompass a range of skills including logical analysis, pattern recognition, algorithmic reasoning, and reflection (Wing, 2006). This comprehensive understanding of the underlying principles provides a basis for demonstrating the relevance and applicability of computational thinking across various academic disciplines.

The following sections of this chapter provide an in-depth examination of the intricate relationship between computational thinking and non-STEM disciplines, drawing on both empirical evidence and illustrative case studies. By scrutinising real-life examples such as the application of algorithmic reasoning in literary analysis or pattern recognition in historical studies, this chapter emphasises the transformative power of computational thinking in enhancing critical thinking, analysis, and creativity across a wide range of subjects (Grover & Pea, 2013; Kurland et al., 2019).

An integral part of this investigation involves presenting practical strategies for educators to effectively integrate computational thinking into their non-STEM curricula. This encompasses the development of versatile lesson plans, inventive classroom activities, and project ideas that highlight the adaptability of computational thinking concepts in non-STEM settings (Barr & Stephenson, 2011).

Assessing the effects of computational thinking on student learning outcomes is a central element of this chapter. By investigating the relationship between computational thinking and critical thinking, problem solving, and analytical abilities, we aim to illustrate how incorporating computational thinking strategies can contribute.

In conclusion, this chapter advocates for a profound shift in educational paradigms, urging educators to embrace a more interconnected and computationally informed approach to teaching and learning. By reaffirming the significance of expanding the application of computational thinking beyond STEM, this chapter contributes to the ongoing discourse on preparing students for a diverse and interconnected world in which algorithmic and abstract thinking prove invaluable across various fields (Wing, 2014).

BACKGROUND

Bridging Computational leadership and Non-STEM Disciplines

The fundamental tenets of computational reasoning play a pivotal role in transcending the conventional boundaries of the STEM disciplines. This section critically examines the relevance of computational reasoning across diverse non-STEM domains, elucidating its core principles and dispelling prevalent misconceptions (Tariq, 2024).

Essential Principles of Computational leadership

Computational leadership encompasses more than just programming or coding; rather, it entails a set of cognitive skills that are critical across a wide range of academic disciplines (Wing 2006). Computational reasoning involves logical analysis, pattern recognition, algorithmic reasoning, and reflection (Grover and Pea 2013). These fundamental principles are similar to intellectual tools that can be applied beyond computer science and are crucial in areas as diverse as literature, history, art, and social sciences.

For example, in literary analysis, computational reasoning can be demonstrated through algorithmic approaches to identify patterns within texts, revealing layers of meaning and functioning with a nuanced understanding of the narrative structures. This application transcends the conventional boundaries of computational spaces and illustrates how the fundamental principles of computational reasoning can be seamlessly integrated into the academic fabric of non-STEM disciplines.

Exploring Misinterpretations

A fundamental aspect of integrating computational reasoning into non-STEM fields is dispelling misconceptions. Computational reasoning is often mistakenly equated with coding or programming, which restricts its perceived applicability to STEM disciplines (Wing, 2006). This section critically investigates these misconceptions, emphasising the comprehensive scope of computational reasoning and its potential beyond mere coding.

For instance, computational reasoning can be employed to identify intricate patterns and trends in historical data, thus enhancing the analytical capabilities of historians. By applying algorithmic reasoning to historical events, scholars can discover the causal relationships between these events more effectively. By challenging the notion that computational reasoning is limited to coding, historians can integrate cognitive skills into their conventional methodologies, thereby enriching their research (Tariq, 2024).

Emphasising General Significance:

The discussion surrounding the integration of computational reasoning with non-STEM disciplines highlights their widespread relevance. Reasoning, pattern detection, algorithmic thinking, and abstraction are intellectual resources that traverse disciplinary limitations and play pivotal roles in various fields (Grover & Pea, 2013; Wing, 2006). For instance, in the arts, computational reasoning can be used to analyse visual patterns, investigate algorithmic art, and delve into the abstract nature of creative expressions.

Additionally, incorporating computational reasoning into data organisation in the social sciences promotes a more systematic and analytical approach for comprehending societal complexities. By emphasising the universal nature of these cognitive skills, this section endeavours to dismantle artificial barriers that restrict computational reasoning in the domain of STEM disciplines.

In conclusion, connecting computational reasoning with non-STEM disciplines transcends theoretical hypotheses. This involves a change in perspective among educators, practitioners, and researchers regarding the application of computational reasoning across diverse academic contexts. By critically examining and refuting misconceptions, this section strives to clarify a more nuanced understanding of computational reasoning's universal importance in shaping scholarly landscapes beyond the traditional confines of STEM.

Exemplification of Computational Leadership Abilities Across Disciplines: Real Examples

The discussion surrounding computational reasoning underscores the embodiment of fundamental skills, such as logical analysis, pattern recognition, algorithmic reasoning, and abstraction. This section provides examples of how these skills are vital in various disciplines (Tariq, 2024).

Logical Analysis in Literature:

In literary studies, the application of computational reasoning in logical analysis is of paramount importance. For instance, when examining the plays of William Shakespeare, it is essential to adopt a systematic approach to identify recurring themes and logical patterns. By employing computational reasoning, literary scholars can conduct a logical analysis of character development, plot structures, and linguistic devices, thus enhancing their understanding of individual works and contributing to a broader understanding of the evolution of literary styles across different historical periods (Wing 2006).

Pattern Recognition in Historical Studies

Historical research can benefit greatly from the aptitude of computational reasoning for pattern detection. For instance, in the examination of historical datasets, recognising patterns in events and timeframes may reveal concealed connections. With the aid of computational reasoning, historians can discern patterns in economic transformations and political movements, thereby illuminating the interconnectedness of historical events. This approach transcends the conventional narrative-based historical analysis and imparts a quantitative aspect to historical scholarship (Grover & Pea, 2013).

Algorithmic Reasoning in Art

The realm of art exemplifies the application of algorithmic reasoning. Artists and designers often use computational algorithms to generate complex patterns and visualisations. Generative art, a genre that relies on algorithms to create visual compositions, is a manifestation of algorithmic reasoning within the artistic domain. This approach allows artists to explore novel forms of expression and challenges conventional notions of creativity, demonstrating how computational reasoning expands the horizons of artistic creation (Wing, 2006).

Abstraction in Social Sciences

In social sciences, computational reasoning's emphasis on abstraction facilitates a more precise analysis of complex societal phenomena. For instance, when dealing with vast datasets in sociology, researchers use abstraction to distil essential elements and identify general trends. Computational models that abstract social interactions enable researchers to simulate and analyse various scenarios, contributing to a deeper understanding of social dynamics and policymaking (Grover & Pea, 2013).

These examples highlight the interdisciplinary nature of computational reasoning skills. They demonstrate that logical analysis, pattern recognition, algorithmic reasoning, and abstraction are not confined to a specific discipline, but permeate various fields. By incorporating computational reasoning, scholars and practitioners in the literature, history, art, and social sciences have gained novel perspectives, enriching their respective domains with a computational lens (Tariq, 2024).

REAL LIFE CASE STUDIES: INTEGRATION OF COMPUTATIONAL REASONING IN NON-STEM SUBJECTS

Algorithm Reasoning in the Literary Analysis

An exemplary case study integrating computational reasoning into non-STEM subjects is evident in literary analysis. Researchers at Stanford University have applied algorithmic reasoning to analyse the works of Shakespeare. Using natural language processing algorithms, they identified semantic patterns, recurring themes, and subtle details across various plays. This computational approach provided a quantitative dimension to literary analysis and uncovered new insights into Shakespearean literature, showcasing the significant potential of computational reasoning in enhancing humanities (Wing, 2006).

Pattern Recognition in Historical Studies

In historical studies, pattern-recognition techniques have effectively integrated computational reasoning. A case study conducted at Harvard University utilised computational algorithms to analyse vast historical datasets and discern patterns in economic change over several centuries. By identifying recurring patterns and correlations, historians have gained a more nuanced understanding of economic history, complementing traditional qualitative approaches. This case study highlights how pattern recognition, a crucial component of computational reasoning, enhances the depth and accuracy of historical studies (Grover & Pea, 2013).

Data Organising in the social sciences

The incorporation of computational reasoning in social sciences is evident in a case study conducted at MIT. Researchers have employed computational techniques for data organisation in large-scale social interaction studies. By organising and analysing vast datasets of social interactions, they unveiled hidden patterns in human behaviour, shedding light on social dynamics. This case study demonstrates how computational reasoning, particularly data organising, contributes to a more systematic and insightful analysis of social phenomena, transcending traditional qualitative approaches in the social sciences (Grover & Pea, 2013).

Algorithmic Creativity in Art

Computational reasoning has also been applied to art to facilitate algorithmic creativity. An illustrative case study involves the collaboration between artists and computer scientists at the Massachusetts College of Art and Design. Using algorithmic techniques, artists generate unique visual compositions and explore the intersection of computation and creative expressions. This case study highlights how algorithmic reasoning can expand the horizons of creativity, challenge traditional artistic paradigms, and foster innovative forms of expression (Wing 2006).

These case studies underscore the versatility and transformative potential of computational reasoning in non-STEM subjects. Integrating algorithmic reasoning, pattern recognition, and data organisation enhances comprehension, analysis, and creativity from literary analysis and historical studies to the social sciences and art. However, a critical examination of the challenges and ethical considerations is essential to ensure responsible and effective integration in diverse educational settings (Tariq, 2024).

Critical Examination of Case Studies: Integration of Computational Reasoning in Non-STEM Subjects

Integrating computational reasoning into non-STEM subjects through real case studies offers a transformative approach to academic disciplines, traditionally rooted in qualitative methods. This critical examination assesses the implications, challenges, and ethical considerations of case studies presented in the literature, historical studies, social sciences, and art.

Algorithm Reasoning in the Literary Analysis

The use of algorithmic reasoning in case studies of literary analysis highlights the potential for quantitative analysis in a field that is primarily qualitative. However, this approach raises questions regarding the subjectivity of algorithmic interpretations. The complexity of the literature makes it challenging for algorithms to accurately reflect their nuances. Furthermore, the risk of oversimplification and loss of the humanistic perspective in literary appreciation must be considered (Wing, 2006). Although computational reasoning can improve the efficiency of an analysis, it is important to carefully consider how to preserve the creative and interpretive nature of the literature.

Pattern Recognition in Historical Studies

The incorporation of computational reasoning in historical research, particularly in the area of pattern recognition, introduces a quantitative dimension to a discipline that has traditionally been characterised by narrative interpretation. The case study demonstrates the potential for uncovering hidden connections, but also raises questions about the nature of historical causation. While correlation can be a useful starting point, it is important to recognise that complex and context-dependent factors often play a significant role in determining causation in historical events. The danger lies in oversimplifying the intricate historical narratives that shape our understanding of the past, and which historians strive to uncover rigor and precision (Grover & Pea, 2013).

Data Organising in the social sciences

A case study that examines data organisation in the social sciences shows the potency of computational reasoning in handling extensive datasets. Nevertheless, ethical considerations have come to the forefront of this research. The organisation of social interaction data presents concerns regarding privacy, consent, and the potential for unintended consequences. Ethical guidelines in social science research should be advanced in parallel with technological advancements to safeguard participants and ensure responsible data use (Grover & Pea, 2013). The difficulty lies in striking a balance between the advantages of computational tools and ethical considerations in the rapidly evolving technological environment.

Algorithmic Creativity in Art

The integration of computational reasoning into art offers a fascinating perspective on algorithmic creativity. Although the case study demonstrates the potential for striking visual compositions, it raises questions about the essence of creativity and the role played by human agency. There is a risk of diminishing creative expression in algorithmic outcomes, which may neglect the subjective and emotional aspects inherent in artistic creation. It is crucial to exercise caution when collaborating between artists and algorithms to maintain the integrity of artistic endeavours (Wing, 2006).

Common Themes and Ethical Considerations

Several common themes were identified in the case studies. The importance of interdisciplinary collaboration between domain experts and computational specialists is highlighted. Educators and practitioners must address the challenges of adapting computational reasoning to non-STEM disciplines, addressing resistance, and promoting a comprehensive understanding (Bocconi et al., 2020). Ethical considerations, including privacy, bias, and consent, should be central to integrating computational tools, necessitating ongoing vigilance and adaptation of ethical guidelines in response to advanced technologies (Grover & Pea, 2013).

While case studies provide compelling evidence of the advantages of computational reasoning in non-STEM subjects, a thorough analysis reveals potential drawbacks. Oversimplification, ethical considerations, and risk of diminishing humanistic aspects must be recognised. The integration of computational reasoning should be pursued with a nuanced comprehension of its implications, ensuring that it enriches rather than diminishes the depth, richness, and ethical integrity of non-STEM disciplines (Tariq, 2024).

STRATEGIES FOR INTEGRATION

Incorporating Computational Thinking into Non-STEM Curricula

This section presents practical strategies and approaches for educators to seamlessly integrate computational thinking into non-STEM curricula. By providing diverse sample plans, classroom activities, and project ideas, the goal is to demonstrate the versatile application of computational thinking concepts across various disciplines. The emphasis lies in fostering adaptable and flexible approaches and empowering educators to tailor these methods to different subjects and educational levels.

Adaptable Sample Plans:

The development of versatile sample plans is indispensable for achieving seamless integration. These plans must be crafted with adaptability in mind, catering to the diverse learning preferences, rhythms, and experiences of students. This adaptability is exemplified in a high school literature course where a sample plan employs algorithmic reasoning. Students evaluated a novel's narrative framework by employing flowcharts, delineating the sequence of events, and discerning recurring patterns. This versatile sample plan enriches their literary interpretations and effortlessly incorporates computational thinking concepts (Wing 2006).

Diverse Classroom Activities

Incorporating computational thinking into non-STEM subjects requires the implementation of engaging and diverse classroom activities. For instance, a history class project could involve the use of data visualisation tools to map historical trends. By organising and visualising historical data, students enhance their computational thinking skills and gain a deeper understanding of their historical narratives. These activities cater to various learning preferences, ultimately making computational thinking an essential component of the learning experience (Grover & Pea, 2013).

Project-Based Learning:

The application of project-based learning was found to be a reliable method for integrating computational thinking into non-STEM subjects. For example, in an art class, students can engage in a project that merges algorithmic creativity with conventional artistic techniques. By employing generative algorithms to generate the original visual arrangements, students can simultaneously explore computational concepts and cultivate a synergistic connection between technology and innovative artistry. This approach to project-based learning fosters a comprehensive grasp of computational thinking within the confines of non-STEM disciplines (Sands et al., 2018).

Adapting to educational level

Educators are faced with the challenge of adapting computational thinking methods to suit various educational levels. In elementary school science classes, a personalised approach might involve introducing basic coding concepts through interactive storytelling. This approach not only makes computational thinking accessible to younger students but also lays the groundwork for future research. Conversely, at the university level, a customised approach could involve collaborative interdisciplinary projects that encourage students to apply computational thinking across different subjects, fostering high-level analytical and problem-solving skills (Pulimood et al., 2016).

History's Problem Decomposition

Problem decomposition is an effective method for incorporating computational thinking into the history curriculum. To better comprehend the underlying causes and effects of complex historical events, this strategy involves breaking them down into smaller and more manageable parts. Students can break down important aspects of World War II, such as political alliances, economic conditions, significant battles, and the roles of major figures. By investigating every of these components exclusively, understudies can more readily comprehend how they interrelate and add to a more extensive account of the conflict. This method not only helps students comprehend the intricate details of historical events but also improves their capacity to methodically dissect and analyse intricate issues (Silveira & Deshmukh, 2022).

Using Algorithms in Language Arts

Through the use of algorithmic thinking, which entails developing step-by-step procedures for approaching tasks, such as writing and text analysis, computational thinking can be integrated into language arts. For instance, students can be instructed to develop a structured algorithm for analysing a poem that consists of the following steps: first, familiarising themselves with the poem by reading it multiple times; second, identifying and listing the literary devices that are used; third, determining the theme of the poem; fourth, analysing how the literary devices contribute to this theme; and fifth, writing a paragraph that explains their findings. Students' overall comprehension and analytical abilities improve as a result of taking this methodical approach, which enables them to tackle challenging literary analysis tasks with greater clarity and precision (Tagare, 2023)

Understanding social studies patterns

Pattern recognition, which entails identifying recurring patterns within social and cultural phenomena, is another method of incorporating computational thinking into subjects that are not STEM-related. Students might, for instance, investigate migration trends in a sociology class to discover patterns, such as push and pull factors, migration routes, and demographic shifts. Students can gain a deeper understanding of the causes of migration and their effects on society by analysing data and identifying these patterns. This approach assists understudies in figuring out authentic and recent developments by featuring fundamental examples and patterns along these lines, improving their insightful abilities and appreciation of social elements. By encouraging systematic analysis, structured problem solving, and pattern recognition, these strategies demonstrate how computational thinking can enhance non-STEM subjects and ultimately improve students' analytical and critical thinking skills (Sondakh et al., 2022).

Critical Examination

The introduction of computational thinking in non-STEM subjects presents several advantages; however, some important aspects require careful consideration. One of the main issues is the discrepancy in computational proficiency among educators, necessitating the implementation of professional development programs to equip teachers with appropriate skills and knowledge. Furthermore, it is essential to scrutinise the potential to reinforce gender and nationality stereotypes and ensure that computational thinking strategies are universally accessible and inclusive for all students (Bocconi et al., 2020). Establishing a balance between promoting computational literacy and avoiding unintended bias is critical for successful integration (Tsortanidou et al., 2023).

Impact on Learning and Critical Analysis

This section investigates the profound consequences of integrating computational thinking into students' learning experiences in non-STEM disciplines. A detailed analysis of the discourse uncovers the implications of nurturing critical thinking, problem-solving, and analytical abilities in various academic fields. Furthermore, this section assesses the interactions between computational thinking and conventional learning techniques with the intention of shedding light on the potential for a more inclusive educational atmosphere.

Development of Critical Thinking

The incorporation of computational thinking into non-STEM subjects serves as a catalyst for the development of critical thinking skills. A close examination of this idea shows that computational thinking encourages students to tackle problems by using a logical and systematic approach. For instance, in a literature class, students might employ algorithmic thinking to analyse narrative structures, which enhances their understanding of literary works and instills critical thinking skills, as they identify patterns and draw conclusions. When computational thinking is skillfully integrated into educational experiences, it becomes a potent tool for fostering a nuanced and reflective approach to various subjects (Wing, 2006).

Enhancement of Problem-solving Abilities

The text highlights the significance of computational thinking in enhancing problem-solving abilities across various disciplines. An extensive examination revealed that algorithmic approaches, which are characteristic of computational

thinking, offer a systematic method for problem decomposition and solution formulation. Students who employ computational methods to analyse intricate historical data in historical studies exhibit improved problem-solving skills. By breaking down complex issues into logical components and applying algorithmic thinking, students can cultivate a problem-solving mindset that is beneficial beyond the boundaries of computational environments. This approach not only enhances academic performance, but also equips students with valuable problem-solving skills applicable to real-world situations (Grover & Pea, 2013).

Development of Analytical Skills

The section under scrutiny posits that computational thinking contributes to the development of analytical skills. A closer examination revealed that computational methods, such as data organising and pattern recognition, foster a systematic and analytical approach. For example, students organising and analysing social interaction data in the social sciences gain insights into cultural patterns. This enhances how they interpret social peculiarities and elevate analytical skills, as they discern correlations and reach informed conclusions. When critically analysed, integrating computational thinking into non-STEM subjects emerges as an educational approach that transcends rote learning, fostering analytical skills essential for academic and professional success (Grover & Pea, 2013).

Interactions with Traditional Learning Strategies

A critical analysis of the interactions between computational thinking and traditional learning methods reveals great potential for a more holistic educational milieu. Computational thinking is not portrayed as a replacement, but as a complement to existing educational approaches. Traditional problem-solving techniques may be coupled with algorithmic thinking in math classes, providing students with diverse approaches to tackle mathematical challenges. This integration of computational and traditional methods creates a symbiotic relationship, enhancing educational experience by leveraging the strengths of both approaches. However, a nuanced examination is critical to avoid potential pitfalls such as overreliance on computational methods at the expense of fundamental understanding (Bocconi et al., 2020).

Challenges and Considerations

The integration of computational thinking into non-STEM domains has been recognised as having a positive impact on student development, fostering critical thinking, problem-solving, and analytical skills. However, it is important to critically evaluate the challenges and considerations associated with this integration, such as the need for educators to bridge the gap in computational literacy among students and teachers and the risk of exacerbating inequalities related to access to technology. A thorough assessment of these challenges is crucial for refining implementation strategies and ensuring equitable access to the benefits of computational thinking (Bocconi et al., 2020).

The assimilation of computational thinking into non-STEM domains has the potential to significantly impact student development and enhance critical thinking, problem-solving, and analytical skills through the application of computational concepts. The interaction between computational thinking and traditional learning methods offers a promising avenue for fostering a more comprehensive educational environment. However, it is vital to continuously engage in critical analysis to navigate potential challenges, refine implementation strategies, and ensure that the integration of computational thinking enhances rather than diminishes the quality of education (Vlahović & Biškupić, 2023).

Challenges and Solutions

This section comprehensively addresses the challenges of integrating computational thinking into non-STEM subjects. It explores obstacles, such as resistance from instructors unfamiliar with computational concepts and the perceived insignificance of these skills in certain disciplines. Furthermore, this section provides comprehensive solutions to overcome these challenges, emphasising professional development for teachers, interdisciplinary collaboration, and the development of resources and tools to facilitate the seamless integration of computational thinking in non-STEM subjects.

Resistance from Instructors New to Computational Ideas

A significant challenge in integrating computational thinking is the resistance encountered by teachers unfamiliar with computational concepts. This obstacle may arise from a lack of exposure or training in computational skills, resulting in scepticism about the relevance and feasibility of integrating these concepts into non-STEM subjects. Targeted professional development programs are crucial to address this challenge. These programs should equip instructors with the necessary knowledge and skills to navigate computational thinking, fostering confidence and enthusiasm in adopting these concepts within their teaching practices (Bocconi et al., 2020).

Real-World Example

An exemplary model of successful professional development is the Code.org Professional Learning System. This program offers teachers training in computational thinking concepts, providing them with tools and knowledge to integrate these skills into various subjects. By empowering teachers with computational literacy, resistance diminishes, laying the groundwork for a more favourable environment for integration (Bocconi et al., 2020).

Perceived Insignificance in Specific Disciplines

The perception of the insignificance of computational thinking skills in certain disciplines poses a substantial challenge. Teachers and peers may question the relevance of these skills in traditionally considered nontechnical fields. To overcome this challenge, it is essential to provide tangible examples and case studies that demonstrate the transformative impact of computational thinking across different subjects. Highlighting how algorithmic reasoning, pattern recognition, and data organising enhance critical thinking and problem solving in literature, history, and art can reshape this perception. Additionally, teachers should emphasise the inclusiveness of computational thinking, underscoring its role in nurturing essential skills irrespective of discipline (Wing, 2006).

Real-World Example:

The Scratch platform, developed by the MIT Media Lab, is a compelling example. While primarily designed for teaching coding, Scratch's visual interface allows students in nontechnical disciplines to create interactive stories, animations, and games. By engaging in these activities, students develop computational thinking skills and witness their practical application in creative projects, dispelling of the notion of insignificance (Bocconi et al., 2020).

Teachers' professional development

Comprehensive professional development for teachers is a crucial solution for overcoming resistance and facilitating successful integration. This involves providing students with the technical aspects of computational thinking and instilling a pedagogical understanding of how these concepts align with non-STEM subjects. Workshops, seminars, and online courses tailored to teachers' specific needs can bridge the knowledge gap and build a community of practice. Continuous learning opportunities ensure that teachers remain adept at integrating computational thinking into evolving curricular landscapes (Grover & Pea, 2013).

Interdisciplinary Collaboration

Another pivotal solution is to foster interdisciplinary collaboration. By encouraging instructors from different disciplines to collaborate, share insights, and co-create lesson plans, the integration of computational thinking becomes a collective effort. This collaboration enhances the learning experience and provides diverse perspectives on how computational thinking can be applied across subjects. Interdisciplinary collaboration is particularly effective in addressing the perceived insignificance challenge by demonstrating the interconnectedness of computational thinking across various fields (Grover & Pea, 2013).

Development of Resources and Tools

This section advocates the development of resources and tools tailored to teachers and students to facilitate seamless integration. This includes the creation of curriculum guides, lesson plans, and interactive platforms aligned with non-STEM subjects. Open-source resources and user-friendly tools enable teachers to integrate computational thinking without being overwhelmed by technical complexities. By investing in creating open resources, educational institutions can alleviate challenges associated with resource scarcity and provide a robust environment for integration (Bocconi et al., 2020).

Critical Examination

Although these solutions offer promising avenues for overcoming challenges, a critical examination is essential. The success of professional development programs depends on their alignment with teachers' needs and the sustained commitment of educational institutions to supporting ongoing learning initiatives. While beneficial, interdisciplinary collaboration requires a cultural shift within institutions, necessitating time and resources for teachers to engage actively. Moreover, developing resources and tools requires careful consideration of accessibility, usability, and inclusivity to ensure equitable integration across diverse educational settings (Bocconi et al., 2020; Grover & Pea, 2013).

In conclusion, addressing the challenges of integrating computational thinking into non-STEM subjects is crucial for fostering a holistic educational environment. Solutions such as professional development, interdisciplinary collaboration, and development of resources and tools present a comprehensive framework. However, nuanced and ongoing critical analysis is essential for the continuous refinement of these solutions. By judiciously navigating challenges, educators can usher in a transformative era, in which computational thinking becomes an integral part of non-STEM education (Wahab et al., 2021).

CONCLUSION

The pinnacle of this section underscores the imperative need to extend the application of computational thinking beyond the traditional confines of STEM subjects, advocating its integration across all academic disciplines. This assertion is substantiated by a thorough examination of the challenges, solutions, and real-world examples presented throughout the chapter.

FOUNDATION FOR A DIVERSE AND INTERCONNECTED WORLD

The rationale for expanding computational thinking stems from its role in preparing students for a diverse and interconnected world. As explained in the preceding sections, computational thinking equips students with essential critical thinking, problem solving, and analytical reasoning skills. In the current intricate and interconnected society, where information is abundant and rapidly evolving, the ability to think algorithmically and conceptually is invaluable across various fields. In the literature, history, art, and social sciences, computational thinking enhances students' capacity to navigate and contribute critically to the complex challenges of the contemporary world (Bocconi et al., 2020; Grover & Pea, 2013).

PARADIGM SHIFT IN EDUCATION

This conclusion underscores the necessity of a paradigm shift in educational approaches. It critically evaluates the challenges and solutions presented earlier, emphasising that the integration of computational thinking should not be perceived as an isolated initiative, but as a fundamental component of a broader educational transformation. This shift requires educators to adopt a more interconnected and computationally informed approach to teaching and learning, transcending traditional disciplinary boundaries.

The call for this paradigm shift resonates with real-world examples that demonstrate the profound impact of computational thinking across disciplines. As previously mentioned, the Code.org Professional Learning System stands out as an exemplary illustration of teachers' successful professional development. By equipping teachers with computational literacy, this program facilitates the integration of computational thinking into various subjects, breaking down traditional silos and fostering a more interconnected educational environment (Bocconi et al., 2020).

Moreover, platforms such as Scratch from the MIT Media Lab showcase how computational thinking can be seamlessly integrated into nontechnical disciplines. Students use coding concepts to engage in creative projects such as storytelling and art. These examples highlight the tremendous potential of computational thinking to reshape educational practices and open new avenues for interdisciplinary exploration (Bocconi et al., 2020).

A critical examination of the section's overarching message revealed nuanced considerations. Although the imperative of extending computational thinking is evident, challenges such as teacher resistance and perceived irrelevance in certain disciplines require ongoing attention. The proposed solutions, including professional development and interdisciplinary collaboration, offer a robust framework; however, their success hinges on sustained commitment, adaptability, and equitable implementation.

Furthermore, the advocated paradigm shift necessitates a comprehensive re-evaluation of school systems. This calls for changes in curriculum design, adjustments in assessment methods, and a redefinition of the roles and expectations of educators. Such a profound shift requires time, resources, and collective commitment from educational institutions, policymakers, and stakeholders to ensure successful implementation.

Overall, the imperative to expand computational thinking across academic disciplines is a compelling directive for educators, institutions, and policymakers. The transformative potential of computational thinking, as exemplified by real success stories, underscores its relevance in shaping a future-ready generation. However, the journey toward integration must be approached carefully, considering challenges, critically analysing proposed solutions, and committing to fostering an educational landscape that prepares students for the complexities of an interconnected world.

REFERENCES

Apostolou, P. P., & Avgerinou, M. D. (2021). The coding maestros project: Blending steam and non-steam subjects through computational thinking. In *Handbook of research on K-12 blended and virtual learning through the i²Flex classroom model* (pp. 504–518). IGI Global. DOI: 10.4018/978-1-7998-7760-8.ch029

Barboza, L., & Teixeira, E. S. (2020). Effect of data science teaching for non-stem students: A systematic literature review. *ICSEA*, 2020, 128.

Bocconi, S., Chioccariello, A., Dettori, G., Ferrari, A., Engelhardt, K., Robson, R., & Underwood, J. (2020). Computational thinking in K-9 education: A review. *Computers in Human Behavior*, 102, 56–67.

Chen, P., Yang, D., Metwally, A. H. S., Lavonen, J., & Wang, X. (2023). Fostering computational thinking through unplugged activities: A systematic literature review and meta-analysis. *International Journal of STEM Education*, 10(1), 47. DOI: 10.1186/s40594-023-00434-7

Cutumisu, M., Adams, C., & Lu, C. (2019). A scoping review of empirical research on recent computational thinking assessments. *Journal of Science Education and Technology*, 28(6), 651–676. DOI: 10.1007/s10956-019-09799-3

Czerkawski, B. C., & Lyman, E. W.III. (2015). Exploring issues about computational thinking in higher education. *TechTrends*, 59(2), 57–65. DOI: 10.1007/s11528-015-0840-3

De Santo, A., Farah, J. C., Martínez, M. L., Moro, A., Bergram, K., Purohit, A. K., Felber, P., Gillet, D., & Holzer, A. (2022). Promoting computational thinking skills in non-computer-science students: Gamifying computational notebooks to increase student engagement. *IEEE Transactions on Learning Technologies*, 15(3), 392–405. DOI: 10.1109/TLT.2022.3180588

Farah, J. C., Moro, A., Bergram, K., Purohit, A. K., Gillet, D., & Holzer, A. (2020). Bringing computational thinking to non-STEM undergraduates through an integrated notebook application. In *15th European Conference on Technology Enhanced Learning*.

Freudenthal, E., Ogrey, A. N., Roy, M. K., & Siegel, A. (2010, April). A computational introduction to STEM studies. In *IEEE EDUCON 2010 Conference* (pp. 663-672). IEEE.

Grover, S., & Pea, R. (2013). Computational thinking in K–12: A review of the state of the field. *Educational Researcher*, 42(1), 38–43. DOI: 10.3102/0013189X12463051

Haines, S., Krach, M., Pustaka, A., Li, Q., & Richman, L. (2019). The effects of computational thinking professional development on STEM teachers' perceptions and pedagogical practices. *Athens Journal of Sciences*, 6(2), 97–122. DOI: 10.30958/ajs.6-2-2

Huang, W., Looi, C. K., & Yeter, I. H. (2022). Comparison of STEM, non-STEM, and mixed-disciplines pre-service teachers' early conceptions about computational thinking.

Israel-Fishelson, R., & Hershkovitz, A. (2022). Studying interrelations of computational thinking and creativity: A scoping review (2011–2020). *Computers & Education*, 176, 104353. DOI: 10.1016/j.compedu.2021.104353

Kakavas, P., & Ugolini, F. C. (2019). Computational thinking in primary education: A systematic literature review. *Research on Education and Media*, 11(2), 64–94. DOI: 10.2478/rem-2019-0023

Kenny, R., & Gunter, G. (2015). Building a competency-based STEM curriculum in non-STEM disciplines: A sySTEMic approach. In *The design of learning experience: Creating the future of educational technology* (pp. 181-198). DOI: 10.1007/978-3-319-16504-2_13

Knie, L., Standl, B., & Schwarzer, S. (2022). First experiences of integrating computational thinking into a blended learning in-service training program for STEM teachers. *Computer Applications in Engineering Education*, 30(5), 1423–1439. DOI: 10.1002/cae.22529

Liao, C. H., Chiang, C. T., Chen, I. C., & Parker, K. R. (2022). Exploring the relationship between computational thinking and learning satisfaction for non-STEM college students. *International Journal of Educational Technology in Higher Education*, 19(1), 43. DOI: 10.1186/s41239-022-00347-5

Looi, C. K., Chan, S. W., Huang, W., Seow, P. S. K., & Wu, L. (2020). Preservice teachers' views of computational thinking: STEM teachers vs non-STEM teachers.

Lu, C., Macdonald, R., Odell, B., Kokhan, V., Demmans Epp, C., & Cutumisu, M. (2022). A scoping review of computational thinking assessments in higher education. *Journal of Computing in Higher Education*, 34(2), 416–461. DOI: 10.1007/s12528-021-09305-y

Lyon, J. A., & Magana, A. J. (2020). Computational thinking in higher education: A review of the literature. *Computer Applications in Engineering Education*, 28(5), 1174–1189. DOI: 10.1002/cae.22295

Pacella, D., Fabbricatore, R., D'Enza, A. I., Galluccio, C., & Palumbo, F. (2022). Teaching STEM subjects in non-STEM degrees: An adaptive learning model for teaching statistics. In *Artificial intelligence in STEM education: The paradigmatic shifts in research, education, and technology* (pp. 61–75). CRC Press. DOI: 10.1201/9781003181187-6

Pulimood, S. M., Pearson, K., & Bates, D. C. (2016, February). A study on the impact of multidisciplinary collaboration on computational thinking. In *Proceedings of the 47th ACM technical symposium on computing science education* (pp. 30-35). DOI: 10.1145/2839509.2844636

Saad, A., & Zainudin, S. (2022). A review of project-based learning (PBL) and computational thinking (CT) in teaching and learning. *Learning and Motivation*, 78, 101802. DOI: 10.1016/j.lmot.2022.101802

Sands, P., Yadav, A., & Good, J. (2018). Computational thinking in K-12: In-service teacher perceptions of computational thinking. In *Computational thinking in the STEM disciplines: Foundations and research highlights* (pp. 151-164).

Silveira, I., & Deshmukh, A. (2022). Computational thinking, history and non-formal learning-A well-crafted blend!.

Sondakh, D. E., Kom, S., Pungus, S. R., & Putra, E. Y. (2022). Indonesian undergraduate students' perception of their computational thinking ability. *CogITo Smart Journal*, 8(1), 68–80. DOI: 10.31154/cogito.v8i1.387.68-80

Tagare, D. (2023). *Factors that predict K-12 teachers' ability to apply computational thinking skills*. ACM Transactions on Computing Education.

Tang, X., Yin, Y., Lin, Q., Hadad, R., & Zhai, X. (2020). Assessing computational thinking: A systematic review of empirical studies. *Computers & Education*, 148, 103798. DOI: 10.1016/j.compedu.2019.103798

Tariq, M. U. (2024). Multi-Agent Models in Healthcare System Design. In Dall'Acqua, L. (Ed.), *Bioethics of Cognitive Ergonomics and Digital Transition* (pp. 143–170). IGI Global., DOI: 10.4018/979-8-3693-2667-1.ch008

Tariq, M. U. (2024). Social Innovations for Improving Healthcare. In Chandan, H. (Ed.), *Social Innovations in Education, Environment, and Healthcare* (pp. 302–317). IGI Global., DOI: 10.4018/979-8-3693-2569-8.ch015

Tariq, M. U. (2024). Leveraging AI for Entrepreneurial Innovation in Healthcare. In Özsungur, F. (Ed.), *Generating Entrepreneurial Ideas With AI* (pp. 192–216). IGI Global., DOI: 10.4018/979-8-3693-3498-0.ch009

Tariq, M. U. (2024). Leading Smart Technologies and Innovations for E-Business 5.0: Applications and Management Frameworks. In Popkova, E. (Ed.), *Smart Technologies and Innovations in E-Business* (pp. 25–46). IGI Global., DOI: 10.4018/978-1-6684-7840-0.ch002

Tariq, M. U. (2024). Crafting Authentic Narratives for Sustainable Branding. In Rodrigues, P. (Eds.), *Compelling Storytelling Narratives for Sustainable Branding* (pp. 194–229). IGI Global., DOI: 10.4018/979-8-3693-3326-6.ch011

Tariq, M. U. (2024). The role of AI in skilling, upskilling, and reskilling the workforce. In Doshi, R., Dadhich, M., Poddar, S., & Hiran, K. (Eds.), *Integrating generative AI in education to achieve sustainable development goals* (pp. 421–433). IGI Global., DOI: 10.4018/979-8-3693-2440-0.ch023

Tariq, M. U. (2024). AI-powered language translation for multilingual classrooms. In Doshi, R., Dadhich, M., Poddar, S., & Hiran, K. (Eds.), *Integrating generative AI in education to achieve sustainable development goals* (pp. 29–46). IGI Global., DOI: 10.4018/979-8-3693-2440-0.ch002

Tariq, M. U. (2024). AI and the future of talent management: Transforming recruitment and retention with machine learning. In Christiansen, B., Aziz, M., & O'Keeffe, E. (Eds.), *Global practices on effective talent acquisition and retention* (pp. 1–16). IGI Global., DOI: 10.4018/979-8-3693-1938-3.ch001

Tariq, M. U. (2024). Application of blockchain and Internet of Things (IoT) in modern business. In Sinha, M., Bhandari, A., Priya, S., & Kabiraj, S. (Eds.), *Future of customer engagement through marketing intelligence* (pp. 66–94). IGI Global., DOI: 10.4018/979-8-3693-2367-0.ch004

Tariq, M. U. (2024). The role of AI ethics in cost and complexity reduction. In Tennin, K., Ray, S., & Sorg, J. (Eds.), *Cases on AI ethics in business* (pp. 59–78). IGI Global., DOI: 10.4018/979-8-3693-2643-5.ch004

Tariq, M. U. (2024). Challenges of a metaverse shaping the future of entrepreneurship. In Inder, S., Dawra, S., Tennin, K., & Sharma, S. (Eds.), *New business frontiers in the metaverse* (pp. 155–173). IGI Global., DOI: 10.4018/979-8-3693-2422-6.ch011

Tariq, M. U. (2024). Neurodiversity inclusion and belonging strategies in the workplace. In J. Vázquez de Príncipe (Ed.), *Resilience of multicultural and multigenerational leadership and workplace experience* (pp. 182-201). IGI Global. https://doi.org/DOI: 10.4018/979-8-3693-1802-7.ch009

Tariq, M. U. (2024). AI and IoT in flood forecasting and mitigation: A comprehensive approach. In Ouaissa, M., Ouaissa, M., Boulouard, Z., Iwendi, C., & Krichen, M. (Eds.), *AI and IoT for proactive disaster management* (pp. 26–60). IGI Global., DOI: 10.4018/979-8-3693-3896-4.ch003

Tariq, M. U. (2024). Empowering student entrepreneurs: From idea to execution. In Cantafio, G., & Munna, A. (Eds.), *Empowering students and elevating universities with innovation centers* (pp. 83–111). IGI Global., DOI: 10.4018/979-8-3693-1467-8.ch005

Tariq, M. U. (2024). The transformation of healthcare through AI-driven diagnostics. In Sharma, A., Chanderwal, N., Tyagi, S., Upadhyay, P., & Tyagi, A. (Eds.), *Enhancing medical imaging with emerging technologies* (pp. 250–264). IGI Global., DOI: 10.4018/979-8-3693-5261-8.ch015

Tariq, M. U. (2024). The role of emerging technologies in shaping the global digital government landscape. In Guo, Y. (Ed.), *Emerging developments and technologies in digital government* (pp. 160–180). IGI Global., DOI: 10.4018/979-8-3693-2363-2.ch009

Tariq, M. U. (2024). Equity and inclusion in learning ecosystems. In Al Husseiny, F., & Munna, A. (Eds.), *Preparing students for the future educational paradigm* (pp. 155–176). IGI Global., DOI: 10.4018/979-8-3693-1536-1.ch007

Tariq, M. U. (2024). Empowering educators in the learning ecosystem. In Al Husseiny, F., & Munna, A. (Eds.), *Preparing students for the future educational paradigm* (pp. 232–255). IGI Global., DOI: 10.4018/979-8-3693-1536-1.ch010

Tariq, M. U. (2024). Revolutionizing health data management with blockchain technology: Enhancing security and efficiency in a digital era. In Garcia, M., & de Almeida, R. (Eds.), *Emerging technologies for health literacy and medical practice* (pp. 153–175). IGI Global., DOI: 10.4018/979-8-3693-1214-8.ch008

Tariq, M. U. (2024). Emerging trends and innovations in blockchain-digital twin integration for green investments: A case study perspective. In Jafar, S., Rodriguez, R., Kannan, H., Akhtar, S., & Plugmann, P. (Eds.), *Harnessing blockchain-digital twin fusion for sustainable investments* (pp. 148–175). IGI Global., DOI: 10.4018/979-8-3693-1878-2.ch007

Tariq, M. U. (2024). Emotional intelligence in understanding and influencing consumer behavior. In Musiolik, T., Rodriguez, R., & Kannan, H. (Eds.), *AI impacts in digital consumer behavior* (pp. 56–81). IGI Global., DOI: 10.4018/979-8-3693-1918-5.ch003

Tariq, M. U. (2024). Fintech startups and cryptocurrency in business: Revolutionizing entrepreneurship. In Kankaew, K., Nakpathom, P., Chnitphattana, A., Pitchayadejanant, K., & Kunnapapdeelert, S. (Eds.), *Applying business intelligence and innovation to entrepreneurship* (pp. 106–124). IGI Global., DOI: 10.4018/979-8-3693-1846-1.ch006

Tariq, M. U. (2024). Multidisciplinary service learning in higher education: Concepts, implementation, and impact. In S. Watson (Ed.), *Applications of service learning in higher education* (pp. 1-19). IGI Global. https://doi.org/DOI: 10.4018/979-8-3693-2133-1.ch001

Tariq, M. U. (2024). Enhancing cybersecurity protocols in modern healthcare systems: Strategies and best practices. In Garcia, M., & de Almeida, R. (Eds.), *Transformative approaches to patient literacy and healthcare innovation* (pp. 223–241). IGI Global., DOI: 10.4018/979-8-3693-3661-8.ch011

Tariq, M. U. (2024). Advanced wearable medical devices and their role in transformative remote health monitoring. In Garcia, M., & de Almeida, R. (Eds.), *Transformative approaches to patient literacy and healthcare innovation* (pp. 308–326). IGI Global., DOI: 10.4018/979-8-3693-3661-8.ch015

Tariq, M. U. (2024). Leveraging artificial intelligence for a sustainable and climate-neutral economy in Asia. In Ordóñez de Pablos, P., Almunawar, M., & Anshari, M. (Eds.), *Strengthening sustainable digitalization of Asian economy and society* (pp. 1–21). IGI Global., DOI: 10.4018/979-8-3693-1942-0.ch001

Tariq, M. U. (2024). Metaverse in business and commerce. In Kumar, J., Arora, M., & Erkol Bayram, G. (Eds.), *Exploring the use of metaverse in business and education* (pp. 47–72). IGI Global., DOI: 10.4018/979-8-3693-5868-9.ch004

Tsarava, K., Moeller, K., Román-González, M., Golle, J., Leifheit, L., Butz, M. V., & Ninaus, M. (2022). A cognitive definition of computational thinking in primary education. *Computers & Education*, 179, 104425. DOI: 10.1016/j.compedu.2021.104425

Tsortanidou, X., Daradoumis, T., & Barberá-Gregori, E. (2023). Unplugged computational thinking at K-6 education: Evidence from a multiple-case study in Spain. *Education 3-13, 51*(6), 948-965.

Vlahović, I., & Biškupić, I. O. (2023, May). Fostering critical and computational thinking in the field of primary and secondary education in non-STEM subjects by using data sets and applications. In *2023 46th MIPRO ICT and Electronics Convention (MIPRO)* (pp. 672-677). IEEE. DOI: 10.23919/MIPRO57284.2023.10159750

Wahab, N. A., Talib, O., Razali, F., & Kamarudin, N. (2021). The big why of implementing computational thinking in STEM education: A systematic literature review. [MJSSH]. *Malaysian Journal of Social Sciences and Humanities*, 6(3), 272–289.

Wing, J. M. (2006). Computational thinking. *Communications of the ACM*, 49(3), 33–35. DOI: 10.1145/1118178.1118215

Chapter 4
Navigating Policy and Management in Academic Institutions

Urmila Yadav

Sharda School of Law, Sharda University, Greater Noida, India

R. Pitchai

https://orcid.org/0000-0002-3759 -6915

Department of Computer Science and Engineering, B.V. Raju Institute of Technology, Telangana, India

V. Gopal

Department of Mechanical Engineering, KCG College of Technology, Karappakkam, India

K. R. Senthil Kumar

Department of Mechanical Engineering, R.M.K. College of Engineering and Technology, Puduvoyal, India

Mitali Talukdar

https://orcid.org/0000-0003-2799 -0043

Amity Business School, Amity University, Kolkata, India

Sampath Boopathi

https://orcid.org/0000-0002-2065 -6539

Department of Mechanical Engineering, Muthyammal Engineering College, Namakkal, India

ABSTRACT

Higher education leadership requires adept navigation of intricate policy and management landscapes to ensure institutional success and sustainability. Academic leaders must balance internal governance with compliance to external regulations while fostering environments conducive to academic excellence, innovation, and inclusivity. This paper explores the pivotal roles and responsibilities of higher education leaders, emphasizing strategic planning, stakeholder engagement, fi-

DOI: 10.4018/979-8-3693-9215-7.ch004

nancial management, and policy implementation. Through examining case studies and current trends, the paper provides insights into effective leadership practices that drive institutional growth. It addresses challenges such as funding, regulatory compliance, and evolving educational demands, offering strategies for leaders to manage these complexities. The findings highlight the importance of adaptive leadership, collaborative decision-making, and proactive policy management in navigating the dynamic higher education sector.

INTRODUCTION

Higher education leadership encompasses a broad range of roles and responsibilities that are essential for the successful operation and growth of academic institutions. These leaders, including university presidents, deans, provosts, and department heads, must navigate complex organizational structures and diverse stakeholder interests to create an environment conducive to learning, research, and community engagement. Their ability to balance strategic vision with operational efficiency is crucial in addressing the multifaceted challenges faced by modern higher education institutions(Ruben et al., 2023a).

At the core of higher education leadership is the development and implementation of a strategic vision. Leaders must craft long-term plans that align with the institution's mission and values while also being adaptable to the dynamic nature of the higher education landscape. This involves setting clear goals, prioritizing initiatives, and ensuring that resources are allocated effectively. Strategic planning is not a solitary activity but a collaborative process that involves input from faculty, staff, students, and external stakeholders. By engaging these groups, leaders can build a sense of shared purpose and commitment to the institution's objectives(Kezar, 2023).

Another critical aspect of higher education leadership is governance. Effective governance structures are essential for making informed decisions and maintaining accountability. Leaders must work within established frameworks to ensure transparency and inclusivity in decision-making processes. This includes adhering to regulatory requirements and institutional policies while also being responsive to the needs and concerns of the academic community. Effective governance fosters a culture of trust and collaboration, which is vital for the smooth operation of the institution(Ash et al., 2020).

Financial management is another cornerstone of higher education leadership. Academic leaders must oversee budgeting, financial planning, and resource allocation to ensure the institution's financial health and sustainability. This involves managing tuition revenues, government funding, research grants, and philanthropic contributions. In an era of declining public funding and increasing financial pressures, leaders must be innovative in identifying new revenue streams and cost-saving measures. Sound financial management practices enable institutions to invest in their core mission areas, such as academic programs, research, and student services. Stakeholder engagement is also paramount in higher education leadership. Leaders must build and maintain relationships with a wide range of stakeholders, including students, faculty, staff, alumni, government agencies, and the broader community(Mohr & Purcell, 2020). Effective communication and collaboration with these groups are essential for garnering support and achieving institutional goals. By fostering strong connections and partnerships, leaders can enhance the institution's reputation, attract resources, and create opportunities for growth and development.

Promoting academic excellence and innovation is a fundamental responsibility of higher education leaders. This involves creating an environment that supports high-quality teaching, cutting-edge research, and the development of new knowledge. Leaders must ensure that faculty have the resources and support they need to excel in their scholarly pursuits and that students receive a transformative educational experience. Encouraging innovation in pedagogy, curriculum design, and research methodologies is essential for keeping pace with the evolving demands of the academic world(Leal Filho et al., 2020).

Inclusivity and diversity are also critical priorities for higher education leaders. Institutions must strive to create a welcoming and inclusive environment for all members of the academic community. This involves developing policies and initiatives that promote diversity in hiring, admissions, and campus life. Leaders must also address issues of equity and access, ensuring that all students have the opportunity to succeed regardless of their background. In conclusion, higher education leadership is a multifaceted and dynamic field that requires a blend of strategic vision, operational expertise, and interpersonal skills. Leaders must navigate a complex landscape of internal and external challenges while fostering an environment that supports academic excellence, innovation, and inclusivity(Antonopoulou et al., 2020). By effectively managing resources, engaging stakeholders, and promoting a culture of collaboration and trust, higher education leaders can drive their institutions toward success and sustainability in an ever-changing world.

Policy and management play pivotal roles in the functioning and success of higher education institutions. These elements are integral to establishing a framework within which academic and administrative activities can be conducted efficiently and effectively. The importance of policy and management in higher education can be seen in how they influence strategic planning, resource allocation, regulatory compliance, and the overall educational experience. Effective policy-making provides a structured approach to governance and operations within higher education institutions. Policies establish clear guidelines and standards that govern various aspects of institutional life, from academic integrity and research ethics to admissions and campus safety(Smith, 2020). These guidelines help ensure consistency, fairness, and transparency, which are essential for maintaining trust and account-ability within the academic community. Without well-defined policies, institutions may face ambiguity and inconsistency in decision-making, leading to potential conflicts and inefficiencies.

Management, on the other hand, is the process by which policies are implemented and operationalized. Effective management involves planning, organizing, directing, and controlling institutional resources and activities to achieve strategic objectives. In the context of higher education, this means managing academic programs, faculty and staff, finances, facilities, and student services. Skilled management ensures that resources are used efficiently, goals are met, and the institution can adapt to changing circumstances and demands(Hale, 2023).

Strategic planning is a critical area where policy and management intersect. Higher education leaders must develop long-term strategies that align with the institution's mission and vision while being responsive to external trends and challenges. Policies provide the framework for these strategies, outlining priorities and establishing the rules for their implementation. Management then translates these strategic plans into actionable initiatives, coordinating efforts across different departments and ensuring that resources are allocated appropriately(Wilkinson, 2020). This align-ment between policy and management is crucial for achieving institutional goals and sustaining growth.

Resource allocation is another vital aspect of higher education that underscores the importance of policy and management. Institutions must make decisions about how to distribute limited resources, such as funding, personnel, and physical space, to support their academic and operational priorities. Policies guide these decisions by setting criteria for resource distribution, such as funding formulas for academic departments or guidelines for hiring and promotion. Effective management ensures that these policies are applied consistently and that resources are allocated in a way that maximizes their impact. This is particularly important in times of financial constraint when institutions must make difficult choices about where to invest and where to cut back(Akanji et al., 2020).

Regulatory compliance is a critical area where policy and management are essential. Higher education institutions must adhere to a myriad of regulations and standards set by government agencies, accrediting bodies, and other external enti-ties. Policies help ensure that institutions meet these requirements by establishing procedures for compliance and accountability. Effective management is necessary to implement these policies, monitor compliance, and address any issues that arise. Failure to comply with regulations can result in legal and financial penalties, damage to the institution's reputation, and loss of accreditation(Chankseliani et al., 2021). The overall educational experience of students is profoundly influenced by effective policy and management. Policies related to curriculum development, grading, academic support, and student conduct help create a structured and supportive learning environment. Management ensures that these policies are implemented consistently and that students receive the services and support they need to succeed. By fostering a positive educational experience, institutions can enhance student satisfaction, retention, and success.

Thus, policy and management are fundamental to the success of higher education institutions. They provide the framework and processes necessary for effective governance, strategic planning, resource allocation, regulatory compliance, and the overall quality of the educational experience. Higher education leaders must prioritize the development and implementation of sound policies and management practices to ensure that their institutions can navigate the complexities of the academic landscape and achieve their goals.

The primary objectives of this chapter are to explore the critical roles and responsibilities of higher education leaders and to highlight the importance of policy and management in academic institutions. It aims to:

- Examine how higher education leaders develop and implement strategic plans to align with institutional missions and respond to evolving educational demands.
- Discuss effective governance and decision-making processes essential for maintaining accountability and fostering collaboration.
- Detail the significance of robust financial management practices in ensuring institutional sustainability and growth.
- Explain the importance of engaging with various stakeholders to build support and achieve institutional goals.
- Address strategies for fostering an environment that supports academic innovation, inclusivity, and diversity.

ROLES AND RESPONSIBILITIES OF HIGHER EDUCATION LEADERS

Higher education leaders play pivotal roles in guiding institutions through strategic planning, establishing effective governance structures, and ensuring sound financial management. These responsibilities are critical for fostering academic excellence, maintaining institutional sustainability, and addressing the diverse needs of stakeholders within the academic community(Ruben et al., 2023b). The figure 1 depicts the roles and responsibilities of higher education leaders.

Figure 1. Roles and Responsibilities of Higher Education Leaders

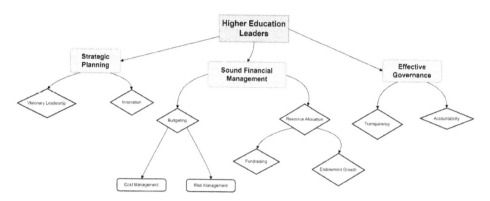

Strategic Planning

Strategic planning is fundamental to the role of higher education leaders as it sets the course for institutional development and growth. Leaders must formulate long-term goals and objectives that align with the institution's mission and vision. This involves analyzing internal strengths and weaknesses, identifying external opportunities and threats, and determining strategic initiatives to achieve desired outcomes.

Effective strategic planning in higher education includes:

- Mission Alignment: Ensuring that all strategic initiatives are aligned with the core mission and values of the institution.
- Stakeholder Engagement: Engaging faculty, staff, students, alumni, and external stakeholders in the planning process to gather diverse perspectives and build consensus.
- Adaptability: Developing plans that are flexible and responsive to changing educational trends, economic conditions, and societal needs.
- Implementation Oversight: Monitoring progress, evaluating outcomes, and making adjustments as necessary to achieve strategic objectives.

Strategic planning not only guides academic and administrative priorities but also enhances institutional coherence and fosters a shared vision among stakeholders.

Governance Structures

Governance structures in higher education are essential for effective decision-making, transparency, and accountability. Higher education leaders must establish and maintain governance frameworks that facilitate collaborative leadership and institutional integrity. The significant aspects of governance include:

- Policy Development: Establishing policies and procedures that govern academic programs, student affairs, research activities, and administrative operations.
- Decision-Making Processes: Implementing inclusive decision-making processes that involve input from faculty, staff, and students to ensure diverse perspectives are considered.
- Accountability: Holding individuals and departments accountable for their actions and decisions through clear roles, responsibilities, and performance metrics.
- Compliance and Ethics: Ensuring compliance with legal and regulatory requirements, ethical standards, and institutional policies to maintain credibility and trust.

Effective governance promotes institutional stability, fosters a culture of ethical behavior, and supports academic freedom and innovation.

Financial Management

Financial management is critical for the sustainability and growth of higher education institutions. Leaders must oversee budgeting, resource allocation, fundraising, and financial planning to ensure the efficient use of resources and the achievement of strategic goals.

- Budget Development: Developing annual budgets that align with strategic priorities and support academic programs, research initiatives, and student services.
- Resource Allocation: Allocating financial resources based on institutional priorities, enrollment trends, and revenue projections.
- Diversification of Revenue: Identifying and pursuing diverse revenue streams, including tuition, government funding, research grants, philanthropy, and partnerships.

- Financial Oversight: Monitoring financial performance, conducting regular audits, and implementing internal controls to safeguard assets and mitigate financial risks.

In an era of financial challenges and economic uncertainties, effective financial management enables institutions to invest in academic excellence, maintain competitive tuition rates, and support faculty and staff development.

The roles and responsibilities of higher education leaders in strategic planning, governance structures, and financial management are crucial for guiding institutions toward excellence and sustainability. By developing clear strategic plans, fostering effective governance, and implementing sound financial practices, leaders can enhance institutional reputation, support academic innovation, and meet the evolving needs of students and society. These responsibilities require visionary leadership, collaborative decision-making, and a commitment to advancing the mission and values of higher education.

NAVIGATING EXTERNAL REGULATIONS AND COMPLIANCE

Navigating external regulations and compliance is a critical responsibility for higher education leaders to ensure institutional integrity, legal adherence, and accountability. This involves understanding regulatory requirements, implementing effective compliance strategies, and maintaining proactive measures to mitigate risks(Martin & Marion, 2005). The figure 2 illustrates the process of navigating external regulations and compliance for higher education leaders.

Figure 2. Process of Navigating External Regulations and Compliance for Higher Education Leaders

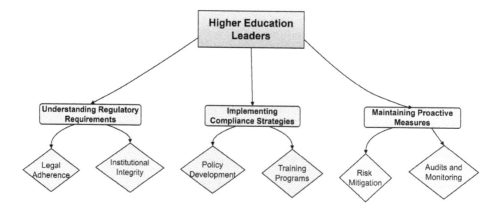

Understanding Regulatory Requirements

Higher education institutions are subject to a wide range of regulatory requirements from governmental agencies, accrediting bodies, and industry standards. These regulations cover areas such as:

- **Academic Standards**: Requirements related to curriculum development, program accreditation, and academic credentials.
- **Financial Management**: Regulations governing financial aid, tuition pricing, budgeting, and accounting practices.
- **Student Rights and Privacy**: Compliance with laws like FERPA (Family Educational Rights and Privacy Act) that protect student privacy and information security.
- **Ethical Standards**: Adherence to ethical guidelines in research, human subjects protection, and intellectual property rights.
- **Diversity and Inclusion**: Requirements related to affirmative action, Title IX compliance, and promoting diversity within the institution.

Higher education leaders must stay informed about these regulations, which may vary by jurisdiction and evolve over time. This requires ongoing monitoring of legislative changes, regulatory updates, and best practices within the industry. Collaborating with legal counsel, compliance officers, and industry associations can provide valuable insights and guidance on interpreting and implementing regulatory requirements effectively.

Implementing Compliance Strategies

Implementing compliance strategies involves developing policies, procedures, and practices to ensure adherence to regulatory requirements and mitigate compliance risks. Main components of effective compliance strategies include:

- **Policy Development**: Creating clear and comprehensive policies that reflect regulatory requirements and institutional values. Policies should outline responsibilities, procedures for reporting violations, and mechanisms for review and updates.
- **Training and Awareness**: Providing regular training sessions and educational programs to faculty, staff, and students on regulatory compliance issues. This includes workshops on data privacy, ethical conduct, and reporting obligations.

- **Monitoring and Auditing**: Establishing mechanisms for monitoring compliance with policies and conducting regular audits to assess adherence and identify areas for improvement.
- **Risk Management**: Developing strategies to identify, assess, and mitigate compliance risks proactively. This may involve conducting risk assessments, implementing controls, and developing contingency plans.
- **Collaboration and Communication**: Fostering a culture of compliance through open communication, collaboration across departments, and promoting ethical behavior. Leaders should encourage reporting of concerns and ensure non-retaliation policies are in place.

Effective compliance strategies not only ensure legal and regulatory compliance but also enhance institutional reputation, build trust with stakeholders, and mitigate potential financial and legal liabilities. By embedding compliance into the institutional culture and operations, leaders demonstrate a commitment to ethical practices and responsible governance.

Navigating external regulations and compliance is a complex but essential aspect of higher education leadership. By understanding regulatory requirements, implementing robust compliance strategies, and fostering a culture of integrity and accountability, leaders can safeguard institutional interests, protect student and employee rights, and uphold the highest standards of academic and operational excellence. Continuous monitoring, proactive risk management, and collaboration with legal and compliance experts are key to navigating the evolving regulatory landscape effectively. As higher education institutions face increasing scrutiny and regulatory complexity, strong leadership in compliance is indispensable for ensuring institutional success and sustainability in a competitive global environment.

INTERNAL GOVERNANCE AND DECISION-MAKING

Internal governance and decision-making processes are foundational to the effective operation and management of higher education institutions. They encompass organizational structures, decision-making processes, and the delicate balance between academic and administrative priorities. Leaders in higher education must navigate these complexities to foster a culture of collaboration, accountability, and strategic alignment(Beerkens & van der Hoek, 2022). The figure 3 depicts the process of internal governance and decision-making.

Figure 3. Internal Governance and Decision-Making

Organizational Structures

Organizational structures in higher education institutions define roles, responsibilities, and reporting relationships among faculty, staff, administrators, and governing bodies. The structure typically includes academic departments, administrative units, and central leadership positions such as presidents, provosts, deans, and department heads.

- **Hierarchical Framework**: Establishing clear lines of authority and accountability to ensure effective communication and decision-making.
- **Functional Units**: Organizing departments and units based on academic disciplines, administrative functions (e.g., finance, human resources), and student services to optimize operational efficiency.
- **Governance Bodies**: Structuring governing boards, committees, and councils to oversee policy development, strategic planning, and institutional oversight.
- **Matrix Relationships**: Facilitating cross-functional collaboration and interdisciplinary initiatives through matrix management structures that integrate diverse perspectives and expertise.

Effective organizational structures promote transparency, streamline operations, and facilitate collaboration across departments and units. They also support strategic initiatives by aligning resources and capabilities with institutional priorities.

Decision-Making Processes

Decision-making processes in higher education involve assessing options, evaluating risks and benefits, and reaching consensus on courses of action. These processes are influenced by institutional policies, governance structures, stakeholder input, and regulatory considerations:

- **Inclusive Participation**: Engaging stakeholders, including faculty, staff, students, and external partners, in decision-making processes to ensure diverse perspectives are considered.
- **Data-Driven Insights**: Utilizing data and analytics to inform decisions, monitor performance, and forecast trends in enrollment, finances, and academic outcomes.
- **Strategic Alignment**: Aligning decisions with institutional goals, mission, and values to ensure coherence and effectiveness in achieving desired outcomes.
- **Timely Execution**: Implementing decisions in a timely manner while maintaining flexibility to adapt to changing circumstances and emerging opportunities.

Leaders must foster a culture of shared governance and collaboration to enhance decision-making effectiveness and promote institutional agility. This involves creating forums for dialogue, establishing decision-making protocols, and empowering stakeholders to contribute meaningfully to the decision-making process.

Balancing Academic and Administrative Priorities

Balancing academic and administrative priorities is a continuous challenge for higher education leaders amidst evolving educational demands and resource constraints. Academic priorities typically include curriculum development, teaching excellence, research innovation, and student success, while administrative priorities encompass financial management, facilities planning, regulatory compliance, and institutional sustainability.

- **Resource Allocation**: Allocating financial, human, and physical resources to support both academic and administrative functions based on institutional goals and strategic priorities.
- **Collaborative Leadership**: Collaborating across academic and administrative units to integrate planning, align initiatives, and leverage synergies.

- **Adaptive Strategies**: Developing adaptive strategies that respond to external challenges, market trends, and technological advancements while preserving academic rigor and institutional values.
- **Stakeholder Engagement**: Engaging stakeholders in dialogue and decision-making processes to build consensus and support for balanced priorities.

Leaders must adopt a holistic approach to governance that integrates academic and administrative perspectives, fosters innovation, and enhances institutional effectiveness. By aligning resources, optimizing workflows, and fostering a culture of mutual respect and collaboration, leaders can navigate complex challenges and position their institutions for sustained success.

Internal governance and decision-making processes are fundamental to the effective leadership of higher education institutions. By establishing clear organizational structures, facilitating inclusive decision-making processes, and balancing academic and administrative priorities, leaders can promote transparency, accountability, and strategic alignment. Continuous adaptation to changing educational landscapes and stakeholder expectations is essential for fostering a culture of innovation and excellence in higher education. As institutions navigate future challenges and opportunities, strong governance and effective decision-making will remain critical to advancing their missions and achieving sustainable growth.

STAKEHOLDER ENGAGEMENT

Stakeholder engagement is crucial in educational management as it fosters collaboration, transparency, and effective decision-making. This article explores the process of identifying key stakeholders, building collaborative relationships, and communicating effectively with stakeholders within educational institutions(Gigliotti & Ruben, 2017). The figure 4 depicts the process of stakeholder engagement in educational management.

Figure 4. Process of Stakeholder Engagement in Educational Management

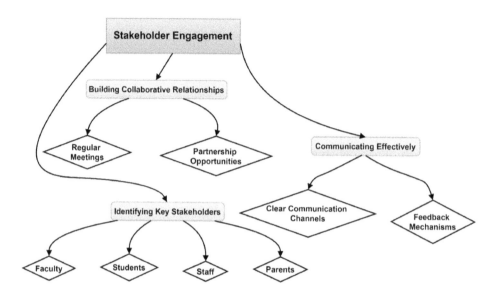

Identifying Important Stakeholders

Identifying key stakeholders in educational management involves recognizing individuals or groups who have a vested interest or influence in the institution's activities and outcomes. These stakeholders can include:

- **Internal Stakeholders**: This group comprises administrators, faculty members, students, and non-teaching staff who directly contribute to the institution's operations and academic environment.
- **External Stakeholders**: External stakeholders may include parents, alumni, community members, government agencies, regulatory bodies, industry partners, and donors who impact or are impacted by the institution's activities.
- **Special Interest Groups**: These are entities such as educational associations, advocacy groups, and professional organizations that advocate for specific interests or causes related to education.

Identifying stakeholders involves conducting stakeholder analysis to prioritize their influence, interests, and expectations. This process helps educational leaders allocate resources effectively and tailor engagement strategies to meet diverse stakeholder needs.

Building Collaborative Relationships

Building collaborative relationships with stakeholders is essential for fostering trust, mutual understanding, and support for educational initiatives.

- **Engagement Platforms**: Establishing formal channels, such as advisory committees, focus groups, and forums, where stakeholders can provide input and participate in decision-making processes.
- **Partnership Development**: Collaborating with external stakeholders, such as industry partners or community organizations, to enrich educational programs, secure funding, or enhance students' learning experiences.
- **Transparency and Accountability**: Ensuring transparency in communication and decision-making processes builds credibility and enhances stakeholders' confidence in the institution's leadership.
- **Conflict Resolution**: Addressing conflicts or disagreements promptly and constructively to maintain positive relationships and minimize disruptions to educational goals.
- **Continuous Engagement**: Maintaining ongoing communication through newsletters, social media, town hall meetings, and personal interactions to keep stakeholders informed and engaged in the institution's progress and challenges.

Successful collaboration requires educational leaders to be proactive listeners, empathetic communicators, and facilitators of inclusive decision-making processes.

Communicating with Stakeholders

Effective communication is central to stakeholder engagement in educational management.

- **Clear and Timely Communication**: Providing stakeholders with accurate, relevant information in a timely manner through various communication channels, such as email updates, newsletters, and official announcements.
- **Two-Way Communication**: Encouraging feedback and dialogue by actively soliciting input, conducting surveys, and responding to queries and concerns promptly.
- **Tailored Messaging**: Adapting communication strategies to resonate with diverse stakeholder groups' interests, preferences, and communication styles.

- **Education and Awareness**: Educating stakeholders about institutional goals, policies, and achievements to foster a shared sense of purpose and commitment to the institution's mission.
- **Crisis Communication**: Developing contingency plans and protocols for managing crises or sensitive issues transparently and responsibly to maintain stakeholders' trust and confidence.

By prioritizing effective stakeholder engagement strategies, educational leaders can cultivate a supportive and collaborative environment that enhances institutional effectiveness, student success, and community impact.

In conclusion, stakeholder engagement is a dynamic process that requires proactive leadership, effective communication, and collaborative relationship-building to align diverse interests and achieve shared educational goals. Educational institutions that prioritize stakeholder engagement foster a culture of transparency, accountability, and innovation that enhances their ability to adapt to evolving challenges and opportunities in the educational landscape.

FOSTERING ACADEMIC EXCELLENCE AND INNOVATION

Achieving academic excellence and fostering innovation are key goals for educational institutions aiming to enhance learning outcomes, research impact, and overall institutional reputation. This article explores strategies to promote research and scholarship, encourage teaching and learning innovations, and support faculty development within the framework of academic excellence and innovation(Kalaiselvi et al., 2024; Saravanan et al., 2024; Singh Madan et al., 2024).

Figure 5. Achieving Academic Excellence and Fostering Innovation

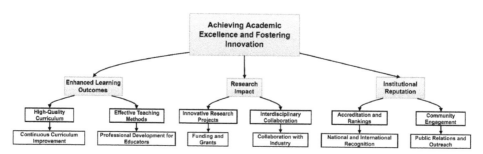

Promoting Research and Scholarship

Promoting research and scholarship is essential for advancing knowledge, addressing societal challenges, and contributing to academic discourse.

- **Research Funding and Grants**: Providing financial support through grants, fellowships, and awards to facilitate faculty research projects, collaborations, and scholarly publications.
- **Research Infrastructure**: Investing in state-of-the-art laboratories, libraries, and research facilities to support faculty and student research activities across disciplines.
- **Collaborative Research Initiatives**: Encouraging interdisciplinary research collaborations and partnerships with industry, government agencies, and international institutions to tackle complex issues and promote knowledge transfer.
- **Publication and Dissemination**: Supporting faculty in publishing their research findings in reputable journals, presenting at conferences, and engaging in public dissemination activities to maximize research impact and visibility.
- **Research Ethics and Integrity**: Promoting ethical standards and integrity in research practices through institutional policies, training programs, and oversight mechanisms.

By fostering a vibrant research culture, educational institutions can empower faculty and students to make significant contributions to their fields and society at large.

Encouraging Teaching and Learning Innovations

Encouraging teaching and learning innovations is crucial for adapting to evolving educational trends, engaging students effectively, and enhancing learning outcomes.

- **Technology Integration**: Incorporating educational technologies, such as learning management systems (LMS), virtual reality (VR), and artificial intelligence (AI), to create interactive and personalized learning experiences.
- **Active Learning Strategies**: Promoting active learning methodologies, including flipped classrooms, collaborative projects, problem-based learning (PBL), and experiential learning opportunities that empower students to apply theoretical knowledge in practical contexts.

- **Curriculum Development**: Updating and diversifying curricula to reflect emerging fields, interdisciplinary approaches, and real-world challenges, ensuring relevance and currency in educational offerings.
- **Assessment and Feedback**: Implementing formative and summative assessment strategies, providing timely feedback, and using data analytics to monitor student progress and tailor instructional interventions.
- **Faculty Training and Support**: Offering professional development workshops, mentoring programs, and teaching awards to empower faculty in adopting innovative pedagogical practices and enhancing their teaching effectiveness.

By fostering a culture of innovation in teaching and learning, educational institutions can optimize student engagement, retention, and academic success while preparing graduates for future professional challenges.

Supporting Faculty Development

Supporting faculty development is critical for maintaining teaching excellence, advancing research productivity, and promoting institutional leadership(Kalaiselvi et al., 2024; Saravanan et al., 2024; Singh Madan et al., 2024).

- **Professional Development Opportunities**: Offering sabbaticals, workshops, seminars, and conferences that enable faculty to enhance their disciplinary expertise, pedagogical skills, and research methodologies.
- **Mentorship Programs**: Pairing junior faculty with experienced mentors who provide guidance, support, and career advice to foster professional growth and academic success.
- **Recognition and Rewards**: Acknowledging faculty achievements through tenure and promotion processes, teaching excellence awards, research grants, and opportunities for leadership roles within the institution.
- **Work-Life Balance Initiatives**: Implementing policies and programs that support faculty well-being, such as flexible scheduling, childcare assistance, and health and wellness resources.
- **Collaborative Leadership**: Cultivating a collaborative leadership culture where faculty participate in decision-making processes, governance structures, and strategic planning initiatives to shape institutional direction and priorities.

By investing in faculty development, educational institutions can cultivate a talented and motivated faculty workforce that drives innovation, fosters academic excellence, and sustains institutional growth over the long term.

Hence, fostering academic excellence and innovation requires a multifaceted approach that integrates robust research support, innovative teaching practices, and comprehensive faculty development initiatives. By prioritizing these strategies, educational institutions can strengthen their competitive edge, enrich the student learning experience, and contribute meaningfully to knowledge creation and societal advancement.

ENSURING INCLUSIVITY AND DIVERSITY

Ensuring inclusivity and diversity in educational institutions is imperative for fostering a supportive and equitable learning environment, promoting social justice, and preparing students to thrive in diverse global societies. This article explores strategies for developing inclusive policies, implementing diversity initiatives, and examines case studies that highlight successful practices in promoting inclusivity(Das et al., 2024; Durairaj et al., 2023; Sharma et al., 2024).

Developing Inclusive Policies

Developing inclusive policies involves creating frameworks and guidelines that promote equity, respect diversity, and eliminate barriers to participation and success for all members of the educational community.

- **Policy Review and Revision**: Conducting regular reviews of existing policies to identify and address gaps in inclusivity, ensuring they reflect current best practices and legal requirements.
- **Non-Discrimination and Equal Opportunity**: Establishing policies that prohibit discrimination based on race, ethnicity, gender identity, sexual orientation, disability, socioeconomic status, or other protected characteristics, and ensuring equitable access to educational resources and opportunities.
- **Accessibility and Accommodation**: Implementing policies that promote accessible facilities, technologies, and services to accommodate diverse needs and ensure inclusivity for students, faculty, and staff with disabilities.
- **Cultural Competence Training**: Providing training programs and resources to enhance cultural competence among faculty, staff, and administrators, enabling them to effectively engage with diverse populations and address implicit biases.

- **Support Services and Resources**: Developing policies that prioritize the provision of support services, such as counseling, mentoring, and academic advising, to assist students from underrepresented backgrounds in achieving their educational goals.

By embedding inclusivity into institutional policies and practices, educational institutions can create a welcoming and supportive environment where all individuals feel valued, respected, and empowered to succeed.

Implementing Diversity Initiatives

Implementing diversity initiatives involves proactive efforts to recruit, retain, and support a diverse student body, faculty, and staff, reflecting the institution's commitment to equity and inclusivity(Agrawal et al., 2023; Durairaj et al., 2023).

- **Diversity Recruitment Strategies**: Developing targeted recruitment efforts to attract students, faculty, and staff from underrepresented groups, including outreach programs, scholarships, and partnerships with community organizations.
- **Retention and Support Programs**: Establishing retention programs and initiatives that provide mentorship, networking opportunities, and cultural affinity groups to support the success and well-being of diverse students, faculty, and staff.
- **Curriculum Diversity**: Integrating diverse perspectives, histories, and cultural contexts into the curriculum to enrich learning experiences, foster critical thinking, and prepare students to thrive in multicultural societies.
- **Celebrating Diversity**: Organizing events, celebrations, and awareness campaigns that promote cultural diversity, raise awareness about social justice issues, and celebrate the contributions of diverse communities within the institution and beyond.
- **Institutional Accountability**: Establishing metrics, benchmarks, and accountability mechanisms to monitor progress toward diversity goals, assess the impact of diversity initiatives, and ensure continuous improvement in fostering inclusivity.

By embracing diversity as a strength and implementing comprehensive initiatives, educational institutions can cultivate an inclusive campus culture that promotes learning, innovation, and social responsibility.

Case Studies on Inclusivity

Examining case studies provides insights into effective practices and outcomes of inclusivity initiatives within educational institutions. Examples include:

- **University of California, Berkeley**: Implemented a comprehensive diversity plan focused on increasing diversity among students and faculty, enhancing campus climate through cultural competency training, and promoting inclusive curriculum development.
- **Georgetown University**: Established the Initiative on Diversity, Equity, and Student Success, which includes targeted recruitment strategies, mentoring programs, and institutional policies to support the academic and social integration of diverse student populations.
- **University of Cape Town, South Africa**: Addressed historical inequities and promoted inclusivity through initiatives such as the Critical Race Theory curriculum, diversity scholarships, and community engagement programs aimed at fostering understanding and reconciliation.
- **McGill University, Canada**: Developed a Disability Policy and Accessible Learning Services that provide accommodations, support services, and advocacy for students with disabilities, ensuring equitable access to education and campus resources.
- **Stanford University**: Launched the Diversity and Access Office, which coordinates diversity initiatives across campus, including recruitment strategies, retention programs, and cultural competence training for faculty, staff, and students.

These case studies illustrate diverse approaches to promoting inclusivity and diversity within educational settings, highlighting the importance of strategic planning, community engagement, and institutional commitment to achieving equitable outcomes.

Hence, ensuring inclusivity and diversity in educational institutions requires proactive leadership, comprehensive policies, and sustained commitment to equity and social justice. By developing inclusive policies, implementing diversity initiatives, and learning from successful case studies, educational institutions can create a vibrant and inclusive campus environment that enriches learning experiences, fosters innovation, and prepares students to contribute positively to a diverse and interconnected world.

FINANCIAL MANAGEMENT AND SUSTAINABILITY

Financial management and sustainability are critical aspects of ensuring the long-term viability and success of educational institutions(Dhanya et al., 2023; Mohanty et al., 2023; Vijaya Lakshmi et al., 2024). This article explores key strategies in budgeting and resource allocation, fundraising and development, and ensuring long-term financial health.

Budgeting and Resource Allocation

Effective budgeting and resource allocation are essential for maximizing financial resources and supporting institutional priorities.

- **Strategic Planning**: Aligning budget priorities with institutional goals and strategic plans to ensure resources are allocated efficiently to support academic programs, faculty development, infrastructure improvements, and student services.
- **Transparency and Accountability**: Establishing transparent budgeting processes that involve stakeholders, such as faculty, staff, and student representatives, to promote accountability and foster trust in financial decision-making.
- **Cost Management**: Implementing cost-effective measures, such as energy efficiency initiatives, centralized procurement systems, and operational efficiencies, to optimize spending and reduce institutional expenses.
- **Risk Management**: Identifying and mitigating financial risks through contingency planning, financial reserves, and insurance policies to protect against unforeseen economic challenges or disruptions.
- **Monitoring and Evaluation**: Regularly monitoring budget performance, assessing outcomes against financial goals, and adjusting resource allocations as needed to ensure alignment with evolving institutional needs and priorities.

By prioritizing strategic budgeting and resource allocation practices, educational institutions can enhance financial stability and support sustainable growth and development.

Fundraising and Development

Fundraising and development efforts play a crucial role in securing additional financial resources and enhancing institutional capacity.

- **Development Campaigns**: Launching comprehensive fundraising campaigns, capital campaigns, and annual giving initiatives to solicit philanthropic support from alumni, parents, foundations, and corporate partners.
- **Grant Writing and Research Funding**: Identifying and pursuing grant opportunities from government agencies, research foundations, and private donors to support research projects, faculty initiatives, and institutional programs.
- **Major Gifts and Endowment Growth**: Cultivating relationships with major donors and planned giving prospects to secure major gifts, endowment contributions, and legacy commitments that provide long-term financial stability.
- **Corporate Partnerships and Sponsorships**: Establishing partnerships with businesses, industry leaders, and community organizations to sponsor research initiatives, scholarship programs, and campus events that align with institutional priorities.
- **Alumni Engagement**: Engaging alumni through networking events, reunions, and mentorship programs to foster a culture of giving, volunteerism, and lifelong connections with the institution.

Effective fundraising and development strategies diversify revenue streams, strengthen institutional relationships, and support initiatives that enhance educational quality and student success.

Ensuring Long-Term Financial Health

Ensuring long-term financial health requires proactive management and sustainable practices to navigate economic uncertainties and achieve financial sustainability.

- **Financial Planning and Forecasting**: Conducting regular financial assessments, forecasting revenue trends, and developing long-term financial plans that account for inflation, enrollment fluctuations, and market conditions.
- **Endowment Management**: Prudently managing endowment funds and investment portfolios through diversified asset allocation strategies, investment oversight, and adherence to fiduciary responsibilities.
- **Debt Management**: Strategically managing institutional debt, including refinancing opportunities, debt service coverage ratios, and leveraging debt for capital projects that generate long-term returns on investment.
- **Revenue Diversification**: Exploring new revenue streams, such as online programs, professional development courses, and continuing education offerings, to supplement traditional sources of funding and support institutional growth.

- **Sustainability Initiatives**: Integrating sustainability principles into financial decision-making, including energy conservation measures, sustainable building practices, and environmentally responsible investments that reduce operational costs and enhance institutional resilience.

By adopting proactive financial management practices and embracing sustainability principles, educational institutions can strengthen their financial position, support mission-critical initiatives, and ensure long-term viability and success.

Hence, financial management and sustainability are integral to achieving institutional goals, supporting academic excellence, and enhancing the overall student experience. By prioritizing strategic budgeting, effective fundraising, and sustainable financial practices, educational institutions can navigate challenges, seize opportunities, and thrive in an evolving higher education landscape.

CHALLENGES AND OPPORTUNITIES IN HIGHER EDUCATION LEADERSHIP

Higher education leadership faces a dynamic landscape characterized by challenges such as funding constraints, changing educational demands, and the need to leverage technology for institutional growth. This article examines these issues and explores strategies to turn them into opportunities for institutional advancement(Prabhuswamy et al., 2024; Singh Madan et al., 2024).

Addressing Funding Constraints

Funding constraints pose significant challenges to higher education institutions, affecting their ability to maintain academic quality, support faculty development, and invest in infrastructure.

- **Diversifying Revenue Streams**: Exploring alternative revenue sources such as philanthropic donations, corporate partnerships, continuing education programs, and research grants to supplement traditional funding sources.
- **Cost Optimization**: Implementing cost-saving measures through operational efficiencies, energy conservation initiatives, and strategic procurement practices to maximize financial resources.
- **Advocacy and Fundraising**: Engaging in advocacy efforts with government agencies, alumni, and community stakeholders to secure public funding, grants, and endowments that support institutional priorities.

- **Financial Planning**: Developing robust financial planning and forecasting processes to anticipate budgetary challenges, prioritize spending, and allocate resources effectively based on institutional goals and strategic priorities.

By proactively addressing funding constraints and diversifying revenue streams, higher education leaders can strengthen financial resilience and enhance institutional sustainability amidst economic uncertainties.

Adapting to Changing Educational Demands

Changing educational demands driven by technological advancements, globalization, and evolving student expectations present both challenges and opportunities for higher education institutions. Strategies to adapt include:

- **Curricular Innovation**: Updating curricula to incorporate emerging fields, interdisciplinary approaches, and real-world applications that prepare students for future careers and societal challenges.
- **Flexible Learning Models**: Offering flexible learning options such as online courses, hybrid programs, and competency-based education to accommodate diverse student needs, enhance accessibility, and promote lifelong learning.
- **Student-Centered Approaches**: Adopting student-centered teaching methodologies, personalized learning experiences, and support services that promote engagement, retention, and academic success.
- **Internationalization**: Expanding international partnerships, study abroad programs, and cultural exchange initiatives to foster global citizenship, diversity, and cross-cultural understanding among students and faculty.

By embracing educational innovation and flexibility, higher education institutions can meet the evolving needs of students, enhance learning outcomes, and maintain competitiveness in a globalized knowledge economy.

Leveraging Technology for Institutional Growth

Technology plays a transformative role in higher education, offering opportunities to enhance teaching effectiveness, improve operational efficiency, and expand institutional reach(Karthikeyan et al., 2024; Saravanan et al., 2024). Strategies to leverage technology include:

- **Digital Learning Platforms**: Implementing robust learning management systems (LMS), virtual classrooms, and educational technologies that support interactive learning experiences, collaboration, and content delivery.
- **Data-Driven Decision Making**: Utilizing data analytics and business intelligence tools to inform strategic planning, enrollment management, student retention initiatives, and resource allocation decisions.
- **Research and Innovation**: Investing in research infrastructure, high-performance computing resources, and digital libraries that support faculty research, innovation, and knowledge dissemination.
- **Administrative Efficiency**: Streamlining administrative processes through enterprise resource planning (ERP) systems, online registration systems, and automated workflows to reduce paperwork, enhance productivity, and improve service delivery.

By embracing technology-enabled solutions and fostering a culture of innovation, higher education leaders can drive institutional growth, enhance academic excellence, and create transformative learning experiences for students and faculty alike.

In conclusion, navigating the challenges and seizing the opportunities in higher education leadership requires visionary leadership, strategic planning, and a commitment to innovation and adaptability. By addressing funding constraints, adapting to changing educational demands, and leveraging technology effectively, higher education institutions can position themselves for sustainable growth, academic excellence, and positive societal impact in an increasingly complex and interconnected world.

FUTURE TRENDS IN HIGHER EDUCATION LEADERSHIP

Higher education leadership is evolving rapidly in response to emerging trends such as new leadership models, the impact of globalization, and predictions for the future. This article explores these trends and their implications for shaping the future of educational institutions worldwide(Besterfield-Sacre et al., 2004; Herrera-Pavo, 2021; Holmes et al., 2007; Kartam, 1998).

Emerging Leadership Models

Future trends in higher education leadership are reshaping traditional models and emphasizing innovative approaches that prioritize collaboration, diversity, and adaptability.

- **Collaborative Leadership**: Moving away from hierarchical structures towards collaborative leadership models that promote teamwork, shared decision-making, and collective problem-solving among administrators, faculty, staff, and students.
- **Transformational Leadership**: Emphasizing visionary leadership that inspires institutional change, fosters a culture of innovation, and drives strategic initiatives to enhance academic excellence, student success, and institutional reputation.
- **Inclusive Leadership**: Promoting inclusive leadership practices that value diverse perspectives, cultivate equitable opportunities, and empower individuals from underrepresented backgrounds to contribute effectively to institutional governance and decision-making.
- **Adaptive Leadership**: Embracing adaptive leadership strategies that enable institutions to navigate complex challenges, anticipate future trends, and proactively respond to disruptions in higher education, such as technological advancements and demographic shifts.
- **Data-Driven Leadership**: Leveraging data analytics and evidence-based decision-making to inform strategic planning, optimize resource allocation, and enhance operational efficiency across academic, administrative, and student support functions.

By adopting these innovative leadership models, higher education institutions can foster resilience, agility, and sustainable growth in a rapidly changing global landscape.

Impact of Globalization

Globalization is profoundly influencing higher education leadership by expanding opportunities for international collaboration, student mobility, and cross-cultural learning experiences.

- Internationalization Strategies: Developing comprehensive internationalization strategies that attract diverse student populations, recruit talented faculty from around the world, and establish global partnerships for research collaboration and knowledge exchange.
- Cross-Border Education: Embracing cross-border education initiatives, such as branch campuses, joint degree programs, and online courses, to extend institutional reach, enhance global competitiveness, and meet the educational needs of a globalized workforce.

- Cultural Competence: Promoting cultural competence among faculty, staff, and students through intercultural training, language proficiency programs, and cross-cultural exchange opportunities that foster mutual understanding and respect.
- Global Citizenship: Educating students to become global citizens who are socially responsible, culturally aware, and equipped to address global challenges through interdisciplinary education, service-learning projects, and community engagement initiatives.
- Policy and Regulatory Challenges: Addressing policy and regulatory challenges related to academic standards, accreditation, student visas, and intellectual property rights in cross-border education partnerships and international collaborations.

Globalization presents both opportunities and challenges for higher education leaders to promote diversity, expand institutional influence, and contribute to global knowledge economies through innovative educational programs and strategic international partnerships.

Predictions for the Future

Looking ahead, several predictions for the future of higher education leadership are shaping strategic priorities and institutional planning efforts:

- **Digital Transformation**: Continued integration of technology into teaching, learning, and administrative processes, with a focus on enhancing accessibility, flexibility, and personalized learning experiences through artificial intelligence, virtual reality, and digital learning platforms.
- **Lifelong Learning**: Expansion of lifelong learning opportunities, micro-credentials, and continuous professional development programs that cater to diverse learner needs and support career advancement in a rapidly evolving job market.
- **Sustainability Initiatives**: Heightened emphasis on sustainability practices, environmental stewardship, and social responsibility within higher education institutions through green campus initiatives, sustainable development goals, and ethical investment strategies.
- **Student-Centered Approaches**: Increasing adoption of student-centered educational models that prioritize personalized learning pathways, holistic student support services, and inclusive campus environments that promote student engagement, retention, and academic success.

- **Strategic Partnerships**: Strengthening strategic partnerships with industry, government agencies, nonprofit organizations, and community stakeholders to address societal challenges, foster innovation, and create pathways for experiential learning and workforce development.

By embracing these future-oriented trends, higher education leaders can navigate uncertainties, capitalize on opportunities, and position their institutions as leaders in fostering academic excellence, innovation, and societal impact in the 21st century.

Hence, future trends in higher education leadership underscore the importance of visionary leadership, strategic foresight, and adaptive capacity to drive institutional transformation, address global challenges, and prepare students for success in a rapidly changing world. By embracing emerging leadership models, leveraging the benefits of globalization, and anticipating future trends, educational institutions can uphold their missions, enhance educational quality, and contribute meaningfully to global knowledge and prosperity.

CONCLUSION

In conclusion, the landscape of higher education leadership is rapidly evolving, driven by emerging trends that emphasize innovation, collaboration, and adaptability. Leaders in higher education must navigate challenges such as funding constraints, changing educational demands, and the integration of technology while leveraging opportunities presented by globalization and future-oriented strategies.

In navigating these trends, higher education leaders have the opportunity to shape the future of education, empower diverse student populations, and contribute to global knowledge economies. By embracing innovation, fostering inclusivity, and adapting proactively to emerging challenges, institutions can thrive in an increasingly interconnected and competitive environment, ultimately fulfilling their missions of advancing learning, research, and societal impact.

REFERENCES

Agrawal, A. V., Pitchai, R., Senthamaraikannan, C., Balaji, N. A., Sajithra, S., & Boopathi, S. (2023). Digital Education System During the COVID-19 Pandemic. In *Using Assistive Technology for Inclusive Learning in K-12 Classrooms* (pp. 104–126). IGI Global. DOI: 10.4018/978-1-6684-6424-3.ch005

Akanji, B., Mordi, C., Ituma, A., Adisa, T. A., & Ajonbadi, H. (2020). The influence of organisational culture on leadership style in higher education institutions. *Personnel Review*, 49(3), 709–732. DOI: 10.1108/PR-08-2018-0280

Antonopoulou, H., Halkiopoulos, C., Barlou, O., & Beligiannis, G. N. (2020). Leadership types and digital leadership in higher education: Behavioural data analysis from University of Patras in Greece. *International Journal of Learning. Teaching and Educational Research*, 19(4), 110–129.

Ash, A. N., Hill, R., Risdon, S., & Jun, A. (2020). Anti-racism in higher education: A model for change. *Race and Pedagogy Journal: Teaching and Learning for Justice*, 4(3), 2.

Beerkens, M., & van der Hoek, M. (2022). Academic leaders and leadership in the changing higher education landscape. In *Research Handbook on Academic Careers and Managing Academics* (pp. 121–136). Edward Elgar Publishing. DOI: 10.4337/9781839102639.00017

Besterfield-Sacre, M., Gerchak, J., Lyons, M. R., Shuman, L. J., & Wolfe, H. (2004). Scoring concept maps: An integrated rubric for assessing engineering education. *Journal of Engineering Education*, 93(2), 105–115. DOI: 10.1002/j.2168-9830.2004. tb00795.x

Chankseliani, M., Qoraboyev, I., & Gimranova, D. (2021). Higher education contributing to local, national, and global development: New empirical and conceptual insights. *Higher Education*, 81(1), 109–127. DOI: 10.1007/s10734-020-00565-8 PMID: 33173242

Das, S., Lekhya, G., Shreya, K., Shekinah, K. L., Babu, K. K., & Boopathi, S. (2024). Fostering Sustainability Education Through Cross-Disciplinary Collaborations and Research Partnerships: Interdisciplinary Synergy. In *Facilitating Global Collaboration and Knowledge Sharing in Higher Education With Generative AI* (pp. 60–88). IGI Global.

Dhanya, D., Kumar, S. S., Thilagavathy, A., Prasad, D., & Boopathi, S. (2023). Data Analytics and Artificial Intelligence in the Circular Economy: Case Studies. In *Intelligent Engineering Applications and Applied Sciences for Sustainability* (pp. 40–58). IGI Global.

Durairaj, M., Jayakumar, S., Karpagavalli, V., Maheswari, B. U., & Boopathi, S. (2023). Utilization of Digital Tools in the Indian Higher Education System During Health Crises. In *Multidisciplinary Approaches to Organizational Governance During Health Crises* (pp. 1–21). IGI Global. DOI: 10.4018/978-1-7998-9213-7.ch001

Gigliotti, R. A., & Ruben, B. D. (2017). Preparing higher education leaders: A conceptual, strategic, and operational approach. *Journal of Leadership Education*, 16(1), 96–114. DOI: 10.12806/V16/I1/T1

Hale, F. W. (2023). *What makes racial diversity work in higher education: Academic leaders present successful policies and strategies.* Taylor & Francis. DOI: 10.4324/9781003448662

Herrera-Pavo, M. Á. (2021). Collaborative learning for virtual higher education. *Learning, Culture and Social Interaction*, 28, 100437. DOI: 10.1016/j.lcsi.2020.100437

Holmes, M., Rulfs, J., & Orr, J. (2007). Curriculum Development And Integration For K 6 Engineering Education. *2007 Annual Conference & Exposition*, 12–436. DOI: 10.18260/1-2--2812

Kalaiselvi, D., Ramaratnam, M. S., Kokila, S., Sarkar, R., Anandakumar, S., & Boopathi, S. (2024). Future Developments of Higher Education on Social Psychology: Innovation and Changes. In *Advances in Human and Social Aspects of Technology* (pp. 146–169). IGI Global. DOI: 10.4018/979-8-3693-2569-8.ch008

Kartam, N. A. (1998). Integrating design into a civil engineering education. *International Journal of Engineering Education*, 14(2), 130–135.

Karthikeyan, M., Vigilia, J. K. N., Sequeira, S. L., Vidhya Priya, P., Ghamande, M. V., & Boopathi, S. (2024). NBA Implementation Across Engineering Disciplines for Driving Social Changes in India. In *Advances in Human and Social Aspects of Technology* (pp. 240–265). IGI Global. DOI: 10.4018/979-8-3693-2569-8.ch012

Kezar, A. J. (2023). *Rethinking leadership in a complex, multicultural, and global environment: New concepts and models for higher education.* Taylor & Francis. DOI: 10.4324/9781003446842

Leal Filho, W., Eustachio, J. H. P. P., Caldana, A. C. F., Will, M., Lange Salvia, A., Rampasso, I. S., Anholon, R., Platje, J., & Kovaleva, M. (2020). Sustainability leadership in higher education institutions: An overview of challenges. *Sustainability (Basel)*, 12(9), 3761. DOI: 10.3390/su12093761

Martin, J. S., & Marion, R. (2005). Higher education leadership roles in knowledge processing. *The Learning Organization*, 12(2), 140–151. DOI: 10.1108/09696470510583520

Mohanty, A., Venkateswaran, N., Ranjit, P., Tripathi, M. A., & Boopathi, S. (2023). Innovative Strategy for Profitable Automobile Industries: Working Capital Management. In *Handbook of Research on Designing Sustainable Supply Chains to Achieve a Circular Economy* (pp. 412–428). IGI Global.

Mohr, S., & Purcell, H. (2020). Sustainable Development of Leadership Strategies in Higher Education. In *Introduction to Sustainable Development Leadership and Strategies in Higher Education* (pp. 55–66). Emerald Publishing Limited. DOI: 10.1108/S2055-364120200000022007

Prabhuswamy, M., Tripathi, R., Vijayakumar, M., Thulasimani, T., Sundharesalingam, P., & Sampath, B. (2024). A Study on the Complex Nature of Higher Education Leadership: An Innovative Approach. In *Challenges of Globalization and Inclusivity in Academic Research* (pp. 202–223). IGI Global. DOI: 10.4018/979-8-3693-1371-8.ch013

Ruben, B. D., De Lisi, R., & Gigliotti, R. A. (2023a). *A guide for leaders in higher education: Concepts, competencies, and tools.* Taylor & Francis.

Ruben, B. D., De Lisi, R., & Gigliotti, R. A. (2023b). *A guide for leaders in higher education: Concepts, competencies, and tools.* Taylor & Francis.

Saravanan, S., Chandrasekar, J., Satheesh Kumar, S., Patel, P., Maria Shanthi, J., & Boopathi, S. (2024). The Impact of NBA Implementation Across Engineering Disciplines: Innovative Approaches. In *Advances in Higher Education and Professional Development* (pp. 229–252). IGI Global. DOI: 10.4018/979-8-3693-1666-5.ch010

Sharma, D. M., Ramana, K. V., Jothilakshmi, R., Verma, R., Maheswari, B. U., & Boopathi, S. (2024). Integrating Generative AI Into K-12 Curriculums and Pedagogies in India: Opportunities and Challenges. *Facilitating Global Collaboration and Knowledge Sharing in Higher Education With Generative AI*, 133–161.

Singh Madan, B., Najma, U., Pande Rana, D., & Kumar, P. K. J., S., S., & Boopathi, S. (2024). Empowering Leadership in Higher Education: Driving Student Performance, Faculty Development, and Institutional Progress. In *Advances in Educational Technologies and Instructional Design* (pp. 191–221). IGI Global. DOI: 10.4018/979-8-3693-0583-6.ch009

Smith, D. G. (2020). *Diversity's promise for higher education: Making it work.* JHU Press. DOI: 10.56021/9781421438405

Vijaya Lakshmi, V., Mishra, M., Kushwah, J. S., Shajahan, U. S., Mohanasundari, M., & Boopathi, S. (2024). Circular Economy Digital Practices for Ethical Dimensions and Policies for Digital Waste Management. In *Harnessing High-Performance Computing and AI for Environmental Sustainability* (pp. 166–193). IGI Global., DOI: 10.4018/979-8-3693-1794-5.ch008

Wilkinson, J. (2020). Educational leadership as practice. In *Oxford research encyclopedia of education*. DOI: 10.1093/acrefore/9780190264093.013.613

KEY TERMS

- **FERPA:** Family Educational Rights and Privacy Act
- **LMS:** Learning Management System
- **VR:** Virtual Reality
- **AI:** Artificial Intelligence
- **PBL:** Project-Based Learning
- **ERP:** Enterprise Resource Planning

Chapter 5
Strategic Retention Management Approach to Academic Migration and Attrition With Policy Implications and Educational Leadership Reimagined

Bolapeju Mary Agboola

https://orcid.org/0000-0003-0763-2599

The University of the West Indies, Mona, Jamaica

ABSTRACT

This chapter investigated academics' perceptions of migration and attrition rates in Jamaican and Nigerian universities using mixed methods. Data on attrition were generated using a checklist and academics' perceptions data were obtained with an open-ended questionnaire survey while ensuring confidentiality of the participant's identity and information. Data were analysed with inferential statistics and thematic analysis. The results revealed that academic attrition rates of lecturers and below were higher than senior lecturers and professors, with males higher than females. Job status, organizational factors, and weak retention policy statistically significantly influence attrition and migration decisions. In conclusion, differences exist among academic attrition rates, consequently, the researcher's strategic retention management model identifies factors that induce migration/attrition and their implications for leadership reimagination and the development of retention policies

DOI: 10.4018/979-8-3693-9215-7.ch005

and proactive support practices to manage academics.

INTRODUCTION

The brain drain of academics globally has been a major challenge threatening the competence, scholarship, and sustainable development of many universities. The reports on attrition of academics and migration to other countries with better job prospects and work environments (Khan, Buhari, Tsaramirsis & Rasheed, 2021; National University Commission NUC, 2022; Ming & Christian, 2022). The university system's sustainability is threatened by scarcity of academic functions in knowledge production, teaching, research, and community service (Federal Ministry of Education: FME, 2021). Khan, et al. (2021) explained the significant role university plays in building stronger academic institutes, creating a friendly work environment wherein academics can continuously nurture and enhance their research skills, teaching knowledge, and experience that could help retain their positions.

The chapter focus on Jamaica and Nigeria because both occupy strategic places in the Caribbean and African development respectively. The university systems in both countries share a similar history of colonisation by Britain, had indigenous university started in 1948, gained independence in the 1960s and experienced brain drain in the '70s and '80s. Fafunwa, (1991) and Sasu, (2023) reported the considerable growth of universities in Nigeria, from one to 202 between 1948 and 2022, and in Jamaica, from 1 to 7 universities in 2023 with seven public, while three private. (Ministry of Education, MOE, 2023; Wikipedia, 2024: June 10). However, Sasu (2023) and Beckles & Richards-Kennedy (2021) reported that both countries' higher education sectors have been facing challenges of economic crunches, a steady decline in the number of academics, and a lack of capacity to meet the rapid technological, political, and social changes. Ekanem & Uchendu (2012) and Agboola & Adeyemi (2013) attributed the increasing poor-quality graduates and youth unemployment in Nigeria to migration or attrition of academics and poor leadership in the universities. Similarly, youth not in employment, education or training (NEET) comprised 28 per cent of Jamaica's total youth population (ILO,2015). Sives, et al (2006) reported that the small island state of Jamaica has a long experience of teacher migration which has resulted in high unemployment and informal employment. Dennis (2022) reported that educator migration is on the rise and will continue to be until the government and educational leaders address the critical factors that trigger migration. Ming & Christian (2022) described the migration of teachers in 2022 as the modern-day exodus in Jamaica that has seemingly crept upon the nation like the rising sun and caught many by surprise.

To address the academic migration and attrition issues at the universities, the Nigeria government established various policies on higher education (FME, 2021; FRN, 2013), and Jamaica did the same with a national higher education policy draft approved by the Cabinet in 2021 (Morris, 2021). Despite their efforts, Dennis's (2022) report about the Jamaica Teachers' Association published by Jamaica Observer showed that over 400 academics moved out of secondary and tertiary institutions, and in 2022 over 167 teachers have resigned from their jobs in Jamaica. The decline of productive academics across universities in Nigeria and Jamaica raises concern among the education key stakeholders on how to close the immensurable gaps caused by academic migration. Likewise in other countries, Michael & Crispen, (2014) reported an increasing competition among the universities in South Africa to retain their best academics. Various kinds of incentives are used to outwit other organizations attracting academics.

The long-standing concern of the stakeholders is that the calibre of academics required to drive the vision and university goals in Nigeria and Jamaica is becoming scarcer because of the migration of specialized, skilled, and productive faculty and the retirement of old academics from the universities. Also, the death of some academics from the COVID-19 pandemic has created a gap that is becoming hard to fill. The issue of attrition and migration among academics cuts across various ranks, genders, staff categories, and so on (UNESCO, 2022).

Overview and Significance

By understanding the historical evolution, structure, and key features of Jamaica and Nigeria's development from the colonial era, readers gain a deeper appreciation for the complexities and nuances of the countries' education systems. Recognizing both countries' challenges and opportunities provides the basis to engage in informed discussions and collaborate toward addressing attrition-induced factors and building a lasting framework for the retention of academics.

Academic attrition/migration is a global problem which portends danger for the healthy growth of the university system with attendant implications. Selesho & Naile (2014) listed these as quality, consistency, and stability of education enterprises and quality of graduates produced. Literature has linked academic migration to poor planning and unsustainable policies on recruitment and conditions of service in universities. Academics in many developing countries are the least remunerated (Uche & Jack, 2014; Khan, et al., 2021). Selesho & Naile's (2014) study in Kenya affirmed that the high turnover rate of academic staff poses a major challenge to higher education institutions. Also in South Africa, Ng'ethe, Iravo & Namusonge (2012) reported an increase in demand and competition for academics with higher education qualifications because these categories of academics are repositories of the most specialised skills.

Academic attrition portrays the insensitivity of university leaders and the government to address the plights of academics over the past years. Ming & Christian (2022) attributed personal, job, and retention related policy as reasons why productive and experienced academics are migrating elsewhere for better prospects. Despite this phenomenon, politicians in developing countries are receiving bogus salaries and allowances, and government establishes more universities without due policy consideration for the resources, academic' availability, remuneration, and support for academic career growth (Praslova, 2023 and Dennis, 2022). The migration situation has continued to put a lot of work pressure on the available academics thus triggering discouragement among the pool of young and experienced intellectuals and facilitating their attrition tendencies. Vnoučková (2012) affirmed that unsuitable human resources and personnel relations practices of higher institutions caused employee disaffection fluctuation and eventual turnover, and suggested that to retain their employees, more attention should be on recruitment, management styles favoured by employees, correlate remuneration and employee performance.

According to Khan, et al., (2021) one of the most important retention factors for an academic may be their job status. That is the academic appointment status that could be tenure-tracked, permanent, contract-based, temporary, adjunct, and so on. The authors opined that college managers should know that retention of permanent/ tenured academics would be higher than that of untenured because the academic staff members on contract-based or adjunct would search for better opportunities. Bibi, et al., (2018) and Lyman, et al., (2020) reported that other factors such as career training and development, the support of the supervisors, work environment, benefits and rewards, and psychological safety influence retention. Migration has been recognised as means of pursuing dignity, access to rights, and opportunity.

Ban Ki-moon (2013), the former Secretary General of the United Nations aptly said: "Migration is an expression of the human aspiration for dignity, safety and a better future," Mr. Ban said. "It is part of the social fabric, part of our very make-up as a human family. It would be naive to overlook the costs, including the human costs. Yet even skeptics have to recognize that migration has become a fundamental part of our globalized world." (p. 2).

The US Department of Education studies of 1990-1991 and Khan, et al. (2021) revealed that migration occurs when teachers move between schools, and attrition occurs when leave the teaching profession completely. In education, academics change jobs in their chosen profession during their professional lives or even leave their profession altogether for various reasons. UNESCO (2022) citing Knight-Grofe & Rauh (2016), reported that the mobility of academics plays a key role in internationalizing higher education, fosters international cooperation and intercultural integration, provides comparative perspectives into education, and boosts international profiles of institutions through publications and projects tied to their networks. The ever-increasing attrition rates and migration of academics from one university/college to another, and from one nation to another is a relatively new phenomenon. Sibonde & Dassah (2021) attributed academic migration to global competition between higher education institutions to recruit and maintain a higher calibre of academics. Chirikov (2016) draws a connection between the migration of academics and the development of the "knowledge economy" worldwide and the impact of globalization.

Gartner cited in Tupper & Ellis (2022) reported that the pace of employee turnover is 50–75 percent higher than what companies have previously experienced, while it takes 18 percent longer to fill roles than pre-pandemic. International academics constituted 25 percent of new academic positions in the United States (Institute of International Education, 2022). Muma, et al. (2019) reported human resourcing and retention as the top challenges while Osibanjo & Adeniji, (2012) affirmed that many organizations face high rates of turnover of employees as a concern in developing and developed countries. Analyzing the literature on academic migration/attrition in Jamaica and Nigeria revealed that the migration of health employees was the most reported and researched in both countries. However, there exists a gap in the literature and limited empirical evidence on the current attrition rates and migration phenomenon in the Caribbean and African regions. Thus, this study was undertaken to fill the knowledge gap, develop a framework to address academic migration and generate recommendations and useful strategies that can support academic retention.

The significance of this study to higher education includes developing a retention framework and creating a new pathway for policy analysis and initiatives on education mission and goal alignment that view educators as the key stakeholders in the education business, decision making, etc, provide tools for the government and educational leaders in charge of management to ensure quality in the Caribbean and Nigeria universities to increase academics commitment and retention. The outcomes of this study can be also used by educational leaders to begin conversations with teachers on issues surrounding migration and the implementation of policies regarding retention strategies and staff support.

Aims/Objectives

The chapter aims to investigate academic attrition rates and explore how the academics perceived the migration-induced factors in Jamaican and Nigerian universities. Specifically, the objectives are to (i). identify the migration-induced factors that promote attrition among academics, (ii). determine the difference in the attrition rates based on the academics' characteristics, (iii). develop a strategic retention management approach as a framework for policy initiatives to manage academic attrition and migration in a broad context while considering the existing educational policy and practices that promote social injustice in the university, and (iv). Making recommendations to address academic attrition and migration-indued factors based on the insights provided by the academics relating to their migration experiences and retention.

Research Questions

This chapter raised quantitative and qualitative research questions and formulated one null hypothesis based on the study's objectives.

1. What are the ratings of attrition and migration-induced factors from academics' perspectives in Jamaican and Nigeran universities?
2. How does the attrition rate of academics differ by demographic and institutional variables?

Hypothesis

$H0_1$: Attrition rates of academics do not differ based on demographics and institution variables.

3. What insights (explanations and related recommendations) can academics provide relating to their migration experiences and retention?

Literature Review

The reviews in this study are premised on scholarly opinions, reports, and extensive literature related to the variables examined.

Academic Attrition and Migration Factors

Attrition is the opposite concept of retention, and it is often used interchangeably as the churn rate or turnover in the university/college. Sibonde & Dassah (2021) see attrition as an indicator of workforce depletion that helps educational managers calculate academic attrition as a percentage of the total number of academics in the institution at a particular period. The attrition rate alerts the university managers to start planning and recruiting for vacant positions (). The cost implications of high attrition and migration of academics are of interest to all stakeholders because they portend grave danger to the future growth of any nation's education sector. Consequently, Ng'ethe, et al. (2012) see academic attrition as a subject for policy discussions and studies on strategies to improve the management of academic retentions.

Academics are an inimitable, valuable, scarcest, non-substitutable, and most crucial productive human capital asset that can create a competitive and longest-lasting advantage for educational institutions. It takes an average of 18 years to produce an assistant lecturer and over 25 years to produce an experienced academic. However, the recent phenomenon of academic migration and attrition is causing brain drain across the globe and raising concern among the stakeholders. While the demand for academics is increasing, their retention is becoming an almost impossible task for many managers of universities. Mamman-Daura, (2022) and Udi (2010) attributed the recent forced academic migration in developing countries to developmental issues. Jamaica ranked second out of 177 countries as reported by McKenzie (2022) citing Black Immigrant Daily News, while the Statistical Institute of Jamaica (Statin) 2021 data revealed that Jamaica's "net migration" numbers were 269,991 from 2002 to 2019.

Migration-induced factors for the Jamaican educators reported by Dennis (2022) include salary, lack of resources, excessive workload, and other related issues like disorganization in the Ministry of Education, frustration created by school administrators/senior educators, and a lack of opportunities for professional growth. Dennis further said that until the root causes of educator migration have been addressed, the problem will continue into perpetuity, thus "let's treat the causes, not the symptoms of migration."

Several pieces of literature on academics' migration-promoted factors were reviewed by the researcher. Tupper & Ellis (2022) provided some reasons why people decide to leave an organization or remain in the same. They include a lack of career progression, job dissatisfaction, work environment, and governance, among other factors Bamiro (2012) and Johnes, et al. (2017) identified the high teacher-student ratio, and university/college inefficiency in terms of quality support for teachers to improve their experiences, professional exposure, and morale as reasons for the exodus of teachers.

Sugden (2010) reported that in Canada, teachers' attrition is connected to (a) the workloads of teachers (b) non-teaching roles are becoming significantly more intensive, and (c) the taking of responsibilities not trained for. In addition, integration of new technology; lack of teacher support by the government; and outcomes-based curriculum). Khan, et al., (2021) found that academic staff workloads were far beyond the acceptable work hour per week. University of Connecticut (UC, 2022) reported that the policy on normal work expectation of a 39-hour week and the academics' management of their own time to achieve their job objectives is often only on paper. Many Deans and heads of departments do not apply the principles of workload. The UC (2022) proposed that formal minimum workloads for academics should be 20, 40, 10, and 10 percent for each of teaching, librarianship, scholarly work, and service.

Other studies have found more consistently positive and stronger demographic characteristics among academics to be predictors of attrition or retention disposition than other commonly measured school attributes. Ekanem's (2011) study showed that age, gender, and job status correlate with teachers' predisposition toward migration. Wilcox's (2023) study on the first 20 years of an academic member's career post-Ph.D. in the US revealed that attrition rates range from 2% to 5%. The attrition rates for women at all stages are higher and the gender gap also increases with seniority in rank. Wilcox found that women who are full professors are 19% more likely than men to leave academia at the same career stage. Making a comparison, 6% of women assistant professors and 10% of associate professors leave their academic jobs. Also, attrition rates were higher for women academics at less prestigious schools and in non-STEM fields.

Carr, Raj, Kaplan, Terrin, Breeze & Freund's (2018) study to identify predictors of advancement, retention, and leadership for women faculty. The authors surveyed a cohort of 1,273 academics at 24 medical schools in the continental United States using regression models to adjust for covariates like seniority, department, academic setting, and race/ethnicity. Carr, et al. (2018) findings revealed that to achieve the rank of a professor, women were less likely than men. However, there were no statistically significant differences in academics gender retention and attainment of senior rank, and the male academics were more likely to hold senior leadership positions after adjusting for their publications.

Michael & Crispen's (2013) study examined how certain work attributes impact the retention of 255 senior academic staff in 10 universities across South African universities using a survey design. Michael, et.al found that the teacher-student mix influences retention in tertiary institutions where there are many programs and in a critical situation where courses include hours of practice and teaching. The results on academics and retention in the universities by Sibonde & Dassah (2021) showed that academics placed greater importance on challenging work, interpersonal relationships, access to research resources, and job security for their retention.

Salau, Worlu, et. al (2020) found that retention strategies determinants had significant impacts on the academic staff's sustainable performance. In addition, a direct correlation existed between sustainable performance and academic retention in Nigerian government-owned universities.

Uche & Jack's (2014) study between 2007 and 2013 was to determine the development and mobility of randomly sampled 150 female academics selected from the population of 300 female academic staff in three colleges and ten faculties at the University of Port Harcourt. The authors generated data with a questionnaire, structured interview, and document analysis. The findings revealed that female academic development schemes were lower than their male counterparts, while job-related stress, bloated workload, time, and family interference trigger female academic mobility. Selesho & Naile (2014) determined factors that influence the poor retention rate of academics at selected universities in South Africa. The authors randomly sampled 80 academics who had worked at higher education institutions for 10 years. The result showed that factors keeping academic staff in their profession include job satisfaction and working conditions, career growth, and academic development. Okello & Lamaro's (2015) quantitative approach used a cross-sectional survey design to randomly sample 134 full-time academic staff (105 males and 29 females) from Gulu University, Uganda. The authors found that pay inadequacy was the major reason for turnover intention among the academic staff

Bashayreh, et al. (2016) carried out a study on the relationship between dimensions of organizational culture and employees' job satisfaction among academics at four higher education institutes in Malaysia. The authors randomly sampled 310 academics using a questionnaire. The data analysed with multiple regression statistics showed a non-significant relationship between employee organizational supportiveness, innovation, stability, and communication and retention. Correspondingly, Manogharan, et al. (2018) found that the reasons for the high turnover of academics and push factors in the migration of academics in Malaysian private higher institutions include tasks and workload, conflict of role, underpay, and other intrinsic factors. The UC (2022) proposed fairly distributed workloads between academics in an open and consultative way, and employer-driven work within socially acceptable working hours while considering individual needs and circumstances.

Alo & Dada (2020) conducted survey research on employee turnover, causes, effects, and remedies among 120 academic staff at selected private universities in Ondo State, Nigeria using a logistic regression model to test the hypotheses. The authors' findings revealed that job dissatisfaction, selection policies, job security, and career development influenced the turnover intentions of academic staff in Nigeria's private universities. Coldwell (2017, as cited in Khan et al., 2021) and Garcia Torres (2019, as cited in Khan et al., 2019) affirmed that there exists a relationship between three factors: distributed leadership and professional collaboration, which are associated with job satisfaction, and collaborative professional development. The authors affirmed that professional development is usually for promotion and leadership skill enhancement and could have a direct link with staff retention.

According to several authors, migration issues require school-based studies and surveys on the analysis of why academics stay, leave, and choose one higher education institution over another, and how a strategic retention approach should address grail areas that intertwine with a lack of commitment and dissatisfaction that arise in areas such as uncompetitive, inequitable or unfair pay systems to develop efficacious strategies for academic retentions (Okello & Lamaro, 2015; Powell, 2010; Tettey, 2009).

Manogharan, (2018) linked the migration of educators relocating from one geographic area to another to reasons like improved work conditions, financial benefits, career advancement, personal preferences, work and family balance, workload, and long holiday/time off (Khan, et al., 2021). Consequently, the researcher concludes that attracting and retaining the best intellectuals because of cost implications and the impact on the institution's overall growth and performance requires a manager's critical skills in organizational leadership. See Figure 1 for the conceptualisation framework of the academic migration and attrition factors model.

Figure 1. Conceptualisation Framework of Migration and Attrition Factors

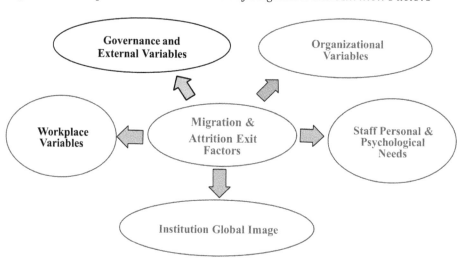

Figure 1 shows the interrelatedness of academics' migration and attrition push and pull factors. Governance (education laws, political and other external factors); Organisational variables (organisational size, structure, climate, culture, internal policies, leadership style, ethics/justice); Workplace variables (physical safety, relationship/belonging, workload, psychological/social support, career growth; work-life balance, engagement); Staff personal and psychological needs (Intrinsic and Extrinsic needs). Khan, et al., (2021) and Sasu, 2023) opine that strategic integration and self-goal actualization in the higher education plan could promote the retention of the best of its pool of employees.

Theoretical Framework

The study is premised on theories on retention by Bean (1975); social equity theory by Adams (1963, 1965), Locke's (1990) goal-setting theory, and Herzberg's (1959) hygiene motivator theory (motivator-hygiene). The theory of retention by Bean (1975) affirmed that the retention intention of employees depends largely on how well the institution can provide them with a conducive social environment for proper integration and self-goal actualization within the coffer of the institution. The institution's policy on recruitment, promotion, organizational justice, and a good work environment could influence employees' intention to stay or leave.

Social equity and justice theory by Adams (1965) asserted that a balance strike between an employee's efforts (inputs: hard work, skills, enthusiasm, etc,) put into their work and the results (output: salary, recognition, responsibility, etc) they get in return could ensure that an employee feels satisfied and motivated, contributing to their productivity and retention. This is in line with Adams's (1963) quotation which stated:

"Equity, or inequity, is a pervasive concern of industry, labour, and government. Yet its psychological basis is probably not fully understood. Evidence suggests that equity is not merely a matter of getting "a fair day's pay for a fair day's work," nor is inequity simply a matter of being underpaid. The fairness of an exchange between employee and employer is not usually perceived by the former purely and simply as an economic matter. An element of relative justice is involved that supervenes economics and underlies perceptions of equity or inequity."(p.422)

When employees are advantageously treated by their organizations, they are motivated and are more likely to stay in their workplace and vice versa. High morale equals high motivation and increased retention while unmotivated employees tend to leave their jobs because of job insecurity, organizational culture, justice, and so on (1963). This theory is relevant when leaders of educational institutions employ justice and equity in addressing and supporting the needs of academics.

Also found relevant is the two-factor theory or the motivator-hygiene theory by Herzberg (1959) which states that some job factors prevent dissatisfaction, while other job factors result in satisfaction. On the one hand, hygiene includes factors such as organisation environment, employees' status, job safety, fair, equal, and reasonable pay or salary structure in the same occupation and level; organisation policies and rules that are fair, flexible, nor ambiguous and create room for adjustment in areas such as working hours, time off, vacation, and fringe benefits prevent employees' dissatisfaction. On the other hand, motivators or satisfiers are the hygiene factors that symbolize the psychological needs of the employees. Motivators look at the job itself, ensuring it's interesting and that employees can progress within their roles. The motivators include recognition of staff by the employer; providing a sense of achievement; growth and promotional opportunities; and delegating responsibilities which gives employees a sense of ownership of the work and engenders accountability. Motivator-hygiene theory is relevant to this study as it provided a framework to understand how academics need to be satisfied with both 'hygiene' factors and 'motivators' if they are to be committed to long-term employment within the university system. Migration constitutes a multifaceted decision encompassing variables such as legal procedures, cultural assimilation, and economic hurdles. This complexity can significantly influence the timing and planning of migration. Those academics considering migration often invest significant effort in comprehending and navigating this complexity.

Through Locke's goal-setting theory, migration can be viewed as behaviour driven by goals. The process of migration and the preparatory phases leading up to it can be impacted by the specificity, challenge, feedback, commitment, and complexity inherent in the goals migrants set for themselves. Whether driven by economic prospects, educational pursuits, safety concerns, or personal aspirations, the underlying goals provide a framework that propels and guides the decision to migrate. Hence the relevance of these theories underpinning the paper.

Methodology

The paper adopted a mixed methods explanatory sequential approach to determine and explore the migration of academics from selected three public universities in Jamaica and Nigeria. This approach is a two-phase design that involves collections of both quantitative and qualitative data, and analysis of data integration from both designs (Creswell & Creswell, 2018). Quantitative data are collected and analysed first, after which the collected qualitative data are used to explain the quantitative data for a profound exploration of the unique personal experiences these academics connected to their migration. A quantitative cross-sectional survey design consisting of documentary analysis, questionnaires, and qualitative structured interviews (Creswell, 2014). Quantitatively, a sample of 537 (Jamaica-153; Nigeria-384) academics were purposively and randomly selected across six faculties and three public universities in Jamaica and Nigeria (Jamaica:1. Nigeria: 2). The proportion 1:2 was used because of the difference in the number of public universities and academics population in Jamaica and Nigeria (UWI, 2024, NUC, 2023). The academics were stratified using academic field, demographics, and institutional variables. Cross-sectional secondary quantitative data were collected with the documentary checklist entitled: "Academic Recruitment and Attrition Rates Checklist" (ARARC) to generate data on academic demographics, and attrition/migration rates. The qualitative data were collected from a sample of 35 academics with a structured open-ended "Academic Migration Induced Questionnaire" (AMIQ) comprising 36 items to explore the academics' perceptions about attrition/migration factors. Eligibility criteria for inclusion in the study include rank and qualification. Ethical procedures were adhered to using written and signed informed consent forms and pseudonyms instead of the names of the participants to ensure confidentiality and protection of the participant's identity and information. Williams & Moser (2019) said that the qualitative data were coded to enable a progressive and verifiable mechanism for establishing codes, their origins, relationships to each other, and integration resulting in themes used to construct meaning. The qualitative data for this study were analysed based on the themes and objectives.

The Cronbach Alpha's statistic was used to test for the reliability of the AMIQ questionnaire on migration-induced variables which gave an overall reliability coefficient of 0.95 (an indication of a strong internal consistency among the items). One-way ANOVA statistic was used to analyse the quantitative data generated and the F ratio to test the hypotheses at the significant level of $p = 0.05$. The UNESCO Institute of Statistics (2023) formula was adopted to calculate the attrition rate.

Similarly, the integration analysis of participants' response item predictive validity and reliability were found using Pearson's correlation statistic to analyse the data at a significance level of .05. The outcome of predictive validity was determined by comparing the rxy value with the r-table value. A. The correlation count value obtained for all the items, rxy > r table value (.273), and significant at $0.0000 < 0.05$, the items are valid. The validity is presented in Table 1 and the reliability in Table 2.

Table 1. Correlation of Academics Migration or Attrition Push and Pull Factors

	1	2	3	4	5	6
Promotion Prospect	–	.809**	.931**	.853**	.876*	.745**
Recruitment Policy		–	.729**	.675**	.489*	.596*
Job Status (tenure/non-tenure)			–	.790**	.915**	.849**
Work Environment & Organisational Justice				–	.692**	.767**
Career Growth & Professional Development					–	.788**
University Culture						–

** Correlation is significant at the 0.01 level,
* Correlation is significant at the 0.05 level (2-tailed)

Table 2. Internal Consistency of the Migration or Attrition-Induced Factors

Factors/Variables	Item #	N	Mean	SD	α
Recruitment & Condition of Service	6	35	17.30	3.74	.71
Career Growth & Professional Development	6	35	17.80	3.99	.83
Work Environment & Organisational Justice	6	35	18.45	4.12	.82
Promotion Prospect	6	35	17.25	4.18	.85
University Culture	6	35	17.65	3.79	.75
Job Status	6	35	17.64	3.88	.81
Overall Migration-Induced Factors	36	35	106.10	20.19	.95

Results

Research Question 1: What are the ratings of attrition and migration-induced factors from academics' perspectives in Jamaican and Nigeran universities?

The academics responded to structured questionnaire items and rated the factors that could induce migration and attrition. The ethical guidelines were duly complied with to protect the respondents' identities. Descriptive statistics like frequency counts and ranking in Tabe 3 were used to explain the results.

Table 3. The Participants' Ratings of Attrition and Migration-Induced Factors (N= 35)

S/N	Migration-Induced Variables	Frequency Count	Responses Percent	Ranking Order
1	Promotion Prospect	34	97.1	1st
2	Work Environment & Organizational Justice	26	74.3	5th
3	Job Status (Tenure/non-tenure)	32	91.4	2nd
4	Remuneration & Conditions of Services Policy	30	85.7	3rd
5	Career / Staff Development	29	82.9	4th
6	Institutional Culture	23	65.7	6th
	Total	35		

Source: Researcher field survey.

In Table 3, the academics ranked migration/attrition-induced factors from the highest to the lowest as promotion, job status, remuneration, conditions of service, etc. The most challenging factor that threatens the retention of academics is the promotion prospect with some eligible academics stagnating in a position due to lopsidedness and disengagement between the government's education policy and the institution's internal policy (Manogharan, et al, 2018).

Research Question 2: How does the attrition rate of academics differ by demographic and institutional variables?

$H0_1$: Attrition rates of academics do not differ based on demographics and institution variables.

The differences in academic attrition rates were determined using One-Way ANOVA because of one dependent variable (attrition rates) versus many factors (independent variables). See Tables 4 and 5 for the quantitative analysis of the attrition rates of university academics in Jamaica and Nigeria.

Table 4. Descriptive Statistics Of Attrition Rates and Demographic Profile Of Academics (n= 537)

Factors	Categories	N	Mean	SD
Gender	Male	328	23.11	5.10
	Female	209	18.77	1.60
Qualification	PhD	172	23.90	4.99
	Master	365	18.82	1.95
Rank Mix	Professors & Readers	84	22.44	8.83
	Senior Lecturers	183	36.98	7.30
	Lecturer & Others	270	28.79	6.55
Job Status	Non-Tenured	259	23.54	5.05
	Tenured	278	18.85	1.97
Location	Rural	147	21.83	4.99
	Urban	390	16.81	1.95

Source. Research field data

Table 4 results reveal that the mean attrition rates of academics differ by categories of gender, rank mix, qualification, job status, and institution location. Differences in the attrition rates by all categories are statistically significant at $P \leq 0.05$. Thus, all categories of variables are attrition-induced factors. Male academics have a high attrition and migration rate. The mean attrition by rank mix of Senior Lecturer is higher than Professor and Lecturer and others. Furthermore, the mean attrition of non-tenured academics is higher than those with tenured appointments while the mean attrition of lecturers with a PhD is higher than those with a master's degree. Finally, the mean attrition/migration of academics differs by institution location. Academic migration/attrition at institutions in the rural is higher than that of institutions in the urban. To determine the significance of the difference, the data were tested with One-way ANOVA statistics. See the results in Table 5.

Table 5. One-Way ANOVA Hypothesis Testing of Difference in Academic Attrition Rates by Profiles

ANOVA						
		Sum of Squares	df	Mean Square	F	Sig.
Gender	Between Groups	84818.881	40	2120.472	16.416	<.001
	Within Groups	64070.103	496	129.174		
	Total	148888.983	536			
Qualification	Between Groups	57433.271	40	1435.832	7.147	<.001
	Within Groups	99652.866	496	200.913		
	Total	157086.138	536			
Staff Rank Mix	Between Groups	80084.515	40	2002.113	14.966	<.001
	Within Groups	66351.644	496	133.773		
	Total	146436.159	536			
Job Status	Between Groups	82906.816	40	2072.670	15.898	<.001
	Within Groups	64666.742	496	130.376		
	Total	147573.559	536			
Institution Location	Between Groups	57291.725	40	1432.293	7.092	<.001
	Within Groups	100178.201	496	201.972		
	Total	157469.926	536			

*Sig. = Significant at P≤0.05

In Table 5, the testing of hypothesis at P≤0.05, all the factors F-values obtained are greater that critical value of 3.84 while p-value of 0.000 is than less than P = 0.05. This indicated that statistically significant differences exist between the academics profiles and the attrition/migration factors.

Strategic Retention Management Approach to Migration/Attrition-Induced Factors

The competition for top talent in academics is fierce, and quick fixes will not reduce employee turnover. There is a need to grow the retention strategy by creating a healthy workplace to retain top talents. According to International Organisation for Migration, IOM (2023), migration is not a problem to be solved by managers when strategically planned, rather it is a powerful driver of sustainable development, for academics and their institutions in terms of skills, strengthening the labour force, investment, cultural diversity, etc. Frolich et al., (2013) considered strategy as practice as an important approach to understanding the complexity of operations and internal diversity in higher education while scholars have investigated strategy in different types of higher education institutions like universities and colleges (Couper & Stoaker 2010; Fumasoli & Hladchenko, 2023). Egorov & Platonova cited in

Fumasoli & Hladchenko (2023) affirmed that middle managers' perceptions show that a correlation exists between strategic planning and changes in operations and performance of higher education institutions.

Reimagining academic retention is necessary because this is a challenging time for university leaders and managers after COVID-19. According to Tupper & Ellis (2022), managers because of the global changes, economic crisis, and academic migration in recent years are facing a never-ending cycle of reskilling and recruiting employees with cost implications in their day-to-day roles. The rise in hunting for productive academic members by higher institutions across the globe calls for a holistic approach by governments and managers to foster strategic retention plans and policy practices that could advance the academics' socioeconomic well-being, and potentially create a work environment that supports their progress and growth (Khan, et.al 2021; Beckles, et al. 2022; Wilcox, 2022). In addition, the universities are to seek efficient retention tools to respond to dwindling enrolments, academic decline, and budget constraints. Hence, the researcher develops a strategic retention management approach to address academic migration.

The Workforce Planning for Wisconsin State Government (2005) defines retention management as "a systematic effort by employers to create and foster an environment that encourages current employees to remain at the same employer having policies and practices in place that address their diverse needs." Kambi (2015) opined that the strategic retention management approach is a blueprint for the reduction of employee turnover, preventing attrition, increasing retention, and fostering employee engagement. Forrest (1999) and Reddy (2018) gave 5 principles of retention management as i). appreciation, value, and trust, ii). Development/career growth, iii). responsibility, iv) good relationships, and v) success that leads to employee performance satisfaction, and retention. Incorporating strategic retention planning processes at the institution-wide level could strengthen the institution's programs, and image and capacity to retain productive academics (Khan, et al., 2021). In Figure 2 the strategic retention management approach model is presented.

Figure 2. **Strategic Retention Management Approach Model.**

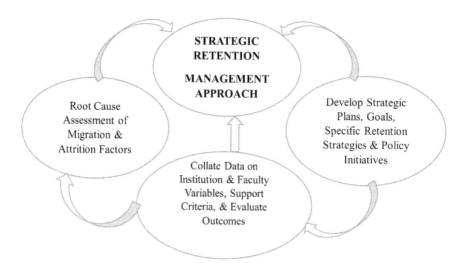

In the Figure 2 model, a strategic retention management approach includes a plan to assess and identify the root causes of academic migration/attrition factors and develop retention strategies to effectively manage these factors. An effective migration management process starts with an understanding of the current academic staff situation and key areas of the academic's needs in the university/college using relevant data and analysis of the extent to which theoretical frameworks and literature shape actions on academic migration/attrition.

The universities/college managers are to plan and make SMART retention strategic goals grounded in the mission and vision fundamental to an organisation's success while ensuring that in-depth analysis of the migration situation, reflection, and processing of formal and informal input from a variety of stakeholders in the university system determine the outcomes. Defining the scope and priorities of policy intervention initiatives and developing retention strategies such as instituting effective and innovative mentoring and collegial collaboration (Khan, et al., 2021; IOM, 2023). Re-evaluating and implementing retention strategies provide current and emerging policy directions to leaders on how these migration factors shape and influence the higher education sector. US National Security Council, (2021) posited that the government and by extension educational leaders need to strengthen cooperative efforts to identify and address the underlying factors leading to academic migration and manage internationalised migration. In addition, the retention planning strategy must be collaborative and prioritization of policy actions. It may be noted, however, that this model cannot stand alone but serves to complement university policy and administrators' leadership and decision-making process skills to manage and enhance academic retention.

Leadership and Strategic Academic Retention Management

The success of educational institutions depends on effective leadership and the strategic planning approach to human resource management (Leithwood, et al., 2020). The higher education system requires transformational leaders who can create and communicate a compelling vision, empower, motivate, and support followers, and model the desired behaviours, values, and attitudes expected of their followers and or subordinates. Fumasoli & Hladchenko (2023:336-337). the authors said that "understanding of the challenges of strategic management in contemporary universities lays the ground for the leaders to delve deeper into the problems associated with expanding various areas of the university. The authors equally shed light on how the university leaders' roles and responsibilities should be shaped to increase the effectiveness of strategic management."

The Center for Organizational Development and Leadership (CODL, 2023:3) citing Shield affirmed that strategic planning in higher education programmes offers a comprehensive approach for leaders in creating, organizing, and implementing the plan to tackle those strategic planning challenges from a leadership perspective. The authors provided step-by-step advice, case studies, and exercises for producing a successful plan, whether it is for an institutional initiative or a departmental review. The planning guide is designed specifically for leaders to be cognizant of the formidable challenges of strategic planning in an educational environment with myriad communication and organizational complexities. Agboola (2024) opined that educational leaders require the utilization of problem-solving, creativity, and innovative skills to effectively administer and manage scarce resources and academics in the universities. In addition, the author reiterated that adopting total quality management could help leaders of higher education manage the after-effects of the pandemic that have stretched educational resources and personnel in many ways. The university leaders applying the right legislative action must focus on the provision of support for academic staff and implement best retention practices. Educational leaders could use the available strategic planning tools, techniques, and models to assess what is the existing situation of academics in the educational systems, to determine where they want the systems to be in the near future and the key metrics and initiatives they would use to track, pursue and to achieve the stated target. Conrad (2020) identified PEST analysis as a planning tool to identify the political, economic, sociocultural, and technological factors that could inform academic intentions to migrate from the universities and could impact negatively the sustainability of education development. Furthermore, PEST could help the leaders to organise the strategic planning team as representatives with a working knowledge of the component factors that could cause academic attrition.

Kupriyanova, Estermann & Sabic (2018) reiterated that while leadership commitment, institutional autonomy, and staff engagement are among the key enablers of efficiency, institutional reluctance to change, financial constraints for investment into efficiency programmes (e.g. technology and staff training) as well as quality concerns are the most common barriers that trigger migration intention. In the context of the management of academics and other educational resources, efficiency measures are found to have both tangible and intangible outcomes in the short and long term, however, this may be limited in terms of their replicability and measurability.

Malachy (2008) reiterated that human migration is a new globalization phenomenon, and it presents a multifaceted test for university leaders, management, and academics. It also provides insight into the fact that academic migration goes beyond the immediate analysis and the existing policy. Consequently, educational leaders need to consider the following areas:

(i) Identifying populations and motivations of new academic immigrants leaving higher educational institutions,
(ii) developing strategic plans that will address what the future educational implications may be,
(iii) developing academic support mechanisms (assisting with access to health care, social welfare systems, etc) and opportunities for professional growth.
(iv) co-creating policies through participative planning and academic perspective-based research and development of innovative social and educational responses sensitive to the needs and current challenges of academics

Research Question 3: What insights (explanations and related recommendations) can academics provide relating to their migration experiences and retention?

Integration of Quantitative & Qualitative Thematic Analysis of Academics Migration Perceptions, Insights and Policy Implications

The scholarly views and literature reviewed in this paper in addition to the responses from the academics revealed an increasingly obvious and emerging set of contested challenges for institutions of higher education globally and in both countries of interest. By integrating and synthesizing insights from literature and data on institutional leadership, the effectiveness of migration management, and academic retention policies. It explores the relationship between migration-induced pull and push factors, migration policies, and trends to disentangle policy effects from determinants of migration among academics. The article, The Teacher Attrition and Mobility Results from the 2021–22: Teacher Follow-up Survey to the National Teacher and Principal Survey by Petraglia, Green, Taie, Ferg, et.al (2023) published by the Institute of Education Sciences provided the integration framework needed for the study. The thematic analysis of academics' migration-induced variables provided insight for the universities' principals, administrators, and management about the decision to provide support for the academics.

The quantitative and qualitative information base on migration and mobility of academics in higher education was examined under quantitative domains of (i) institution management and organisation (i.e., professional leadership, work environment & organizational justice, institutional culture, and job status (Tenure/non-tenure). (ii) Staff support and School policy (i.e., remuneration & conditions of services policy, staff support (health, personal, academic, etc.,), professional development, research financial support, and collaboration. See Figure 3 for the quantitative analysis chart

Figure 3. Quantitative Analysis Chart of Responses to Migration-Induced Factors

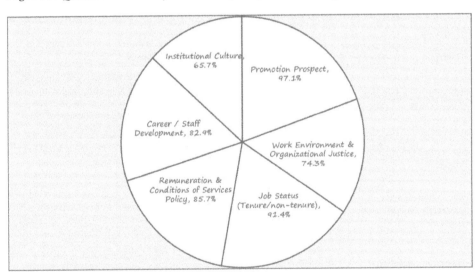

Qualitatively, some scholars made relevant remarks on educators' migration that helped integrate the participants' responses. Some of these statements include:

"I think the best single indicators of the overall quality of life of a state are statistics on net migration. If lots of people move into an area, it is reasonable to assume that they think that place is overall a good place to live —better than the place that they left. Out-migration is a sign that for some reason(s) people perceive that the place in which they have been living is less desirable than their new destination" (Richard Vedder, 2021: January 11).

"The reality is that, as a developing country, we lack certain financial resources to retain productive academics; however, we must place greater value on those whose love, dedication, and sacrifices have played a major part in who and where we are today as a nation. Above all things, we should listen to our teachers. Let's treat the causes, not the symptoms of migration" (Jadio Dennis, 2022: August 30).

Acosta & Freier (2023) said that leaders should adopt a reflexive lens of academic staff on migration policies, relevant institutional definitions of key categories, and the discursive knowledge they carry. The authors while quoting Amelina (2021) stated: *"How specific configurations of discursive knowledge become inscribed in the organizational and institutional routines of migration and integration policies."* (p. 2)

The migration-induced variables explored through the lens of academics are similar to the article by Ming & Christian (2022). These authors also provided insights on the migration push factors. See Table 4 for the thematic responses of the academics.

Table 6. Through the Lens of Academics: Exploring Migration and Attrition-Induced Variables

Themes	Participants Responses
Promotion prospect and career growth	The faculty agreed that promotion processes and requirements are politicized, prolonged, and shrouded in secrecy and off-handedness by leadership. Academics most times do not get promoted as fast as they deserve, and management shows little commitment to the quality development of the faculty and no opportunities to improve their career.
Job Status (Tenure/Non-Tenure)	Almost all the academics responded that the process of becoming a tenured staff in the universities is slow and cumbersome, thus staying in a job for many years without the prospect of job security is a risk they will not take.
Poor remuneration and unattractive condition of service	This is a major push factor for the mass teacher migration in Jamaica and Nigeria. The payment method for faculty in government-owned universities is complex and not encouraging. Many academics are unable to meet their needs sufficiently and live comfortably today amidst high inflation rates.
The lack of educational resources	The lack of educational resources in many universities results in less satisfactory working conditions for educators. This also negatively impacts their teaching capacity and abilities. In addition, the absence of resources affects students' learning and the quality of university outputs.
Poor leadership and management abilities displayed by school administrators	Some university leaders lack the management and interpersonal skills needed to effectively communicate with their academic staff. Lack of cordiality, feeling of unappreciation, undermining teacher's voice, etc.
Little to no psychosocial support for teachers	Academics need personal and academic support to carry on their tasks effectively. The affective domain is an area of concern for teachers. Many university leaders inflict psychological, and emotional traumas and frustrations on academics through their disposition, actions, and policies

Discussion of Findings/Policy Implications

The mixed methods approach provided both quantitative and qualitative information to examine migration holistically. The findings reveal that the attrition rates of academics in the two countries were statistically significant differences based on the demographics of the academics and the institutional variables. Male academics have higher migration/attrition rates than female academics, which Carr, et al. (2018) attributed to male traits of seeking higher work challenges, greener pastures, and better job prospects. In the same vein, attrition rates are high for senior lecturers, PhD degree holders, non-tenured, and academics in rural area institutions. Alo & Dada (2020) affirmed that low attrition rates of academics at the professorial rank tenured and in urban-located institutions are because they are at the peak of their career, while those with master's degrees, lecturers, and others may not be able to get better offers for lack of experience and expertise.

An increase in academic migration could be a result of an increase in demand for academics from other sectors and organisations (Khan, et al., 2021). The findings also revealed that academics' disposition to attrition is influenced by their academic qualifications, experience, lack of job security (non-tenured), school location, better performance, and better job prospects (Ming & Christian, 2023). While gender, rank mix, program/course, etc may lead to migration or attrition (Selesho & Naile, 2014; Tupper & Ellis, 2018).

Globally, university managers are spending more time and resources searching for high-profile academic recruits in an expensive and competitive market. Consequently, academic retention should have short-term and long-term implications for universities' management, leaders, and government agencies to develop the right strategic retention plans, initiate retention and migration policies, and apply best global practices to address the migration-induced factors and staff agitations in key areas of disagreement between the employer, government and the academics. Colos (2023) affirmed that when leaders implement effective human resource policies and procedures, they can ensure that their employees remain engaged, and committed to the organization, and improve their retention.

Tupper & Ellis (2022) recommended that university leaders need to refocus their efforts on retention strategies to drive staff performance, and they need to reimagine retention from the leadership perspective, not a quick-fix solution to the challenge of educator migration that school managers are facing, but an urgent call to develop the right mindset and strategic plan to attract and retain top intellectuals.

CONCLUSION/RECOMMENDATIONS

Based on the researcher's findings, there are insufficient current and accurate data on academic attrition rates, and retention policy documents to curtail academic migration in Jamaica and Nigeria, and more surprisingly for several years of academic brain drain phenomenon in both countries in the '80s. The migration-induced variables examined in this study have a statistically significant influence on academics' migration/attrition rate thus, the researcher concludes that intricate factors influencing academic migration/attrition extend beyond the scope of using a few theories. For this reason, the study has implications for university leaders and the government. Strategic planning in higher education clearly articulates a proven methodology that will yield strategic thinking from groups and move universities in an innovative direction. Consequently, both the government and their agencies and higher education leaders need to develop a comprehensive database on academics, adopt the right retention management approach, and initiate policies to address the needs of academics in Jamaica and Nigeria.

Furthermore, there is a need to address the policy discourse on academic satisfaction and motivation variables in universities. Internationalization of the migration management process should be at the heart of economic and social development policies by the government, while the policy initiatives by the leaders at the university level should address the personal and institutional variables to support academics.

According to the Center for Organizational Development and Leadership (2023) paying attention to planning imperatives by university leaders could address academic migration and other educational issues by following these steps.

- Create a diverse leadership team with deep organizational knowledge from a variety of perspectives to develop an understanding of decision-making powers and boundaries
- Foster readiness, receptivity, and a shared sense of the need for change among the stakeholders,
- Gain a historical perspective on efforts to change an organisation's migration narratives –and how perceptions of previous retention planning efforts may exert an influence on current initiatives.
- Anticipate concerns about the retention planning process and develop strategies to address those concerns
- Engage faculty and other groups to make sure the process is seen as open, inclusive, and worthwhile, thereby setting the stage for a commitment to the retention planning process
- Identify needed resources to support the faculty.

In summary, the strategic retention management approach through affirmative action to policy practices could also help educational leaders and government to holistically:

i). Assess academic needs and plan action.

ii). Address the ambiguous nature of migration policies and retention reform.

iii). Manage and administer institutional factors to improve retention

iv). Develop a supportive policy environment for career growth and

v). Institute global best retention policies and practices to enhance capacities and resilience building through partnerships/collaboration. These would discourage attrition and reduce the drivers of forced migration.

REFERENCES

Acosta, D., & Freier, L. F. (2023). Expanding the Reflexive Turn in Migration Studies: Refugee Protection, Regularization, and Naturalization in Latin America. *Journal of Immigrant & Refugee Studies*, 21(4), 597–610. DOI: 10.1080/15562948.2022.2146246

Adams, J. S. (1963). Toward an understanding of inequity. *Journal of Abnormal and Social Psychology*, 67(5), 422–436. https://ia800704.us.archive.org/view_archive.php?archive=/24/items/wikipedia-scholarly-sources-corpus/10.1037%252Fh0034974.zip&file=10.1037%252Fh0040968.pdf. DOI: 10.1037/h0040968 PMID: 14081885

Agboola, B. M. (2024). Total Quality Management (TQM) Approach to Administration of Higher Education Institutions: Implications for Leadership Effectiveness in Jamaica. In Afzal, S. M., Uzoechi, N., & Yahaya, A. (Eds.), *Edited book on Promoting Crisis Management and Creative Problem-Solving Skills in Educational Leadership. Publisher.* IGI Global.

Agboola, B. M., & Adeyemi, J. K. (2013). Projecting enrolment for effective academic staff planning in Nigerian universities. *Educational Planning,* 21(1), 6-17. https://isep.info/wp[REMOVED HYPERLINK FIELD]content/uploads/2015/12/21-1_1ProjectingEnrollment.pdf

Alo, E. A., & Dada, D. A. (2020). Employees' Turnover Intention: A Survey of Academic Staff of Selected Private Universities in Ondo State, Nigeria. *International Journal of Scientific and Research Publications*, 10(2), 263–268. DOI: 10.29322/IJSRP.10.02.2020.p98377

Amutuhaire, T. (2010). Terms of service and job retention among academic staff at Makerere University. Master of Arts in Higher Education Studies Thesis, Makerere University, Kampala.

Ki-Moon, B. (2013). *Secretary-General's Remarks to High-Level Dialogue on International Migration and Development*. United Nations.

Bashayreh, A. M., Assaf, N., & Qudah, M. (2016). Prevailing organizational culture and effect on academic staff satisfaction in the Malaysian higher education institutes. *International Journal of Statistics and Systems*, 11(1), 89–102. https://www.ripublication.com/ijss16/ijssv11n1_09.pdff

Bean, J. P. (1980). Dropouts and Turnover: The Synthesis and Test of a Causal Model of Student Attrition. *Research in Higher Education*, 12(2), 155–187. DOI: 10.1007/BF00976194

Beckles, H., & Richards-Kennedy, S. (2021). Accelerating the Future into the Present: Reimagining Higher Education in the Caribbean in Land, A. Corcoran & D-C. Lancu (Eds.). *The Promise of Higher Education.*https://link.springer.com/chapter/10.1007/978-3-030[REMOVED HYPERLINK FIELD]67245-4_54

Carr, P. L., Raj, A., Kaplan, S. E., Terrin, N., Breeze, J. L., & Freund, K. M. (2018). Gender Differences in Academic Medicine: Retention, Rank, and Leadership Comparisons from the National Faculty Survey. *Academic Medicine*, 93(11), 1694–1699. https://pubmed.ncbi.nlm.nih.gov/29384751/. DOI: 10.1097/ACM.0000000000002146 PMID: 29384751

Center for Organizational Development and Leadership. (CODL, 2023). Strategic Planning in Higher Education: A Guide for Leaders, 1-12. Publisher: the Department of University Relations, the State University of New Jersey, Rutgers. https://www2.cortland.edu/offices/institutional-research-and-assessment/planning-and-assessment-support/file-uploads/RutgersPlanning.pdf

Chirikov, I. (2016). *How global competition is changing universities: Three theoretical perspectives. Research & Occasional Paper Series.* Center for Studies of Higher Education, University of California., https://escholarship.org/content/qt50g3t797/qt50g3t797_noSplash_c538a92a248d853a236c 6d2147b0bbde.pdf?t=ohtfhs

Colos, L. (2023: February, 03) How HR Policies and Procedures Can Help Improve Employee Retention. Pitchgrade publication. https://pitchgrade.com/blog/hr-policies-procedures-improve-employee-retention

Conrad, A. (December 22, 2020). 4 Strategic Planning Tools and Models for 2021 and Beyond. https://www.softwareadvice.com/resources/strategic-planning-tools/

Creswell, J. W. (2014). *Research Design: Qualitative, Quantitative, and Mixed Methods Approaches* (4th ed.). Sage.

Creswell, J. W., & Creswell, J. D. (2018). Mixed methods procedures. In *Research design: Qualitative, quantitative, and mixed methods approaches* (5th ed., pp. 213–246). SAGE Publications, Inc.

David, J. Forrest (1999). Employer Attitude. The Foundation of Employee Retention http://www.keepemployees.com/WhitePapers/attitude.pdf

Dennis, J. (2022, August 30). Jamaica teacher migration: Treating the symptoms and not the causes. *The Jamaica Observer*. https://www.jamaicaobserver.com/2022/08/30/jamaica-teacher-migration-treating-the-symptoms-and-not-the-causes/

Ekanem, E. E., & Uchendu, C. C. (2012). University academic staff service delivery quality and vision 2020 attainment in Nigeria. *Journal of National Library and Information Practitioners CRS*, 3(2), 13–143.

Federal Ministry of Education. (2021). Nigerian University System Statistical Digest 2018 & 2019. https://education.gov.ng/wp-content/uploads/2021/09/2019 -NIGERIAN[REMOVED HYPERLINK FIELD]UNIVERSITY-SYSTEM-STATISTICAL-DIGEST.pdf

Federal Republic of Nigeria. (2013). *National Policy on Education* (6th ed.). NERDC Press Lagos.

Fumasoli, T., & Hladchenko, M. (2023). Strategic management in higher education: Conceptual insights, lessons learned, emerging challenges. *Tertiary Education and Management*, 29(4), 331–339. DOI: 10.1007/s11233-024-09134-5

ILO. (2015). Global employment trends for youth: Scaling up investments in decent jobs for youth. https://www.ilo.org/publications/global-employment-trends-youth -2015-scaling-investments-decent-jobs-youth

International Organization for Migration. (IOM, 2023). How to "solve" migration: A practical guide. IOM UN Migration, Regional Office for Central, North America and the Caribbean. https://rosanjose.iom.int/en/blogs/how-solve-migration-practical -guide

Jacob, M. Selesho & Naile, I. (2014). Academic staff retention as a human resource factor: University Perspective. *The International Business & Economics Research Journal*, 13(2), 295304.

Khan, F. Q., Buhari, S. M., Tsaramirsis, G., & Rasheed, S. (2021). A study of faculty retention factors in educational institutes in context with ABET. *Frontiers in Education*, 6, 678018. https://www.frontiersin.org/articles/10.3389/feduc.2021 .678018/full. DOI: 10.3389/feduc.2021.678018

Kupriyanova, V., Estermann, T., & Sabic, N. (2018). Efficiency of Universities: Drivers, Enablers and Limitations. In Curaj, A., Deca, L., & Pricopie, R. (Eds.), *European Higher Education Area: The Impact of Past and Future Policies*. Springer., DOI: 10.1007/978-3-319-77407-7_36

Leithwood, K., Harris, A., & Hopkins, D. (2020). Seven strong claims about successful school leadership revisited. [Crossref.]. *School Leadership & Management*, 40(1), 5–22. DOI: 10.1080/13632434.2019.1596077

Malahy, M. M. (2008). Contested Challenges: universities, globalisation, and human migration. Proceedings of the 4th International Barcelona Conference on Higher Education, 8. *Higher education and citizenship, participation and democracy.* Barcelona: GUNI. http://www.guni-rmies.net

Mamman-Daura, F. (2022). Forced migration in Nigeria is a development issue. *OECD- Development Matters.*https://oecd-development-matters.org/2022/02/02/forced-migration[REMOVED HYPERLINK FIELD]in-nigeria-is-a-development-issue/

Manogharan, M. W., Thivaharan, T., & Rahman, R. A. (2018). Academic staff retention in private higher education institute – a case study of private colleges in Kuala Lumpur. *International Journal of Higher Education*, 7(3), 52. Advance online publication. DOI: 10.5430/ijhe.v7n3p52

McKenzie, N. (Sep 29, 2022). Migrant teachers' perspectives. Jamaica Observer, https://www.jamaicaobserver.com/columns/migrant-teachers-perspectives/

Metcalf, H., Rolfe, P., Stevens, P., & Weale, M. (2005). *Recruitment and Retention of Academic Staff in Higher Education.* National Institute of Economic and Social Research, Research Report RR658.

Ming, D., & Christian, C. (August 30, 2022) Teacher migration in Jamaica: Exploring the causes, effects, and solutions. Publisher: Leadership Reimagination Enterprise. https://leadershipreimagination.com/uncategorized/teacher-migration-in-jamaica-exploring-the-causes-effects-and-solutions/

Morris, A. (2021). Cabinet approves development of national higher-education policy. Jamaica Information Service.https://jis.gov.jm/cabinet-approves-development-of-national-higher[REMOVED HYPERLINK FIELD]education-policy/

Muma, M.M., Nzulwa, D.J., Ombui, D.K., Odhiambo, R.O., Wekesa, D.S., Omondi, M., Lumiti, P.A., Ochego, C., & Charles, M. (2019). Influence of recruitment strategies on retention of employees in universities in Kenya.

National Security Council. (2021). Collaborative migration management strategy. US White House, Washington. https://www.whitehouse.gov/wp-content/uploads/2021/07/Collaborative-Migration-Management-Strategy.pdf

Ng'ethe, M., Iravo, M. E., & Namusonge, G. S. (2012). Determinants of Academic Staff Retention in Public Universities in Kenya: Empirical Review Jane. *International Journal of Humanities and Social Science*, 2(13), 205–212. https://www.ijhssnet.com/journals/Vol_2_No_13_July_2012/22.pdf

Norma, A. Sugden (2010). Teacher workload: and Formula to maximize teacher job performance and well-being. (Unpublished Dissertation) Walden University. https://pdfs.semanticscholar.org/f928/9b4ff7320fece395aa488df2ee5de916b175.pdf?_ga=2. 188060136.119827029.1588006256-311954297.1581345624

Okello, N. G., & Lamaro, G. (2015). Perceptions on remunerations and turnover intentions in public universities in Uganda. *International Journal of Developmental Research*, 5(01), 3061–3068. https://hdl.handle.net/20.500.14270/434

Petraglia, E., Green, J., Taie, S., Ferg, R., Hubbell, K., Salinas, V., Greene, A., & Lewis, L. (2023). User's Manual for the 2020–21 National Teacher and Principal Survey: Vol. 1–4. *(NCES 2022-061rev through 2022-064rev). U.S. Department of Education.* National Center for Education Statistics., https://nces.ed.gov/pubs2024/2024039SummaryM.pdf

Powell, W. W. (2010). Understanding attrition and predicting employment durations of former staff in a public social service organization. *Journal of Social Work : JSW*, 10(4), 407–435. DOI: 10.1177/1468017310369606

Praslova, L. N. (2023: January 10). Today's Most Critical Workplace Challenges Are About Systems. Published by *Havard Business Review*. https://hbr.org/2023/01/todays-most-critical-workplace-challenges-are-about-systems

Salau, O., Worlu, R., Osinbanjo, A., Adeniji, A., Atolagbe, T., & Salau, J. (2020). Determinants of retention strategies and sustainable performance of academic staff of government-owned universities in Nigeria. *F1000Research*, 1-19. DOI: 10.12688/f1000research.25011.1

Samuel, M. O., & Chipunza, C. (2013). Higher Learning in South Africa: The Strategies, Complexities and Realities. *Journal of Social Sciences*, 35(2), 97–109. DOI: 10.1080/09718923.2013.11893151

Sasu, D. D. (2023). Immigration in Nigeria - statistics & facts: Africa Migration flow. Statista. https://www.statista.com/topics/7865/immigration-in-nigeria/

Sives, A., Morgan, W. J., & Simon Appleton, S. (2006). Teacher migration from Jamaica: Assessing the short-term impact. Caribbean Journal of Education, 27(1), 85-111. https://www.researchgate.net/publication/274017514_Teacher_Migration_from_Jamaica_assessing_the_short_term_impact

Tettey, W. J. (2009). Deficits in academic staff capacity in Africa and challenges of developing and retaining the next generation of academics. *Partnership for higher education in Africa.* https://www.semanticscholar.org/paper/DEFICITS -IN-ACADEMIC-STAFF-CAPACITY-IN-AFRICA-AND-Tettey/acf6a510cb ce13b2f21449623103ccbaf3b38ee7

Tupper, H., & Ellis, S. (2022). It's time to reimagine employee retention. *Havard Business Review.*https://hbr.org/2022/07/its-time-to-reimagine-employee-retention

Uche, C. M., & Jack, I. F. (2014). Level of female academic staff development and mobility in the University of Port Harcourt. *Research Journal in Organizational Psychology & Educational Studies* 3(3) 152-158. www.emergingresource.orgg

Udi, G. (2010). Determinants of Staff Retention in Service Organisations. A Case of Consumer Insight Ltd. Master's thesis, Jomo Kenyatta University of Agriculture and Technology.

UNESCO. (2019). Migration, displacement, and education: Building bridges, not walls. *Global Education Monitoring Report.* https://unesdoc.unesco.org/ark:/48223/ pf0000265866.page=117

University of Connecticut. (2022). Guidelines for the Development of Faculty Workload Assignment Policies. Provost Office Document. https://policy.uconn .edu/wp-content/uploads/sites/243/2022/08/Guidelines-for-the[REMOVED HY-PERLINK FIELD]Development-of-Faculty-Workload-Assignment-Policies-Final-8-22-22.pdf# U.S. Department of Education (1990-91). Teacher Supply, Teacher Turnover, and Teacher Qualifications. *National Center for Education Statistics, 1990-91 (NCES 95-744).*https://nces.ed.gov/pubs95/web/95770.asp# Vedder, R. (2021, January,11). Migrants Flee States With Highly Educated People: Why? Publisher: Forbes, Leadership Education. https://www.forbes.com/sites/richardvedder/ 2021/01/11/migrants-flee-states-with-highly-educated-people-why/

Vnoučková, L. (2012). Monitoring labour mobility as a way to competitiveness. *Journal of Competitiveness*, 4(3), 105–121. https://www.cjournal.cz/files/111.pdf. DOI: 10.7441/joc.2012.03.08

Wilcox, C. (2023). Women faculty feel 'pushed' from academia by poor workplace climate. *Science.* Advance online publication. DOI: 10.1126/science.caredit.adl4899

Workforce Planning for Wisconsin State Government. (2005). Employee retention http://workforceplanning.wi.gov/category.asp?linkcatid=15&linkid=18

Chapter 6
Insights for Administrators, Faculty, and Policymakers

Mete Sipahioglu
https://orcid.org/0000-0003-2196-5533
Samsun University, Turkey

ABSTRACT

This chapter examines the connections between leadership strategies and enhanced student achievement at higher education institutions. As pressures grow around outcomes, affordability and inclusion, effective leadership has become key to accelerating reforms focused on student success, including increased retention, progression, degree completion and career readiness. Theories explored include transformational, distributed and culturally responsive models. Competencies for contemporary contexts cover cultural competence, change leadership, talent development and data literacy. Examples of successful initiatives promoted include predictive analytics, transition programs, pathway redesigns, early intervention systems and student-centric cultures. Vision, community-building, resource optimization and change management provide frameworks to facilitate progress despite complexity. Findings synthesize scholarship and practice into recommendations translating leadership capabilities to institutional environments enabling all students to thrive.

OVERVIEW

This chapter examines the instrumental role effective leadership plays in enhancing student success in higher education. As colleges and universities face mounting pressures to demonstrate outcomes around retention, progression, attainment, career

DOI: 10.4018/979-8-3693-9215-7.ch006

readiness and more, leadership has become mission critical to driving systemic reforms that enable these student achievement aims. The chapter provides higher education administrators, teams and policymakers research-backed principles to translate leadership vision, strategy and capabilities into tangible initiatives and cultural change that help all students thrive.

First, the chapter explores prevalent leadership theories like transformational, distributed and culturally responsive models to equip leaders with nuanced understanding of diverse, evidence-based approaches. Specific competencies such as strategic planning, data fluency, community building, talent development and equity advancement are highlighted as vital for contemporary higher education contexts. Real-world examples illustrate connections between leadership decisions and increased student success. Initiatives covered range from implementing holistic analytics platforms that identify at-risk students early for targeted supports; establishing summer bridge programs and peer communities to ease transitions; redesigning guided pathways that keep students on track; expanding emergency funding and resources to eliminate structural barriers; building inclusive campus environments that foster belonging; aligning curricula and experiences to career needs; and creating early intervention systems informed by predictive data to sustain momentum.

While multifaceted strategies exist, change often stalls due to insufficient commitment, communication breakdowns, misused data or misaligned structures. Principles grounded in vision, partnership, optimization and change management counteract these pitfalls. The chapter synthesizes current literature with practice-based evidence into a leadership toolkit. Recommendations guide administrators in elevating student achievement through initiatives, policies, practices and cultures tailored to their institutional environments. Concluding insights discuss emerging challenges leaders must creatively navigate, such as demographic shifts, funding constraints, remote learning and calls for even greater equity or reform.

With pressure on higher education mounting, the need for strategic leadership committed to student advancement has never been more acute or consequential. This chapter seeks to inform this charge.

INTRODUCTION

The role of leadership in higher education is pivotal, with institutions facing rising demands for accountability (Bryman, 2007). This chapter explores effective leadership strategies for enhanced student success in higher education. Leadership effectiveness impacts both the institution and its stakeholders, especially students (Choudhary, & Paharia, 2018). The evolving landscape of higher education requires adaptable and innovative leaders (Orr et al., 2020). Higher education institutions now contribute to social mobility and economic development alongside traditional objectives (McNair et al., 2011). Student success is defined by academic achievement and persistence (Tinto, 1993), as well as satisfactory participation in valuable activities (Kuh et al., 2006). Effective leadership strategies create environments conducive to student success by promoting quality teaching, fostering inclusive communities, and enabling engagement opportunities (McCormick et al., 2013). They also influence policy development impacting student outcomes (Day et al., 2016). Various leadership models have been explored: transformative (Dantley & Tillman, 2007), servant (Greenleaf & Spears, 2002), distributed (Bolden et al., 2008), and situational (Hersey & Blanchard, 1969). This chapter bridges the gap between these models and their practical application for enhancing student success. The chapter explores leadership models, their impact on student success, and provides practical insights for administrators. It includes case studies and discusses current challenges and future directions for leadership in higher education

Context and Importance of Student Success

Student success prioritization in higher education has gained unprecedented attention over the past decade (Calhoun, 1996; Matthews, 2018). Historically, institutional success was measured by scholarly output and reputation. However, evolving societal expectations and economic challenges led to a paradigm shift (Labaree, 2022). Key metrics like retention (Astin, 1997), graduation rates, and post-graduation outcomes (Borden, 2005) have become integral to assessing institutional performance and accountability (Cullen et al., 2003). Driving forces include rising education costs, student debt (Bonet & Walters, 2016), and performance-based funding models (Hillman et al., 2018). Demographic shifts (Grawe, 2021) and workforce alignment (Torres et al., 2014) further amplify the significance of student success. Leadership in higher education must adopt a strategic and student-centric approach to navigate these challenges effectively.

Outline of Key Objectives and Topics

In navigating higher education, this chapter illuminates the role of effective leadership in advancing student achievement. It aims to provide administrators and educational teams with actionable principles and recommendations. The chapter analyzes prevailing leadership theories, models, and competencies relevant to higher education (Bolman & Deal, 2017; Cetin & Kinik, 2016). It explores transformational, distributed, and servant leadership approaches and their impact on student outcomes. Building on theoretical foundations, it examines specific strategies employed by effective leaders to enhance student success. This includes visioning, collaboration, resource management, and diversity and inclusion strategies. The chapter show-cases real-world institutional initiatives that have increased student achievement, offering practical insights into how successful leadership translates into tangible outcomes. Acknowledging challenges, it discusses common leadership pitfalls that can impede progress, such as lack of long-term commitment, poor communication, and misaligned incentives. Finally, it provides comprehensive guidelines and best practices for maximizing leadership impact on student success, empowering leaders with knowledge and tools to systematically improve student outcomes within their educational contexts.

Defining Student Success

Common Metrics

In the intricate tapestry of higher education, the definition of student success is intricately woven with quantifiable markers that extend beyond the diverse perspectives and values held by educational institutions (Lane et al., 2019). While the conceptu-alization of success in education is subjective, the prevailing trend emphasizes the significance of quantifiable metrics as pivotal indicators that colleges and universities meticulously track. These quantifiable markers not only serve as benchmarks for individual student achievement but also play a crucial role in shaping institutional viability through its impact on performance funding, student recruitment, workforce alignment, and public perceptions of educational quality (Labaree, 2020).

Quantifiable Benchmarks as Key Performance Indicators

Among the array of quantifiable benchmarks, retention rates and graduation rates stand out as primary indicators that institutions use to gauge student success (Barbera et al., 2020; Kuh et al., 2006). Retention rates, denoting the percentage of first-time undergraduate students who persist at the same institution from year to year, serve as a crucial metric. High retention rates signify that students are persisting in their academic programs as expected, progressing towards completion. The tracking of fall-to-fall retention, particularly for first-time, full-time student cohorts, provides institutions with valuable insights into the persistence patterns of their students (Craig & Ward, 2008).

Similarly, graduation rates play a fundamental role in assessing student success (Kuh et al., 2006). This metric reflects the percentage of first-time undergraduate students who successfully complete their academic program and earn a degree or certificate within a specified time frame after initial enrollment, typically 4, 6, or 8 years. Like retention rates, graduation rates are derived from longitudinal tracking of entering fall cohorts, offering institutions a comprehensive view of the outcomes of their academic programs.

Critiques and Limitations of Quantitative Metrics

While these numerical metrics form the backbone of accountability frameworks, scholarly discourse underscores their limitations (Labaree, 2020). One notable critique center around the potential consequences of overly narrow definitions of success, which predominantly focus on completion and job outcomes. Some scholars advocate for broader conceptualizations of success that encompass multidimensional aims such as civic competence, and community engagement (Torney-Purta et al., 2015). These broader perspectives challenge the singular emphasis on completion rates, urging institutions to consider a more holistic view of student success.

Navigating Complexity: Beyond Numbers to Holistic Success

Critics also caution against the unintended consequences that may arise if metrics become overemphasized, potentially leading to institutional decisions that prioritize numerical outcomes over the holistic development of students (Zepke, 2014). As the landscape of education evolves, so too must our understanding of success. Recent research suggests taking a more comprehensive, multidimensional view of student achievement that goes beyond quantitative metrics (York et al., 2015). The subsequent sections of this chapter will delve into the nuanced factors influencing student success, transcending the confines of quantitative metrics to embrace a more comprehensive and multidimensional view of student achievement. By doing so, we aim to provide administrators, policymakers, and educators with a holistic framework for understanding and enhancing student success in higher education.

Influencing Factors

Delving into the fabric of student success reveals a rich tapestry woven from the intricate interplay of myriad factors, both quantitative and qualitative. While prevailing definitions often center on quantitative outcomes, the qualitative dimensions of students' experiences wield profound influence over their motivation, sense of belonging, learning trajectories, and overall persistence within the educational journey (Strayhorn, 2018).

Pre-College Academic Readiness as a Foundation

The bedrock of student success lies in pre-college academic readiness, spanning crucial areas such as mathematics, reading, writing, and study skills (Conley, 2007). This foundational phase establishes the groundwork upon which students build their academic endeavors (Byrd & MacDonald, 2005). Academic preparedness, measured through standardized testing and other assessment tools, not only influences early academic success but also serves as a predictor for students' ability to navigate the challenges of higher education (Camara, 2013).

Intra-Institutional Experiences: Classroom and Beyond

Once enrolled, students traverse a multifaceted landscape of experiences inside and outside the classroom, each wielding an impact on their mindsets, behaviors, and the acquisition of skills necessary for progression (Zhao & Kuh, 2004). The quality of relationships formed with faculty and advisors emerges as a critical factor influencing student success. These relationships contribute significantly to students' academic engagement, providing guidance, mentorship, and a support system crucial for overcoming challenges (Jones, 2008).

Moreover, the significance of peer connections cannot be overstated. Engaging with a diverse and supportive peer community fosters a sense of belonging and collaboration, positively influencing the overall student experience (Wilcox et al., 2005). However, the journey is not without its hurdles, and students grapple with financial and life challenges that can significantly impact their ability to persist and succeed in their academic pursuits (Britt et al., 2017). Campus climate, particularly regarding inclusion and diversity, further shapes the overall environment in which students navigate their educational journeys (Campbell-Whatley et al., 2015).

Leadership Decisions and Institutional Support

Crucially, the decisions made by institutional leaders play a pivotal role in shaping the landscape of student success. Leadership choices regarding resource allocation for support services, early interventions, curricular reforms, and faculty professional development have far-reaching consequences (Cruickshank, 2017). These decisions directly influence the level of support available to students, impacting their ability to overcome challenges, access necessary resources, and engage in a curriculum that aligns with their academic and career aspirations.

Balancing Academic and Non-Academic Factors

While completion metrics often take center stage, it is essential to recognize the intricate web of academic and non-academic factors that underlie these outcomes. This multifaceted perspective acknowledges that student success is not solely a product of academic prowess but is intricately linked to a holistic approach that considers the diverse and evolving needs of students.

As we navigate through the subsequent sections of this chapter, we will unravel the layers of effective leadership strategies that address these influencing factors, providing administrators and educators with a nuanced understanding of how leadership decisions can positively impact the complex landscape of student success in higher education.

Rising Priority

In higher education, student success has become an urgent, multidimensional priority, driven by converging pressures on retention, progression, attainment, and post-graduation outcomes (Sipahioglu, 2020). Heightened scrutiny from stakeholders demands transparency and accountability in educational outcomes (Kelchen, 2018). Challenges include funding declines, demographic shifts, and questioning of higher education's return on investment. The call for equitable and inclusive environments necessitates intentional leadership efforts to create an atmosphere where all students can thrive (Black & Simon, 2014; Young, 2015). Effective leadership is crucial for enhancing student success rates (Delener, 2013). Leaders must strategically align institutional resources and priorities to foster an environment where students persist, thrive academically, pursue meaningful careers, and receive necessary support. The following sections will explore leadership strategies and competencies needed to address the challenges posed by the rising priority of student success in higher education.

Leadership Theories and Competencies

Transformational, distributed, and culturally responsive leadership models offer frameworks for fostering student success in higher education (Bass & Riggio, 2006; Spillane, 2006; Khalifa et al., 2016). Integrating these models addresses multifaceted student needs (Leithwood et al., 2020). Diversity and inclusion within leadership is crucial for equity and student success (Bensimon, 2018). Case studies provide insights into successful diversity initiatives (Harper & Simmons, 2019). Interdisciplinary perspectives enhance leadership strategies. Organizational psychology improves team building (Northouse, 2021), while educational sociology informs student engagement (Tierney, 2008). Team leadership facilitates professional learning communities (Koeslag-Kreunen et al., 2018). Distributed leadership engages stakeholders in collaborative decision-making (Harris, 2013a). Culturally responsive leadership (CRL) promotes inclusive campuses fostering belonging among marginalized students (Santamaría, 2014). Servant leadership prioritizes group interests through ethical stewardship (Noland & Richards, 2015; Parris and Peachey, 2013). Both philosophies advance justice through systemic changes supporting minoritized learners.

In contrast to solely hierarchical, outcomes-driven paradigms, strengths-based leadership focuses on nurturing human potential in higher education. As Hewitt et al. (2014) discuss, this student-centric model encourages a holistic approach that acknowledges and develops the unique talents of individuals within the educational community. Similarly, in times of disruption and change, visionary and ethical leadership proves vital (Shapiro & Gross, 2013). As Shapiro and Gross (2013) articulate, ethical leaders promote clarity of vision, courageous advocacy, inclusiveness, empathy, and respect to navigate uncertainty. They consolidate fragmented voices into coherent, principled stances upholding institutional mission when facing external criticism. By channeling persuasive narratives, they continue advancing equitable access and pluralism despite short-term setbacks. Visionary, ethical leaders ultimately inspire followers' best selves while furthering just purposes, especially when inconvenient. Their steadfast adherence to morality resisting compromise counterbalances pragmatic tendencies (Komives & Dugan, 2010). Thus, strengths-building and visionary ethical leadership counterbalance other paradigms, keeping institutions firmly rooted in human dignity.

Key Competencies

Scholarship underscores key capabilities driving effective leadership specifically within educational contexts. Developing a compelling moral vision emerges as a vital competency for leaders to motivate and unify stakeholders (Starratt, 2005). This requires articulating aspirational futures grounded in ethical convictions that tap into followers' intrinsic motivations. Additionally, fluency in planning and managing strategic initiatives proves essential to channel ambitions into feasible action (Bolman & Deal, 2017). Here, delineating logical connections between activities, outputs, and desired outcomes provides guardrails for improvement cycles. Data literacy also enables evidence-based decisions, requiring leaders to translate statistics into contextual insights for responsive adaptations (Mandinach & Jimerson, 2016). Further, cultural competence building inclusive environments proves critical, involving identity consciousness, dismantling biases, and multicultural community bridging (Coleman & Lumby, 2007). Finally, leading change through uncertainty constitutes a key competency, demanding adaptive skills to mobilize collective mobilization amid discomfort (Heifetz et al., 2009). By developing these research-based capabilities, education leaders can profoundly expand their impact.

Moral Purpose & Vision: Guiding with Ethical Clarity

At the heart of effective leadership lies the ability to articulate a moral purpose and vision that resonates with followers. Research emphasizes that conveying a hopeful vision firmly anchored to ethical values not only inspires but also taps into followers' intrinsic motivations (Komives & Wagner, 2017; Northouse, 2021). Leaders who communicate a compelling future and sense of purpose are better able to motivate teams and foster engagement (Komives & Wagner, 2017). Northouse (2021) states that "Leadership requires envisioning attractive, though perhaps difficult, future states that inspire others to pursue a common goal."

The process of establishing a credible moral vision involves reflection to clarify values and determine principles that guide decision-making (Komives & Wagner, 2017). Leaders thoughtfully consider how to articulate this vision to resonate with diverse perspectives (Northouse, 2021). Communicating with clarity and inviting input helps consolidate viewpoints. Effective leaders embody the vision through consistent modeling of ethical behaviors anchored in shared principles (Komives & Wagner, 2017; Northouse, 2021). This builds credibility over time.

Research shows that visions centered around values like fairness and care can cultivate compassionate, empowering cultures (Starratt, 2005). When visions emphasize intrinsic purposes rather than solely outcomes, they foster creativity and risk-taking needed for growth (Komives & Wagner, 2017). A strong moral vision grounded in ethics serves as an anchor during turbulent times (Northouse, 2021). Overall, conveying credible moral visions represents effective leadership capable of inspiring positive change.

Strategic Planning: Aligning Aspirations with Action

A crucial capability enabling effective leaders to advance student success involves strategic planning to systematically progress toward goals. As Machado and Taylor (2010, p. 12) note, "any form of leadership is better guided with a plan, a road map, or a navigational compass." Concrete roadmaps with stepwise milestones maintain momentum across implementation timelines (Paris, 2003). Developing rigorous logic models elucidates how current activities link contextually to short and long-term performance indicators, allowing for evidence-based adaptations (Taylor-Powell & Henert, 2008). Moreover, environmental scanning facilitates pattern recognition and agenda setting aligned to potentialities, helping institutions balance ambition with pragmatism (Morrison, 1992). Through data-informed public engagement and transparent goal-setting, inclusive strategic planning bridges aspirational vision with actionable next steps (Lake & Mrozinski, 2011). By codifying collective intentions, strategy tangibly drives desired futures centered on access, affordability, and student thriving. Thus, sound planning actualizes the promise of higher education.

Data Literacy: Informed Decision-Making

Data literacy is the ability to read, understand, analyze, and communicate with data. It is a crucial skill for effective leadership in higher education, as it enables informed decision-making based on evidence, insights, and best practices. Data literacy also fosters a culture of learning and innovation, as leaders can use data to identify problems, evaluate solutions, monitor progress, and adapt to changing circumstances. In this section, we will discuss the importance of data literacy for higher education leaders, the challenges and opportunities of data-informed decision-making, and the strategies and competencies that can enhance data literacy across the organization.

As analytics and predictive modeling increasingly inform student success initiatives, developing leadership data literacy emerges as pivotal (Daniel, 2015). This requires statistical fluency to translate metrics into actionable insights and assess validity within local contexts (Picciano, 2012). Skilled interpretation of dashboard indicators allows administrators to recognize patterns, identify problems proactively, and select appropriate interventions (Mandinach & Gummer, 2016a). Equally crucial is understanding limitations of data-based decision-making to augment rather than replace professional judgment and avoid oversimplified framing of complex realities (Picciano, 2012). Beyond dashboards, strengthening evaluation capacity to assess efforts' efficacy through methodical inquiry sustains continuous enhancement (Mandinach & Gummer, 2016b). By balancing analytics with awareness of political nuances and ethical complexities, data-informed leaders can nurture cultures of evidence-based, equity-advancing educational improvements.

Cultural Competence: Fostering Inclusive Environments

As campuses diversify amid demographic shifts, cultural competence building inclusive environments emerges as an imperative leadership capability (Coleman & Lumby, 2007). This requires conscientization raising awareness of diversity issues and systemic barriers facing marginalized groups (Arday, 2018). Identity consciousness then informs efforts promoting equity-minded teaching, anti-racist programming, and support resources reducing opportunity gaps for minority students (Bartlett, 2021). Further elements include enacting restorative justice dismantling biases embedded in policies, practices, and procedures that disadvantage under-represented populations (Snively, 2021). Leaders additionally play a key role in fostering intercultural socialization through campus spaces that encourage cross-racial relationship building (Bowman, 2013). Taken together these competencies can create institutional climates where all students feel valued and able to thrive personally and intellectually.

Change Leadership: Navigating Transformation

The dynamic landscape of higher education necessitates that competent leaders embrace adaptability and change management skills (Fullan & Scott, 2009). This involves normalizing discomfort during transitions and cultivation of growth mindsets focused on possibility rather than constraint (Heifetz et al., 2009). Change leaders adeptly sequence messaging and frame challenges as opportunities for stakeholder input and co-creation of solutions (Kezar, 2018). They employ flexibility in implementation yet persistently nudge cultural shifts over time through inquiry and pilot testing of innovations (Cels et al., 2012). Additionally, savvy change stewardship retains cultural continuity honouring past wisdom while revealing its limits in addressing emergent complexities (Coates et al., 2019). Rather than imposing directives, distributed engagement convenes partners across hierarchies to re-envision systems upholding collective interests (Kezar et al., 2019). By gracefully surfacing contradictions and convening coalitions for redress, change trailblazers manifest aspirational realities advancing access, sustainability and justice.

Talent Cultivation: Multiplying Leadership Impact

Effective leaders recognize that talent development multiplies institutional capability to advance student success (Fullan, 2009). This competency involves taking inventory of teams' complementary strengths and areas for growth to align roles leveraging unique aptitudes (Paris, 2003). Facilitating mentoring relationships and communities of practice fosters intergenerational knowledge sharing critical for scaling innovations (Wenger, 2011). Sponsorship platforms additionally provide visibility encouraging aspirational mobility across hierarchies. Further, distributed leadership models share agency, building leadership muscles throughout the organizational ecosystem (Harris, 2013b). Together these human infrastructure investments elevate collective expertise. As Cardichon et al. (2020) underscore, ongoing renewal of skills for evolving contexts and coaching in trauma-invested, healing-centered practices equips staff resilience. By simultaneously developing people and shaping cultures that ignite their altruistic commitments, values-aligned leaders compound returns benefiting institutional sustainability.

LEADERSHIP STRATEGIES TO PROMOTE STUDENT SUCCESS

Background on Leadership Strategies

Leadership strategies in higher education are crucial for fostering an environment conducive to student success. Effective leadership strategies encompass a variety of approaches aimed at improving institutional performance, enhancing student engagement, and ensuring academic achievement. These strategies include transformational leadership, distributed leadership, and culturally responsive leadership, among others. Each of these strategies brings unique benefits and challenges, shaping the educational landscape in significant ways.

Transformational Leadership

Transformational leadership focuses on inspiring and motivating staff and students to exceed expectations and embrace change (Bass & Riggio, 2006). It is characterized by the ability to create a vision for the future, foster a supportive and inclusive environment, and encourage innovation and creativity. This leadership style has been shown to positively influence student outcomes by promoting a culture of excellence and high expectations (Leithwood & Jantzi, 2005).

Distributed Leadership

Distributed leadership emphasizes shared responsibility and collaborative decision-making processes (Spillane, 2006). This approach can lead to more inclusive and participatory governance structures, enhancing the sense of ownership and accountability among faculty and staff. Distributed leadership has been linked to improved student outcomes as it leverages the collective expertise of the institution's members to address complex challenges (Harris, 2013a).

Culturally Responsive Leadership

Culturally responsive leadership involves recognizing and addressing the diverse cultural backgrounds of students to create an inclusive educational environment (Khalifa et al., 2016). This strategy is particularly effective in promoting equity and reducing achievement gaps among different student groups. By fostering a culturally sensitive atmosphere, leaders can ensure that all students feel valued and supported, which is critical for their academic success (Gay, 2018).

Indicators of Effective Leadership Strategies

The indicators of effective leadership strategies include increased student retention and graduation rates, enhanced student engagement, improved academic performance, and a positive campus climate. These indicators can be measured through various metrics such as student satisfaction surveys, academic achievement records, and institutional performance evaluations.

Perspectives on Leadership Strategies

Perspectives on leadership strategies vary across different stakeholders in higher education. Faculty members may value strategies that promote academic freedom and collaborative governance, while students may prioritize approaches that enhance their learning experience and provide support services. Administrators might focus on strategies that improve institutional efficiency and accountability. Understanding these diverse perspectives is essential for developing comprehensive and effective leadership strategies.

Conceptual Model of Leadership Strategies and Student Success

To highlight the relationships among the various leadership strategies and student success, a conceptual model can be used. This model should illustrate how transformational, distributed, and culturally responsive leadership strategies influence key indicators of student success. For example, transformational leadership might directly impact student motivation and engagement, which in turn affects retention and academic performance. Distributed leadership can enhance faculty collaboration and innovation, leading to improved teaching practices and student outcomes. Culturally responsive leadership ensures an inclusive environment, reducing barriers for marginalized students and supporting their academic achievement.

Connection Between Leadership Theories and Strategies

The connection between leadership theories and strategies needs to be clearly articulated. Leadership theories provide the foundational principles and frameworks that inform specific leadership strategies. For instance, transformational leadership theory underpins strategies that focus on vision-building and inspiring change. Similarly, distributed leadership theory supports strategies that emphasize shared governance and collaborative decision-making. By aligning leadership theories with practical strategies, leaders can more effectively address the complex challenges of higher education.

Justification for Change Management in Transformative Leadership

Change management is a critical component of transformational leadership as it involves guiding institutions through significant changes in a systematic and effective manner. The focus on change management within the context of transformative leadership is justified by the need to adapt to rapidly evolving educational environments, technological advancements, and shifting student demographics. Effective change management strategies can help institutions navigate these changes while maintaining stability and achieving desired outcomes.

Removing Barriers and Expanding Access

Socioeconomic stressors, such as poverty and discrimination, disproportionately impact historically excluded groups, necessitating leadership strategies that demonstrate institutional care while eliminating structural barriers (Iwasaki, 2005; Larey, 2021; Plowden, 2003; Williams, 1980). These stressors can lead to social exclusion and resilience as frameworks for stress and coping (Iwasaki, 2005), and are influenced by sociostructural factors such as kinship, resource accessibility, ethnohealth beliefs, and a caring environment (Plowden, 2003). Therefore, effective leadership in addressing these stressors should prioritize the needs of historically excluded groups and work towards creating a more equitable and inclusive society.

In addition to addressing basic needs and academic barriers, leadership can impact access by evaluating policies and practices that may disadvantage certain student populations. For example, reviewing financial aid awarding criteria to support those with greater financial need. Standardizing credit transfer processes so credits are not lost through changes in majors or institutions. Ensuring accessibility of campus facilities, online platforms and course materials for students with disabilities.

Leaders should also consider less tangible but influential barriers like perceived belonging or experiences of microaggressions on campus. Initiative to promote diversity, equity and inclusion in campus culture and curriculum send the important message that all students are valued members of the learning community (El-Amin, 2022).

These retention-enhancing supports send a powerful message of institutional commitment to unlocking each learner's potential. They demonstrate that challenges outside the classroom will not derail educational goals, fostering student resilience and motivation to succeed.

Building Inclusive Environments

As higher education institutions diversify, fostering inclusive cultures becomes pivotal for equitable student thriving (Arday, 2018). Identity-conscious leaders play a key role in auditing biases embedded in norms, policies, curricula and conduct that alienate minority groups. Reform requires confronting historical privilege and enacting restorative practices that embrace pluralism (Grant, 1997). Strategies like diversifying faculty and leadership to reflect served communities signals valuations, as does displaying cultural representation in iconography and architecture. Revising Eurocentric content and pedagogies by incorporating non-dominant voices enhances relevance. And resolving equity gaps in achievement via reallocated resources exhibits priorities through actions, not just words. Beyond mirroring and curricular enhancements, designing gathering spaces that facilitate intercultural relationship building across difference combats segregation. Taken together, these strategies create environments where all students feel safe, seen and able to fully participate without assimilation pressures.

Workforce Alignment and Career Readiness

Leadership strategies tightening alignment between higher education and workforce needs enhance motivation and real-world preparation, fueling persistence and post-graduation trajectories (Hein, 2020). Program offerings integrating industry-relevant competency development ensure marketable skills application. Work-integrated platforms like cooperative education, internships and client-sponsored capstones bridge the academic-occupational divide through experiential learning (Jackson, 2017). Industry advisory boards refreshing curricula based on projected trends keep content current. Career exposure events and profiles of alumni pathways reinforce purpose and networking. Additionally, leadership-championed centers coaching students in conveying transferable competencies to multiple fields builds resilience (Artess et al., 2017). And reforming overly rigid degree maps grants self-directed learners agency in optimizing skill-building for emerging economic shifts. By aligning higher education experiences with workforce realities, leaders invest in graduate success beyond the first job.

Student-Centric Cultures and Policies

Distributed and transformative leadership philosophies advocate engaging student input to enhance experiential quality and support redesign (Marshall, 2016). Elevating student governance through formal advisory roles in decision-making bodies fosters ownership in policy reforms (Lizzio & Wilson, 2009). Design thinking panels, user experience surveys and focus groups to solicit perspectives across academic journeys inform empathetic improvements in advising, instruction, evaluations or campus interfaces (Huq & Gilbert, 2017). Co-creation processes grant agency while tapping lived expertise from primary end-users. Message framing emphasizing partnership and peer accountability nurtures achievement norms. And reinforcing student communities as incubators of change leadership develops capacity for current and prospective enhancement. By upholding "nothing about us without us" principles, institutions manifest cultures where all learners feel invested in collective advancement.

ADDRESSING LEADERSHIP CHALLENGES

While research emphasizes the multifaceted nature of strategies to enhance student success, change initiatives often face impediments (Kezar & Eckel, 2002). Common barriers include lack of commitment, poor communication, limited data use, and misaligned structures (Smith, 2014).

To preempt obstacles, leaders must understand challenges within their context. Surveys and interviews can assess change readiness across units (Holt et al., 2007). Reviewing policies against reform goals reveals misalignments (Paulsen & Smart, 2001).

With deeper insight, leaders design enactment strategies tailored to their institution (Kezar, 2018). Support networks strengthen long-term change capacity (Anderson & Anderson, 2010). Building data literacy across the organization establishes shared goals. Reexamining incentives aligns goals and rewards (Lane, 2007).

Commitment and Engagement

Launching student success programs without dedicated resources or sustained attention risks collapse when the initial urgency fades. Staff burnout, initiative fatigue, and cultural inertia can drag down momentum. Leaders must publicly convey constancy of purpose through both words and actions to counteract this phenomenon. Consistent messaging, reminding all stakeholders of the "why" behind institutional reforms, galvanizes continuity (Bolman & Deal, 2017). Securing multi-year budgets, sunsetting legacy activities to free up capacity, and crystallizing accountability structures help maintain focus as staff or student turnover occurs. Savvy leaders also nurture growth by breaking large goals into milestone markers, allowing for the celebration of small wins (Fullan & Scott 2009).

Broad stakeholder participation is also essential to increase engagement, a factor crucial for sustainability (Sipahioglu, 2020). Initiatives launched without active input from students, faculty, and advisors may face unconscious resistance. Involving stakeholders through surveys, focus groups, and participatory planning bodies not only grants influence but also gathers insights from end-users. Co-creation and transparency about how voices shaped decisions build collective investment. As key success partners, equipping teams across functional silos with the tools to enact desired improvements empowers leadership agency.

Communication and Collaboration

Inadequate communication can fuel misperceptions and suboptimize coordinated resource use (Bolman & Deal, 2017). Information gaps can result in duplicated efforts by one department unknown to another, mixed messaging can cause confusion, and opaque decision processes can breed mistrust. Proactive communication strategies, including upward transparency around progress reports, allow for adaptation. Informal knowledge-sharing networks pooling insights across units can exacerbate synergies. Clear delineation of departmental roles prevents service gaps or the diffusion of responsibilities. Broad messaging, utilizing diverse platforms and messengers, reinforces unified strategic priorities.

Siloed structures that isolate experts also inhibit the cross-disciplinary collaboration increasingly vital for complex student support (Pennington, 2008). Joint training programs, rotational assignments between departments, interdepartmental action research, and embedded integrative leadership roles bridge divides. Advisory councils consolidating multi-stakeholder perspectives guide decisions benefiting from collaborative wisdom. Breaking down barriers so interdependent functions align and integrate around shared goals enhances student experiences.

Data Utilization

Suboptimal data literacy can derail evidence-based interventions (Pullin & Stewart, 2006). Disjointed systems that cannot integrate indicators from fragmented sources limit insights. Lack of time, training, or analytical capacity keeps many practitioners from capitalizing on predictive modeling or disaggregating trends by student segments. Misinterpretation of statistics or empathy gaps around qualitative nuances also constrain responsive planning. Critical leadership responsibilities include updating systems, building teams' skills in making meaning from metrics, and closing loopholes that allow students to slip through cracks without triggering appropriate supports (Jr & Uline, 2005).

While data analytics empower precision intervention, over-reliance on algorithms risks dehumanizing cultures. Numbers should always augment rather than replace professional judgment grounded in an ethical commitment to student well-being. Assessment and care must take equal priority. Leaders must continually resist internal and external demands for simplistic data that forfeit richness (Daft & Lengel, 1983). Nuanced analysis of behavior in context demonstrates responsiveness, just as relational advising complements prescriptive nudging. Holism balances efficiencies.

Incentive Alignment

Incongruent policies, practices, and procedures can sabotage desired outcomes despite formal vision statements proclaiming their centrality. Lingering legacy recruiting tactics conveying false images of campus life set unrealistic expectations that hamper transition and retention. Faculty rewards valuing narrow research output over teaching excellence inhibit the adoption of inclusive pedagogies. Graduation pathway reforms falter without corresponding shifts in scheduling, course availability, or advising models that operationalize intended redesigns. Austerity measures stratifying access to supports along lines unrelated to student needs disproportionately disadvantage certain groups. Aligning espoused values with the allotment of time, space, and compensation renders coherence.

Principles for Enhancing Leadership Effectiveness

Student success reforms face barriers, but effective leadership principles can drive improvements. Key strategies include:

- Grounding initiatives in a clear vision reflecting institutional identity and priorities.
- Leveraging partnerships across departments and with external organizations to expand resources and expertise.
- Strategic resource allocation to directly support the vision, prioritizing initiatives based on impact.
- Utilizing change management frameworks to navigate resistance and structure reforms.

Continuous evaluation and refinement prevent initiatives from losing momentum. Effective leadership applies these principles at all levels to shepherd wide-scale reforms productively, focusing on improving student outcomes despite challenges.

Vision and Planning

A compelling institutional vision channels stakeholder motivations while stabilizing cultures during disruption (Bolman & Deal, 2017). By portraying uplifting environments where all students can flourish, leaders prompt investment in realizing that future vision (Kalsbeek, 2013). Inclusive inquiry building communal aspirations prevents fragmentation. Concrete operationalization of strategic priorities through measurable action plans translates ideals into attainable objectives (Paris, 2003). Well-developed logic models clarify interconnections between immediate activities, outputs generated, and long-range goals, enabling evidence-based adaptations (Taylor-Powell & Henert, 2008). Rigorous milestone tracking ensures implementation fidelity. Environmental scanning facilitates pattern anticipation, so plans evolve fittingly (Morrison, 1992). Vision thus orients change, while planning actualizes systemic reforms that foster access, equity, and achievement. In concert, these foundations secure institutional purpose.

Community and Partnership

Students rarely persist in isolation. Networks of peers, faculty, advisors, and family filling relational needs substantially impact outcomes (Strayhorn, 2018). Internal partnerships within institutions similarly determine the quality of teaching, support programs, and cultural environments shaping achievement. Leaders thus carry responsibility for nurturing collaborative communities advancing every learner.

Externally, connections with feeder schools, employers, and community groups expand capability. K-12 alignment allows earlier intervention around student readiness while clarifying expectations. Workforce partnerships contextualize relevance, provide platforms for project-based learning, and open avenues for career exposure. Municipal alliances marshal resources addressing non-academic factors like housing, transportation, and neighborhood safety. Weaving holistic ecosystems synthesizes strengths from partners filling institutional gaps Through reciprocity, the collective whole becomes greater than isolated impact. Leadership spanning boundaries to enhance a sense of belonging, scaffold skill-building, and meet needs more comprehensively produces multiplier effects on student success.

Resource Optimization

Elevating teaching excellence expands capacity efficiently by leveraging faculty and graduate students for high-touch roles advising, tutoring, and mentoring traditionally staffed through external hires. Cross-training also pools talent across siloes. For instance, financial aid officers could provide basic advising during peak registration cycles while faculty teach first-year transition seminars. Eliminating duplicated efforts similarly frees resources for functions directly enabling student progress.

Leaders must additionally consider sources beyond operating budgets. Grants underwrite supplemental initiatives while incentivizing cross-unit collaboration required during proposal development. Public-private partnerships with industry groups, community organizations, and philanthropic entities generate essential revenue amid declining state support. And land acknowledgments opening events should translate into scholarships, internships, and supply chain contracts upholding commitments by conferring opportunity to excluded populations. Resources encompass more than dollars allotted.

Change Management in Higher Education: Navigating Transformational Leadership

Change is an inherent aspect of the dynamic landscape in higher education, necessitating effective strategies to manage transitions and foster adaptability. Change management in the context of higher education demands a nuanced approach, considering the complex interplay of academic, organizational, and cultural factors. This section explores key principles and strategies for implementing successful change initiatives, providing insights for administrators, faculty, and policymakers.

The Imperative of Change in Higher Education

The need for change in higher education is underscored by a myriad of factors, including technological advancements, shifting demographics, and evolving pedagogical paradigms. Bensimon and Neumann (2017) emphasize that institutions must proactively engage with change to remain responsive to societal needs and ensure the continued relevance of their educational offerings.

Transformational Leadership as a Catalyst for Change

Effective change management often hinges on leadership that goes beyond transactional approaches. Bass and Riggio (2006) argue that transformational leadership, characterized by visionary thinking, inspiration, intellectual stimulation, and individualized consideration, provides a robust framework for navigating change in higher education. Leaders who embody these qualities can inspire a shared vision for change, fostering a collective commitment among stakeholders.

Building a Change-Ready Culture

Creating a culture that embraces change is pivotal for successful implementation. Fullan (2014) contends that a change-ready culture is characterized by trust, collaboration, and a collective sense of efficacy. Administrators play a crucial role in cultivating such a culture by fostering open communication channels, involving faculty in decision-making processes, and providing professional development opportunities that equip stakeholders with the skills needed to adapt.

Stakeholder Engagement and Communication

Engaging stakeholders throughout the change process is fundamental to garnering support and mitigating resistance. Bryson (2018) underscores the importance of transparent communication, involving stakeholders at various stages of decision-making, and addressing concerns empathetically. Leaders must articulate the rationale behind change initiatives, emphasizing the shared benefits and aligning the proposed changes with the institution's mission and values.

Assessing and Addressing Resistance

Resistance to change is a common challenge in higher education settings (Kezar, 2018). Acknowledging and addressing resistance requires a nuanced understanding of its sources, which may include concerns about workload, fear of the unknown, or perceived threats to autonomy. Leaders must proactively address these concerns through ongoing dialogue, providing clear information, and involving faculty and staff in the decision-making process.

Evaluation and Continuous Improvement

Change initiatives should be viewed as iterative processes that require ongoing evaluation and refinement. Kotter (1996) proposes a dual-operating system for change, combining a hierarchy that manages day-to-day operations with a network that encourages innovation and adaptation. This dual approach ensures that the institution remains responsive to emerging challenges and opportunities.

In conclusion, effective change management in higher education demands a holistic and collaborative approach, rooted in transformational leadership principles. By cultivating a change-ready culture, engaging stakeholders, addressing resistance, and maintaining a commitment to ongoing evaluation, institutions can navigate the complexities of change and enhance student success.

CONCLUSION AND FUTURE DIRECTIONS

This chapter serves as a synthesis of research on leadership strategies that have demonstrated efficacy in enhancing student success, while also addressing common implementation obstacles and providing guiding principles for institutional improvements. In the face of challenges related to affordability, outcomes, and inclusion, effective leadership has proven instrumental in accelerating reforms that realize retention, timely progression, and completion objectives. Despite this, change initiatives often encounter obstacles without concerted commitment, communication, data literacy, and structural alignment. The presented evidence-based principles, focusing on vision, community, resources, and change management, aim to counteract these challenges.

The contextual backdrop established the urgent priority of student achievement metrics, considering the pressures colleges face around affordability, outcomes, and inclusion. The chapter explored key quantitative indicators and the complex, interdependent factors shaping outcomes, while acknowledging their limitations. Leadership theories relevant to contemporary higher education, including hierarchical, distributed, transformative, and culturally conscious models, provided a framework for evaluating competencies, decisions, and behaviors.

Specific initiatives were then presented as examples, illustrating how leaders can directly improve persistence, certificate or degree conferral, and career entry. Data-informed supports were shown to foster seamless transitions, while belonging and inclusion cultivated campus climates where all students thrive. Streamlined pathways, needs-based access, and career integration were highlighted as strategies preventing frustration and departure, promoting human flourishing and societal prosperity by enabling learner growth.

Foreseeable impediments were acknowledged, emphasizing the need for leaders to intentionally safeguard reforms through committed focus, transparent communication, contextual data literacy, and structural harmonization. Principles were subsequently introduced to imbue efforts with meaning, harness collective expertise, direct funds responsibly, and shepherd institutional evolution. Despite the complexity of change, the chapter underscored the importance of steadfast leadership in ensuring students receive the support they need.

Equity was emphasized as a central moral and practical priority. The demographic landscape amid global interconnectedness positions diversity as a valuable asset that higher education cannot afford to squander. Economic mobility, community health, civic innovation, and national security rely on robust human capital development, making the improvement of outcomes for underserved learners imperative. Leaders seeking transformative change must embrace bold social justice advocacy as central to their mission based on these ethical realities.

The COVID-19 pandemic highlighted the fragility of existing models, creating urgency for institutions to demonstrate greater agility in meeting evolving student and societal needs. The importance of technology supports, competitive differentiation, alignment with economic shifts, and resource prioritization were underscored. Visionary leadership was identified as vital to navigating disruptive crosscurrents and ensuring the continued success of higher education institutions.

In summation, higher education plays a uniquely influential role in cultivating talents that elevate communities. However, persistent outcome disparities demand principled leaders who challenge assumptions. This chapter has illuminated practical strategies, common obstacles, and guiding frameworks to invigorate efforts centered on enabling all students' aspirations through equitable, relevant learning. While pressures and uncertainty persist, the singular importance of human potential makes investments in student success indelible. Graduates whose gifts fully activate through supportive institutions return dividends across generations.

REFERENCES

Anderson, L. A., & Anderson, D. (2010). *The change leader's roadmap: How to navigate your organization's transformation* (Vol. 384). John Wiley & Sons.

Arday, J. (2018). Understanding mental health: What are the issues for black and ethnic minority students at university? *Social Sciences (Basel, Switzerland)*, 7(10), 196. DOI: 10.3390/socsci7100196

Artess, J., Mellors-Bourne, R., & Hooley, T. (2017). Employability: A review of the literature 2012-2016. https://www.advance-he.ac.uk/knowledge-hub/employability -review-literature-2012-2016

Astin, A. W. (1997). How "good" is your institution's retention rate? *Research in Higher Education*, 38(6), 647–658. DOI: 10.1023/A:1024903702810

ation quarterly, 52(2), 221-258.

Barbera, S. A., Berkshire, S. D., Boronat, C. B., & Kennedy, M. H. (2020). Review of Undergraduate Student Retention and Graduation Since 2010: Patterns, Predictions, and Recommendations for 2020. *Journal of College Student Retention*, 22(2), 227–250. DOI: 10.1177/1521025117738233

Bartlett, T. (2021). The antiracist college. *The Chronicle of Higher Education,* ●●●, 2021.

Bass, B. M., & Riggio, R. E. (2006). *Transformational Leadership* (2nd ed.). Lawrence Erlbaum Associates. DOI: 10.4324/9781410617095

Bensimon, E. M. (2018). Reclaiming Racial Justice in Equity. *Change*, 50(3-4), 95–98. DOI: 10.1080/00091383.2018.1509623

Bensimon, E. M., & Neumann, A. (2017). *Diversity's Promise for Higher Education: Making it Work*. Johns Hopkins University Press.

Black, W. R., & Simon, M. D. (2014). Leadership for all students: Planning for more inclusive school practices. *The International Journal of Educational Leadership Preparation*, 9(2), 153–172.

Bolden, R., Petrov, G., & Gosling, J. (2008). Distributed leadership in higher education: Rhetoric and reality.Educational Management Administration & Leadership. https://doi.org/ Bolman, L. G., & Deal, T. E. (2017). *Reframing organizations: Artistry, choice, and leadership*.John Wiley & Sons.DOI: 10.1177/1741143208100301

Bonet, G., & Walters, B. R. (2016). High impact practices: Student engagement and retention. *College Student Journal*, 50(2), 224–235.

Borden, V. M. (2005). Using alumni research to align program improvement with institutional accountability. *New Directions for Institutional Research*, 2005(126), 61–72. DOI: 10.1002/ir.148

Bowman, N. A. (2013). How much diversity is enough? The curvilinear relationship between college diversity interactions and first-year student outcomes. *Research in Higher Education*, 54(8), 874–894. DOI: 10.1007/s11162-013-9300-0

Britt, S. L., Ammerman, D. A., Barrett, S. F., & Jones, S. (2017). Student Loans, Financial Stress, and College Student Retention. *Journal of Student Financial Aid*, 47(1), 3. DOI: 10.55504/0884-9153.1605

Bryman, A. (2007). Effective leadership in higher education: A literature review. *Studies in Higher Education*, 32(6), 693–710. DOI: 10.1080/03075070701685114

Bryson, J. M. (2018). *Strategic planning for public and nonprofit organizations: A guide to strengthening and sustaining organizational achievement.* John Wiley & Sons.

Byrd, K. L., & MacDonald, G. (2005). Defining college readiness from the inside out: First-generation college student perspectives. *Community College Review*, 33(1), 22–37. DOI: 10.1177/009155210503300102

Calhoun, J. C. (1996). The student learning imperative: Implications for student affairs. *Journal of College Student Development*, 37(2), 188–122.

Camara, W. (2013). Defining and measuring college and career readiness: A validation framework. *Educational Measurement: Issues and Practice*, 32(4), 16–27. DOI: 10.1111/emip.12016

Campbell-Whatley, G. D., Wang, C., Toms, O., & Williams, N. (2015). Factors affecting campus climate: Creating a welcoming environment. *New Waves-Educational Research and Development Journal*, 18(2), 40–52.

Cardichon, J., Darling-Hammond, L., Yang, M., Scott, C., Shields, P. M., & Burns, D. (2020). *Inequitable Opportunity to Learn: Student Access to Certified and Experienced Teachers.* Learning Policy Institute.

Cels, S., De Jong, J., & Nauta, F. (2012). *Agents of change: Strategy and tactics for social innovation.* Rowman & Littlefield.

Cetin, M., & Kinik, F. S. F. (2016). Effects of Leadership on Student Success through the Balanced Leadership Framework. *Universal Journal of Educational Research*, 4(4), 675–682. DOI: 10.13189/ujer.2016.040403

Choudhary, M., & Paharia, P. (2018). Role of leadership in quality education in public and private higher education institutions: A comparative study. *GYANODAYA: The Journal of Progressive Education*, 11(1), 17. Advance online publication. DOI: 10.5958/2229-4422.2018.00004.X

Coates, H., & Matthews, K. E. (2018). Frontier perspectives and insights into higher education student success. *Higher Education Research & Development*, 37(5), 903–907. DOI: 10.1080/07294360.2018.1474539

Coleman, M., & Lumby, J. (2007). Leadership and diversity: Challenging theory and practice in education. *Leadership and Diversity*, 1-160.

Conley, D. T. (2007). Redefining college readiness. Educational Policy Improvement Center. https://eric.ed.gov/?id=ED539251

Craig, A. J., & Ward, C. V. (2008). Retention of Community College Students: Related Student and Institutional Characteristics. *Journal of College Student Retention*, 9(4), 505–517. DOI: 10.2190/CS.9.4.f

Cruickshank, V. (2017). The Influence of School Leadership on Student Outcomes. *Open Journal of Social Sciences*, 5(9), 115–123. DOI: 10.4236/jss.2017.59009

Cullen, J., Joyce, J., Hassall, T., & Broadbent, M. (2003). Quality in higher education: From monitoring to management. *Quality Assurance in Education*, 11(1), 5–14. DOI: 10.1108/09684880310462038

Daft, R., & Lengel, R. (1983). Information Richness. A New Approach to Managerial Behavior and Organization Design. *Research in Organizational Behavior*. Advance online publication. DOI: 10.21236/ADA128980

Dantley, M. E., & Tillman, L. C. (2006). Social justice and moral transformative leadership. *Leadership for social justice: Making revolutions in education*, 16-30.

Day, C., Gu, Q., & Sammons, P. (2016). The impact of leadership on student outcomes: How successful school leaders use transformational and instructional strategies to make a difference. *Educational administr*

Delener, N. (2013). Leadership excellence in higher education: Present and future. *Journal of Contemporary Issues in Business and Government*, 19(1), 19–33. DOI: 10.7790/cibg.v19i1.6

Douglass, J. A., Roebken, H., & Thomson, G. (2020). The immigrant university: Assessing the dynamics of race, major and socioeconomic characteristics at the University of California. Center for Studies in Higher Education. https://cshe .berkeley.edu/publications/immigrant-university-assessing-dynamics-race-major -and-socioeconomic-characteristics

El-Amin, A. (2022). *Improving Organizational Commitment to Diversity, Equity, Inclusion, and Belonging.* Social Justice Research Methods for Doctoral Research., DOI: 10.4018/978-1-7998-8479-8.ch010

Fullan, M. (2007). *Leading in a culture of change.* John Wiley & Sons.

Fullan, M. (2009). Leadership development: The larger context. *Educational Leadership*, 67(2), 45–49.

Fullan, M., & Scott, G. (2009). *Turnaround leadership for higher education.* John Wiley & Sons.

Gay, G. (2018). *Culturally Responsive Teaching: Theory, Research, and Practice* (3rd ed.). Teachers College Press.

Grant, N. (1997). Some Problems of Identity and Education: A comparative examination of multicultural education. *Comparative Education*, 33(1), 9–28. DOI: 10.1080/03050069728613

Grawe, N. D. (2018). *Demographics and the demand for higher education.* JHU Press.

Greenleaf, R. K. (2002). *Servant leadership: A journey into the nature of legitimate power and greatness.* Paulist Press.

Harper, S. R., & Simmons, I. (2019). *Black students at public colleges and universities: A 50-state report card.* University of Southern California, Race and Equity Center.

Harris, A. (2013a). *Distributed leadership matters: Perspectives, practicalities, and potential.* Corwin Press. DOI: 10.4324/9780203607909

Harris, A. (2013b). Distributed leadership: Friend or foe? *Educational Management Administration & Leadership*, 41(5), 545–554. DOI: 10.1177/1741143213497635

Heifetz, R. A., Grashow, A., & Linsky, M. (2009). *The practice of adaptive leadership: Tools and tactics for changing your organization and the world.* Harvard business press.

Hein, V. L. (2020). *Combatting the Drive Deficit: An Exploration of Conative Skill Inclusion in College and Career Readiness Policy* (Doctoral dissertation, DePaul University).

Hersey, P., & Blanchard, K. H. (1969). Life cycle theory of leadership. *Training and Development Journal*.

Hewitt, P. M., Denny, G. S., & Pijanowski, J. C. (2014). Teacher preferences for alternative school site administrative models. *Administrative Issues Journal: Connecting Education, Practice, and Research*, 2(1), 35–47. DOI: 10.5929/2011.2.1.5

Hillman, N. W., Hicklin Fryar, A., & Crespín-Trujillo, V. (2018). Evaluating the impact of performance funding in Ohio and Tennessee. *American Educational Research Journal*, 55(1), 144–170. DOI: 10.3102/0002831217732951

Holt, D. T., Armenakis, A. A., Feild, H. S., & Harris, S. G. (2007). Readiness for organizational change: The systematic development of a scale. *The Journal of Applied Behavioral Science*, 43(2), 232–255. DOI: 10.1177/0021886306295295

Huq, A., & Gilbert, D. (2017). All the world's a stage: Transforming entrepreneurship education through design thinking. *Education + Training*, 59(2), 155–170. DOI: 10.1108/ET-12-2015-0111

Iwasaki, Y., Bartlett, J., MacKay, K., Mactavish, J., & Ristock, J. (2005). Social exclusion and resilience as frameworks of stress and coping among selected non-dominant groups. *International Journal of Mental Health Promotion*, 7(3), 4–17. DOI: 10.1080/14623730.2005.9721870

Jackson, D. (2017). Exploring the challenges experienced by international students during work-integrated learning in Australia. *Asia Pacific Journal of Education*, 37(3), 344–359. DOI: 10.1080/02188791.2017.1298515

Johnson, J. F. Jr., & Uline, C. L. (2005). Preparing educational leaders to close achievement gaps. *Theory into Practice*, 44(1), 45–52. DOI: 10.1207/s15430421tip4401_7

Jones, W. A. (2011). Faculty involvement in institutional governance: A literature review. *Journal of the Professoriate*, 6(1), 118–135.

Kalsbeek, D. H. (Ed.). (2013). *Reframing Retention Strategy for Institutional Improvement: New Directions for Higher Education, Number 161*. John Wiley & Sons.

Kelchen, R. (2018). *Higher education accountability*. JHU Press. DOI: 10.1353/book.58123

Kezar, A. (2018). *How colleges change: Understanding, leading, and enacting change*. Routledge. DOI: 10.4324/9781315121178

Kezar, A., & Eckel, P. D. (2002). The effect of institutional culture on change strategies in higher education: Universal principles or culturally responsive concepts? *The Journal of Higher Education*, 73(4), 435–460. DOI: 10.1080/00221546.2002.11777159

Kezar, A., Fries-Britt, S., Kurban, E., McGuire, D., & Wheaton, M. M. (2019). Speaking Truth and Acting with Integrity: Confronting Challenges of Campus Racial Climate (2018). http://hdl.handle.net/10919/90753

Khalifa, M. A., Gooden, M. A., & Davis, J. E. (2016). Culturally Responsive School Leadership: A Synthesis of the Literature. *Review of Educational Research*, 86(4), 1272–1311. DOI: 10.3102/0034654316630383

Komives, S. R., & Dugan, J. P. (2010). Contemporary leadership theories. *Political and civic leadership: A reference handbook, 1*, 111-120.

Komives, S. R., & Wagner, W. (Eds.). (2016). *Leadership for a better world: Understanding the social change model of leadership development*. John Wiley & Sons.

Kotter, J. P. (1996). Leading Change, Harvard Business School Press, Boston. *Search in*.

Kuh, G. D., Kinzie, J. L., Buckley, J. A., Bridges, B. K., & Hayek, J. C. (2006). *What matters to student success: A review of the literature* (Vol. 8). National Postsecondary Education Cooperative.

Labaree, D. F. (2020). *A perfect mess: The unlikely ascendancy of American higher education*. University of Chicago Press.

Lake, R. S., & Mrozinski, M. D. (2011). The conflicted realities of community college mission statements. *Planning for Higher Education*, 39(2), 5–14.

Lane, J. E. (2007). The spider web of oversight: An analysis of external oversight of higher education. *The Journal of Higher Education*, 78(6), 615–644. DOI: 10.1080/00221546.2007.11772074

Lane, M., Moore, A. J., Hooper, L., Menzies, V. J., Cooper, B., Shaw, N., & Rueckert, C. (2019). Dimensions of student success: A framework for defining and evaluating support for learning in higher education. *Higher Education Research & Development*, 38(5), 954–968. DOI: 10.1080/07294360.2019.1615418

Larey, D. P., Le Roux, A., & Jacobs, L. (2021). Evoking edupreneurial leadership towards social justice among historically disadvantaged communities. *International Journal of Leadership in Education*, ●●●, 1–17. DOI: 10.1080/13603124.2021.1882700

Leithwood, K., Harris, A., & Hopkins, D. (2020). Seven strong claims about successful school leadership revisited. *School Leadership & Management*, 40(1), 5–22. DOI: 10.1080/13632434.2019.1596077

Leithwood, K., & Jantzi, D. (2005). Transformational leadership. In Davies, B. (Ed.), *The Essentials of School Leadership* (pp. 31–43). SAGE Publications.

Lizzio, A., & Wilson, K. (2009). Student participation in university governance: The role conceptions and sense of efficacy of student representatives on departmental committees. *Studies in Higher Education*, 34(1), 69–84. DOI: 10.1080/03075070802602000

Machado, M. D. L., & Taylor, J. S. (2010). The struggle for strategic planning in European higher education: The case of Portugal. *Research in Higher Education*.

Mandinach, E. B., & Gummer, E. S. (2016a). *Data literacy for educators: Making it count in teacher preparation and practice*. Teachers College Press.

Mandinach, E. B., & Gummer, E. S. (2016b). What does it mean for teachers to be data literate: Laying out the skills, knowledge, and dispositions. *Teaching and Teacher Education*, 60, 366–376. DOI: 10.1016/j.tate.2016.07.011

Mandinach, E. B., & Jimerson, J. B. (2016). Teachers learning how to use data: A synthesis of the issues and what is known. *Teaching and Teacher Education*, 60, 452–457. DOI: 10.1016/j.tate.2016.07.009

Marshall, S. (2016). *A handbook for leaders in higher education: Transforming teaching and learning*. Routledge. DOI: 10.4324/9781315693798

Matthews, K. E. (2018). Engaging students as participants and partners: An argument for partnership with students in higher education research on student success. *International Journal of Chinese Education*, 7(1), 42–64. DOI: 10.1163/22125868-12340089

McCormick, A. C., Kinzie, J., & Gonyea, R. M. (2013). Student engagement: Bridging research and practice to improve the quality of undergraduate education. In *Higher Education: Handbook of Theory and Research* (Vol. 28, pp. 47–92). Springer Netherlands., DOI: 10.1007/978-94-007-5836-0_2

McNair, D. E., Duree, C. A., & Ebbers, L. (2011). If I knew then what I know now: Using the leadership competencies developed by the American Association of Community Colleges to prepare community college presidents. *Community College Review*, 39(1), 3–25. DOI: 10.1177/0091552110394831

Morrison, J. L. (1992). Environmental scanning. *A primer for new institutional researchers*, 86-99.

Noland, A., & Richards, K. (2015). Servant teaching: An exploration of teacher servant leadership on student outcomes. *The Journal of Scholarship of Teaching and Learning*, 15(6), 16–38. DOI: 10.14434/josotl.v15i6.13928

Northouse, P. G. (2021). *Leadership: Theory and practice*. Sage publications.

Orr, D., Luebcke, M., Schmidt, J. P., Ebner, M., Wannemacher, K., Ebner, M., & Dohmen, D. (2020). *Higher education landscape 2030: A trend analysis based on the ahead international horizon scanning.* Springer Nature., DOI: 10.1007/978-3-030-44897-4

Paris, K. A. (2003). Strategic planning in the university. *University of Wisconsin System Board of Regents, USA.* https://www.uwsa.edu/opar/reports/primer-2003.pdf

Parris, D. L., & Peachey, J. W. (2013). A systematic literature review of servant leadership theory in organizational contexts. *Journal of Business Ethics*, 113(3), 377–393. DOI: 10.1007/s10551-012-1322-6

Paulsen, M. B., & Smart, J. C. (Eds.). (2001). *The finance of higher education: Theory, research, policy, and practice.* Algora Publishing.

Pennington, D. (2008). Cross-Disciplinary Collaboration and Learning. *Ecology and Society*, 13(2), 8. DOI: 10.5751/ES-02520-130208

Plowden, K. O., & Young, A. E. (2003). Sociostructural factors influencing health behaviors of urban African-American men. *Journal of National Black Nurses' Association. Journal of National Black Nurses' Association*, 14(1), 45–51. PMID: 15259998

Pullin, A., & Stewart, G. (2006). Guidelines for Systematic Review in Conservation and Environmental Management. *Conservation Biology*, 20(6), 1647–1656. Advance online publication. DOI: 10.1111/j.1523-1739.2006.00485.x PMID: 17181800

Santamaría, L. J. (2014). Critical change for the greater good: Multicultural perceptions in educational leadership toward social justice and equity. *Educational Administration Quarterly*, 50(3), 347–391. DOI: 10.1177/0013161X13505287

Shapiro, J. P., & Gross, S. J. (2013). *Ethical educational leadership in turbulent times:(Re) solving moral dilemmas.* Routledge. DOI: 10.4324/9780203809310

Sipahioğlu, M. (2020). *Yükseköğretimde kurumsal itibar yönetimi.* İksad Yayınevi.

Smith, W. K. (2014). Dynamic decision making: A model of senior leaders managing strategic paradoxes. *Academy of Management Journal*, 57(6), 1592–1623. DOI: 10.5465/amj.2011.0932

Snively, E. (2021). Diversity, Equity, and Inclusion vs. Social Justice Positioning in Higher Education: Identifying communication strategies that serve both the institution and society. https://doi.org/DOI: 10.17615/m4fv-nk38

Spillane, J. P. (2006). *Distributed Leadership.* Jossey-Bass.

Starratt, R. J. (2005, June). Responsible leadership. In *The educational forum* (Vol. 69, No. 2, pp. 124-133). Taylor & Francis Group. https://doi.org/DOI: 10.1080/00131720508984676

Strayhorn, T. L. (2018). *College students' sense of belonging: A key to educational success for all students*. Routledge. DOI: 10.4324/9781315297293

Taylor-Powell, E., & Henert, E. (2008). Developing a logic model: Teaching and training guide. *Benefits*, 3(22), 1–118.

Tierney, W. G. (2008). *The Impact of Culture on Organizational Decision-Making: Theory and Practice in Higher Education*. Stylus Publishing, LLC.

Tinto, V. (2012). *Leaving college: Rethinking the causes and cures of student attrition*. University of Chicago press.

Torney-Purta, J., Cabrera, J. C., Roohr, K. C., Liu, O. L., & Rios, J. A. (2015). Assessing civic competency and engagement in higher education: Research background, frameworks, and directions for next-generation assessment. *ETS Research Report Series*, 2015(2), 1–48. DOI: 10.1002/ets2.12081

Torres-Coronas, T., Vidal-Blasco, M. A., & Simón-Olmos, M. J. (2014). Aligning educational outcomes to boost employment and workforce employability. In *Handbook of research on education and technology in a changing society* (pp. 407–417). IGI Global., DOI: 10.4018/978-1-4666-6046-5.ch031

Wenger, E. (2011). Communities of practice: A brief introduction. https://www.nsf.gov/pubs/2012/nsf12544/nsf12544.pdf

Wilcox, P., Winn, S., & Fyvie-Gauld, M. (2005). 'It was nothing to do with the university, it was just the people': The role of social support in the first-year experience of higher education. *Studies in Higher Education*, 30(6), 707–722. DOI: 10.1080/03075070500340036

Williams, D. H., Bellis, E. C., & Wellington, S. W. (1980). Deinstitutionalization and social policy: Historical perspectives and present dilemmas. *The American Journal of Orthopsychiatry*, 50(1), 54–64. DOI: 10.1111/j.1939-0025.1980.tb03262.x PMID: 6986789

York, T. T., Gibson, C., & Rankin, S. (2019). Defining and measuring academic success. *Practical Assessment, Research & Evaluation*, 20(1), 5. DOI: 10.7275/hz5x-tx03

Young, M. D. (2015). The leadership challenge: Supporting the learning of all students. *Leadership and Policy in Schools*, 14(4), 389–410. DOI: 10.1080/15700763.2015.1073330

Zepke, N. (2014). Student engagement research in higher education: Questioning an academic orthodoxy. *Teaching in Higher Education*, 19(6), 697–708. DOI: 10.1080/13562517.2014.901956

Zhao, C. M., & Kuh, G. D. (2004). Adding value: Learning communities and student engagement. *Research in Higher Education*, 45(2), 115–138. DOI: 10.1023/B:RI-HE.0000015692.88534.de

KEY TERMS AND DEFINITIONS:

Student Success: Satisfactory participation in academic and extracurricular activities that promote learning and development, leading to outcomes like degree completion.

Leadership Strategies: Approaches and tactics employed by administrators, faculty, and policymakers to guide an institution and influence student success.

Predictive Analytics: Use of data modeling and machine learning algorithms to identify patterns and assess risk factors, enabling early intervention for at-risk students.

Strategic Planning: Systematic process of defining goals and objectives, and aligning actions and resources to achieve them over specified time periods.

Data Literacy: Ability to collect, analyze, and apply insights from institutional data to make evidence-based decisions.

Cultural Competence: Awareness of diversity issues, commitment to promoting inclusion and equity, and capacity to foster supportive campus environments.

Talent Cultivation: Strategies such as mentorship, leadership development, and skills training to maximize the contributions of faculty, staff and administrators over time.

Chapter 7
A Comprehensive Analysis of Servant Leadership's Role in Enhancing School Effectiveness

Athanasios Tsarkos
https://orcid.org/0000-0002-3486-3416
Aegean University, Greece

ABSTRACT

This chapter delves into the transformative potential of Servant Leadership in advancing school effectiveness, exploring its theoretical underpinnings and practical implications within educational settings. By prioritizing empathy, inclusivity, and ethical governance, Servant Leadership fosters environments conducive to the holistic development of students and educators alike. Through a nuanced analysis of relational dynamics, professional development, and organizational health, the text offers insights into overcoming implementation challenges and underscores the model's capacity to navigate the complexities of contemporary education. Looking ahead, it posits a future where Servant Leadership principles guide institutions towards societal contributions, highlighting its role in cultivating a generation of ethical, engaged citizens.

DOI: 10.4018/979-8-3693-9215-7.ch007

INTRODUCTION

In the evolving landscape of educational theory and practice, there is a pressing need to address critical issues affecting school effectiveness, such as student achievement gaps, teacher retention, and the integration of socio-emotional learning. The quest for leadership models that transcend traditional metrics of success and cultivate environments of inclusivity, empathy, and holistic development has become increasingly salient. Within this pursuit lies the exploration of leadership philosophies adept at navigating the complex interplay between fostering academic excellence and nurturing the socio-emotional well-being of the educational community (Krise, 2023). Servant leadership, characterized by its foundational premise of serving others as the core tenet of leadership, proposes an inversion of conventional leadership hierarchies, placing the growth, development, and welfare of individuals and the collective at the heart of its philosophy (D'Ascoli & Piro, 2022; Eva et al., 2019).

The domain of educational effectiveness presents a unique canvas for the application of servant leadership. The dynamics of educational leadership, encompassing the intricate balance between administrative responsibilities and the imperative to foster a nurturing learning environment, underscore the significance of adopting leadership models that champion the holistic development of students, educators, and administrators alike (Bellei et al., 2020). Servant leadership, with its emphasis on empathy, stewardship, and communal growth, offers a compelling lens through which to view and navigate these challenges. It beckons educational leaders to embody principles that not only aspire toward academic excellence but also advocate for the creation of learning environments that are responsive, inclusive, and conducive to the comprehensive development of every member of the school community.

This chapter seeks to delve into the transformative potential of servant leadership in enhancing school effectiveness at the primary and secondary education levels. By focusing on these critical stages of education, the chapter aims to address specific challenges such as student engagement, academic achievement, and the development of socio-emotional skills. It aims to dissect the theoretical foundations of servant leadership within the context of education, elucidate its practical applications in fostering environments of empathy and mutual respect, and explore strategies for surmounting the obstacles to its implementation. Through this exploration, the chapter aspires to offer a roadmap for educational leaders, advocating for a paradigm of leadership that is reflective, empathetic, and undeniably dedicated to serving the holistic needs of students and educators in the complex landscape of contemporary education.

CONCEPTUAL FOUNDATIONS

Defining School Effectiveness

School effectiveness constitutes a pivotal area of inquiry within educational research, oriented towards elucidating the determinants that underpin a school's capacity to deliver quality education and engender favorable student outcomes. This chapter focuses on these issues at the K-12 education level. This domain of study is inherently multifaceted, examining a confluence of both external and internal factors that collectively contribute to the operational efficacy of educational institutions. Notably, the internal dynamics, including aspects such as teacher satisfaction -identified by Duan et al. (2018) as a mediating factor of school effectiveness -underscore the integral role of teacher well-being and contentment in amplifying a school's overall performance. This recognition aligns with the broader understanding that the effectiveness of schools is inexorably linked to the nuances of school culture and climate.

According to Konstantinou (2015), an educational institution's capacity for attaining its designated objectives encapsulates the concept of school effectiveness. He delineates a school's mission through essential inquiries that probe both pedagogical and societal obligations:

- What constitutes the school's foundational mission in fostering educational and societal responsibility?
- How should a school equip its students and contribute to society?

Within the discourse presented by Konstantinou (2015), two prevailing theoretical frameworks emerge concerning the school's mission. The initial perspective, deeply rooted in pedagogical theory, posits that a school is a pivotal institution obligated to impart knowledge and cultivate a student's competencies and skills. This preparation aims to equip students for active and informed participation as future citizens in various economic and social spheres. Conversely, the second perspective prioritizes the necessity of aligning the educational process with the student's needs and interests, advocating for the holistic development of their personas whenever feasible.

Amidst the array of factors influencing school effectiveness, several have been prominently featured in the literature, including the adoption of innovative teaching methodologies (e.g. Breaux et al., 2002), the significance of school leadership and climate (e.g. Huber & Muijs, 2010), and the maintenance of high expectations (e.g. Reynolds, 2010). Additionally, the importance of progress monitoring (e.g. DeMatthews et al., 2020), fostering cooperative relationships among school members (e.g. Bellei et al., 2020), ensuring staff stability (e.g. Hallinger & Heck, 2011), and prioritizing professional development (e.g. Sims & Fletcher-Wood, 2021) further underscores the multifactorial nature of school effectiveness. The conceptualization of schools as learning organizations (e.g. Papazoglou & Koutouzis, 2020) alongside the emphasis on well-being encapsulates the comprehensive approach required to navigate and enhance the complex landscape of school effectiveness.

Principles of Servant Leadership

This foundational premise, meticulously introduced by Robert K. Greenleaf in 1970, pioneers an inversion of the normative leadership hierarchy by suggesting that the essence of true leadership is rooted in a foundational desire to serve rather than to lead (Spears, 1998; Russell & Stone, 2002; Ehrhart, 2004; Liden et al., 2008; Sendjaya et al., 2008; Van Dierendonck, 2011; Chughtai, 2016). The collective body of work by these scholars endeavors to operationalize Greenleaf's conceptualization within diverse organizational contexts, emphasizing the servant leader's inherent dedication to fostering the growth and potential of subordinates above personal gain or prestige (D'Ascoli & Piro, 2022). The relational dynamic underscored by Russell and Stone (2002) and Liden et al. (2008), mirroring Greenleaf's original articulations, posits a leadership style characterized by empathy, foresight, and stewardship.

However, the journey toward a universally accepted operationalization of servant leadership has encountered significant conceptual ambiguities, presenting a challenge for empirical investigations into its efficacy and applicability (Eva et al., 2019; Van Dierendonck, 2011). The lack of a precise definition has historically hindered the advancement of research aimed at unraveling the practical manifestations and outcomes of servant leadership. To navigate these conceptual hurdles, Eva et al. (2019) proposed a definition encapsulating servant leadership as an outward-oriented leadership approach, characterized by a focus on followers' needs and a systemic shift from self-centered motivations to a broader concern for the collective welfare of organizational members and the community.

The principles of servant leadership extend beyond the foundational aspects of empathy, listening, and stewardship, encompassing a broader spectrum of qualities that are essential for a leader who serves first (Owens & Hekman, 2016). Recent empirical studies have reinforced the efficacy of these principles. For instance, research by Chiniara and Bentein (2017) suggests that servant leadership positively impacts organizational citizenship behavior, enhancing employees' willingness to go above and beyond their formal responsibilities. Furthermore, Eva et al. (2019) have consolidated previous findings to suggest that the integration of these principles not only improves individual and organizational performance but also contributes to societal well-being.

Servant leadership, with its emphasis on service, humility, authenticity, and community, offers a transformative approach that challenges conventional leadership paradigms and inspires leaders to foster environments where everyone can excel. Research has shown that servant leadership is a multidimensional construct that can be applied in various contexts, including healthcare, education, and crisis management (Silver & Martín, 2021; Simon et al., 2022). It has been globally embraced as a follower-centered transformational leadership paradigm that values beliefs such as openness, accountability, and a willingness to learn (D'Ascoli & Piro, 2022; Simon et al., 2022). Servant leadership principles have been integrated into different sectors, such as higher education and religious organizations, to reduce turnover intentions, promote learner-centered education, and develop new leaders (Krise, 2023).

Servant leadership has been associated with positive organizational behavior, psychological well-being, and work performance, emphasizing the importance of fairness, radical equality, and supporting organization members to reach their full potential (Hendrikz & Engelbrecht, 2019; Choi, 2021; Ullah, 2021). The concept of servant leadership aligns with ethical principles, emphasizing moral, legal, and normative behavior, and encouraging individuals to act in a similar manner (Choi, 2021). Additionally, servant leadership has been suggested as a tool to achieve sustainable development goals and enhance leaders' performance in various settings (Ogunsola et al., 2020).

Servant Leadership in Educational Settings

In educational contexts, particularly at the primary and secondary levels, the implementation of servant leadership involves a profound reorientation of the roles and relationships between educators, administrators, and students. This approach seeks to address issues such as student engagement, teacher burnout, and the development of a supportive school culture. It eschews hierarchical dynamics and instead promotes a culture of mutual respect, shared responsibility, and collective decision-making. Such an approach not only democratizes the educational process but also significantly enhances the educational experience by making it more responsive to the needs and aspirations of the student body (Aboramadan et al., 2020). The emphasis on fostering an inclusive environment is crucial in higher education where servant leadership is pivotal in enhancing academic outcomes and job satisfaction, underscoring the transformative impact of this leadership style across educational strata (Dami et al., 2022).

One of the cardinal principles of servant leadership in education is the prioritization of students' growth—both academic and personal—over institutional metrics or personal accolades for leaders themselves (Liden et al., 2008). This student-centered focus necessitates that educational leaders exhibit a high degree of empathy, actively listening to and understanding the unique needs and challenges faced by their students. Servant leadership, therefore, enables leaders to create and implement strategies that support students' holistic development, including emotional, social, and ethical dimensions, alongside intellectual growth (D'Ascoli & Piro, 2022). The mediating role of trust and leader-member exchange significantly enhances these outcomes, facilitating a nurturing and supportive educational atmosphere (Feng, 2023).

Servant leadership encourages an ethos of stewardship, where educational leaders see themselves as caretakers of their institution's mission and values. This perspective involves a commitment to sustainable practices, ethical conduct, and the long-term well-being of the educational community. It also calls for a dedication to transparency and accountability, ensuring that the institution's resources are utilized in ways that align with its educational goals and the broader interests of society. The fostering of fair workplace environments and organizational citizenship behaviors under this leadership model is crucial, as it promotes trust among followers and enhances organizational health (Almutairi et al., 2020).

The application of servant leadership in educational settings engenders a strong sense of community. Through the promotion of collaborative practices, shared governance, and open communication, this leadership style fosters a sense of belonging and mutual care among students, faculty, and staff. This environment not only improves the quality of the educational experience but also prepares students to engage in civic life with a sense of responsibility and a commitment to the common good (Tasker-Mitchell & Attoh, 2019).

The servant leadership model advocates for the professional development and empowerment of educators and administrative staff. Recognizing and nurturing the talents and potential of faculty members creates an environment that encourages innovation, continuous learning, and pedagogical excellence. This approach is seen as suitable for academic leaders and significantly impacts student learning experiences, indicating its wide applicability and potential to enhance academic offerings and contribute to a vibrant educational community (Purwaningtyas et al., 2023). Additionally, servant leadership is also instrumental in transforming groups into learning organizations (Tsarkos, 2023). Furthermore, the literature points to its efficacy in enhancing career competencies, adaptability, and psychological safety among employees (Samo et al., 2023).

The impact of servant leadership extends beyond the immediate educational setting, influencing the broader community and society at large. By cultivating leaders who are empathetic, ethical, and committed to serving others, educational institutions can play a pivotal role in addressing societal challenges and contributing to the development of a more just and compassionate world. The characteristics of servant leadership have been identified as essential in various educational settings, including Islamic institutions, suggesting its compatibility with modern educational philosophies (Imaduddin et al., 2022).

In conclusion, the adoption of servant leadership within educational settings represents a comprehensive and transformative approach to leadership and management. It challenges conventional models by placing the needs and well-being of students and the community at the forefront of educational practice. Through its emphasis on empathy, stewardship, and community building, servant leadership not only enriches the educational experience but also fosters the development of responsible, ethical, and engaged citizens. As such, it offers a visionary and effective framework for leadership that aligns with the fundamental values and goals of education.

ENHANCING SCHOOL EFFECTIVENESS THROUGH SERVANT LEADERSHIP

Relational Dynamics

Empathetic Congruence and Comprehension

The influence of servant leadership in enhancing school effectiveness is notably profound when examined through the lenses of empathetic congruence and comprehension. These dimensions underscore the importance of leaders' ability to understand and resonate with the emotional and intellectual needs of their constituents, a principle that is particularly vital in educational settings.

Empathetic congruence refers to the alignment between a leader's empathy towards others and their actions. In the context of K-12 education, servant leaders demonstrate a deep understanding of teachers', students', and parents' emotional and educational needs, addressing key issues such as student motivation, teacher retention, and parental involvement, and facilitating an environment where each individual feels valued and understood. This emotional resonance not only fosters a supportive school culture but also enhances collective efficacy. Servant leadership in education emphasizes the importance of qualities such as empathetic congruence and comprehension. Empathetic congruence involves being genuine, showing unconditional positive regard, and understanding others' perspectives (Guo & Kroll, 2014). This empathetic understanding is crucial in educational settings, especially when working with students (Bugaj et al., 2019). As Laub (2010) notes, the servant leader's focus on understanding and valuing community members' perspectives contributes to a positive school climate, which is a critical factor in school effectiveness.

Comprehension, in this framework, involves the leader's ability to grasp complex educational challenges and navigate them effectively. Servant leaders in schools employ active listening and reflective thinking to understand these challenges, enabling them to develop inclusive and innovative solutions (Khan et al., 2021). Their comprehension of educational dynamics is instrumental in implementing strategies that promote academic excellence and holistic development. Comprehension is vital for effective communication and ensuring that information is understood (Breese et al., 2007). Servant leaders' strategic foresight, grounded in a comprehensive understanding of educational needs and trends, significantly impacts school performance and student outcomes.

In the context of education, the pedagogy of authenticity highlights the significance of congruence as a core condition for meaningful learning and growth (Dietlin et al., 2019). This aligns with the principles of servant leadership, where authenticity and genuine care for others are central tenets. Additionally, the application of human comprehensive development theory in innovative education emphasizes the holistic development of students (Zhang, 2020). This holistic approach resonates with the servant leadership philosophy of serving others' needs and promoting their overall well-being. Furthermore, empirical studies, such as that by Cerit (2009), demonstrate the positive correlation between servant leadership practices in schools and various indicators of school effectiveness, including teacher satisfaction, student achievement, and parental involvement. These findings underscore the role of empathetic congruence and comprehension in cultivating an environment that nurtures academic and social-emotional growth.

In essence, servant leadership's emphasis on empathetic congruence and comprehension not only enriches the educational experience for all stakeholders but also propels schools toward achieving higher levels of effectiveness. Through fostering empathy and understanding, servant leaders in education pave the way for more responsive, inclusive, and adaptive learning environments.

Communicative Transparency and Trustworthiness

Communicative transparency and trustworthiness constitute fundamental pillars in the realm of servant leadership, particularly within the context of education. These elements are critical in forging strong, trust-based relationships between educators and stakeholders, thereby enhancing the overall effectiveness of educational institutions (Joo et al., 2022). Communicative transparency refers to the open and forthright exchange of information, where leaders share knowledge, intentions, and feedback with clarity and honesty. This transparency is pivotal in creating a culture of trust, respect, and mutual understanding within schools, allowing for more effective collaboration and decision-making processes among educators, students, and parents. Servant leadership enhances followers' perceptions of leader trustworthiness, which in turn influences organizational trust levels (Sendjaya & Pekerti, 2010). By demonstrating humility, authenticity, interpersonal acceptance, and stewardship, servant leaders build trust and credibility among their team members (Dierendonck, 2010). This trust is further reinforced by the mediating role of affective and cognitive trust in the relationship between servant leadership and team performance (Schaubroeck et al., 2011).

Trustworthiness, intertwined with communicative transparency, is characterized by leaders' integrity, reliability, and benevolence. In educational settings, a leader's trustworthiness is demonstrated through consistent ethical behavior, the fulfillment of promises, and a genuine commitment to the well-being of the school community (Joo et al., 2022). Such trustworthiness not only reinforces the bonds between faculty and leadership but also cultivates a sense of security and belonging among students and staff, essential for a conducive learning environment. Moreover, servant leadership is associated with job satisfaction, as it fosters trust and positive leader-member exchanges, ultimately leading to increased job satisfaction among employees (Dami et al., 2022). Servant leaders promote openness, transparency, empowerment, and sharing of ownership, fostering a culture of trust and communication (Simon et al., 2022).

The synergy between communicative transparency and trustworthiness enhances the efficacy of servant leadership in schools by fostering an atmosphere where open communication flourishes and ethical leadership is the norm. This environment supports a dynamic educational community where all members feel valued, understood, and engaged, thereby contributing to the overall goal of school effectiveness through improved relational dynamics and educational outcomes.

Communal Cohesion and Inclusivity

Communal cohesion and inclusivity stand as pivotal principles within the framework of servant leadership, particularly in the educational sphere. These concepts emphasize the importance of fostering a sense of belonging and unity among all members of a school community, ensuring that diverse perspectives and backgrounds are not only acknowledged but celebrated. Servant leadership plays a crucial role in promoting communal cohesion by prioritizing the needs, values, and aspirations of teachers, students, and parents alike, thereby creating an environment where every individual feels an integral part of the collective mission.

Servant leadership has been increasingly recognized as a valuable approach in fostering communal cohesion and inclusivity within educational settings. Studies have highlighted the alignment of servant leadership with communal emphases on stakeholders and relationships, indicating potential advantages for job performance, especially through prosocial motivation and follower behaviors (Lemoine & Blum, 2019). This leadership style has been proposed as highly relevant in higher education, emphasizing the importance of serving the community, creating value, and promoting academic excellence (Ghasemy et al., 2021; Dami et al., 2022).

Inclusivity, as a complement to communal cohesion, involves adopting policies and practices that embrace diversity in all its forms, including cultural, linguistic, and socio-economic diversity. By actively seeking to understand and incorporate the unique contributions of each community member, servant leaders enhance the educational experience, making it more enriching and representative of the broader society. This approach not only boosts the morale and engagement of students and staff but also prepares students to thrive in a globalized world.

The implementation of communal cohesion and inclusivity within schools contributes significantly to creating a supportive and positive learning environment. It reduces instances of bullying and discrimination, promotes equity, and fosters mutual respect among students and educators. Ultimately, by embedding these values into the fabric of school culture, servant leaders lay the groundwork for a more empathetic, understanding, and cooperative educational community. Furthermore, servant leadership has been associated with gender-integrative and partnership-oriented leadership principles, emphasizing a sense of community, teamwork, and power-sharing (Reynolds, 2011). These aspects are critical for advancing communal cohesion and fostering an inclusive environment that values and leverages the strengths of all members.

PROFESSIONAL DEVELOPMENT AND EMPOWERMENT

Autonomy and Teacher Empowerment

Within the ambit of enhancing school effectiveness through servant leadership the twin pillars of autonomy and teacher empowerment are seminal (Van der Hoven et al., 2021). This paradigm posits that by vesting educators with the autonomy to navigate curricular and instructional decisions, and by empowering them through sustained support and resources, a conducive atmosphere for pedagogical innovation and student-centric learning is cultivated. Autonomy herein is conceptualized as the degree of self-governance granted to teachers, allowing them the creative freedom to adapt teaching methodologies to the nuanced needs of their students (Khan et al.,

2021). This autonomy is instrumental in fostering a sense of professional agency and intrinsic motivation among educators, which is pivotal for educational excellence.

Empowerment complements autonomy by providing the requisite infrastructural and moral support that enables teachers to actualize their pedagogical strategies effectively. This encompasses not just access to resources and professional development opportunities but also a supportive leadership structure that values teacher input in decision-making processes, thereby enhancing their sense of efficacy and commitment to the educational mission (Georgolopoulos et al., 2018). The interplay between autonomy and empowerment thus nurtures a dynamic educational environment where teachers feel valued and students benefit from highly engaged and motivated educators.

The research underscores that schools embracing this model of autonomy and empowerment not only witness improved educational outcomes but also cultivate a more satisfied and resilient teaching workforce. Such an environment is conducive to innovation, with teachers feeling both capable and motivated to implement instructional practices that best meet their students' learning needs (Khan et al., 2021). Hence, in the broader context of servant leadership within education, fostering teacher autonomy and empowerment is paramount for achieving sustained school effectiveness and transformative educational experiences.

Continual Professional Advancement

Professional development is pivotal in the domain of education, underscoring the essence of ongoing learning and growth for educators (D'Ascoli & Piro, 2022). This commitment not only enriches their professional journey but also significantly elevates the educational experiences provided to students. Within the servant leadership framework, there's a pronounced emphasis on nurturing and empowering teachers, recognizing them as both learners and educators. This leadership style fosters an environment where continual professional advancement is not just encouraged but is seen as integral to the school's ethos.

Servant leadership facilitates the creation of professional development programs specifically designed to meet the evolving needs of educators. These programs are instrumental in equipping teachers with the latest knowledge, teaching strategies, and insights into educational research and technology. Such dedication to continual learning is crucial for fostering innovation and excellence within the educational sphere (Khan et al., 2021), ensuring that educators are well-prepared to navigate the complexities of modern teaching (Darling-Hammond et al., 2017). The impact of servant leadership extends beyond the immediate classroom, influencing various aspects of educational settings including employee resilience, mentoring competencies, and overall job satisfaction, thereby enhancing the educational experience for both teachers and students alike (Peng et al., 2022).

The servant leadership model champions a collaborative learning environment, where teachers share insights, engage in reflective practice, and collectively contribute to the pedagogical community. This collaborative ethos bolsters individual growth and amplifies the collective competency of the teaching staff. By embedding mutual support and continuous improvement into the fabric of the school culture, servant leaders directly influence student achievement and school success. In essence, servant leadership's approach to professional development—centered on empowerment, community building, and addressing individual needs—plays a critical role in preventing educator burnout and fostering a vibrant work environment (Harris & Jones, 2019; Dami et al., 2022).

The overarching goal of continual professional advancement within the servant leadership paradigm is to cultivate a culture of lifelong learning among educators. By prioritizing the professional growth of teachers, servant leaders ensure a dynamic, adaptive, and responsive educational setting conducive to the holistic development of students (D'Ascoli & Piro, 2022). This approach reflects a broader vision of education that values the development of all community members, demonstrating that servant leadership positively impacts not only career satisfaction but also the satisfaction with life among educators, thereby sustaining a healthy and thriving educational ecosystem (Haider et al., 2020).

In sum, the servant leadership framework, with its focus on reflective practices and supporting individuals with minoritized social identities, offers a robust model for enhancing the educational landscape through the continual professional advancement of teachers (Sims, 2018). This integrated approach ensures that educators are not only equipped to meet the demands of their profession but are also empowered to lead with empathy, innovation, and a deep commitment to student success.

Leadership Capacitation

This process involves equipping current and aspiring leaders with the skills, knowledge, and mindset necessary to embody the principles of servant leadership effectively. The aim is to create a culture where leadership is not confined to positional authority but is distributed throughout the organization, empowering every educator and staff member to take on leadership roles in their respective domains. The concept of leadership capacitation underscores the belief that leadership potential exists within every individual, and with the right support and opportunities, this potential can be unleashed to contribute positively to the school's mission and vision. This involves comprehensive professional development programs that go beyond traditional leadership training to include mentoring, coaching, and experiential learning opportunities. These programs are designed to foster key servant leadership qualities such as empathy, active listening, stewardship, and a commitment to the growth of others (Liden et al., 2008; Spears, 1998).

Leadership capacitation emphasizes the importance of reflective practice as a tool for personal and professional growth. Leaders are encouraged to engage in continuous self-assessment and reflection to deepen their understanding of their leadership style and its impact on others. This reflective process is crucial for cultivating the self-awareness and humility that are hallmark traits of effective servant leaders (van Dierendonck & Patterson, 2015). By investing in leadership capacitation, schools can build a resilient leadership pipeline that ensures continuity and stability in leadership roles. This approach also fosters a collaborative and inclusive school culture, where decision-making is shared and all voices are valued. The distributed leadership model, inherent in leadership capacitation, enhances the organizational capacity to innovate, adapt, and respond effectively to the diverse needs of students and the broader school community (Harris, & Jones, 2019).

In essence, leadership capacitation within the servant leadership paradigm is a strategic investment in the human capital of educational institutions. It prepares educators not only to lead with competence and confidence but also to inspire and nurture the next generation of leaders.

ORGANIZATIONAL HEALTH AND CLIMATE

Positive Educational Milieu

A positive educational milieu, as a fundamental aspect of a thriving academic setting at the primary and secondary levels, emerges distinctly within the framework of servant leadership, which is centered around nurturing and prioritizing the holistic welfare of the educational community. This approach aims to tackle challenges like bullying, diversity, and student well-being. Servant leaders, with their profound commitment to the emotional and intellectual flourishing of all members—students, teachers, and staff alike—meticulously cultivate an atmosphere imbued with trust, mutual respect, and a deep-seated sense of value and motivation for each individual. Such a meticulously crafted environment not only significantly amplifies student engagement and elevates academic outcomes but also plays a pivotal role in retaining teachers by nurturing a profound sense of professional satisfaction and a feeling of belonging within the educational ecosystem.

The strategic emphasis placed on empathy, coupled with the practice of active listening by servant leaders, transforms the educational setting into a sanctuary conducive to both effective teaching and profound learning experiences. This not only substantiates the educational milieu as a critical element in bolstering the overall school effectiveness and efficiency but also highlights the indispensable role of servant leadership in fostering an educational atmosphere where the collective welfare and development of the school community are placed at the forefront. Through such leadership, the educational milieu becomes not just a backdrop for academic pursuits but a vibrant, dynamic space where growth, learning, and mutual respect flourish, thereby ensuring the sustenance and enhancement of school effectiveness.

Conflict Resolution and Harmonious Cohabitation

The servant leadership paradigm champions a resolution process that emphasizes empathy, active engagement, and a deep commitment to mutual understanding. This philosophy is built on the foundation that true resolution comes from addressing the root causes of conflict with compassion and a genuine desire for peace (Obi et al., 2021). Servant leaders, by embodying these principles, serve as exemplars of effective communication and problem-solving, thereby fostering a climate where disputes are viewed as opportunities for growth and deeper understanding.

In this context, servant leadership facilitates an educational atmosphere where every member feels heard, respected, and valued, creating a sense of security and trust (Eva et al., 2019). This trust, in turn, encourages individuals to express their concerns openly, knowing that issues will be approached with fairness and a focus on equitable solutions. Such an environment not only enhances the relational dynamics within the school but also significantly contributes to a positive learning atmosphere conducive to student success. Moreover, the commitment to harmonious cohabitation underlines the importance of a united school community, where diversity is celebrated and differences are bridged through dialogue and shared goals. Servant leaders actively work to cultivate an inclusive culture that transcends individual differences, fostering a sense of belonging and unity among all stakeholders. This inclusive approach not only mitigates conflicts but also strengthens the fabric of the school community, ensuring resilience in the face of challenges (Jit et al., 2016).

Ultimately, the practice of conflict resolution and harmonious cohabitation within the servant leadership model is a testament to the transformative power of leading by example (Innocentina-Marie et al., 2020). Through their dedication to understanding, reconciliation, and mutual respect, servant leaders create a fertile ground for a thriving educational community. This proactive and compassionate stance on conflict resolution ensures that the school remains a nurturing space where every individual can achieve their fullest potential, underscoring the indispensable role of servant leadership in enhancing school effectiveness and fostering a harmonious educational milieu.

Innovation and Adaptability

Innovation and adaptability stand as pivotal pillars for educational institutions endeavoring to align with the dynamic requisites of their students and the expansive educational sphere. Within the framework of servant leadership, these attributes flourish, driven by a profound commitment to the collective well-being and growth of the school community. Servant leadership, with its foundational ethos of altruism and service, inherently fosters an organizational culture ripe for innovation (Khan et al., 2021). This leadership style empowers educators and learners alike, encouraging them to venture into the exploration of novel ideas, pedagogies, and methodologies, thereby sowing the seeds of creativity and innovation across the educational landscape.

Empowerment in education is closely tied to creating a nurturing environment that celebrates risk-taking and experimentation. This environment is crucial, as it enables teachers and students to transcend traditional educational paradigms and embrace the uncertainties and potential of innovation. Encouraging risk-taking is supported by a robust system that alleviates the fear of failure, positioning innovation as a vital aspect of the educational process (Khan et al., 2021). Additionally, the adaptability of educational institutions is greatly enhanced through servant leadership, a model characterized by a steadfast commitment to continuous learning and self-improvement at both individual and institutional levels. Servant leaders foster a culture of adaptability by embodying lifelong learning, ensuring the institution remains agile and responsive to evolving educational challenges and societal demands. This adaptability is anticipatory, allowing schools to proactively address future trends and shifts in the educational landscape.

Overall, innovation and adaptability, as nurtured by servant leadership, are indispensable for the sustained effectiveness and relevance of educational institutions in an increasingly complex and rapidly changing world (Khan et al., 2021). Through fostering a culture that values creative exploration and is resilient in the face of change, servant leaders ensure that schools can continue to provide a high-quality, relevant, and engaging education that meets the needs of all students. This approach not only enhances the immediate learning environment but also prepares students and educators to thrive in a future marked by continuous change and innovation.

STUDENT-CENTERED OUTCOMES IN THE CONTEXT OF SERVANT LEADERSHIP

Scholastic Achievement

The influence of servant leadership on scholastic achievement is profound, albeit indirect. By prioritizing the creation of optimal learning environments and fostering the holistic development of learners, servant leadership sets the stage for academic excellence. This leadership style cultivates an atmosphere where students are encouraged to explore, question, and assimilate knowledge in a manner that resonates with their intrinsic motivations and learning styles (McQuade et al., 2020). Furthermore, by addressing the individual needs of students and ensuring they feel valued and understood, servant leaders enhance students' ability to focus, persist, and excel academically. Thus, the servant leadership approach indirectly but significantly bolsters scholastic achievement by nurturing an educational setting ripe for intellectual engagement and discovery (Topal, 2022).

Socio-Emotional Flourishing

Servant leadership profoundly impacts the socio-emotional well-being of students by creating a supportive and empathetic school culture (Balti & Karoui Zouaoui, 2023). The emphasis on understanding and meeting the emotional needs of students fosters a sense of security and belonging, which are crucial for socio-emotional development. Through servant leadership, students are encouraged to develop resilience, empathy, and robust interpersonal skills—qualities essential for navigating the complexities and challenges of the modern world. This focus on socio-emotional well-being equips students not only for academic success but also for life beyond the classroom, preparing them to become compassionate, adaptable, and emotionally intelligent individuals (Balti & Karoui Zouaoui, 2023).

Engaged Participation

Under the guidance of servant leadership, students are encouraged to take an active role in school governance and participate in extracurricular activities (Topal, 2022). This engagement is not merely about involvement in additional activities but signifies a deeper level of educational investment and ownership over the learning experience. By involving students in decision-making processes and offering opportunities for leadership and collaboration outside the traditional academic curriculum, servant leaders foster a sense of responsibility and community among students (Topal, 2022). Such engaged participation enhances the vibrancy of the school community, promoting a culture where students are motivated to contribute positively and take initiative in their educational journey and beyond.

In conclusion, servant leadership ensures that students are not only academically prepared but also emotionally and socially equipped to meet the demands and opportunities of the future, thereby embodying the true essence of comprehensive education.

STRATEGIC VISION AND INSTITUTIONAL INTEGRITY

Visionary Stewardship

Within the academic echelons of leadership at the K-12 level, visionary stewardship epitomizes the strategic foresight and judicious administration of educational resources, aimed at actualizing the institution's overarching aspirations. It embodies the development and promulgation of an aspirational vision that synergizes with the institution's foundational ethos and objectives. This stewardship is underscored by a proactive, forward-looking leadership philosophy, wherein leaders not only prognosticate the future contours of the educational sector but also adeptly maneuver the institution to optimally engage with forthcoming challenges and opportunities. Such an approach ensures the harmonization of institutional goals, resources, and endeavors, directing them towards achieving sustained academic distinction and operational relevance.

Ethical Governance

Ethical Governance within the sphere of educational administration signifies a steadfast commitment to the principles of justice, transparency, and accountability that govern decision-making and administrative protocols. This dimension of institutional integrity is anchored in the establishment of rigorous ethical frameworks that dictate the conduct of the school's constituents, fostering an environment steeped in moral rectitude. By prioritizing ethical governance, leaders cultivate an ethos of integrity, where ethical quandaries are navigated with an unwavering allegiance to ethical standards and the collective well-being of the educational community. Such dedication to principled leadership not only preserves the institution's credibility but also fortifies its foundational trustworthiness, a critical pillar for enduring institutional success.

Sustainability and Legacy Planning

Sustainability and legacy planning in the context of educational strategy involves insightful anticipation and planning for the institution's long-term viability and impact. This strategy encompasses a commitment to multifaceted sustainability—environmental, financial, and communal—guaranteeing the institution's capacity to serve successive generations effectively. Legacy planning transcends the immediacy of scholastic achievement to encompass a broader contribution toward societal betterment and the cultivation of a sustainable future. This expansive view implicates educational institutions in the duty of not only championing academic excellence but also advancing societal welfare and sustainable development, thereby enshrining a lasting legacy that reverberates through the annals of educational history.

Table 1. Enhancing School Effectiveness through Servant Leadership

Dimensions	Sub-Dimensions	Synopsis
Relational Dynamics	Empathetic Congruence and Comprehension	Foster leaders' ability to deeply understand and connect with the emotions and intellectual needs of the school community.
	Communicative Transparency and Trustworthiness	Promote open sharing of knowledge and feedback to build a foundation of trust and mutual understanding.
	Communal Cohesion and Inclusivity	Encourage practices that enhance the sense of belonging and unity among school community members, embracing diversity.
Professional Development and Empowerment	Autonomy and Teacher Empowerment	Encourage autonomy and provide resources and support for educators to innovate and engage students effectively.
	Continual Professional Advancement	Implement ongoing professional development to keep teachers informed, motivated, and proficient in the latest educational practices.
Organizational Health and Climate	Positive Educational Milieu	Cultivate an environment that promotes mutual respect, engagement, and academic excellence.
	Conflict Resolution and Harmonious Cohabitation	Develop and implement strategies for effective conflict resolution that promote a cohesive and harmonious school climate.
	Innovation and Adaptability	Encourage a culture of innovation that embraces change and seeks continuous improvement in educational practices.

continued on following page

Table 1. Continued

Dimensions	Sub-Dimensions	Synopsis
Student-Centered Outcomes	Scholastic Achievement	Enhance academic excellence through supportive learning environments and personalized educational strategies.
	Socio-Emotional Flourishing	Support the development of students' socio-emotional skills, resilience, and well-being.
	Engaged Participation	Promote active student involvement in school governance and extracurricular activities for a richer educational experience.
Strategic Vision and Institutional Integrity	Visionary Stewardship	Develop and articulate a clear, forward-looking vision that aligns with the institution's goals and community values.
	Ethical Governance	Emphasize ethical decision-making, transparency, and accountability in all leadership actions and policies.
	Sustainability and Legacy Planning	Plan for the long-term sustainability of the institution, focusing on environmental, financial, and community impact.

NAVIGATING SCHOOL EFFECTIVENESS: CHALLENGES ENCOUNTERED BY SERVANT LEADERS AND RECOMMENDATIONS

The endeavor to institutionalize servant leadership within K-12 educational paradigms encounters multifarious challenges, each necessitating strategic and nuanced responses to facilitate its effective integration and realization of its full potential in enhancing school effectiveness. First among these challenges is the pervasive adherence to traditional hierarchical and autocratic leadership models, which starkly contrasts with the servant leadership ethos that prioritizes service over authority (Krise, 2023). This paradigmatic dissonance necessitates a deliberate cultural recalibration within educational institutions, fostering a milieu that embraces the ethos of servant leadership as a normative guiding principle. In addressing this, a concerted effort towards cultivating a broad-based institutional commitment to servant leadership is imperative. This can be achieved through the development and dissemination of a shared vision that clearly articulates the value and principles of servant leadership, coupled with a comprehensive change management strategy designed to facilitate the transition towards a more inclusive and collaborative leadership culture (D'Ascoli & Piro, 2022).

A second challenge lies in the paucity of tailored professional development opportunities that specifically aim to nurture the competencies requisite for effective servant leadership. The complexity and nuance of servant leadership demand a sophisticated understanding of its principles and practices, a gap that existing professional development programs often fail to bridge adequately. To surmount this, there is a pressing need for the design and implementation of bespoke professional development initiatives that are meticulously tailored to the exigencies of servant leadership in educational settings. These programs should encompass a blend of theoretical exploration and practical application, ensuring that educational leaders are both cognitively and experientially prepared to embody servant leadership in their professional praxis (Krise, 2023).

The challenge of quantifying the impact of servant leadership on school effectiveness presents a significant obstacle. The inherently qualitative benefits of servant leadership, such as enhanced school climate and socio-emotional development, elude easy quantification, rendering it difficult to empirically substantiate its efficacy within the prevailing data-driven educational policy landscape. In response to this challenge, the development of innovative metrics and evaluation frameworks that adeptly capture the multidimensional impact of servant leadership is crucial. These frameworks should integrate both qualitative and quantitative methodologies to provide a holistic assessment of servant leadership's efficacy, facilitating a more nuanced understanding of its contributions to school effectiveness.

Furthermore, the integration of servant leadership within educational institutions often encounters resistance due to entrenched institutional norms and individual skepticism. Overcoming this resistance necessitates a strategic approach that emphasizes stakeholder engagement and the demonstration of servant leadership's tangible benefits to the school community. To this end, it is recommended that institutions adopt a phased implementation strategy that allows for the gradual introduction of servant leadership practices, coupled with robust communication efforts that transparently articulate the rationale, processes, and anticipated outcomes of this transformative leadership model.

Lastly, the sustainability of servant leadership initiatives poses a challenge, given the potential for fluctuation in leadership and educational policy priorities. Ensuring the long-term integration and practice of servant leadership requires the establishment of structural supports and policies that institutionalize its principles within the fabric of educational governance and operational modalities. Addressing this challenge calls for the embedding of servant leadership principles into the strategic planning processes and policy frameworks of educational institutions. This could involve the integration of servant leadership competencies into leadership evaluation criteria, the incorporation of servant leadership principles into curriculum and pedagogical standards, and the establishment of servant leadership as a core component of school culture and ethos.

By meticulously addressing these challenges with strategic and thoughtfully crafted responses, educational institutions can effectively harness the transformative potential of servant leadership to enhance school effectiveness, thereby contributing to the cultivation of a more equitable, responsive, and empowering educational landscape.

Table 2. Complexities and Strategic Interventions: Enhancing School Effectiveness through Servant Leadership

Challenges	Strategic Recommendations
Adherence to Traditional Leadership Models	Cultivate an institutional commitment to servant leadership through shared vision development and change management strategies to transition towards inclusive leadership cultures.
Lack of Tailored Professional Development	Design bespoke professional development programs that combine theoretical exploration and practical application, specifically tailored to the demands of servant leadership in education.
Quantifying Impact on School Effectiveness	Develop innovative metrics and evaluation frameworks that integrate both qualitative and quantitative methodologies to holistically assess the efficacy of servant leadership.
Resistance to Change	Adopt phased implementation strategies for servant leadership practices and enhance stakeholder engagement through transparent communication of benefits and processes.
Sustainability of Initiatives	Embed servant leadership principles into strategic planning, policy frameworks, and school culture to ensure long-term integration and practice within educational institutions.

PROSPECTIVE TRAJECTORIES OF SERVANT LEADERSHIP IN NAVIGATING CONFLICT DYNAMICS

The future trajectory of servant leadership within K-12 education is poised to embody a transformative shift, characterized by a deeper integration of ethical and inclusive leadership practices that prioritize the holistic development of all stakeholders. This shift will address pressing issues such as equity, inclusion, and student-centered learning, ensuring that educational institutions are equipped to meet the challenges of a diverse and rapidly changing world. This evolving paradigm is anticipated to be driven by an increasing recognition of the interconnectedness of educational outcomes and the socio-emotional well-being of students, educators, and communities. As educational institutions increasingly embrace servant leadership, a marked shift towards more empathetic, responsive, and community-oriented educational environments is expected, fostering spaces where mutual respect, collaboration, and a shared sense of purpose thrive (Krise, 2023).

In this emerging landscape, the role of technology and digital platforms in facilitating servant leadership practices is likely to expand, offering novel avenues for enhancing communication, professional development, and stakeholder engagement. The digitalization of education, accelerated by global challenges such as the COVID-19 pandemic, presents both opportunities and challenges for servant leadership. On one hand, it offers the potential to democratize access to educational resources and leadership development; on the other hand, it necessitates a reevaluation of how servant leadership principles are applied in increasingly virtual learning environments of Education 4.0.

The imperative for educational systems to address complex global issues, including sustainability, equity, and social justice, will further entrench the relevance of servant leadership. By fostering leaders who are deeply attuned to the ethical dimensions of their roles and committed to serving the greater good, educational institutions can become catalysts for societal transformation. This aligns with the broader trend towards sustainability and social responsibility in education, highlighting the role of servant leaders in championing initiatives that contribute to the well-being of the planet and future generations.

In sum, the future of servant leadership in education is intrinsically linked to the evolving demands of a rapidly changing world. As educational institutions navigate these shifts, the principles of servant leadership - emphasizing empathy, stewardship, and community engagement - will be increasingly central to their mission, shaping a future where education not only imparts knowledge but also cultivates wisdom, compassion, and a commitment to the collective good.

CONCLUSIONS

This chapter has explored the transformative role of servant leadership in enhancing school effectiveness, particularly within K-12 education. By prioritizing empathy, inclusivity, and ethical practices, servant leadership directly addresses key issues such as academic achievement, teacher satisfaction, and socio-emotional learning. The application of servant leadership principles fosters positive school climates, improves relational dynamics, and empowers educators through professional development, ultimately leading to improved student outcomes and a more engaged school community. By embedding servant leadership into educational practices, schools can navigate challenges such as resource allocation, diversity, and resistance to change, creating environments where students and educators thrive. This approach not only elevates academic standards but also promotes holistic development, ensuring that schools fulfill their mission to nurture well-rounded, ethical, and engaged citizens.

The chapter outlines strategic recommendations for implementing servant leadership to sustain its positive impact on school effectiveness, paving the way for educational institutions to adapt and excel in a rapidly changing world. Servant leadership thus emerges as a compelling framework for educational excellence, aligning with contemporary demands for equity, innovation, and community engagement in schools.

REFERENCES

Aboramadan, M., Dahleez, K. A., & Hamad, M. H. (2020). Servant leadership and academics outcomes in higher education: The role of job satisfaction. *The International Journal of Organizational Analysis*, 29(3), 562–584. DOI: 10.1108/ijoa-11-2019-1923

Balti, M., & Karoui Zouaoui, S. (2023). Employee and manager's emotional intelligence and individual adaptive performance: The role of servant leadership climate. *Journal of Management Development*, 43(1), 13–34. DOI: 10.1108/JMD-04-2021-0117

Barbuto, J. E., & Wheeler, D. W. (2006). Scale development and construct clarification of servant leadership. *Group & Organization Management*, 31(3), 300–326. DOI: 10.1177/1059601106287091

Bellei, C., Morawietz, L., Valenzuela, J. P., & Vanni, X. (2020). Effective schools 10 years on: Factors and processes enabling the sustainability of school effectiveness. *School Effectiveness and School Improvement*, 31(2), 266–288. DOI: 10.1080/09243453.2019.1652191

Breaux, G., Danridge, J., & Pearson, P. D. (2002). Scott Elementary School: Homegrown school improvement in the flesh. In Taylor, B. M., & Pearson, P. D. (Eds.), *Teaching reading: Effective schools, accomplished teachers* (pp. 217–236). Lawrence Erlbaum.

Breese, P., Burman, W. J., Goldberg, S., & Weis, S. E. (2007). Education level, primary language, and comprehension of the informed consent process. *Journal of Empirical Research on Human Research Ethics; JERHRE*, 2(4), 69–79. DOI: 10.1525/jer.2007.2.4.69

Bugaj, T. J., Blohm, M., Schmid, C., Koehl, N., Huber, J., Huhn, D., Herzog, W., Krautter, M., & Nikendei, C. (2019). Peer-assisted learning (PAL): Skills lab tutors' experiences and motivation. *BMC Medical Education*, 19, 353. DOI: 10.1186/s12909-019-1760-2

Cerit, Y. (2009). The Effects of Servant Leadership Behaviours of School Principals on Teachers' Job Satisfaction. *Educational Management Administration & Leadership*, 37(5), 600–623. DOI: 10.1177/1741143209339650

Chiniara, M., & Bentein, K. (2017). The servant leadership advantage: When perceiving low differentiation in leader-member relationship quality influences team cohesion, team task performance, and service OCB. *The Leadership Quarterly*, 29(3), 333–345. DOI: 10.1016/j.leaqua.2017.05.002

Choi, H. (2021). Effect of chief executive officer's sustainable leadership styles on organization members' psychological well-being and organizational citizenship behavior. *Sustainability*, 13(24), 13676. DOI: 10.3390/su132413676

Chughtai, A. A. (2016). Servant leadership and follower outcomes: Mediating effects of organizational identification and psychological safety. *The Journal of Psychology*, 150(7), 11–15. DOI: 10.1080/00223980.2016.1170657

D'Ascoli, S., & Piro, J. (2022). Educational servant-leaders and personal growth. *Journal of School Leadership*, 33(1), 26–49. DOI: 10.1177/10526846221134001

Dami, Z. A., Imron, A., & Supriyanto, A. (2022). Servant leadership and job satisfaction: The mediating role of trust and leader-member exchange. *Frontiers in Education*, 7. Advance online publication. DOI: 10.3389/feduc.2022.1036668

Darling-Hammond, L., Hyler, M. E., & Gardner, M. (2017). *Effective Teacher Professional Development*. Learning Policy Institute.

DeMatthews, D., Billingsley, B., McLeskey, J., & Sharma, U. (2020). Principal leadership for students with disabilities in effective inclusive schools. *Journal of Educational Administration*, 58(5), 539–554.

Dietlin, O. R., Loomis, J. S., & Preffer, J. (2019). Pedagogy of authenticity in the online learning environment: An interdisciplinary overview. In Kyei-Blankson, L., Blankson, J., & Ntuli, E. (Eds.), *Care and Culturally Responsive Pedagogy in Online Settings* (pp. 214–229)., DOI: 10.4018/978-1-5225-7802-4.ch011

Duan, X., Du, X., & Yu, K. (2018). School culture and school effectiveness: The mediating effect of teachers' job satisfaction. *International Journal of Learning. Teaching and Educational Research*, 17(5), 15–25. DOI: 10.26803/ijlter.17.5.2

Ehrhart, M. G. (2004). Leadership and procedural justice climate as antecedents of unit-level organizational citizenship behavior. *Personnel Psychology*, 57(1), 61–94. DOI: 10.1111/ j.1744-6570.2004.tb02484.x

Eva, N., Robin, M., Sendjaya, S., Van Dierendonck, D., & Liden, R. C. (2019). Servant leadership: A systematic review and call for future research. *The Leadership Quarterly*, 30(1), 111–132. DOI: 10.1016/j.leaqua.2018.07.004

Gao, R., & Li, B. (2023). Avoiding the scenario of "The farmer and the snake": The dark side of servant leadership and an intervention mechanism. *Journal of Managerial Psychology*, 38(4), 289–302. DOI: 10.1108/JMP-02-2022-0062

Georgolopoulos, V., Papaloi, E., & Loukorou, K. (2018). Servant leadership as a predictive factor of teachers' job satisfaction. *European Journal of Education*, 1(2), 15. DOI: 10.26417/ejed.v1i2.p15-28

Ghasemy, M., Mohajer, L., Frömbling, L., & Karimi, M. (2021). Faculty members in polytechnics to serve the community and industry: Conceptual skills and creating value for the community—the two main drivers. *SAGE Open*, 11(3), 215824402110475. DOI: 10.1177/21582440211047568

Greenleaf, R. K. (1970). *Center for Applied Studies.*

Greenleaf, R. K. (2002). *Servant leadership: A journey into the nature of legitimate power and greatness.* Paulist Press.

Guo, Y., & Kroll, B. M. (2014). A review of studies on Rogerian rhetoric and its implications for English writing instruction in East Asian countries. *Theory and Practice in Language Studies*, 4(3), 481–488. DOI: 10.4304/tpls.4.3.481-488

Haider, A., Khan, M. A., & Taj, T. (2020). Impact of servant leadership on teaching effectiveness: A study of public sector universities, KP, Pakistan. *Global Regional Review*, V(I), 509–518. DOI: 10.31703/grr.2020(v-i).54

Harris, A., & Jones, M. (2019). Leading professional learning with impact. *School Leadership & Management*, 39(1), 1–4. DOI: 10.1080/13632434.2018.1530892

Hendrikz, K., & Engelbrecht, A. (2019). The principled leadership scale: An integration of value-based leadership. *SA Journal of Industrial Psychology*, 45. Advance online publication. DOI: 10.4102/sajip.v45i0.1553

Huber, S. G., & Muijs, D. (2010). School leadership effectiveness: The growing insight into the importance of school leadership for the quality and development of schools and their pupils. In S. Huber (Ed.), *School Leadership - International Perspectives (Studies in Educational Leadership*, vol. 10). Springer, Dordrecht. https://doi.org/DOI: 10.1007/978-90-481-3501-1_4

Imaduddin, I., Putra, H. G., Tukiyo, T., Wahab, A., & Nurulloh, A. (2022). The effect of servant leadership on the quality of education through the characteristics of millennial teachers. Al-Tanzim. *Jurnal Manajemen Pendidikan Islam*, 6(4), 1092–1102. DOI: 10.33650/al-tanzim.v6i4.4069

Innocentina-Marie, O., Bollen, K., Aaldering, H., Robijn, W., & Euwema, M. (2020). Servant leadership, third-party behavior, and emotional exhaustion of followers. *Negotiation and Conflict Management Research.* Advance online publication. DOI: 10.1111/ncmr.12184

Jehn, K. A. (1997). A qualitative analysis of conflict types and dimensions in organizational groups. *Administrative Science Quarterly*, 42(3), 530. DOI: 10.2307/2393737

Jehn, K. A., Greer, L. L., Levine, S. S., & Szulanski, G. (2008). The effects of conflict types, dimensions, and emergent states on group outcomes. *Group Decision and Negotiation*, 17(6), 465–495. DOI: 10.1007/s10726-008-9107-0

Jit, R., Sharma, C. S., & Kawatra, M. (2016). Servant leadership and conflict resolution: A qualitative study. *International Journal of Conflict Management*, 27(4), 591–612. DOI: 10.1108/ijcma-12-2015-0086

Jit, R., Sharma, C. S., & Kawatra, M. (2017). Healing a broken spirit: Role of servant leadership. *Vikalpa*, 42(2), 80–94. DOI: 10.1177/0256090917703754

Joo, B., Yoon, S. K., & Galbraith, D. D. (2022). The effects of organizational trust and empowering leadership on group conflict: Psychological safety as a mediator. *Organizational Management Journal*, 20(1), 4–16. DOI: 10.1108/omj-07-2021-1308

Khan, M. M., Mubarik, M. S., Islam, T., Rehman, A., Ahmed, S. S., Khan, E., Khattak, M. N., Asghar, Z., Mumtaz, F., & Sohail, F.. (2021). How servant leadership triggers innovative work behavior: Exploring the sequential mediating role of psychological empowerment and job crafting. *European Journal of Innovation Management*, 25(4), 1037–1055. DOI: 10.1108/ejim-09-2020-0367

Konstantinou, C. (2015). *To kalo sxoleio, o ikanos ekpaideutikos kai i katallili agogi os pedagogiki theoria kai praksi* [The effective school, the competent teacher, and the appropriate education as pedagogical theory and practice]. Gutenberg.

Krise, R. (2023). Faculty perceptions of how their altruistic and servant teaching behaviors influence student learning. *International Journal of Responsible Leadership and Ethical Decision-Making*, 5(1), 1–14. DOI: 10.4018/ijrledm.317372

Langhof, J. G., & Güldenberg, S. (2020). Servant leadership: A systematic literature review—toward a model of antecedents and outcomes. *German Journal of Human Resource Management*, 34(1), 32–68. DOI: 10.1177/2397002219869903

Laub, J. (2010). The servant organization. In van Dierendonck, D., & Patterson, K. (Eds.), *Servant Leadership*. Palgrave Macmillan., DOI: 10.1057/9780230299184_9

Lemoine, G. J., & Blum, T. C. (2019). Servant leadership, leader gender, and team gender role: Testing a female advantage in a cascading model of performance. *Personnel Psychology*, 74(1), 3–28. DOI: 10.1111/peps.12379

Liden, R. C., Wayne, S. J., Zhao, H., & Henderson, D. (2008). Servant leadership: Development of a multidimensional measure and multi-level assessment. *The Leadership Quarterly*, 19(2), 161–177. DOI: 10.1016/j.leaqua.2008.01.006

Markey, K., Prosen, M., Martin, E., & Repo Jamal, H. (2021). Fostering an ethos of cultural humility development in nurturing inclusiveness and effective intercultural team working. *Journal of Nursing Management*, 29(8), 2724–2728. DOI: 10.1111/jonm.13429

McQuade, K., Harrison, C., & Tarbert, H. (2020). Systematically reviewing servant leadership. *European Business Review*, 33(3), 465–490. DOI: 10.1108/ebr-08-2019-0162

Obi, I., Bollen, K., Aaldering, H., & Euwema, M. (2021). Servant and authoritarian leadership, and leaders' third-party conflict behavior in convents. *International Journal of Conflict Management*, 32(5), 769–790. DOI: 10.1108/ijcma-02-2021-0027

Ogunsola, K. O., Sarif, S. M., & Fonatine, R. A. (2020). Islamic performance instrument: An alternative servant leadership tool for sustainable development goals. *International Journal of Islamic Business Ethics*, 5(1), 1. DOI: 10.30659/ijibe.5.1.1-20

Owens, B. P., & Hekman, D. R. (2016). How does leader humility influence team performance? Exploring the mechanisms of contagion and collective promotion focus. *Academy of Management Journal*, 59(3), 1088–1111. DOI: 10.5465/amj.2013.0660

Papazoglou, A., & Koutouzis, M. (2020). Schools as learning organizations in Greece: Measurement and first indications. *European Journal of Education*, 55(1), 43–57. DOI: 10.1111/ejed.12380

Peng, A. C., Gao, R., & Wang, B. (2023). Linking servant leadership to follower emotional exhaustion through impression management. *Journal of Organizational Behavior*, 44(4), 643–659. DOI: 10.1002/job.2682

Purwaningtyas, E. K., Arifin, Z., Aghniacakti, A., & Hawabi, A. I. (2023). Characteristics of servant leadership in Islamic educational institutions. In *Proceedings of the First Conference of Psychology and Flourishing Humanity (PFH 2022)* (pp. 286-292). DOI: 10.2991/978-2-38476-032-9_29

Reynolds, D. (2010). *School effectiveness*. A&C Black.

Reynolds, K. (2011). Servant-leadership as gender-integrative leadership. *Journal of Leadership Education*, 10(2), 155–171. DOI: 10.12806/v10/i2/rf8

Russell, R. F., & Stone, A. G. (2002). A review of servant leadership attributes: Developing a practical model. *Leadership and Organization Development Journal,* 23(3), 145–157. DOI: 10.1108/01437730210424

Schaubroeck, J., Lam, S. S. K., & Peng, A. C. (2011). Cognition-based and affect-based trust as mediators of leader behavior influences on team performance. *The Journal of Applied Psychology,* 96(4), 863–871. DOI: 10.1037/a0022625

Sendjaya, S., & Pekerti, A. A. (2010). Servant leadership as antecedent of trust in organizations. *Leadership and Organization Development Journal,* 31(7), 643–663. DOI: 10.1108/01437731011079673

Sendjaya, S., Sarros, J. C., & Santora, J. C. (2008). Defining and measuring servant leadership behavior in organizations. *Journal of Management Studies,* 45(2), 402–424. DOI: https://doi.org/10. 1111/j.1467-6486.2007.00761.x

Silver, R., & Martín, M. C. R. d. (2021). Servant leadership and its association with an environment of empathic care: An empirical analysis of the perspectives of mid-level practitioners. *Leadership in Health Services,* 35(1), 116–136. DOI: 10.1108/LHS-06-2021-0052

Sims, C., & Morris, L. R. (2018). Are women business owners authentic servant leaders? *Gender in Management,* 33(5), 405–427. DOI: 10.1108/GM-01-2018-0003

Sims, S., Fletcher-Wood, H., O'Mara-Eves, A., Cottingham, S., Stansfield, C., Van Herwegen, J., & Anders, J. (2021). *What are the characteristics of teacher professional development that increase pupil achievement? A systematic review and meta-analysis.* Education Endowment Foundation.

Spears, L. (1998). *Insights on leadership: Service, stewardship, spirit, and servant leadership.* Wiley.

Tasker-Mitchell, A., & Attoh, P. A. (2019). The mediating effect of faculty trust in principals on the relationship between servant leadership practices and organizational health. *Journal of School Leadership,* 30(4), 297–336. DOI: 10.1177/1052684619884784

Topal, M. R. (2022). The relationship between school principals' servant leadership behaviors and conflict management styles. *SDU International Journal of Educational Studies,* 9(2), 105–136. DOI: 10.33710/sduijes.1200956

Tsarkos, A. (2023). The effect of servant leadership on Greek public secondary schools acting as learning organizations. *International Journal of Leadership in Education,* •••, 1–26. DOI: 10.1080/13603124.2023.2264261

Ullah, S. (2021). Examining the role of grit in the relationship between servant leadership and work performance: An empirical study of the higher education sector of Quetta, Balochistan, Pakistan. *Journal of Development and Social Sciences*, 2(3), 191–201. DOI: 10.47205/jdss.2021(2-III)18

Van der Hoven, A. G., Mahembe, B., & Hamman-Fisher, D. (2021). The influence of servant leadership on psychological empowerment and organizational citizenship on a sample of teachers. *SA Journal of Human Resource Management*, 19(0), a1395. DOI: 10.4102/sajhrm.v19i0.1395

Van Dierendonck, D. (2010). Servant leadership: A review and synthesis. *Journal of Management*, 37(4), 1228–1261. DOI: 10.1177/0149206310380462

Van Dierendonck, D. (2011). Servant leadership: A review and synthesis. *Journal of Management*, 37(4), 1228–1261. DOI: 10.1177/0149206310380462

Van Dierendonck, D., & Patterson, K. (2015). Compassionate Love as a Cornerstone of Servant Leadership: An Integration of Previous Theorizing and Research. *Journal of Business Ethics*, 128, 119–131. DOI: 10.1007/s10551-014-2085-z

Yang, J., Liu, H., & Gu, J. (2017). A multi-level study of servant leadership on creativity. *Leadership and Organization Development Journal*, 38(5), 610–629. DOI: 10.1108/LODJ-10-2015-0229

Zhang, J. (2020). The application of human comprehensive development theory and deep learning in innovation education in higher education. *Frontiers in Psychology*, 11. Advance online publication. DOI: 10.3389/fpsyg.2020.01605

ADDITIONAL READING

Clarence, M., Devassy, V. P., & Jena, L. K.. (2021). The effect of servant leadership on ad hoc schoolteachers' affective commitment and psychological well-being: The mediating role of psychological capital. *International Review of Education*, 67, 305–331. DOI: 10.1007/s11159-020-09856-9

Creemers, B. P., Peters, T., & Reynolds, D. (Eds.). (2022). *School effectiveness and school improvement*. Routledge.

Verhelst, D., Vanhoof, J., & Van Petegem, P. (2023). School effectiveness for education for sustainable development (ESD): What characterizes an ESD-effective school organization? *Educational Management Administration & Leadership*, 51(2), 502–525. DOI: 10.1177/174114322098519

KEY TERMS AND DEFINITIONS

Conceptual skills: In servant leadership, conceptualizing refers to the leader's ability to envision future scenarios and strategic directions for the organization. It involves understanding complex situations deeply, identifying long-term solutions, and guiding the organization towards achieving its vision and goals with foresight and insight.

Education 4.0: Education 4.0 corresponds with the fourth industrial revolution, characterized by the integration of digital technologies, artificial intelligence, and the internet into educational practices. This approach emphasizes personalized learning, real-time feedback, collaborative and interdisciplinary learning experiences, and the preparation of students for future challenges and careers in a highly interconnected and technologically advanced world. It aims to transform traditional educational models to be more flexible, student-centered, and aligned with the skills required in the 21st century.

Empathetic congruence: It refers to the alignment or harmony between an individual's understanding and response to another's emotional state and the actual feelings of that person. It involves accurately perceiving, sharing, and reflecting back the emotions of others, thereby facilitating deep, empathetic connections. This concept is pivotal in therapeutic settings, educational environments, and interpersonal relationships, as it underscores the importance of genuinely understanding and resonating with others' emotional experiences.

Leadership capacitation: The process of developing and enhancing an individual's ability, skills, and knowledge to effectively lead and influence others within an organization or community. It encompasses a wide range of activities, such as training programs, mentorship, experiential learning, and self-directed studies, aimed at preparing leaders to effectively manage teams, drive organizational change, make strategic decisions, and inspire followers towards achieving common goals.

Organizational Citizenship Behaviors (OCBs): OCBs are discretionary actions performed by employees that are not directly recognized by the formal reward system but contribute to the effective functioning of the organization. These behaviors include altruism, conscientiousness, sportsmanship, courtesy, and civic virtue, enhancing workplace environment and organizational performance.

Visionary stewardship: It embodies the fusion of forward-looking leadership with a deep sense of responsibility towards managing and safeguarding resources for future generations. It encompasses strategic foresight, ethical governance, and the sustainable development of organizational or community assets, ensuring their enduring benefit and legacy.

Chapter 8
Leadership's Role in Students' Co-Production of University Brand Features

Mandu Umoren
University of Uyo, Nigeria

ABSTRACT

This paper explored the forms of individual and collective leadership roles in a collaborative network of professional and non-professional co-producers of university brand features. It was discovered that the three identified broad phases in the co-production of brand features (preparation, execution, evaluation/implementation) represent collective activities with implied opportunities for the exercising of collective and individual leadership roles in formal and informal capacities. The paper concluded that the co-production approach to institutional branding can reduce the seeming feeling of marginalisation among university students.

INTRODUCTION

The growing need for recognition of students as partners of a university and brand appears to have amplified the importance of modifying institutional decision-making processes and governance models to assist in the formation of a working relationship that is inclined towards collaboration with staff and administrators. A cursory look at the typical internal governance model of a university shows that it is made up of the visitor, administrative chancellors, senate, academic deans, faculty boards, heads of departments, departmental boards, and usually a platform for students' rep-

DOI: 10.4018/979-8-3693-9215-7.ch008

resentation. This traditional model of university governance signifies the presence of structured hierarchies of administrative groups and the implied distribution of leadership alongside roles that are associated with formal authority; as such, power favourably remains with the professionals. Since professionals have expertise in their academic fields and administration, they tend to have voice dominance and the upper hand in decision-making. Students are merely given opportunities to contribute to decision-making and governance through their representative system (Students Union) or, at most, through ad hoc representation in a few special work groups. However, having been exposed to the academic and social practices of the institution, students have the advantage of current experiential knowledge of the university brand and should be able to contribute to its development.

Earlier, Zimmerman and Burkhart (as cited in Hilliard, 2010) highlighted reported research that indicates a low percentage of leadership opportunities for university students. The fact remains that the interdependent relationship between professionals (administrators and staff) and non-professionals (students) is obvious, but these official interactions appear not to be set for collaborative work on institutional branding, especially in terms of activities that are focused on modifying academic or social practices into uniqueness. From a related perspective, there has been a seeming persistent emphasis on the need to improve customer-organisational relationships in recent times. Given this, a university's responsive action through the adoption of the strategy of co-production for definition, redefinition, or modification of brand features appears to make practical sense.

The idea is that while each university is seeking ways to remain competitively relevant, especially in terms of the uniqueness and value of offered services, the fulfilment of this quality and sustaining it, from the viewpoint of Miller (2017b), is a brand project that should be set as an ongoing way to fulfil a university's overall strategy. Miller (2017a) added that some of the issues with the branding of universities are related to their inability to communicate what differentiates them from competitors and the focus on crafting symbolic cues (visual expressions and verbal statements) rather than on whole-scale strategic branding. One can therefore deduce from Miller's submissions that, with the peculiar characteristics of a university, branding should be adapted accordingly to align with the systemic values. This explains why the features of a university's brand should be more focused on those academic and social practices that are capable of providing distinctiveness and competitive advantages to the institution, while the complementary elements should serve to highlight the values of these unique practices.

Co-production of brand features in this context refers to all voluntary collaborative activities among the non-professionals (students) and professionals of a university (staff, management, or agents) for the purpose of planning, reviewing, identifying, modifying, evaluating, and launching a university's unique academic and social practices. The supportive argument here is that the co-production of academic and social practices can be used as a tool to extend the concept of a brand from the services of a university to the process of branding. Moreover, looking at the contemporary approach to branding (which tends to emphasise consumers' collaboration with the organisation), a university can choose the strategy of co-production of brand features in order to make comparatively better accomplishments from the process. The co-production workstream presents the advantage of ensuring that new ideas are created in collaboration with those who stand to benefit from them (Alden, n.d.). Since students are the direct consumers of the services of a university, their collaborative involvement through the co-production of unique academic and social practices is not only an opportunity for them to utilise their experiences productively, but it can also be used to highlight existing gaps in what is offered and their expectations. This implies that with the strategy of co-production, a university's professionals can exploit the opportunity to collaborate with students, parents, alumni, and other non-professionals for the definition or redefinition of brand features. In line with this, Bright (2019) emphasised the need for formal organisations to run a co-production system where 'experts by experience' and 'experts by profession' can work collaboratively to accomplish specific goals.

Bussu and Galanti (2018) observed that where there is a systemic presence of frequent interactions between service users (non-professionals) and professionals, and, to a large extent, outcomes depend on the success of each interaction, it can be taken that these are indicators of the feasibility of co-production. It can be said of students, therefore, that with a fairly long contact period with the university and frequent interactions with staff or management, the strategy of co-production can be initiated and sustained. For example, the re-analysis of a service redesign project by Radnor et al. (2014) showed that in the case of the institution, staff and students' collaboration for review and the mapping out of students' enrolment processes could yield outputs with potential to improve this aspect of service delivery.

In the literature, there are seemingly few instances where professionals and students at different levels of learning have been involved in co-production work. Consistent with this submission, the results of the study by Garcia et al. (2018) revealed that students' previous experience with this model of activities was very limited. As much as the benefits of co-production are attractive, there are indications in the literature that the implementation and sustenance of this strategy are often challenged by institutional barriers (Ferlie; van Gestel & Grotenbreg, as cited by Regal et al., 2023). Thus, according to the Social Care Institute for Excellence (2019), the practice of co-production is hindered in organisations when there is a lack of knowledge and understanding of this principle; absence of backing by clear policies, legal requirements, or resources; and when the professionals' exhibit resistance to change or power sharing. Other issues reported to limit the success of co-production work include confusion around responsibilities, administrative burden, and pressures on people for whom the implied work is not their primary activity (Gagliardi & Dobrow; Kothari & Mays; Batalden et al., as cited in Alden, n.d.). On this ground, Bussu and Galanti (2018) added that in a setting with a marginalised group of individuals (by extension, co-production requires foundational activities such as staff training and leadership; otherwise, it might turn out to highlight inequalities more.

Recent attention to the initiation or adoption of co-production and maintenance as a viable organisational practice has brought leadership and roles under the spotlight. In line with this, Regal et al. (2023) highlighted the strategic implications of leadership in sustaining cooperative and collective co-production, unlike where a leader's systemic authority and influence over productive efforts are temporary and limited to their time in the organisation. Similarly, Bussu and Galanti (2018) stated that the form of leadership that is favourable to co-production is one with the practices and interactions of different types of roles and individuals. However, Baptista et al. and Engen et al. (as cited in Regal et al., 2023) added that in a cooperative framework, alongside an individual's (leader's) influence, collective dynamics are central to facilitating co-production. There are, however, streams of research on how co-production can be engineered through the initiatives of individual and collective leadership roles in task groups (Ärleskog et al., 2021; Hansson & Polk, 2017; Kjellström et al., 2024). Leadership's role is conceptualised here as the exercising of influence among the professionals (staff or agents) and non-professionals (students) using shared vision, inspiration, and various university-wide practices, conditions, and provisions for the initiation and sustenance of co-production of the university's brand features.

Since all organisational situations are not the same, the approach to co-production of a university's brand features will also be different. This paper draws on the advantages of formal and informal leadership roles for the derivation of a conceptual framework enmeshed with democratic features and opportunities for inclusion of the marginalised groups during institutional branding.

University Brand Features

The American Marketing Association (AMA) defines a brand as a name, term, sign, symbol, design, or combination of them intended to identify the goods and services of one seller or a group of sellers and to differentiate them from those of competitors (Keller, 2013, p. 30). AMA's definition of a brand highlights the wide range and many perspectives of this term (Avis, 2009). To this extent, the components in a brand could vary. Most models of a brand include the symbolic, visual, or physical representations (Aaker; Kapferer; Simões, Dibb, & Fisk, as cited in Black & Veloutsou, 2017); the offered characteristics or the brand personality (Kapferer;

Aaker; Coleman, de Chernatony & Christodoulides, as cited in Black & Veloutsou, 2017). The corporate brand identity perspective, however, has extended the horizon of a brand from the unique products or services of an organisation to the characteristics of the organisation. Thus, Keller (2013) defines a brand as 'anything' that is capable of creating a measure of awareness, reputation, and prominence or from any other distinctive element that can offer a competitive advantage for a product, service, or organisation. There are, however, some major differences between product (service) branding and corporate branding. Likewise, the application of the concept of branding to an educational institution should take on a modified form, with some differences from what is obtained in pure commercial organisations.

Going by the nature of a university as an institution of learning of the highest level, its brand should equally mark it out as a place with this noble quality. Consistent with the foregoing submission, the core features of a university brand should generally be more focused on academic and social practices that are capable of differentiating and providing competitive advantages to the institution. Thus, the complementary elements (logo, institutional name, motto, tagline, and mission statement) should work to highlight and/or bring out the values in a university's unique academic and social practices. The agreeing submission by Hoang and Rojas-Lizana (as cited in Shahnaz & Qadir, 2020) is that where a university wants to establish a brand, the backup with complementary brand features should be exploited as a means of providing concrete evidence to claims of uniqueness.

Figure 1. University Brand Features

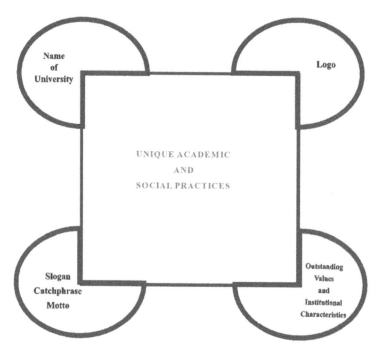

As shown in Figure 1, a university's main brand features should be made up of unique academic and social practices, while the name, logo, slogan, catchphrase, outstanding values, and institutional characteristics constitute the complementary elements. This implicitly relates to the fact that brand consumers should be able to associate these complementary elements with the unique academic and social practices of the university. It has been argued that complementary brand features have bearings on a university's promotional activities; therefore, in terms of derived benefit, they are more useful in attracting prospective students (Mafofo & Banda; Osman; Wells et al., as cited in Shahnaz & Qadir, 2020). But a branded university can gain a range of other benefits from current students and other internal stake-holder groups. Such benefits can manifest individually or collectively as biassed preferential treatments, cooperation, or expressions of support for the institution. Eldegwy et al. (2018) added that a balanced and fulfilling university experience should offer both positive social and academic dimensions.

A university's academic practices are focused on the basic functions (research, teaching, and learning) and performance, but as brand features, these functions should be performed uniquely and differently from all other institutions. In effect, a branded university will exhibit the features and capabilities to perform the basic functional roles, but with identified and adopted university-specific additional dimensions that will enable these functions to be performed uniquely. According to Eldegwy *et al.* (2018), social practices are the activities of the university whose major aim is to facilitate social interactions among students, alumni, faculty, or other relevant external brand consumers. A branded university should be perceived clearly by students, staff, and other stakeholders as one with characteristics and features that depict a typical university but embodied with unique qualities in academic and social practices for obvious differences from all other universities.

Institutional Branding

Initially, institutions of learning were not consciously inclined towards branding; however, logos were designed and used by them as a representative symbol (Osman, as cited in Shahnaz & Qadir, 2020). One can state that at the early stage of university branding, logos and mottos were the most commonly used forms of institutional distinction. With time, and as indicated by Randall (as cited in Shahnaz & Qadir), the parameters of the brand in the old and traditional universities were focused on the personality of the institution, and branding entailed the provision of quality education, while the name was considered sufficient as a mark of distinction.

With the conceptualisation of branding as a comprehensive process that should cover all the activities that can be used to create distinctiveness and to set an institution as one that is unique, there are a wide range of parameters that can be exploited. With evolution in the perspective of brand management, there comes a new approach that considers branding as a social process that involves many stakeholders (Iglesias *et al.*, 2013). Branding is presented in the literature as a set of collaborative and social activities that occurs within a network of many relevant participants (Mühlbacher & Hemetsberger, 2008). The argument is that the concept of a brand leans more towards the consumer's perspective than the marketer's (or the organisation's).

In addition, the channels for corporate organisations to use and disseminate information or spread their brand values have changed with the availability and wider access to modern communication media. In the contemporary approach to branding, the advantages of technology and the adaptation of social interactive platforms for communication and other forms of customers' engagement are executed easily in line with organisationally determined intentions (Meltzer, 2018). Moreover, students have access to modern media of communication, they tend to exhibit high expectations about the brand and, as well, show greater socially related behaviours among the network of brand consumers. A university, therefore, can easily connect and strategically work with their experienced customers for the production, provision, and sustenance of unique academic and social practices. Thus, institutional branding in this paper is described as a dynamic, social, and interactive process where the professionals (university staff and administrators) collaborate with the non-professionals (students) to creatively and jointly produce and provide unique academic and social practices (brand features).

The Concept of Co-production

Co-production is an evolving concept that is believed to have found its way simultaneously into policy and practices in various fields (Bandola-Gill *et al.*, 2023). As such, this concept exhibits variation in definitions, flexibility (since it is open to a wide variety of participants and contexts of application), as well as differences in objectives and usage strategies. Consequently, there are controversies on both the effects and benefits of co-production, and this has also created issues around the generalisation of findings from related research among scholars and practitioners (Needham & Carr, 2009).

The concepts of co-production and customer participation are related but distinctively different. On customer participation, Brandt *et al.* (as cited in Bandola-Gill *et al.*, 2023) stated that it can be adapted to take the form of information (one-way communication), consultation, collaboration, and empowerment (where practitioners have decision-making authority). The argument, however, is that merely increasing the quantity or quality of the aforementioned participatory activities does not transmute into practicing co-production.

Customer co-production and customer participation can also be differentiated in terms of level of effort, nature of tasks (simple or continuous), and type of project (extensive or not, novel or routine) (Hsiuju, Kevin, & Wanru; Ng, Mauli, & Yip, as cited in Norsiah, 2015). Thus, according to Hsiuju *et al.*; Ng et al. (as cited in Norsiah), customer participation behaviours are associated with tasks that are simple or merely routine and would require a low level of effort, and they are more applicable to projects that are not extensive or novel. Customer co-production behaviours take the form of high-level efforts, deal with complex, continuously evolving tasks, and are more suitable for projects that are extensive or novel.

Co-production is a term that is generally used to describe various formalised (productive) activities conducted jointly between laypeople and professionals (Nabatchi *et al.*, 2017; Pestoff, 2014). In formal settings, the central ideas in the concept of co-production converge around its being as a form of active productive involvement of customers in the work of an organisation. Parks *et al.* (as cited in Jakobsen & Anderson, 2013) added that opportunities for these joint productive activities may occur directly, involving coordinated efforts in the same production process, or indirectly through independent yet related efforts of regular producers and consumer producers.

In order to simplify the meaning of co-production, Nabatchi *et al.* (2017) broke the term into the 'co' and 'production' dimensions. Thus, according to Nabatchi *et al.*, 'co' here conveys collaborative efforts, and two sets of actors or participants are involved: the professionals and the citizens (lay producers). Furthermore, Nabatchi *et al.* explained that the professionals ordinarily should be the regular producers or their agents, and the lay producers may be clients, customers, service beneficiaries, community members, and such others. Based on this submission, laypeople ordinarily should be consumers of outputs from professionals, but with co-production, they can collaborate at three levels: individual, group, and collective (Bradney and England, as cited in Tuurnas, 2016). Furthermore, 'production' in the term 'co-production' generally describes what occurs during co-production; with the shift from the initial focus on service delivery, it has been expanded to include other productive activities within the public service cycle and in other areas (Nabatchi *et al.*, 2017).

The following four service cycle phases and benefits have been identified in co-production (Nabatchi *et al.*, 2017, p. 8):

Co-commissioning refers to activities used prospectively to decide on or prioritise needed public services, outcomes, and users. Co-design refers to activities used to create, plan for, or arrange prospective or concurrent public services. Co-delivery refers to activities used to provide or improve the provision of concurrent public services. Co-assessment refers to activities used to retrospectively assess public service quality or outcomes.

The types of co-production can also be distinguished based on the extent to which laypeople are involved in the design of services that they individually receive and whether the co-production concerns core services of the organisation or complementary activities (Brandsen & Honingh, 2015). In addition, co-production operates in a deliberately created network with a two-way channel where organisations both receive and share information and resources with the aim of generating 'empowerment' and 'user-led, transformative innovation' (Osborne & Strokosch, 2013).

The Social Care Institute for Excellence (2013) explained that co-production operates with the principles of equality (where there is an understanding that all participants possess relevant resources and stand to benefit from a proposed project); diversity (where participants as much as possible are selected to represent the community or group); accessibility (where support and opportunities are available for interested participants); and reciprocity (where there is an understanding of mutual benefits for all participants). The presence of these four principles in a productive network therefore, distinguishes co-production from customer participation. Thus, co-production thrives in a purposefully created democratic system, where all the relevant participants can contribute meaningfully and equally in terms of suggestions, decisions, and implementation activities to a project or service (The Social Care Institute for Excellence, 2013).

In this context, co-production of university brand features refers to all voluntary collaborations between professionals (staff and administrators) and non-professionals (students) for the purpose of planning, reviewing, identifying, modifying, launching, and evaluating a university's unique academic and social features. A co-production strategy opens up opportunities for continuous improvement of a university's brand features.

Need for Students' Co-production of University Brand Features

A university, both professionals and non-professionals are expected to exhibit shared responsibility towards the attainment of the goals of the university. The strategy of co-production of brand features helps to bring students' perspectives on the academic or social practices of their university into branding. This is important since their perspective may be different from that of the professionals. Moreover, students have a variety of skills, and coupled with the advantage of brand consumption, they can bring experiential knowledge to a university's branding or rebranding processes. Also, in terms of the quality of outputs from such collaborative engagements, it is likely that the co-produced unique academic and social practices will truly represent students' expectations or what may have been overlooked by university professionals. Unlike when the distinguishing components of a university are identified, defined, or redefined internally by the professionals and presented to external audiences, the strategy of co-production of brand features enables a university to exploit both the experiences and expertise of all the collaborative partners.

Through the avenue of co-production, opportunities are created for meaningful communication between university professionals and non-professionals. Similarly, the exchange of information on the university's academic and social practices during the planning and execution phases of co-production creates shared understanding, balances, and strengthens the relationship between the university and students. With the created sense of ownership in the co-produced brand features and responsibility, there is also the possibility that such collaborative involvements can evolve into forms of supportive behaviours like brand advocacy, loyalty, and such others. Thus, gains from students' co-production can be considered in terms of the quality and quantity of brand features that can be generated with this strategy and their bearings on the value or quality of academic and social practices of the university, effects on students' citizenship behaviours, and benefits to the university as a whole.

In line with this, Cumming *et al.* (2023) added that collaborative involvement can foster important affective experiences, inform academic engagement, and contribute to students' sense of themselves as active agents in their own and others' development. On the part of the organisation (the university), ideas, opinions, or suggestions that are based on students' perspectives or points of difference in the academic and social practices of the university help set the tone for top executives' reflection and tend to direct attention to areas that need improvement by management and professionals (Pettersson, as cited in Ärleskog *et al.*, 2021).

The benefits of co-production have been summed up in Vanleene *et al.'s* (2015) exploratory study to include better services, better relationships between the lay producers and the professional organisation, and an improvement in democratic quality. On the whole, the adoption of co-production as a strategy for branding or rebranding will not only modify the traditional top-down approach to governance and power dynamics at a university but will also help to ease the seeming feeling of marginalisation among non-professionals.

Leadership in Co-production: What It Entails and How It Emerges

Co-production, in the context of an organisation or institution, is a socially innovative process that is structured for the realisation of collective outcomes. However, both collective efforts and outcomes require the combined influence of a favourable working relationship between the service providers and users (consumers) and, as well, systemic conditions that are in alignment with the principles of equality, diversity, accessibility, and reciprocity (The Social Care Institute for Excellence, 2013). In a university, co-production of brand features should be structured to generally permit anyone who is eligible and has the desire to work as a partner for this purpose to be invited, granted opportunities for active involvement through the provided platforms, and inspired to bring in their best contributions during the process.

The assumption in co-production is that it should allow variation in perspectives about academic and social practices to be put forward by these two interdependent groups (professionals and non-professionals). It should, as well, permit diverse ideas about academic and social practices to be combined to produce the brand features of the university. This is because co-production is naturally oriented to rely on collaborations, and the partners could come from various groups and different backgrounds. However, the envisioned success of this collaborative approach and the outcome of the combined efforts of the groups depend on the adopted leadership approach.

Leadership in this sense is an influence strategy that works to bring everyone in the team, regardless of formal authority, status, or position, to the point of being inspired by a shared sense of purpose to contribute ideas or actions willingly and at every opportunity towards the branding or rebranding processes of the university. It is important to mention that co-production of brand features in a university is favourably endowed to take on the attention of the entire institution (being that its spotlight is on strategic transformations in the whole system); as such, it should involve multiple leaders and collective actions. This 'leadership in the plural' (Denis *et al.,* 2012) here signifies collective leadership.

Collective leadership, according to Yukl (as cited in Tipurić, 2022), is the process by which individual and collective efforts are directed towards the accomplishment of common goals.Collective leadership is often initiated in an organisational setting through processes and enablings by the organisational top leaders as they work with their team members towards the attainment of collectively set goals.The collective leadership approach can be entrenched in the selected style of leadership and as a strategy whose aim is to work in the sharing of power and responsibility in line with collectively set goals. In line with this, Meindl et al. (as cited in Alsaedi, 2022) noted that collective leadership can be blended into transactional and transformational leadership types due to the reinforcing benefits it offers. Unlike traditional command-and-control leadership, this approach conveys the idea of shared responsibility and mutual accountability by all the partners in a collaborative network (Collar, 2013). In practice, individual leaders (top executives), rather than engaging all the collaborators in the different task groups, preferably deploy a structure where leadership roles can be performed in different capacities, both individually and collectively, by members of the multiple task groups (Paunova, 2015).

There are seemingly hazy conceptualisations of the forms that collective leadership could take. For example, in terms of size or scope of power distribution, an organisation can simply operate with micro- or macro-types of collective leadership. Micro-collective leadership is more of an interpersonal relationship system where the collective activities involve the coming together of a few top executives of the organisation (institution) for decision-making. In the macro collective model, leadership is shared and can be exercised within multiple teams working on a project (Kjellström *et al.,* 2024). Thus, collective leadership is sometimes conceived to simply involve the incorporation of more than one person in leadership roles (co-leadership or team leadership); while in others, it conveys the flow or rotation of leadership roles among individuals as indicated in distributed or shared leadership (Ospina & Foldy, 2016). This explains why leadership approaches in multiple task groups are often portrayed in shared, distributed, pooled, and relational (social) modes (Kjellström *et al.,* 2024).

Ospina and Foldy (2016), however, went further to assert that the 'collective' dimension in the term 'collective leadership' implicates all members of a group rather than one or even several individual members. From this perspective, in a collaborative network, all the participants are potential leaders, and leadership in this sense is conceived in terms of the various roles that can be undertaken by the partners individually and collectively during co-production. With the foundational assumption that any collaborative partner can and should be given the opportunity to lead, leadership in the collective orientation can be undertaken in both formal and informal capacities (O'Neil & Brinkerhoff; Friedrich *et al.,* as cited in Shonk, 2024). This is where the co-production approach to branding favours not just the distribution of leadership in the formal hierarchies of administration (institutional, faculty, and departmental) but also the active involvement of all collaborative partners whose responsibilities are set according to their suitability for the leadership roles. In practice, this brings to the fore a need for important adaptations in the university leadership structures to favour the co-production approach to institutional branding. One of them is the systematic facilitation and establishment of horizontal relationships in the collaborative network(s) of co-producers. This action is a crucial step for the development of genuine interconnectivity, the formation of desirable social relationships among professionals and students, and, indirectly, the accomplishment of set collective goals.

The implication of this is that during the co-production of a university's brand features, the top-level managers will not only help to bring on board all the willing collaborative partners, but will also drive them towards an understanding of the need and willingness to accomplish common purposes and goals. It is therefore the responsibility of the leader's (irrespective of level) to ensure that the set collective goals are realised; however, this requires the tactical deployment of inspiration and motivation for collective actions among the collaborative partners. Leadership in the collective model, according to Drath *et al.* (2008), emerges as a consequence of direction, alignment, and commitment within a task group. Thus, a leader is expected to deploy directive behaviours, inspiration, motivation, and, as well, the mechanism of collaboration.

Informal Leadership Roles in Students' Co-production of Brand Features

Ärleskog *et al.* (2021); Hansson and Polk (2017); Alsaedi (2022); Kjellström *et al.* (2024) identified supporters, facilitators, co-leaders/managers, project leaders, champions, mentors, ambassadors, advocates, coaches, problem-solvers, and motivators as some of the leadership roles in a collective framework. These leadership roles are also essential to co-production work and its success. In a formal organisation, Kjellström *et al.* maintained that some of the roles naturally align with some categories of the collaborative partners, while others could go to any individual during the process, and that leadership roles could occur at different stages of the collective processes or at all time points in various ways.

Table 1. Informal Leadership Roles in Students' Co-production of Brand Features

Informal Leadership Roles	Influence Activities
Facilitators	• Provides sponsorship and resources (time, money, infrastructure, and information).
	• Establishes and maintains enabling conditions
	• Maintains momentum and the status of collaborative networks
	• Addresses tensions and lapses that may arise during the process and on networking platforms.
Champions	• Represents the professional or non-professional groups.
	• Facilitates understanding among institutional managers concerning the importance of co-production.
	• Promotes and defends the use of a co-production approach to branding.
Co-leaders	• Creates dynamic, open, and tolerant processes for co-production.
Project Leaders	• Guides the entire co-production work.
	• Ensures smooth operation in all phases of co-production and in networks.
	• Maintains the collaborative framework and alignment to co-production principles.
	• Manages the steering phase of co-production by co-setting goals, objectives, and timelines.
	• Facilitates the use of collaborative skills (communication, transparent dialogue, etc.)
	• Provides first-hand assessment for group processes and project outputs.
	• Identifies conditions that hinder or support co-production.
	• Manages arising conflicts in the collaborative team and maintains the project's progress.
Ambassadors	• Promotes co-production activities.
	• Volunteers time for capacity building for professionals and non-professionals.
	• Lends credibility to co-production.
Mentors	• Provides advice and counseling based on experience and expertise.
Motivators	• Offers encouragement to the collaborative partners
	• Propels collaborative actions in the teams
Problem-Solvers	• Resolves difficulties arising from co-production processes and teams.
Coaches	• Listens to the collaborative partners.
	• Recognises the non-professionals and their importance as collaborative partners.

As shown in Table 1, every actor has a place in co-production work and opportunities to manifest leadership roles that fit best with the individual's abilities. While collective leadership is not set to eliminate the role or responsibility of the institutional heads or formal leaders, it is, however, shaped first to recognise the skills, abilities, talents, and experiences of every collaborator and second to encourage the development of a mindset where collaborators are seen as active role players in leadership.

Activities in Students' Co-production of Brand Features

Bussu and Galanti (2018) highlighted four basic roles of leadership in coproductive processes: setting the priorities of co-production and clarifying shared goals; guaranteeing greater inclusion; fostering communication and public accountability; and encouraging and supporting innovative practices. According to Kjellström *et al.* (2024), the following nine activities highlight collective leadership roles in the context of health and wellbeing: initiating, power sharing and redistribution, training and development of the collaborative partners, provision of support, establishment of trusting relationships, provision of a networking system, communication, orchestration, and implementation. However, these practices can be condensed to yield three phases of activities with opportunities for collective and individual leadership roles during the co-production. The three phases are: preparation, execution, implementation, and evaluation.

Preparing for Co-production of Brand Features

This is used to describe all the initial activities or arrangements as well as the provisions (conditions and support structures) that necessarily must be put in place before the main co-production work. It covers planning, capacity building, power sharing, the provision of networking platforms, and the provision of co-production supportive infrastructures.

Planning. Once co-production has been considered as the innovative method that will be adopted for branding or rebranding, it is important to formulate the goals clearly, outline the expected outcomes, and specify actions that will lead to the realisation of the goals in the proposed co-production work. At the initial stages of planning, a steering group of co-producers can be adopted to develop the terms of reference, take strategic decisions regarding the formation of task groups or teams (in terms of eligibility requirements and selection processes), the responsibilities of team members, phases in the co-production cycles, intervals of collaborative engagements, and the frequency of co-production of brand features. In order to effectively use time, it is important to recognise that the collaborative partners will also be involved in their primary responsibilities as academics, administrative staff, or students; therefore, the frequency of co-production should be determined at the planning phase. Furthermore, the proliferation of brand features (academic and social practices or complementary components) as a result of too frequent co-production is unhealthy; in the viewpoint of Sela (2023), it will generate 'noise' in the brand environment and could erode the brand, hinder recognition, and weaken its distinctive quality.

In addition, at this stage, failure to develop a shared vision of the goals, set priorities and targets for the expected outputs and outcomes, and communicate this shared vision to actors that may hold very different values can jeopardise the entire co-production work and results (Albrechts; Beebeejaun *et al.*, Richardson, as cited in Bussu and Galanti, 2018). These observations support Gracias et al. (2018), whose study findings showed that organisational hindrances like the lack of time to delve into the tasks, difficulty in exchanging relevant experiences among the participants, and the elaborated scope of the project affected the collaborative work and results. More often than not, the power of the decision at the planning phase lies in the hands of the professionals, as they often select issues or focus areas for co-production work to suit their convenience (Verschuere *et al.*, 2018). This can be checked when the planning activities are properly managed by the steering group of co-producers. One of the strategies is to make the steering co-production group take on a collaborative approach in which both the professionals and students (consumers) of the university brand will be involved.

The collaborators at this stage can rely on contributions from a purposefully derived team or set of stakeholders (staff, students, parents, alumni, or any other relevant others) for the derivation of insights. This means that this set of collaborators may conduct research, review, or evaluate the brand features of the university, come to an understanding of grey areas, and the gained insights will be used to set the foundation, focus, and provide clear themes for the main co-productive engagements. All in all, the top executives have to consider how the aforementioned activities will be captured in the university system.

Overall, the leadership roles of the top executives are variously seen in all phases of the co-production work, as they can function at different times as facilitators, resource providers (sponsors), champions, advocates, mentors, or coaches. For example, top executives provide support during co-production by getting the staff engaged in the process and providing credibility to the project (Chisholm *et al.*, 2018). As resource providers and with the advantage of being in a position to control institutional (organisational) resources, they tend to define the means, methods, and forms of participation (Hämäläinen *et al.*, as cited in Kjellström *et al.*, 2024). Similarly, as champions, top executives can use their expertise to drive or propel co-production work. Interestingly, student leaders can also exhibit individual leadership roles as ambassadors, champions, or co-leaders at this phase of co-production work. Hansson and Polk (2017) highlighted that co-leaders' role is reflected in collaborative efforts from the beginning of a project as the work to create dynamic, open, and tolerant processes for the team.

Capacity Building. This is expressed in a co-production environment as continuous learning efforts whose intentions are to address the collaborative partners' needs for understanding the socially innovative method of working together and maintaining both horizontal and vertical forms of working relationships. One can state that this is one of the systemic provisions that can influence the mental adjustments and behaviours of professionals (staff, institutional leaders) and non-professionals (students and any other group) to favour co-production work.

During branding or rebranding, it is equally important for all the collaborative partners to be adequately informed about the already existing university brand and features and the roles expected from them. Capacity building is an avenue for relevant knowledge on brand features and skills relevant to co-production to be passed to professionals and non-professionals through training programmes. It is possible that knowledge on different leadership roles can emerge from experience, especially from previous co-production work and collaborations; however, Palmer *et al.'s* (2020) viewpoint is that special result-oriented leadership roles like facilitating may require intentionally provided capacity building activities. Regarding this, Kjellström *et al.* (2024) suggested that a process of training and learning will expose the collaborators to co-production principles and applications of this social innovation method. Training and development for the emerging co-production signifies that leadership should be framed to bring out the desired effects among professionals and non-professionals. As such, it is recommended that training for professionals be focused on the process of sharing power with service users or facilitating collaboration; for service users, it should emphasise capacity-building and collaborative procedures (Kjellström *et al.*, 2024).

Power Sharing. A leader's action towards addressing power imbalances among the network of collaborators is a crucial step in co-production work. The idea is that such initiatives should be informed and guided by the leader's reflection on power, which, according to Pettersson (as cited in Ärleskog *et al.*, 2021), is the act of visualising and taking into account the larger context. The need for mutually respectful and reciprocal relationships to be established among the network of collaborators has made it necessary for power imbalances to be addressed during co-production. This, according to Bussu and Galanti (2018), will guarantee greater inclusion for traditionally underrepresented groups and their commitments to group tasks. Power sharing denotes the redistribution of power in alignment with co-production principles, and for the purpose of institutional branding or rebranding, it should be preferably undertaken as system-wide actions. Power in this context is considered to be a resource that can be exercised by individual(s) within a relationship and can also be shared; as such, rather than viewing it as a tool for ruling, it is taken as that which is present and is created whenever there is a relational interface (Franzen,

Lilja, & Vinthagen, as cited in Ärleskog *et al.*, 2021); it can initiate resistance as reactions amongst the concerned interconnected persons.

With leaders' observation of where power is inclined, they can purposely institute mechanisms that facilitate the derivation of insights and ideas from the experiences of the 'less powerful' groups. The administrators of a university must not only believe in the abilities and skills of students but should actualise this position using strategic adaptive structures to create an assumption of influence as would be manifested through their contribution to the development of the university's brand features. Vindrola-Padros et al. (2019) suggested that there is a need for non-professionals to be informed about this power distribution dimension, along with the advantage of influence.

Provision of Networking Platforms. Networking in this context is the process of initiating and maintaining relationships among the collaborative partners during co-production work; the aim is to establish interconnections that should permit the sharing, evaluating, defining, and modification of the academic and social practices of the university into uniqueness. Thus, the networking platforms, which also serve as collaborative platforms, are avenues for both professional and experiential knowledge to be shared about the university brand and features.

Networking platforms can take the form of an advisory panel, collaborative workshop, consultation group, special programmes, debates, or any other appropriate mode. The platforms can also be set at institutional, faculty, or departmental levels, and their activities can be fixed annually or as deemed important, bearing in mind the other commitments that the collaborative partners undertake, either as staff or as students. Also, the organised teams in the university's administrative structure can be adapted for this purpose. For example, the Students' Union Forum (SUF) can be enhanced as a collaborative platform with suitable mechanisms. In harnessing the benefits of the existing structures in the SUF, a students' consultative group can be created through democratic processes, and such elected student consultants can work with the professionals based on the compatibility of their schedules. A major consideration is how the derived collaborative group will reflect a balance in the number of professionals and non-professionals.

It is possible for a university to adopt more than one collaborative platform for co-production. In that case, it is important to consider how the various platforms will be coordinated to avoid chaos and disharmony in efforts and outputs. However, the already established and organised levels of formal leadership in the university governance structure can be used as the unifying platform for these processes.

Establishing Supportive Infrastructures for Co-production. Provision and access to two-way communication and accountability systems are important infrastructures that will facilitate co-production and allow students to have more ownership in the process. Huafang (2019) is of the opinion that in a co-producing network, two-way communication will help to maintain healthy relationships among the collaborative partners and also build mutual trust. In this context, a two-way communication system describes oral and written systems that allow professionals and non-professionals to engage in conversations among themselves about the brand features of the university. With the assumption of asymmetry in information flow and access between the professionals and non-professionals in different organisations (Huafang, 2019), a university can adopt suitable online and offline channels of communication for interactions among the professionals and non-professionals and for the balancing of this asymmetry in communication. The idea is that co-production of brand features and decisions is best taken when there is adequate information on the academic and social practices of the university as well as the learning conditions of students.

Similarly, the accountability system should be designed to maintain a central checklist that can accommodate modifications to the university's academic and social practices. Top leadership's role comes in the consideration of whether students have access to technology and its adaptation for co-production. Furthermore, information preferences and channels that will prove to be the most effective and beneficial to co-production are still decisions that lie on the top executives' tables.

Executing Co-production

The main co-production work should be based on the core collaborative partners' understanding of the task at hand; therefore, it should derive ideas and leverage outputs from the steering co-production group. It is important to mention that the main co-production group(s) may have to also take decisions regarding the formulation of specific task group goals and make outlines of expected outcomes, just like it was done by the steering co-production group. In practice, this main co-production team has to adopt or design suitable networking platforms for their co-production work.

The following three broad activities can be adopted for the execution of co-production of brand features:

(i)   Co-reviewing, co-assessing, and comparative evaluation of the university's academic and social practices;
(ii) Co-identifying and modifying the university's academic and social practices; and
(iii) Co-launching of the co-produced unique academic and social practices.

Each set of activities requires regular dialogue and reflection on goals, outcomes, and impacts. However, the focus of co-production which is on the associated values and benefits of incorporating the perspectives of experience from students and expertise on the part of professionals, must be consciously maintained. The project leaders and facilitators ensure the smooth running of the collaborative project, and they also provide focus in the team for realisation of expected immediate outcomes from the group tasks (Chisholm *et al.*, 2018).

Evaluation and Implementation of Outcomes

Evaluation here implies that careful assessment of the results of co-production in terms of outputs, outcomes, and impacts (Palmer *et al.*, 2020) will be done. However, the impacts of co-production can be assessed in terms of different orders of effects; thus, the first-order effects of co-production are assessed in terms of immediate products (outcomes) and accrued benefits to the collaborative partners in individual and collective capacities (Luederitz *et al.*; Williams; Williams & Robinson, as cited in Palmer *et al.*, 2020).

The impacts on the organisation or institution (in terms of decisions, new policies, and general systemic changes) and the impacts on the wider community and society (in the aspects of new visions or changes in behaviours, norms, and practices as well as consequential expression in new societal imaginations), respectively, represent the second and third orders of effects of co-production (Luederitz *et al.*; Williams; Williams & Robinson, as cited in Palmer *et al.*, 2020). One can therefore state, for example, that the incorporation of the co-produced unique academic and social features into the university's brand components is a second-order effect of co-production. Hansson and Polk (2017) highlighted the project leaders' role as first assessors of project processes, group task outputs, outcomes, and impacts, as well as the conditions and factors that supported or hindered the collaborative efforts.

From the foregoing, implementation can be conceived as a complementary process to evaluation, being that the involved activities are derived from reflections on outputs, outcomes, and impacts of co-production. Relatedly, Bombard *et al.* (2018) highlighted that the outcomes of co-production should be transformed into strategic plans and policies. One can therefore state that the implementation aspect of co-production is actualised when specific actions and decisions are made in order to connect the aforementioned with relevant resources for execution, sponsors, and consideration of similar collaborations or partners.

Figure 2. A Conceptual Framework on Leadership's Role in Students' Co-production of Brand Features

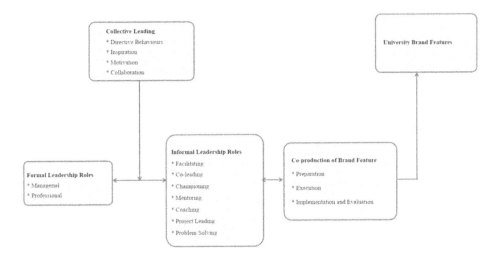

Figure 2 presents a picture of leadership' role in the collaborative activities between students and professionals during the branding or rebranding of a university. As shown in Figure 2, university executives' collective leading is a foundational activity for the initiation of various forms of informal leadership behaviours among the collaborative partners.

Top University Executives' Role in Students' Co-production of Brand Features

Unlike individuals, who, by reason of their position in the organisation exercise maximum authority during group projects and decision-making, the chief executives and other top-level administrators' role during co-production remains more dependent on the support that they can offer in the adopted collective leadership framework. Such supportive roles can come in forms like facilitating, coaching, advocating for, mediating, and championing co-production work (Ärleskog *et al.*, 2021; Kjellström *et al.*, 2024). Leadership here is inclined towards those styles that are driven by outcomes, as such, influence is tilted towards those that will elicit and support productive initiatives and the responsibilities of all collaborative partners. This means that the priority of leaders is directed towards the building of interconnections within and across diverse co-producing teams; thus, relational dynamics are prioritised.

Collar's (2013) summation of leadership roles in the collective orientation shows that it involves leaders's sharing of responsibility and accountability (using the corporate culture and mechanisms that can transform team members into a network of empowered collaborative partners), alignment of strategic direction with talents (skills, expertise, or experience), providing and granting access to opportunities for development, and such other enabling conditions. Thus, the top (formal) executives' roles are redescribed during co-production to reflect being the host of the project, being that they are the initiators, providers, and moderators. Top university executives ensure that silos are broken down in order to allow, first, the sharing of information and other resources among professionals and non-professionals, and second, they encourage collaboration. To accomplish these, they encourage the creation of networking platforms and provide feedback loops where students, staff, and other stakeholders can exchange ideas on brand features and branding processes. Top executives, therefore, constitute a visible part of this broader process that involves many interconnected persons in an emerging and continuously evolving network of relationships; thus, leadership happens at this collective level (Ospina & Foldy, 2016).

Bloemhard (2009) sums up the responsibilities of a top executive (leader) during the process of brand creation as a link person, one who connects the emotional and practical needs of all collaborative partners with the culture and (unique) capabilities of the organisation. With their positions in the organisation, leaders can revisit set goals for branding or rebranding and check them out to ensure that they are in alignment with institutional culture and intended outcomes. Equally, top leaders establish leadership parameters in the co-production team and inspire members' recognition of themselves as active collaborators in leadership. For Gassner and Gofer (2019), leaders's actions (like resource provisions, establishment of collaborative platforms and structures, and ensuring inclusion can facilitate co-production, while the perpetuation of a conservative administrative culture, failure to provide training, or reluctance in the sharing or distribution of power are inhibiting or limiting factors.

At the planning phase of co-production, senior leaders play the role of coaches, as they are expected to listen to users (service or brand consumers), recognise them as part of the collaborating team, and take their needs, desires, and experiences as the starting point for decision-making and actions (The National Board of Health and Welfare; Batalden, as cited in Ärleskog *et al.*, 2021). On the importance of the role of coaches, Mulvale *et al.* and Roos (as cited in Ärleskog *et al.*) maintained that coaches can block or promote user influence and, thus, co-production. In the same vein, as mediators, the top executives' roles revolve around negotiations and other mediating actions that can bring the collaborative partners to points of agreement (especially when there is conflict) throughout the entire co-production work.

CONCLUSION

The conceptual framework outlined for co-production of a university's brand features in this paper highlights a practically relevant approach for the development of a university's brand features. This approach has the potential to modify the traditional model of university governance while permitting the pragmatic provision of opportunities for better inclusion of non-professionals. However, successful implementation of co-production cannot be automatically realised, as both professionals and non-professionals are likely to face significant challenges when attempting to execute this innovative framework. Among other strategies, the initiation of co-production work requires backup policies and the articulation of clear guidelines to direct the project.

Although this framework can inform the design and implementation of co-production in diverse activities and in other groups with features of marginalisation of some categories of individuals, contextual exploration may highlight their peculiar operational requirements. It is necessary for future research to examine how the already established and organised levels of formal leadership in the university governance structure and networks can be used as the unifying platform for the co-production of brand features.

REFERENCES

Alden, S. (n.d). Co-production: Research and practice review full report. https://www.sheffield.ac.uk>... Alsaedi, F. (2022) The important role of collective leadership in the face of change: Literature review. *Open Journal of Leadership*, 11, 1-12. DOI: 10.4236/ojl.2022.111001

Ärleskog, C., Vackerberg, N., & Andersson, A. (2021). Balancing power in co-production: Introducing a reflection model. https://doi.org/.DOI: 10.1057/s41599-02-00790-1

Avis, M. (2009). The problem of brand definition. www. duplication.net.au/---/ANZMAC200

Bandola-Gill, J., Arthur, M., & Ivor Leng, R. (2023). What is co-production? Conceptualising and understanding co-production of knowledge and policy across different theoretical perspectives. *Evidence & Policy*, 19(2), 275–298. DOI: 10.1332/174426421X16420955772641

Black, I., & Veloutsou, C. (2017). Working consumers: Co-creation of brand identity, consumer identity and brand community identity. *Journal of Business Research*, 70, 416–429. DOI: 10.1016/j.jbusres.2016.07.012

Bloemhard, M. (2016). On contemporary leadership and branded organisations. (Doctoral dissertation, Antioch University). https://etd.ohiolink.edu/!etd.send_file?

Bombard, Y., Baker, G. R., Orlando, E., Fancott, C., Bhatia, P., Casalino, S., Onate, K., Denis, J-L., & Pomey, M-P. (2018). Engaging patients to improve quality of care: A systematic review. *Implementation Science*, 13(1), 1–22. 42.

Brandsen, T., & Honingh, M. (2015). Distinguishing different types of co-production: A conceptual analysis based on the classical definitions. *Public Administration Review*, 75(3), 427–435. DOI: 10.1111/puar.12465

Bright, C. (2019). Coproduction and working with experts by experience. https://www. cordisbright.co.uk.A.

Bussu, S., & Galanti, M. T. (2018). Facilitating co-production: The role of leadership in co-production initiatives in the UK. *Policy and Society*, 37(3), 347–367. DOI: 10.1080/14494035.2018.1414355

Chisholm, L., Holttum, S., & Springham, N. (2018). Processes in an experience-based co-design project with family carers in community mental health. *SAGE Open*, 8(4), 2158244018809220. DOI: 10.1177/2158244018809220

Collar, M. (2013). Collective Leadership. https://www.shrm.org>news>col....

Cumming, T. M., Bugge, A. S-J., Kriss, K., McArthur, I., Watson, K., & Jiang, Z. (2023). Diversified: Promoting co-production in course design and delivery. *Front. Educ.* 8:1329810. DOI: 10.3389/feduc.2023.1329810

Denis, J.-L., Langley, A., & Sergi, V. (2012). Leadership in the plural. *The Academy of Management Annals*, 6(1), 211–283. DOI: 10.5465/19416520.2012.667612

Drath, W. H., McCauley, C. D., Palus, C. J., Van Velsor, E., O'Connor, P. M. G., & McGuire, J. B. (2008). Direction, alignment, commitment: Toward a more integrative ontology of leadership. *The Leadership Quarterly*, 19(6), 635–653. DOI: 10.1016/j.leaqua.2008.09.003

Eldegwy, A., Elsharnouby, T. H., & Kortam, W. (2018). How sociable is your university brand? An empirical investigation of university social augmenters' brand equity. *International Journal of Educational Management*, 32(5), 912–930. DOI: 10.1108/IJEM-12-2017-0346

Garcia, I., Noguera, I., & Cortada-Pujol, M. (2018). *Students' perspective on participation in a co-design process of learning scenarios. Journal of.* Educational Innovation Partnership and Change., DOI: 10.21100/jeipc.v4i1.760

Gassner, D., & Gofen, A. (2019). Coproduction investments: Street-level management perspective on co-production. *Cogent Business Management*, 6(1), 1617023. DOI: 10.1080/23311975.2019.1617023

Hansson, S., & Polk, M. (2017). Evaluation of knowledge co-production for sustainable urban development. In: Part I: experiences from project leaders and participants at Gothenburg local interaction platform 2012–2015. www.mistraurbanfutures.org/sites/mistraurban futures.org/files/hansson-polk-wp-2017-2.pdf

Hilliard, A. T. (2010). Student leadership at the university. https://core.ac.uk>pdf.

Huafang, L. (2019). Communication for co-production: A systematic review and research agenda. *Journal of Chinese Governance*, 1695711. Advance online publication. DOI: 10.1080/23812346.2019

Iglesias, O., Ind, N., & Alfaro, M. (2013). The organic view of the brand: A brand value co-creation model. *Journal of Brand Management*, 20(8), 670–688. DOI: 10.1057/bm.2013.8

Jakobsen, M., & Andersen, S. C. (2013). Co-production and equity in public service delivery. *Public Administration Review*, 73(5), 704–713. DOI: 10.1111/puar.12094

Keller, L. L. (2013). *Strategic brand management: Building, measuring and managing brand equity* (4th ed.). Pearson.

Kjellström, S., Sarre, S., & Masterson, D. (2024). The complexity of leadership in co-production practices: A guiding framework based on a systematic literature review. *BMC Health Services Research*, 24(1), 219. Advance online publication. DOI: 10.1186/s12913-024-10549-4 PMID: 38368329

Meltzer, D. (2018). Today's savvy branding mixes traditional and modern strategies. https://www.neur.com>arrti.... Miller, P. (2017a). University branding, but not as we know it. linkedin.com/pulse/university

Miller, P. (2017b). Strategy should reflect the university as a whole. linkedin.com/pulse/university.

Nabatchi, T., Sancino, A., & Sicilia, M. (2017). Varieties of participation in public services: The who, when, and what of co-production. *Public Administration Review*, 77(5), 766–776. DOI: 10.1111/puar.12765

Needham, C., & Carr, S. (2009). Co-production: An emerging evidence base for adult social care transformation. https://ix.iriss.org.uk>content>Co-prod.... Norsiah, A. (2015). The way forward for customer co-production behaviour. *Procedia-Social and Behavioral Sciences*, 224, 238–245.

Osborne, S. P., & Strokosch, K. (2013). It takes two to tango? Understanding the co-production of public services by integrating the services management and public administration perspectives. *British Journal of Management*, 24(S1), 31–47. DOI: 10.1111/1467-8551.12010

Ospina, S. M., & Foldy, E. G. (2016). Collective Dimensions of Leadership. In Farazmand, A. (Ed.), *Global Encyclopedia of Public Administration*. Public Policy, and Governance., DOI: 10.1007/978-3-319-31816-5_2202-1

Palmer, H., Polk, M., Simon, D., & Hansson, S. (2020). Evaluative and enabling infrastructures: Supporting the ability of urban co-production processes to contribute to societal change. *Urban Transformations*, 2(1), 6. DOI: 10.1186/s42854-020-00010-0

Paunova, M. (2015). The emergence of individual and collective leadership in task groups: A matter of achievement and ascription. *The Leadership Quarterly*, 26(6), 935–957. DOI: 10.1016/j.leaqua.2015.10.002

Pestoff, V. (2014). Collective action and the sustainability of co-production. *Public Management Review*, 16(3), 383–401. DOI: 10.1080/14719037.2013.841460

Radnor, Z., Osborne, S. P., Kinder, T., & Mutton, J. (2014). Operationalizing co-production in public services delivery: The contribution of service blueprinting. *Public Management Review*, 16(3), 402–423.

Regal, B., Budjanovcanin, A., van Elk, S., & Ferlie, E. (2023). Organising for co-production: The role of leadership cultures. *Public Management Review*, 2271477. Advance online publication. DOI: 10.1080/14719037

Sela, R. (2023). What is brand dilution? Preventive strategies. https://wwwronsela .com> brand_di.

Shahnaz, A., & Qadir, A. S. (2020). Branding the higher education: Identity construction of universities through logos, mottos and slogans. *Journal of Research in Social Sciences*. .DOI: 10.52015/jrss.8i1.67

Shonk, K. (2024). What is collective leadership? https://www.pon.harvard.edu>daily.

Social Care Institute for Excellence. (2013). Co-production in social care: What it is and how to do it. www.scie.org.uk

Social Care Institute for Excellence. (2019). Breaking down the barriers to co-production. https://www.yhphnetwork.co.uk>... Tipurić, D. (2022). The enactment of strategic leadership, DOI: 10.1007/978-3-031-03799-3_1

Tuurnas, S. (2016). The professional side of co-production. (Academic Dissertation, School of Management, University of Tampere, Finland). https://tampub.uta .fi>bitstream> handle.

Vanleene, D., Verschuere, B., & Voets, J. (2015). Benefits and risks of co-production: A preliminary literature review. https://core.ac. uk>pdf.

Verschuere, B., Vanleene, D., Trui Steen, T., & Brandsen, T. (2018). 18 Democratic co-production: Concepts and determinants. https://www.taylorfrancis.com>

Vindrola-Padros, C., Eyre, L., Baxter, H., Cramer, H., George, B., Wye, L., Fulop, N. J., Utley, M., Phillips, N., Brindle, P., & Marshall, M. (2019). Addressing the challenges of knowledge co-production in quality improvement: Learning from the implementation of the researcher-in-residence model. *BMJ Quality & Safety*, 28, 67–73. doi:10.1136/bmjqs-2017-007127

Zarandi, N., Soares, A. M., & Alves, H. (2022). Student roles and behaviors in higher education co-creation – a systematic literature review. *International Journal of Educational Management*, 36(7), 1297–1320. DOI: 10.1108/IJEM-08-2021-0317

KEY TERMS AND DEFINITIONS

Co-production: This is the process whereby university staff, administrators, agents, and students work together to combine assets of experience, skill, and expertise for the modification of academic and social practices into uniqueness.

Collective Leadership: It is an inclusive approach to leadership and the manifestation of collective understanding of purpose and power sharing among professionals and non-professionals for the purpose of co-producing brand features.

Institutional Branding: This describes the dynamic, social, and collaborative processes involving professionals (university staff, administrators, or agents) and non-professionals (students) for the joint production of unique academic and social practices.

Academic Practices: This refers to the activities that are associated with the basic university functions (research, teaching, and learning) and performance.

Social Practices: This covers all activities at the university whose major aim is to facilitate social interactions among students, alumni, faculty, or other relevant external brand consumers.

Brand Features: A university's brand features describe the unique academic and social practices that are capable of differentiating and providing competitive advantages to the institution.

The Professionals: The professionals are the staff, administrators, or agents of the university who, with expertise in their academic fields and administration, can collaborate with the laypeople for the co-production of brand features.

The Non-professionals: These are the brand consumers, who, with the advantage of brand experience, can collaborate with university professionals for the co-production of brand features.

Chapter 9
Practicing Model of Relationship Between Caring Leadership and Attitude Towards Teaching Profession

Ahmad Najmuddin Azmi
https://orcid.org/0000-0003-1523-3643
University of Malaya, Malaysia

ABSTRACT

Based on the research that has been employed in Malaysia, caring leadership has proven a significant relationship with attitudes towards the teaching profession. As a result, a model of relationship between caring leadership and attitude towards the teaching profession in higher education settings suggests the implementation of this model for future caring leaders. This chapter has proposed eleven steps taken to enhance the caring leadership capacity of existing and future caring leaders in caring leadership practices. Grounded from the implementation of caring using examples, networking, professional development, advocating leadership policy, and also measurement, this chapter offers insight into improving caring leadership among existing leaders and future generations of leaders. All of these steps are taken to solve the issue of caring leadership and teacher retention. Therefore, this chapter is not only to improve leadership but also to cultivate caring future leaders in facing the challenging educational world.

DOI: 10.4018/979-8-3693-9215-7.ch009

INTRODUCTION

Caring leadership is rooted in principles of empathy, support, and relational practices, has gained prominence as an influential leadership style in various fields, including nursing and education (Adhikari et al., 2023; Ozaki, 2023; Tuckwiller et al., 2024; Walls, 2022). In higher education, caring leadership is characterized by leaders who prioritize the emotional and professional needs of their subordinates, thereby creating a supportive and nurturing environment (Smylie et al., 2016). Caring leadership has been brought from nursing sciences to the education field since the importance of caring leadership in promoting well-being to the educators and building a caring community in educational institutions (Adhikari et al., 2023; Ozaki, 2023; Tuckwiller et al., 2024; Walls, 2022).

The theory of human caring by Watson indicated that humans must not be separated from their workforce, nature, or others, even from themselves (Bagheri et al., 2023). In educational institutions, caring leaders have to take care of their subordinates, as mentioned in Noddings's Theory of Care (Adhikari et al., 2023). These caring leadership theories have been connected to each other since the importance of the development of caring leadership with a focus on teachers' well-being is nurtured (Ryu et al., 2022). At the same time, the future of the development of caring leadership also must not be overseen because it is important to create a caring school culture to develop more caring leaders in the future.

Based on the previous literature, caring leadership has been shown to significantly improve teachers' overall well-being. Through the practice of caring leadership, caring leaders who demonstrate empathy and support positively impact teachers' emotional health, which in turn reduces burnout and turnover rates (Dreer, 2024; Ryu et al., 2022; Kelly, 2023). In addition, caring leadership is important since the crisis of shortage of teachers is global (Burke & Ceo-DiFrancesco, 2022; Ledger et al., 2024; Wieser, 2024). Moreover, the declining number of young adults who chose teaching as their profession is a major concern in education society (Dadvand et al., 2024; Guo & Hau, 2024; Kraft & Lyon, 2024). Recent trends show that the leadership abuse have led to a negative perspective of the teaching profession (Li et al., 2022; Odhiambo, 2022; Piest et al., 2024). Leadership is among factors contributing to teacher turnover rates. The 2023 report by UNESCO noted that countries with less supportive leadership and insufficient professional development opportunities face higher teacher turnover rates. The attrition rate from 2015 to 2022 were 4.6% to 9% globally (UNESCO, 2023). Therefore, this literature shows that caring leadership has a significant relationship in determining teachers' situations in the education society.

Furthermore, the issue of power abuse among educational leaders (Khumalo, 2019; Lumby, 2019; Oleksiyenko, 2018; Sam, 2021) and vaguely caring leadership practices in institutes of higher learning (Baker & Burke, 2023; Levay & Andersson Bäck, 2022) is also the major contribution for teacher attrition rates. In 2021 to 2022, research has discovered just a quarter (23.6%) of teachers have a firm stand not to leave their profession (Marshall et al., 2022). Not surprising, leadership is also one of the factors retaining teachers from leaving their positions (DeMatthews et al., 2023; Kilag et al., 2023; Scallon et al., 2023). Perhaps this will also give the bad image to future teachers who want to be involved in the teaching profession. (Kraft & Lyon, 2024) Due to these circumstances, this book chapter suggests a model of relationship caring leadership capacity development with attitude towards the teaching profession. This model is essential given the need for global education to change in order to improve the quality of education. Through research that has been developed by a public university in Malaysia (Azmi, 2024), several strategies have been conceptualised to achieve this goal. The steps that examined in this chapter are: leading by example; implementing caring through networking; caring leadership through professional development; caring leadership focusing on changing leaders; and future leader development. Furthermore, this chapter also suggests changing and promoting caring leadership policy, measurement, evaluation, assessment, and feedback through evaluation, curriculum development to introduce a global perspective in caring leadership, caring leadership promotion and awareness, reflecting recognition and appreciation, and experiential learning and continuous improvement to build leadership capacity in facing global education change.

This chapter also developed a model that gives new insight into deeper understanding of how relational caring leadership practices can influence pre-service teachers' satisfaction, attitudes towards their teaching roles and performance, and ultimately providing valuable implications for policy and practice in higher education.

INTRODUCING THE MODEL OF CARING LEADERSHIP AND ATTITUDE TOWARDS

Teaching Profession.

The model of caring leadership that has been developed shows that caring leadership has a relationship with attitudes towards the teaching profession. The indicators involved in caring leadership that have been measured are academic support, classroom management, interpersonal relationships, and respect and trust. All these indicators have been used to measure caring leadership, which has been shown by future leaders. On the other hand, the attitude towards the teaching profession has three indicators for measuring the attitude that has been displayed by future leaders. The indicators involved in this model are attitudinal development, professional expectation, and professional pride. As shown in the model, the effect of caring leadership on the teaching profession is significant ($\beta = 0.389$, p = 0.000). The outer loadings show that all indicators are in the range of $\beta = 0.746$ to $\beta = 0.899$, which supports that the items in the indicators represent the underlying construct. This has also been supported by previous studies indicating that readings of outer loading must be greater than 0.70 are recommended (Ali et al., 2023; Bagga et al., 2023; Majali et al., 2022).

The significance of this model becomes apparent when considering the current challenges faced by higher education institutions, such as high teacher turnover, burnout, and decreased job satisfaction. By examining the relationship between caring leadership and future pre-service teachers' attitudes, this model aims to provide insights into how leadership practices can be optimised to enhance educational institution well-being and effectiveness. Furthermore, this exploration is timely given the increasing demand for educational leaders to adapt their practices to meet the evolving needs of educational institutions and students. Implementing a caring leadership model may potentially address these challenges by fostering an environment where future leaders feel valued and supported, thus contributing to a more positive and productive academic setting.

Figure 1. The model for the relationship between Caring Leadership on Attitude Towards Teaching Profession

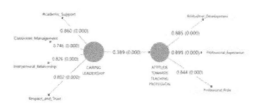

In Table 1, the model shows that caring leadership has the relationship on attitudes towards the teaching profession. Based on this model, results have shown that the relationship between caring leadership on attitude towards the teaching profession is significant ($\beta = 0.389$, t = 8.357, p < 0.05). This model has met the significant threshold value with a *p* value under 0.5 (Ringle et al., 2024)

Table 1. Structural Equation Modelling (SEM) result for Caring Leadership and Attitude towards Teaching Profession Relationship

Path	Original Sample (O)	Sample Mean (M)	Standard Deviation (STDEV)	T Statistics (|O/ STDEV|)	P Values
Caring Leadership -> Attitude Towards Teaching Profession	0.389	0.397	0.047	8.357	0.000

In Table 2, The model of relationship between caring leadership and attitude towards the teaching profession has been through reliability and validity to test the assumption. The mean of square loadings showing the indicator relationship with the construct is greater than 0.5, which demonstrates the acceptable level of convergent validity, and the Cronbach's alpha value is greater than 0.7 or 0.8, which denotes good reliability (Hair et al., 2022; Hair et al., 2024).

Table 2. Table of Reliability and Validity of Construct

	Cronbach's Alpha	rho_A	Composite Reliability	Average Variance Extracted (AVE)
Caring Leadership	0.824	0.830	0.884	0.656
Attitude Towards Teaching Profession	0.776	0.777	0.854	0.597

Overall, the model of the relationship between caring leadership and attitude towards the teaching profession suggested the model is significant to be used to show the relationship between these two indicators. This model has also been supported by other research that shows the relationship between leadership and attitude has always been to be considered (Khan et al., 2023; Walk, 2023; Vermeulen et al., 2023). Based on the developed relationship model, this chapter suggests several steps that should be taken by education institution members, society, management, and stakeholder groups in order to encourage the development of good, caring leadership practices with attitudes towards the teaching profession in higher education settings.

1. Leading through Example.

Higher education leaders and administrators should display caring leadership in their interactions with management, educators, and students (Anderson et al., 2020: Bower & Wolverton, 2023, Leal Filho et al., 2020; Sharma & Jain, 2022). This sets a good example for the educational society in cultivating caring leadership with regard to race, age, academic status, and position. As a leader, steps can be taken through actively listen to the concerns and needs of faculty members. By show empathy and understanding their challenges where support provided when their followers' needed. This could involve offering mentoring, professional development opportunities, or resources to enhance their teaching practices. At the same time, culture of collaboration could be fostered and collegiality among faculty members. Leaders may encourage open communication, collaboration on research projects, and sharing of best practices in teaching. By promoting a supportive and collaborative environment, members of the educational institution can enhance job satisfaction and morale among teaching staff (Ma et al., 2023; Kyangwe et al., 2023; Stoytcheva et al., 2024). This will help the leaders to be as a reference to their educational society when they are seeking for guidance to develop their potential in managing the educational institution towards excellence.

The model of caring leadership also could be in form of interactions with faculty members and other stakeholders. Through demonstrate integrity, transparency, and fairness in decision-making processes leaders are shown their character which can be a good example for the educational society members. In this part, leaders must be accessible, approachable, and responsive to the needs of the academic community. This exemplary leader's actions will serve as a powerful example for others to emulate. In order to build the better attitude towards the teaching profession, caring leaders should demonstrate genuine concern and empathy for their teachers. They actively listen to their concerns, provide emotional support, and acknowledge the challenges they face in their roles. By doing so, they create a culture of trust and support within the educational institution, which can positively influence teachers' attitudes towards their profession. For example, a principal who regularly checks in with teachers, listens to their needs, and offers assistance when needed fosters a sense of belonging and value among the teaching staff. In summary, caring leadership in education can positively influence teachers' attitudes towards their profession by fostering a culture of support, recognition, growth, and well-being. When leaders lead by example through empathy, appreciation, investment in professional development, and promotion of work-life balance, they inspire teachers to remain passionate, motivated, and committed to their roles in shaping the future generation of caring leaders.

2. Implement Caring through Networking.

Caring leadership needs to be cultured through networking among top management and educators (Heffernan et al., 2022; John, 2022; Wei et al., 2020). This shared responsibility to care for others will encourage caring partnerships in educational society to improve morale and engagement among them. Caring for networking implementation suggests third parties to such as parents, get involved in educational practice to ensure society understand the value teachers place in students lives. When parents respect and appreciate the role of educators, it will impact the positivity of building a good attitude among students to become teachers in the future (Marini et al., 2023).

At the same time, it is suggested that higher educational institutions connect with the local community to encourage a caring attitude towards the teaching profession. Higher educational institutions should encourage partnerships with the local community by providing real-world exposure for students to practice caring leadership. This could be done by encourage educators to take on leadership roles within their professional networks and advocate for positive change in education. In this matter, higher education leaders could provide opportunities for their apprentices to lead committees, organize events, and spearhead initiatives that address important issues facing the education community.

On another level, higher education institutions should make connections with global education affiliates and networks. This could give the ideas of the best-practiced caring leaders in the education of the border concept (Aithal & Aithal, 2023; Jang et al., 2023; Rae, 2023). The changing ideas and learning from another educational institution help to give another perspective on practicing caring leadership in organisations. Seminars, colloquium, exhibition or taking part in conferences may help to broaden their view and exchanging opinion on practicing caring leadership in a global level.

By leveraging their networks, leaders can raise awareness of the needs and challenges facing educators and rally support for initiatives that benefit the teaching profession. Whether it's securing funding for professional development opportunities, advocating for policy changes to improve working conditions, or garnering community support for higher education programs, caring leaders demonstrate their commitment to advocating for teachers' interests, which can enhance their morale and sense of value within the profession. This will indirectly shaping the new future leaders attitude.

3. Caring Leadership training through Professional Development.

Professional development helps leaders to be more competent (Lanaj et al., 2022; Mikkonen et al., 2022; Zepeda, 2019) Professional development is suggested to help teachers and future talents teachers develop their teaching skills and instill a passion for their profession. Policymakers should develop a module that emphasises caring leadership continuously. This module and workshop should nurture a sense of empathy, skills on conflict resolution, and communication abilities that are critical in developing positive relationships with the entire educational community.

Base from this theory, this chapter suggests that a mentorship programme to help new leaders develop caring leadership be conducted. This programme should encourage future teachers to practice caring leadership and, at the same time, gain insight into their future profession. This might be included identify individuals within the organization who demonstrate potential for leadership roles and exhibit qualities such as empathy, compassion, integrity, and a genuine concern for others' well-being. Through professional development the competencies and attributes associated with caring leadership, such as empathy, active listening, emotional intelligence, trustworthiness, inclusivity, and ethical decision-making could be thought to the potential leaders. These competencies will serve as the foundation for the training programmes. After that, pairing potential leaders with experienced leaders who exemplify caring leadership principles. Mentors can provide guidance, support, and feedback as participants navigate their leadership journey and apply new skills in their roles.

On the management level, investment in well-being programmes such as stress management and mental health support should be included to promote well-being among educators and society. This is to ensure that the educator feels a sense of being cared for and supported personally. Higher education management also should encourage future teachers who have the potential to be leaders to participate in collaborative projects, webinars, and students exchanging programme that focus on caring leadership and the teaching profession. This exposure might help to open a wider view of different education systems and inspire teachers to have passion for their careers and be caring leaders in the future (Hammoudi Halat et al., 2023; Hartcher et al., 2023; Nwoko et al., 2023).

In conclusion, caring leadership training through professional development can influence teachers' attitudes towards their profession by promoting self-awareness, enhancing interpersonal skills, fostering a growth mindset, emphasizing emotional intelligence, and providing empowerment and support. By equipping educators with the knowledge, skills, and confidence to lead with care and compassion, professional development opportunities inspire a sense of fulfilment, purpose, and satisfaction in the teaching profession.

4. Caring Leadership focusing on Changing Leaders and Future Leaders Development

Future leaders are the hope to determine the future of an organisation (Bodolica & Spraggon, 2021; Forrest & Geraghty, 2022; Moldoveanu & Narayandas, 2019). Management and leaders in higher education should develop their capacity for caring leadership through a student-centred approach. This approach suggests that leaders focus on the needs and care that have been provided to students to foster them into caring leaders. Students interest in caring leadership should be recognised, focused on, and developed to ensure priority is given to cultivating caring leadership.

To achieve this goal organizations can implement caring leadership development initiatives tailored to both current and aspiring leaders. Since students can be trained to be a future caring leader, educational institution could provide leadership training and development programs that emphasize a student-centered approach to leadership. This might include modules on understanding students' perspectives, needs, and challenges, and how leaders can effectively support and advocate for them. At the same time, foster a culture of student empowerment by involving students in decision-making processes at all levels of the organization. This might include the appointment of students' representative in decision making which involve students so their voices and opinion could be heard. Leaders also should be encouraged to seek student input, perspectives, and feedback when making decisions that impact them. This will help the future leader's development indirectly.

The importance of learning environment in developing future leaders are also could not be denied (Hoque & Raya, 2023; Kilag et al., 2023; McCullough et al., 2023). In order to achieve that, the educational management must ensure that organizational policies, practices, and physical environments are conducive to student success and well-being. This can be done by providing resources, support services, and accommodations to address students' diverse needs and promote inclusivity. Through this support, students as a future leaders experience caring and apply caring that they have receive to apply on practicing caring leadership on shaping their attitude towards teaching profession.

5. Changing and advocate Caring Leadership Policy

It is time for the majority of policies that have been developed to focus more on caring leadership practices among educational leaders, society, and future leaders. Policymakers are a body that triggers the phenomenon of change through the development of better policymaking (Cellina et al., 2020; Davidaviciene & Al Majzoub 2022; Zhang et al., 2020). Based on this philosophy, this chapter suggests that caring leadership is viewed as one of the policies that should be in line with global education change. The development of better policies will help to be a catalyst for the goal of developing better future leaders. Policies that support developing a positive attitude in the teaching profession through fair compensation, reviewing a manageable workload, and professional career development opportunities are also an alternative to enhancing the attitude of educational workers. At the same time, policies that support caring leadership values among new future talents and focus on building caring leaders in education should take place. It is suggested that policymakers should engage with educational institutions to promote caring leadership values in every institution involved.

To achieve this goal, educational organisation could constitute committee/task force of key stakeholders, including senior leadership, professionals, and representatives from various departments, to develop the caring leadership policy. The committee established could conduct assessment to understand the current leadership culture and identify gaps in caring leadership practices. This assessment can involve surveys, interviews, focus groups, and analysis of organizational data to gather insights into leadership behaviours and attitudes. From all information that has been gathered, clear objectives and goals for the caring leadership policy, outlining the desired outcomes and impact on leadership development and organizational culture should be developed. These steps taken is to ensure the caring leadership policy is align with the organization's mission, vision, and values.

In the management level, draft policy proposals should be developed to focus and outline specific changes or additions to existing policies to promote caring leadership. These proposals should include clear language, actionable strategies, and measurable outcomes to guide implementation and evaluation. When the caring proposals has been approved, communicate the policy changes effectively to all employees to ensuring clarity on expectations, benefits, and support mechanisms are available. This implementation of changes must be taken out systematically, providing necessary resources, guidance, and support to leaders and employees.

To practicing delegating caring leadership policy, an assessment needs to be conducted to understand the current leadership culture and identify gaps in caring leadership practices (Crawford et al., 2023; Cordova et al., 2024; Fischer & Sitkin, 2024). This assessment can involve surveys, interviews, focus groups, and analysis of organizational data to gather insights into leadership behaviors and attitudes. Through this steps taken, changing and advocating for caring leadership policies can positively influence teachers' attitudes towards their profession by prioritizing teacher well-being, fostering collaborative decision-making, supporting professional development, promoting equity and inclusivity, and celebrating teacher achievements. When teachers feel valued, supported, and empowered by their leaders, they are more likely to have a positive attitude towards their profession and be motivated to make a difference in the lives of their students. With this act, future caring leaders also will be shaped using this mould through practicing of caring leadership like what they have experienced.

6. Measurement, Evaluation Assessment and Feedback.

Leadership capacity should always be measured in order to enhance the quality in leadership capacity building (Awan et al., 2023; Karsono et al., 2022; Qiu et al., 2019). It is suggest that the metrics to measure effort in practising caring leadership coulde be develop to update the caring leadership and attitude towerads the teaching profession among new in service teacher. This data could be a reference in developing improvement and decision make.

This chapter also proposes that comprehensive needs assessments should be employed regularly to understand the current state of leaders and future leaders. Interviews and surveys should be conducted with educational leaders and future leaders to measure leaders' attitudes and their apprentices' attitudes towards the teaching profession. At the same time, caring leadership assessment should always be exercised in order to maintain high levels among leaders and their apprentices. Feedback from existing leaders and apprentices is important to use as a reference to adjust and develop enhancement programmes accordingly. In this part, the development of feedback mechanisms is suggested to help leaders and future leaders take part and feel appreciated for being a part of the decision-making process.

Besides that, organisations should share success stories and celebrate the positive change in caring leadership and positive attitudes in their profession through credits and rewards. It is suggested that this process be done continuously in order to increase the level of caring leadership and foster a positive attitude towards the teaching profession. Evaluation processes encourage teachers to engage in self-reflection and adopt a growth mindset. When teachers are encouraged to reflect on their practice, set goals for improvement, and seek out opportunities for growth, it promotes a sense of ownership and agency in their professional development. Teachers who embrace a growth mindset are more likely to view challenges as opportunities for learning and growth, leading to a more positive attitude towards their profession (Jeffs et al., 2023; Kutasi, 2023; Rissanen & Kuusisto, 2023).

7. Curriculum Development to introduce Global Perspective in Caring Leadership

Using the model of caring leadership and attitude towards the teaching profession, this chapter suggests developing a caring leadership curriculum for the faculty members and their future leaders to boost their knowledge in this area. Curriculum development is essential to understand newly leadership practiced understandings from a new perspective (Al-Husseini et al., 2021; Farrell et al., 2022; Northouse, 2021). In this case, the responsible authority should model these values and practices to change the landscape and view caring leadership as a good practice for developing a positive attitude in the teaching profession.

Teacher training curriculum also needs to be revised where caring leadership subjects could be incorporated to promote caring leadership and attitude towards the teaching profession. It is suggested that courses in caring philosophy, ethics, and social-emotional learning should be developed and taught to the future leaders. At the same time, to ensure the understanding of the chosen career, global issues in education should be thought of by the leaders, and programmes such as collaboration with other institutions can help future leaders view the good examples that could be practices in the future. Institution could lead the change by introducing the global education concept, where issues, cultural diversity, and international teaching practices could be shared to broaden knowledge and change perceptions in order to instil empathy in the hearts of future leaders. This will help the broaden view in caring leadership and attitude towards teaching profession perspective. This can be done by cultivating cultural awareness and sensitivity, promoting global citizenship, encouraging collaboration and connection, inspiring innovation and creativity, and fostering lifelong learning and growth. By embracing a global perspective in their curriculum, teachers feel empowered to prepare students to be compassionate, informed, and engaged global citizens, leading to a sense of purpose and fulfilment in their roles as educators

8. Research and Innovation using Technology to foster Caring Leadership

The development of caring future leaders capacity should consider technology in changing resources, methods, and applications through the global educator network (Bagheri et al., 2022; Dexter & Richardson, 2020Sterrett & Richardson, 2020). Changing methods, programmes, cultures, and knowledge in managing educational institutions embedded with caring leadership may boost the inner selves to develop new talents in educators and prepare them for their future roles as caring leaders. At the same time, in order to develop more leaders in the future, progress can be made to encourage engagement in research and innovation. The management of higher education should focus on supporting the improvement of teaching and designing a curriculum that can attract the talents of future leaders to always have a passion for the teaching profession. This could be done with the assistance of existing technology and online collaboration in order to foster caring leadership.

Research on caring leadership also could be done in order to foster caring leadership. It is already known that research helps to develop better attitude and broaden perspective (Hendrickson & Askew, 2024 ; Liu & Huang, 2023; Rocco & Priest, 2023) The education institution is suggest to conduct research studies to deepen the understanding of caring leadership principles, behaviors, and their impact within the context of higher education. The relationship between caring leadership and organizational outcomes such as employee engagement, student success, and institutional performance could be explored to deepen the understanding of caring leadership. This can be done though the development of assessment tools. In this part the innovation in developing assessment tools, surveys, and instruments to measure caring leadership competencies among aspiring leaders in higher education may be employed through the existing framework which suitable with the education society. These tools can provide valuable insights into individuals' strengths, areas for growth, and readiness to lead with empathy and compassion. The outcome from the new insight may help future leaders to develop their capacity in changing to be a caring leader and also give impact to existing leaders who intent to improve their leadership skills.

The integration into leadership development programs might help the future leaders to prosper in their leadership capacity building. The outcome from the research can be integrated by using the research findings and evidence-based practices into leadership development programs and initiatives for future leaders in higher education. This can be done through designing curriculum modules, workshops, and training sessions that focus on fostering caring leadership skills, behaviours, and mindsets. In this part content from the research and innovation might be reference to leaders in solving their issues in caring leadership development. The use of technology cannot be separated from the new generation (Chan & Lee., 2023; Satam et al., 2023; Twenge, 2023). In this context, leverage technology to enhance leadership development and promote caring leadership among future leaders is useful in developing new caring leaders without technology has been left behind. The development of digital platforms, mobile applications, and online resources that offer interactive learning experiences, virtual simulations, and self-assessment tools to support the development of empathy, compassion, and inclusive leadership practices can be done with the expert of the future caring leaders. This is promising since more and more future generation are capable with the ability to create and developed technology to enhance the usage of online resources to foster caring leadership.

It is important to know weakness and strength properly to implement caring leadership, therefore the future caring leaders might suits their caring leadership ability with the evolvement of caring leadership towards the changing world. By embracing technology as a tool for positive change, caring leaders create supportive and empowering environments where teachers feel valued, supported, and inspired to make a difference in the lives of their students, leading to a more positive attitude towards the teaching profession.

9. Caring Leadership Promotion and Awareness

Awareness of caring leadership and positive attitudes towards the teaching profession could be promoted through social media, work courses, and seminars (Borah et al., 2022; Corbett & Spinello, 2020; Zhang et al., 2020). This could be done through sharing the success stories of established institutions, where their leaders could be a good example of practicing caring leadership and gain excellent academic reputation at the same time. The caring leadership promotion can be done through the creation of social media accounts dedicated the caring leadership and attitude towards teaching profession to develop leaders. This establishes social media accounts or profiles which specifically focused on promoting caring leadership in higher education through sharing knowledge, information or activities related to caring leadership. It is believe that through caring leadership example, young or future leaders may thinks that the post or sharing is useful for them to develop their future caring leadership capacity (Asghar et al., 2023; Khan, 2023; Quaquebeke & Gerpott, 2023). The other platform can be used such as Twitter, LinkedIn, Facebook, and Instagram to reach a diverse audience of students, faculty, staff, alumni, and community members may beneficial to give idea and example for future caring leadership practices.

The usage of social media to create compelling and contents like sharing inspirational quotes, success stories, case studies, research findings, and practical tips for practicing empathy, compassion, and inclusivity in leadership roles might help young leaders to view caring leadership is something essential for their future leadership talent development. Previous literature has discovered that learning from example may assist future leaders to develop their leadership capacity and skill in facing the real world. (Dugan, 2024; Ledlow et al., 2023; Lundqvist et al., 2023). Furthermore, real-life examples sharing in social media might help future leaders to give examples of caring leadership in action within the higher education community. This could be done by highlight individuals, teams, and organizations that exemplify caring leadership principles and practices, showcasing their positive impact on students, faculty, staff, and the wider community. This act can be done to multimedia utilization as well. The utilization of multimedia content such as videos, infographics, podcasts, and live streams might help to convey caring leadership messages effectively. This visual and interactive content tends to be more engaging and shareable, helping to increase awareness and reach a wider audience. Therefore, the caring leadership also could be learned not only by role modelling but also through the interactive content as well.

The future caring leaders should also engage with their audience. Partnering with individuals and organizations that share caring leadership values and objectives can help increase visibility and credibility. Future caring leaders must foster meaningful engagement with their audience by asking questions, soliciting feedback, and responding to comments and messages promptly. This can de done through encourage dialogue, discussion, and sharing of ideas related to caring leadership in higher education. In this part the collaboration with influences and partners is useful in giving new insight of caring leadership. the collaboration can be done with influencers, thought leaders, and partner organizations within the higher education sector to amplify caring message and reach a broader audience.

Undeniably in social media there is some great existing platform to engage with followers could give impact for caring leadership (Asghar et al., 2023; Fowler et al., 2023; Kalra et al., 2023). For example the ability to host Twitter Chats or Face-book Live Sessions is very engaging as well as TikTok. The future leaders might host Twitter chats or Facebook Live sessions to focused on topics related to caring leadership in higher education. Here the invitation of guest speakers, facilitate discussions, and encourage participation from your audience to create interactive and informative experiences. In this involvement of social media, sharing resources and tools is helpful in sharing valuable resources, tools, and practical tips for developing caring leadership skills and fostering a culture of empathy and inclusivity within higher education institutions. Future leaders also could provide links to articles, books, podcasts, webinars, and online courses related to caring leadership. With this social media platform and content, this might be very helpful for create engagement by the leaders to thier followers.

On the other hand, the organizing a summit might be very helpful to promote caring leadership through meeting and sharing their knowledge. The promotion and awareness of caring leadership could start with the selection of clear theme and objectives for the organized summit, such as "Fostering Caring Leadership in Higher Education" or "Empowering Future Leaders with Caring Leadership Skills." In this part, organizers have to ensure that the theme reflects the importance of empathy, compassion, and inclusivity in leadership roles within higher education. At the same time, partnership, mentoring and collaboration also may take part from this session. Clear theme creates clear objective and aims of the journey in organising the summit toward achievable goals. Therefore, sharing knowledge among academia might help to broaden the perspective of caring leadership action and practices. Future leaders or educational institution could invite keynote speakers who are recognized experts in caring leadership or who have demonstrated exemplary practice of caring leadership within the context of higher education. These speakers can provide insights, inspiration, and practical strategies for implementing caring leadership principles. With this sharing, it might helps audiences, leaders or future leaders in understanding clear caring leadership.

Activities such as panel discussions featuring a diverse range of leaders like academic administrators, faculty members, student leaders, and industry experts to share their knowledge and views on caring leadership could promote its awareness. Topics could include the role of caring leadership in promoting student success, fostering a positive organizational culture, and addressing challenges in higher education. Also, workshops and skill-building sessions that focus on developing key caring leadership competences, such as active listening, emotional intelligence, conflict resolution, and inclusive decision-making could help future caring leaders to develop their potential.

It is important to ensure that caring leadership promotion and awareness initiatives influence teachers' attitudes towards their profession by using social media to promote caring leadership, summit organising, highlighting positive examples, celebrating caring leadership, fostering a culture of collaboration and support using online platform, and empowering teachers to lead current practice change. By promoting caring leadership principles and practices, these initiatives inspire educators to cultivate empathy, compassion, and collaboration in their work, leading to a more positive and fulfilling experience in the teaching profession.

10. Reflect Recognition and Appreciation

Recognition and appreciation could help boost morale in the education society (Morales, 2022; Noor & Ampornstira, 2019; Zin et al., 2022). The implementation of a caring leadership programme and recognition for leaders and future leaders could be implemented. This chapter suggest that public appreciation and recognition should always be held to enhance the morale of leaders, and perhaps it could boost their self-esteem to be caring leaders. To build leadership capacity, it is suggested that the management of educational institutions always implement reflective practices among leaders at any level and develop research about caring leadership awards to encourage participation in networking programme. The establish awards or recognition programs to honor individuals or institutions that have demonstrated outstanding commitment to caring leadership in higher education could include young caring leaders awards to recognize achievements in areas such as student support, faculty development, community engagement, and organizational change among future developing leaders.

Appreciation plays a crucial role in fostering caring leadership among future leaders (Aljumah, 2023; Chen et al., 2023; Steilen, & Stone-Johnson, 2023). Theres some appreciation can be specifically utilized to nurture this leadership style. Showing gratitude to future leaders can be practiced in educational organisation. This will teach future leaders the importance of expressing genuine gratitude towards their team members. Future leaders could encourage themselves to regularly thank their colleagues for their contributions, both big and small, to show appreciation for their efforts in prcaticing caring leadership.

The importance to nurture caring leadership is to teach future leaders the importance of self-appreciation and self-care (Cripps, 2023; Martin, 2024; Turner & Tsang, 2023). Educational institution could encourage them to recognize their own accomplishments and to prioritize their well-being, leading by example in practicing self-compassion and self-care. At the same time promote a growth mindset to foster a culture of continuous learning and growth, where mistakes are seen as opportunities for improvement rather than failures. Future leaders should appreciate the learning journey of themselves and their team members, emphasizing progress over perfection. This might include providing support and resources to existing and young future leaders. Educational institution could appreciate the efforts of team members by providing them with the support, resources, and development opportunities they need to succeed. Future leaders also should invest in their professional growth and well-being, demonstrating care and commitment to their success. Leaders should actively seek feedback from their team members on how they can better demonstrate appreciation and support.

11. Experiential Learning and Continuous Improvement

To achieve the goals of building leadership capacity, the leaders in organisations should be able to open their minds and change to be better leaders (Baron, 2019; Crane, 2022; Harvey at al., 2019). In this part, policymakers should always update and improve the curriculum to change leadership training for future leaders in higher education. The evolving needs to make this process true also need to be revised from time to time. Future leaders also need to engage in internships, volunteer work, and leadership-based learning projects. These trainings could assist them in planning and executing improvements related to their future professions.

Future leaders should encourage to stay informed about emerging trends, best practices, and research in the field of leadership and organizational development. Attend conferences, participate in professional networks, and engage with thought leaders to stay current and continuously evolve as leaders is important to keep caring leaders up to date with issues, solutions and practicing caring leadership. These opportunities to recalibrate their approach and set goals for continuous growth and development. To achieve this state, other new ideas that could be implemented is the concept of leadership style characterized by humility, openness, and a willingness to learn from others (Al-Abrrow et al., 2023; Kelemen et al., 2023; Tariq et al., 2023). Future leaders should acknowledge their own limitations, seek input from diverse perspectives, and remain receptive to feedback and new ideas, creating an environment where continuous improvement flourishes. Caring leadership influences attitudes towards the teaching profession through reflective recognition and appreciation by continuous validating efforts, stay informed about emerging trends and inspiring excellence among teachers.

FUTURE RESEARCH DIRECTION/CONCLUSION

This chapter has proposed several steps to be taken by education institution members, society, management, and stakeholders towards developing the future talents of caring leaders. With the insights gained from exploring the relationship between caring leadership and attitudes towards the teaching profession in higher education, several future research directions emerge. These directions aim to deepen the understanding of this dynamic and its implications for educational leadership, institutions, society's well-being, and institutional effectiveness. First, future research should include longitudinal studies to assess the long-term effects of caring leadership on faculty attitudes and outcomes.

In conclusion, promoting caring leadership among future leaders is not only essential for organisational success but also for creating positive work environments where employees feel valued, supported, and motivated to perform at their best. Utilising the principles of empathy, compassion, and respect, future leaders can cultivate a culture of care that fosters trust, collaboration, and employee well-being. To flourish caring leadership among leaders and future caring leaders is to recognise that continuous improvement is also key in this endeavour. As future leaders, they must be willing to reflect on their practices, seek feedback, and adapt to changing circumstances to effectively meet the needs of their teams and organisations.

In essence, using the model of the relationship between caring leadership and the attitude towards the teaching profession to promote caring leadership among future leaders is not just a strategic imperative but also a moral imperative. By prioritising empathy, understanding, and kindness in their leadership approach, future leaders can create workplaces where individuals thrive, collaboration flourishes, and organisational goals are achieved with integrity and compassion. Ultimately, the impact of caring leadership extends far beyond the bottom line, shaping the future of work in a way that prioritises the well-being and dignity of all individuals involved.

REFERENCES

Adhikari, A., Saha, B., & Sen, S. (2023). Nel Noddings' Theory of Care and its Ethical Components. *International Research Journal of Education and Technology*, 5(8), 198-206.

Aithal, P. S., & Aithal, S. (2023). How to increase emotional infrastructure of higher education institutions. [IJMTS]. *International Journal of Management, Technology, and Social Sciences*, 8(3), 356–394. DOI: 10.47992/IJMTS.2581.6012.0307

Al-Abrrow, H., Fayez, A. S., Abdullah, H., Khaw, K. W., Alnoor, A., & Rexhepi, G. (2023). Effect of open-mindedness and humble behavior on innovation: Mediator role of learning. *International Journal of Emerging Markets*, 18(9), 3065–3084. DOI: 10.1108/IJOEM-08-2020-0888

Al-Husseini, S., El Beltagi, I., & Moizer, J. (2021). Transformational leadership and innovation: The mediating role of knowledge sharing amongst higher education faculty. *International Journal of Leadership in Education*, 24(5), 670–693. DOI: 10.1080/13603124.2019.1588381

Ali, A. H., Kineber, A. F., Elyamany, A., Ibrahim, A. H., & Daoud, A. O. (2023). Modelling the role of modular construction's critical success factors in the overall sustainable success of Egyptian housing projects. *Journal of Building Engineering*, 71, 106467. DOI: 10.1016/j.jobe.2023.106467

Aljumah, A. (2023). The impact of extrinsic and intrinsic motivation on job satisfaction: The mediating role of transactional leadership. *Cogent Business & Management*, 10(3), 2270813. DOI: 10.1080/23311975.2023.2270813

Anderson, V., Rabello, R., Wass, R., Golding, C., Rangi, A., Eteuati, E., Bristowe, Z., & Waller, A. (2020). Good teaching as care in higher education. *Higher Education*, 79(1), 1–19. DOI: 10.1007/s10734-019-00392-6

Asghar, M. Z., Barbera, E., Rasool, S. F., Seitamaa-Hakkarainen, P., & Mohelská, H. (2023). Adoption of social media-based knowledge-sharing behaviour and authentic leadership development: Evidence from the educational sector of Pakistan during COVID-19. *Journal of Knowledge Management*, 27(1), 59–83. DOI: 10.1108/JKM-11-2021-0892

Awan, F. H., Dunnan, L., Jamil, K., & Gul, R. F. (2023). Stimulating environmental performance via green human resource management, green transformational leadership, and green innovation: A mediation-moderation model. *Environmental Science and Pollution Research International*, 30(2), 2958–2976. DOI: 10.1007/s11356-022-22424-y PMID: 35939187

Azmi, A. N. (2024). *Relationships Between Lecturers' Caring Leadership And Pre-Service Teachers' Thinking Styles And Attitudes Towards Teaching Profession At Teacher Education Institutes In Kuala Lumpur*[Unpublished Doctoral Thesis]. University of Malaya

Bagga, S. K., Gera, S., & Haque, S. N. (2023). The mediating role of organizational culture: Transformational leadership and change management in virtual teams. *Asia Pacific Management Review*, 28(2), 120–131.

Bagheri, A., Newman, A., & Eva, N. (2022). Entrepreneurial leadership of CEOs and employees' innovative behavior in high-technology new ventures. *Journal of Small Business Management*, 60(4), 805–827. DOI: 10.1080/00472778.2020.1737094

Bagheri, S., Zarshenas, L., Rakhshan, M., Sharif, F., Sarani, E. M., Shirazi, Z. H., & Sitzman, K. (2023). Impact of Watson's human caring-based health promotion program on caregivers of individuals with schizophrenia. *BMC Health Services Research*, 23(1), 711. DOI: 10.1186/s12913-023-09725-9 PMID: 37386572

Baker, S., & Burke, R. (2023). What Is Care? In *Questioning Care in Higher Education: Resisting Definitions as Radical* (pp. 21–58). Springer International Publishing. DOI: 10.1007/978-3-031-41829-7_2

Baron, J. (2019). Actively open-minded thinking in politics. *Cognition*, 188, 8–18. DOI: 10.1016/j.cognition.2018.10.004 PMID: 30366602

Bodolica, V., & Spraggon, M. (2021). Incubating innovation in university settings: Building entrepreneurial mindsets in the future generation of innovative emerging market leaders. *Education + Training*, 63(4), 613–631. DOI: 10.1108/ET-06-2020-0145

Borah, P. S., Iqbal, S., & Akhtar, S. (2022). Linking social media usage and SME's sustainable performance: The role of digital leadership and innovation capabilities. *Technology in Society*, 68, 101900. DOI: 10.1016/j.techsoc.2022.101900

Bower, B. L., & Wolverton, M. (2023). *Answering the call: African American women in higher education leadership*. Taylor & Francis. DOI: 10.4324/9781003443001

Buchanan, R., Mills, T., & Mooney, E. (2022). Working across time and space: Developing a framework for teacher leadership throughout a teaching career. In *Leadership for Professional Learning* (pp. 65–77). Routledge. DOI: 10.4324/9781003357384-5

Burke, B. M., & Ceo-DiFrancesco, D. (2022). Recruitment and retention of world language teacher education majors: Perspectives of teacher candidates and alumni to remedy a global shortage. *Foreign Language Annals*, 55(2), 333–360. DOI: 10.1111/flan.12613

Cellina, F., Castri, R., Simão, J. V., & Granato, P. (2020). Co-creating app-based policy measures for mobility behavior change: A trigger for novel governance practices at the urban level. *Sustainable Cities and Society*, 53, 101911. DOI: 10.1016/j. scs.2019.101911

Chan, C. K. Y., & Lee, K. K. (2023). The AI generation gap: Are Gen Z students more interested in adopting generative AI such as ChatGPT in teaching and learning than their Gen X and millennial generation teachers? *Smart Learning Environments*, 10(1), 60. DOI: 10.1186/s40561-023-00269-3

Chen, S., Zhu, Y., Guo, L., & Liu, W. (2023). The impact of leader gratitude expressions on followers' behaviours: Increasing gratitude and increases proactivity. *Journal of Leadership & Organizational Studies*, 30(2), 187–204. DOI: 10.1177/15480518231151575

Corbett, F., & Spinello, E. (2020). Connectivism and leadership: Harnessing a learning theory for the digital age to redefine leadership in the twenty-first century. *Heliyon*, 6(1), e03250. DOI: 10.1016/j.heliyon.2020.e03250 PMID: 31993523

Cordova Jr, N., Kilag, O. K., Andrin, G., Tañiza, F. N., Groenewald, E., & Abella, J. (2024). Leadership Strategies for Numeracy Development in Educational Settings. *Excellencia: International Multi-disciplinary Journal of Education (2994-9521)*, 2(1), 58-68.

Crane, B. (2022). Leadership mindsets: Why new managers fail and what to do about it. *Business Horizons*, 65(4), 447–455. DOI: 10.1016/j.bushor.2021.05.005

Crawford, J., Cowling, M., & Allen, K. A. (2023). Leadership is needed for ethical ChatGPT: Character, assessment, and learning using artificial intelligence (AI). *Journal of University Teaching & Learning Practice, 20*(3), 02.

Cripps, K. (2023). University Sustainability Career Information Events for Future Leaders. In *Events Management for the Infant and Youth Market* (pp. 55–65). Emerald Publishing Limited. DOI: 10.1108/978-1-80455-690-020231009

Dadvand, B., van Driel, J., Speldewinde, C., & Dawborn-Gundlach, M. (2024). Career change teachers in hard-to-staff schools: Should I stay or leave? *Australian Educational Researcher*, 51(2), 481 496. DOI: 10.1007/s13384-023-00609-9 PMID: 36817651

Davidaviciene, V., & Al Majzoub, K. (2022). The effect of cultural intelligence, conflict, and transformational leadership on decision-making processes in virtual teams. *Social Sciences (Basel, Switzerland)*, 11(2), 64. DOI: 10.3390/socsci11020064

DeMatthews, D. E., Knight, D. S., & Shin, J. (2022). The principal-teacher churn: Understanding the relationship between leadership turnover and teacher attrition. *Educational Administration Quarterly*, 58(1), 76–109. DOI: 10.1177/0013161X211051974

Dexter, S., & Richardson, J. W. (2020). What does technology integration research tell us about the leadership of technology? *Journal of Research on Technology in Education*, 52(1), 17–36. DOI: 10.1080/15391523.2019.1668316

Dreer, B. (2024). Teachers' well-being and job satisfaction: The important role of positive emotions in the workplace. *Educational Studies*, 50(1), 61–77. DOI: 10.1080/03055698.2021.1940872

Dugan, J. P. (2024). *Leadership theory: Cultivating critical perspectives*. John Wiley & Sons.

Farrell, C. C., Penuel, W. R., Allen, A., Anderson, E. R., Bohannon, A. X., Coburn, C. E., & Brown, S. L. (2022). Learning at the boundaries of research and practice: A framework for understanding research–practice partnerships. *Educational Researcher*, 51(3), 197–208. DOI: 10.3102/0013189X211069073

Fischer, T., & Sitkin, S. B. (2023). Leadership styles: A comprehensive assessment and way forward. *The Academy of Management Annals*, 17(1), 331–372. DOI: 10.5465/annals.2020.0340

Forrest, L. L., & Geraghty, J. R. (2022). Student-Led Initiatives and Advocacy in Academic Medicine: Empowering the leaders of tomorrow. *Academic Medicine*, 97(6), 781–785. DOI: 10.1097/ACM.0000000000004644 PMID: 35234719

Fowler, J., Zachry, M., & McDonald, D. W. (2023). Policy recommendations from an empirical study of an online foster care community. *Child Indicators Research*, 16(5), 2033–2054. DOI: 10.1007/s12187-023-10037-x

Guo, L., & Hau, K. T. (2024). Adolescents want to be teachers? Affecting factors and two-decade trends in 39 educational systems. *International Journal of Educational Research*, 123, 102274. DOI: 10.1016/j.ijer.2023.102274

Hair, J. F., Hult, G. T. M., Ringle, C. M., & Sarstedt, M. (2022). *A primer on partial least squares structural equation modeling (PLS-SEM)* (3rd ed.). Sage.

Hair, J. F., Sarstedt, M., Ringle, C. M., & Gudergan, S. P. (2024). *Advanced issues in partial least squares structural equation modeling (PLS-SEM)* (2nd ed.). Sage.

Hammoudi Halat, D., Soltani, A., Dalli, R., Alsarraj, L., & Malki, A. (2023). Understanding and fostering mental health and well-being among university faculty: A narrative review. *Journal of Clinical Medicine*, 12(13), 4425. DOI: 10.3390/jcm12134425 PMID: 37445459

Hartcher, K., Chapman, S., & Morrison, C. (2023). Applying a band-aid or building a bridge: Ecological factors and divergent approaches to enhancing teacher wellbeing. *Cambridge Journal of Education*, 53(3), 329–356. DOI: 10.1080/0305764X.2022.2155612

Harvey, J. F., Johnson, K. J., Roloff, K. S., & Edmondson, A. C. (2019). From orientation to behavior: The interplay between learning orientation, open-mindedness, and psychological safety in team learning. *Human Relations*, 72(11), 1726–1751. DOI: 10.1177/0018726718817812

Heffernan, A., MacDonald, K., & Longmuir, F. (2022). The emotional intensity of educational leadership: A scoping review. *International Journal of Leadership in Education*, ●●●, 1–23.

Hendrickson, K. A., & Askew, K. (2024). Broadening participation in STEM, caring intelligence as a leadership intelligence: Perspectives of HBCU faculty leaders. *Journal of Applied Research in Higher Education*. Advance online publication. DOI: 10.1108/JARHE-08-2023-0368

Hoque, K. E., & Raya, Z. T. (2023). Relationship between principals' leadership styles and teachers' behavior. *Behavioral Sciences (Basel, Switzerland)*, 13(2), 111. DOI: 10.3390/bs13020111 PMID: 36829339

Jang, H. S., Valero, J. N., & Jung, K. (2023). Effective leadership in network collaboration: Lessons learned from continuum of care homeless programs. In *Understanding Nonprofit Organizations* (pp. 150–161). Routledge. DOI: 10.4324/9781003387800-18

Jeffs, C., Nelson, N., Grant, K. A., Nowell, L., Paris, B., & Viceer, N. (2023). Feedback for teaching development: Moving from a fixed to growth mindset. *Professional Development in Education*, 49(5), 842–855. DOI: 10.1080/19415257.2021.1876149

John, E. P. S. (Ed.). (2022). *Co-learning in higher education: Community wellbeing, engaged scholarship, and creating futures.* Taylor & Francis. DOI: 10.4324/9781003310112

Kalra, A., Briggs, E., & Schrock, W. (2023). Exploring the synergistic role of ethical leadership and sales control systems on salesperson social media use and sales performance. *Journal of Business Research*, 154, 113344. DOI: 10.1016/j.jbusres.2022.113344

Karsono, B., Suraji, R., & Sastrodiharjo, I. (2022). The Influence of Leadership Spirituality to Improving the Quality of Higher Education in Indonesia. *International Journal of Social Sciences and Humanities Invention*, 9(01), 6832–6841. DOI: 10.18535/ijsshi/v9i02.06

Kelemen, T. K., Matthews, S. H., Matthews, M. J., & Henry, S. E. (2023). Humble leadership: A review and synthesis of leader expressed humility. *Journal of Organizational Behavior*, 44(2), 202–224. DOI: 10.1002/job.2608

Kelly, H. (2023). *School leaders matter: Preventing burnout, managing stress, and improving wellbeing*. Routledge. DOI: 10.4324/9781003198475

Khan, A. N. (2023). A diary study of social media and performance in service sector: Transformational leadership as cross-level moderator. *Current Psychology (New Brunswick, N.J.)*, 42(12), 10077–10091. DOI: 10.1007/s12144-021-02310-5

Khan, I. U., Idris, M., & Amin, R. U. (2023). Leadership style and performance in higher education: The role of organizational justice. *International Journal of Leadership in Education*, 26(6), 1111–1125. DOI: 10.1080/13603124.2020.1854868

Khumalo, S. S. (2019). Analyzing abusive school leadership practices through the lens of social justice. *International Journal of Educational Management*, 33(4), 546–555. DOI: 10.1108/IJEM-11-2017-0320

Kilag, O. K. T., Uy, F. T., Abendan, C. F. K., & Malbas, M. H. (2023). Teaching leadership: An examination of best practices for leadership educators. *Science and Education*, 4(7), 430–445.

Kraft, M. A., & Lyon, M. A. (2024). *The rise and fall of the teaching profession: Prestige, interest, preparation, and satisfaction over the last half century* (No. w32386). National Bureau of Economic Research.

Kutasi, R. (2023). Cultivating a Classroom Culture of Growth: Nurture the Power of a Growth Mindset. *Acta Marisiensis.Philologia*, 5(5), 91–101.

Kyangwe, L., Onyango, D. O., & Alloph, J. M. (2023). Strategies to Enhance Teachers' Job Satisfaction in Secondary Schools in Butiama District, Mara, Tanzania. *East African Journal of Education Studies*, 6(1), 120–132. DOI: 10.37284/eajes.6.1.1078

Lanaj, K., Jennings, R. E., Ashford, S. J., & Krishnan, S. (2022). When leader self-care begets other care: Leader role self-compassion and helping at work. *The Journal of Applied Psychology*, 107(9), 1543–1560. DOI: 10.1037/apl0000957 PMID: 34647780

Leal Filho, W., Eustachio, J. H. P. P., Caldana, A. C. F., Will, M., Lange Salvia, A., Levay, C., & Andersson Bäck, M. (2022). Caring leader identity between power and powerlessness. *Organization Studies*, 43(6), 953–972. DOI: 10.1177/01708406211006245

Ledger, M., See, B. H., Gorard, S., & Morris, R. (2024). A new approach to understanding the global teacher supply crisis. In *An International Approach to Developing Early Career Researchers* (pp. 160–176). Routledge. DOI: 10.4324/9781003455066-17

Ledlow, G. R., Bosworth, M., & Maryon, T. (2023). *Leadership for health professionals: Theory, skills, and applications*. Jones & Bartlett Learning.

Li, M., Ahmed, A., Syed, O. R., Khalid, N., & Muñoz, J. E.Jr. (2022). Impact of abusive leader behavior on employee job insecurity: A mediating roles of emotional exhaustion and abusive peer behavior. *Frontiers in Psychology*, 13, 947258. DOI: 10.3389/fpsyg.2022.947258 PMID: 36072034

Liu, W., & Huang, C. (2023). The international comparative approach to higher education leadership development: Evaluating the longer-term impacts. *International Journal of Leadership in Education*, ●●●, 1–15. DOI: 10.1080/13603124.2023.2224773

Lumby, J. (2019). Leadership and power in higher education. *Studies in Higher Education*, 44(9), 1619–1629. DOI: 10.1080/03075079.2018.1458221

Lundqvist, D., Wallo, A., Coetzer, A., & Kock, H. (2023). Leadership and learning at work: A systematic literature review of learning-oriented leadership. *Journal of Leadership & Organizational Studies*, 30(2), 205–238. DOI: 10.1177/15480518221133970

Ma, X., Khattak, A., Ghani, B., & Huo, M. (2023). Perceived overqualification in higher education institutions: Enhancing employee innovative behavior via creative self-confidence and harmonious workplace climate. *Current Psychology (New Brunswick, N.J.)*, ●●●, 1–12.

Majali, T. E., Alkaraki, M., Asad, M., Aladwan, N., & Aledeinat, M. (2022). Green transformational leadership, green entrepreneurial orientation and performance of SMEs: The mediating role of green product innovation. *Journal of Open Innovation*, 8(4), 191. DOI: 10.3390/joitmc8040191

Marshall, D. T,, Pressley, T., Neugebauer, N. M., & Shannon, D. M. (2022). Why teachers are leaving and what we can do about it. *Phi Delta Kappan*, 104(1), 6 11. DOI: 10.1177/00317217221123642

Martin, C. (2024). The impact of the pandemic on leaders: A pathway to healing and self-care. *Nursing Management*, 55(1), 12–19. DOI: 10.1097/nmg.0000000000000081 PMID: 38170884

McCullough, L. B., Coverdale, J., & Chervenak, F. A. (2023). Professional virtue of civility and the responsibilities of medical educators and academic leaders. *Journal of Medical Ethics*, 49(10), 674–678. DOI: 10.1136/jme-2022-108735 PMID: 36889908

Mikkonen, K., Kuivila, H. M., Sjögren, T., Korpi, H., Koskinen, C., Koskinen, M., Koivula, M., Koskimäki, M., Lähteenmäki, M.-L., Saaranen, T., Sormunen, M., Salminen, L., Mäki-Hakola, H., Wallin, O., Holopainen, A., Tuomikoski, A.-M., & Kääriäinen, M. (2022). Social, health care and rehabilitation educators' competence in professional education—Empirical testing of a model. *Health & Social Care in the Community*, 30(1), e75–e85. DOI: 10.1111/hsc.13414 PMID: 34009683

Moldoveanu, M., & Narayandas, D. (2019). The future of leadership development. *Harvard Business Review*, 97(2), 40–48.

Morales, J. C. (2022). Transformational Leadership and Teacher Work Motivation in Private Educational Institutions. *International Journal of Research Publications*, 105(1), 578–614. DOI: 10.47119/IJRP1001051720223687

Näsman, Y. (2018). The theory of caritative leadership applied to education. *International Journal of Leadership in Education*, 21(4), 518–529. DOI: 10.1080/13603124.2017.1349183

Noor, A., & Ampornstira, F. (2019). Effect of Leadership on Employee Morale in Higher Education. *International Journal of Business and Social Science*, 10(7), 141–144. DOI: 10.30845/ijbss.v10n7p15

Northouse, P. G. (2021). *Leadership: Theory and practice*. Sage publications.

Nwoko, J. C., Emeto, T. I., Malau-Aduli, A. E., & Malau-Aduli, B. S. (2023). A systematic review of the factors that influence teachers' occupational wellbeing. *International Journal of Environmental Research and Public Health*, 20(12), 6070. DOI: 10.3390/ijerph20126070 PMID: 37372657

Odhiambo, G. (2022). Toxic Leadership in Education: An Understanding of the Dark Side of Leadership. In *Handbook of Research on Educational Leadership and Research Methodology* (pp. 233-255). IGI Global.

Oleksiyenko, A. (2018). Zones of alienation in global higher education: Corporate abuse and leadership failures. *Tertiary Education and Management*, 24, 193–205. DOI: 10.1080/13583883.2018.1439095

Ozaki, H. (2023). Caring and Education. In *Philosophy of Education in Dialogue between East and West* (pp. 1–13). Routledge. DOI: 10.4324/9781003271024-1

Peist, E., McMahon, S. D., Davis-Wright, J. O., & Keys, C. B. (2024). Understanding teacher-directed violence and related turnover through a school climate framework. *Psychology in the Schools*, 61(1), 220–236. DOI: 10.1002/pits.23044

Qiu, S., Alizadeh, A., Dooley, L. M., & Zhang, R. (2019). The effects of authentic leadership on trust in leaders, organizational citizenship behavior, and service quality in the Chinese hospitality industry. *Journal of Hospitality and Tourism Management*, 40, 77–87. DOI: 10.1016/j.jhtm.2019.06.004

Quaquebeke, N. V., & Gerpott, F. H. (2023). The now, new, and next of digital leadership: How Artificial Intelligence (AI) will take over and change leadership as we know it. *Journal of Leadership & Organizational Studies*, 30(3), 265–275. DOI: 10.1177/15480518231181731

Rae, J. (2023). Connecting for creativity in higher education. *Innovative Higher Education*, 48(1), 127–143. DOI: 10.1007/s10755-022-09609-6

Rampasso, I. S., & Kovaleva, M. (2020). Sustainability leadership in higher education institutions: An overview of challenges. *Sustainability (Basel)*, 12(9), 3761. DOI: 10.3390/su12093761

Ringle, C. M., Wende, S., & Becker, J.-M. (2024). *SmartPLS 4. Bönningstedt: SmartPLS*. Retrieved from https://www.smartpls.com

Rissanen, I., & Kuusisto, E. (2023). The role of growth mindset in shaping teachers' intercultural competencies: A study among Finnish teachers. *British Educational Research Journal*, 49(5), 947–967. DOI: 10.1002/berj.3875

Rocco, M. L., & Priest, K. L. (2023). Extending the scope of leadership identity development. *New Directions for Student Leadership*, 2023(178), 107–117. DOI: 10.1002/yd.20559 PMID: 37309859

Ryu, J., Walls, J., & Seashore Louis, K. (2022). Caring leadership: The role of principals in producing caring school cultures. *Leadership and Policy in Schools*, 21(3), 585–602. DOI: 10.1080/15700763.2020.1811877

Sam, C. H. (2021). What are the practices of unethical leaders? Exploring how teachers experience the "dark side" of administrative leadership. *Educational Management Administration & Leadership*, 49(2), 303–320. DOI: 10.1177/1741143219898480

Satam, H., Joshi, K., Mangrolia, U., Waghoo, S., Zaidi, G., Rawool, S., Thakare, R. P., Banday, S., Mishra, A. K., Das, G., & Malonia, S. K. (2023). Next-generation sequencing technology: Current trends and advancements. *Biology (Basel)*, 12(7), 997. DOI: 10.3390/biology12070997 PMID: 37508427

Sharma, P., & Jain, V. (2022). Role of culture in developing transformative leadership for higher education in emerging economies. In *Re-imagining educational futures in developing countries: Lessons from global health crises* (pp. 243–259). Springer International Publishing. DOI: 10.1007/978-3-030-88234-1_13

Smylie, M. A., Murphy, J., & Louis, K. S. (2016). Caring school leadership: A multidisciplinary, cross-occupational model. *American Journal of Education*, 123(1), 1–35. DOI: 10.1086/688166

Steilen, K., & Stone-Johnson, C. (2023, June). "There wasn't a guidebook for this": Caring leadership during crisis. [). Frontiers.]. *Frontiers in Education*, 8, 1183134. DOI: 10.3389/feduc.2023.1183134

Sterrett, W., & Richardson, J. W. (2020). Supporting professional development through digital principal leadership. *Journal of Organizational and Educational Leadership*, 5(2), 4.

Stoytcheva, B., Horissian, K., & You, W. (2024). Factors Affecting Theatre Faculty Job Satisfaction: A Thematic Analysis. *Theatre Topics*, 34(1), 19–31. DOI: 10.1353/tt.2024.a920470

Tariq, H., Abrar, M., & Ahmad, B. (2023). Humility breeds creativity: The moderated mediation model of leader humility and subordinates' creative service performance in hospitality. *International Journal of Contemporary Hospitality Management*, 35(12), 4117–4136. DOI: 10.1108/IJCHM-07-2022-0851

Tuckwiller, E., Fox, H., Ball, K., & St. Louis, J. (2024). More than just a "nod" to care: Expanding Nel Noddings' ethics of care framework to sustain educator resilience. *Leadership and Policy in Schools*, ●●●, 1–18. DOI: 10.1080/15700763.2024.2311249

Turner, S., & Tsang, Y. (2023). Nature versus nurture: What underpins great leadership? The case for nurture. *Clinical Oncology*, 35(1), 6–9. DOI: 10.1016/j.clon.2022.09.053 PMID: 36270863

UNESCO. (2023). *Global report on teachers: addressing teacher shortages*. United Nations Educational, Scientific and Cultural Organization.

Uusiautti, S., & Maatta, K. (2013). Enhancing university students' study success through caring leadership. *European Scientific Journal, 9*(19). Twenge, J. M. (2023). *Generations: The Real Differences Between Gen Z, Millennials [Boomers, and Silents—and What They Mean for America's Future*. Simon and Schuster.]. *GEN*, ●●●, X.

Vermeulen, M., Kreijns, K., & Evers, A. T. (2022). Transformational leadership, leader–member exchange and school learning climate: Impact on teachers' innovative behaviour in the Netherlands. *Educational Management Administration & Leadership*, 50(3), 491–510. DOI: 10.1177/1741143220932582

Walk, M. (2023). Leaders as change executors: The impact of leader attitudes to change and change-specific support on followers. *European Management Journal*, 41(1), 154–163. DOI: 10.1016/j.emj.2022.01.002

Walls, J. (2022). Performativity and caring in education: Toward an ethic of reimagination. *Journal of School Leadership*, 32(3), 289–314. DOI: 10.1177/1052684620972065

Wei, H., Corbett, R. W., Ray, J., & Wei, T. L. (2020). A culture of caring: The essence of healthcare interprofessional collaboration. *Journal of Interprofessional Care*, 34(3), 324–331. DOI: 10.1080/13561820.2019.1641476 PMID: 31390903

Wieser, C. (2024). Teacher qualities that make teachers stay in the profession: Addressing teacher shortage in Nordic countries with ethics of care. *Teacher ethics and teaching quality in Scandinavian schools*, 51-65.

Zepeda, S. J. (2019). *Professional development: What works*. Routledge.

Zhang, F., Peng, X., Huang, L., Liu, Y., Xu, J., He, J., Guan, C., Chang, H., & Chen, Y. (2022). A caring leadership model in nursing: A grounded theory approach. *Journal of Nursing Management*, 30(4), 981–992. DOI: 10.1111/jonm.13600 PMID: 35312131

Zhang, Z., Gao, Y., & Li, Z. (2020). Consensus reaching for social network group decision making by considering leadership and bounded confidence. *Knowledge-Based Systems*, 204, 106240. DOI: 10.1016/j.knosys.2020.106240

Zin, M. L. M., Ibrahim, H., Aman-Ullah, A., & Ibrahim, N. (2022). Transformational leadership, job enrichment and recognition as predictors of job satisfaction in non-profit organizations. *Nankai Business Review International*, 14(2), 338–351.

ADDITIONAL READING

Louis, K. S., Murphy, J., & Smylie, M. (2016). Caring leadership in schools: Findings from exploratory analyses. *Educational Administration Quarterly*, 52(2), 310–348. DOI: 10.1177/0013161X15627678

Noddings, N. (2006). Educational leaders as caring teachers. *School Leadership & Management*, 26(4), 339–345. DOI: 10.1080/13632430600886848

Smylie, M. A., Murphy, J. F., & Louis, K. S. (2020). *Caring school leadership*. Corwin. DOI: 10.4135/9781071872741

Chapter 10
Student Involvement in Leadership Programmes at the UWI, Mona and the Impact They Have on Their Personal and Professional Development

Roger M. Bent

The University of the West Indies, Mona, Jamaica

Shinique J. Walters

The University of the West Indies, Mona, Jamaica

ABSTRACT

It has been highlighted that a lot of our political leaders and various CEO were all a part of some form of student leadership through their sojourn at the U.W.I. This factors has always been an area for higher education institutions, it is also important to determine how students perceive the leadership development programs from which they are meant to benefit. The study is grounded in the Kolbs, 2015 Experimental learning theory. This posits that we all have the ability to become a leader with different experiences and these experiences impact how we deal with challenges and opportunities to become who we are as professionals and leaders. The researchers embarked on an exploratory qualitative assessment where they utilized past students who were once enrolled in the guild to facilitate interviews.

DOI: 10.4018/979-8-3693-9215-7.ch010

The study used a phenomenological methodological approach in assessing the experiences of these students and assessing these various factors with regard to their personal development.

INTRODUCTION

Leadership in the current global landscape has to be flexible to accommodate the fast-paced changes that are occurring in the world around us. The world needs leaders with the skills and qualities that can manoeuvre the complex nature of contemporary societies (Korejan, & Shahbazi, 2016). The role of schools, especially universities, is critical as they are the main portals of learning. Through involvement in leadership programmes and initiatives in these spaces individuals learn valuable skill sets such as emotional intelligence, change management and digital literacy. A critical feature however is the global perspectives that universities in particular expose leaders to. The curriculum and internationalised focus of these institutions demonstrate the interconnected nature of economies and society.

Young leaders who develop a global mind-set will better understand cultures, apply themselves to international best practices and collaborate with groups and entities from various backgrounds (Samad, 2012). These skill sets will impact and shape the world as the labour market is expecting graduates to be armed with these soft skill competencies when they exit institutions of higher learning. The graduates will filter into critical industries such as politics, science, and commerce.

The main components of this chapter examine the role of the Guild of Students, its leadership programme, and its impact on the personal and professional lives of the participants. It has been highlighted that a significant number of our political leaders and various Chief Executive Officers (CEOs) were involved in some form of student leadership throughout their sojourn at The University of the West Indies (UWI). The role of universities to prepare a qualified labour force is an important feature for higher education institutions, it is also important to determine how students perceive the leadership development programmes and their impact on areas such as success and communities. The literature points to how effective leadership can elevate various aspects of society so establishing a connection with leadership training programmes in universities and the world of work is critical to the discourse in this chapter.

The chapter will be guided by the following research questions:

- What are the main factors that have contributed to your personal development while on the Guild of Students?

- What are the main opportunities that you accessed while on the Guild of Students and how has that helped with regards to your professional development?
- What are the main challenges while on the guild and how has that helped with regards to your professional development?
- What factors would you consider encouraging more persons to participate in the Guild of Students and its leadership programme?

Conceptualization

The UWI Guild of Students Council - The UWI Guild of Students (The Guild) is the body that represents the interests of the students via a democratically elected process. While each student has membership in the Guild, the Guild Council which is the decision making arm of the organisation consists of democratically elected student leaders from the UWI who availed themselves to serving their peers (fellow students) by advocating on their behalf and aiding in their development and experience while being students at The UWI. The Guild focuses on promoting, fostering and developing the educational, social, cultural and economic interests of its members at all levels be it local, regional or international (U.W.I., 2024). The Guild as a programme is enshrined in the University's Charter and is overseen by the Office of Student Services and Development whose mandate is to develop student learning and development on all five (5) campuses of the UWI (U.W.I., 2024). Throughout the year various development activities are offered to the Guild Councillors and at the end of the period, an evaluation exercise is conducted as a fit for purpose quality assurance measure. This kind of rigour establishes the intentionality of the university to develop transformational leaders for life and the world of work.

Personal Development - Personal development looks at the awareness and identity, used to develop talents and potential, build human capital that enhances the quality of life, and contribute to the realisation of dreams and aspirations." (Bob, 2010))

Professional Development - Professional development refers to the continuous process of acquiring new knowledge, skills, and experiences that can help individuals advance their careers and enhance their professional capabilities. (Speck & Knipe, 2005)

Conceptual Framework

Leadership plays a critical role in society hence it is a widely studied phenomenon. Leadership is defined as the ability to influence and guide individuals, groups, or entities to achieve mutual gains. The concept extends beyond a position of influence to form character traits that others can admire and emulate such as trust, respect, and confidence.

There are several leadership theories which have developed over time that explore the various facets of leadership and the nuances that make leaders effective. The theory most relevant to this study however is transformational leadership given the established curriculum of The University of the West Indies and the demands in the world of work.

Transformational Leadership

Transformational leadership has gained prominence as the world has evolved into a faster paced environment. The features of this kind of leadership style are adaptive to change, hence its adoption into mainstream society. Transformational leadership inspires not just the individual but those in orbit which makes it applicable in high stress contexts and especially in the business and political realms. These qualities make it a suitable framework for the Guild of Students to design and implement leadership initiatives. Studies in fact have shown a nexus between transformational leadership and organisational performance (Samad, 2012).

The keen interest in locating the value of leadership training in the academy is important as learning institutions play a pivotal role in developing individuals for the world of work. Higher educational institutions in particular, are based on the development stage of students at that level, and sets the foundation for the development of essential skills and qualities that will be advantageous in the world of work. The skill sets often referred to as soft skills, translate into the wider society, manifesting themselves through areas such as innovation and resilience, cultural competence, and social responsibility.

Kolb's Experiential Learning Theory

Kolb's Experiential Learning Theory (ELT) is named after American Educational Theorist David A. Kolb who conceptualised it. He opines that learning is the process whereby knowledge is encouraged through the transformation of experience. It is a widely recognized framework that incorporates a cyclical model of learning, consisting of four stages, namely: concrete experience; observation and reflection; the formation of abstract concepts; and testing in new situations. This theory has been widely used in educational contexts, simulations, co-curricular programmes, and organisational development to create diverse learning experiences.

Kolb's work discusses developmental implications within dimensions of his model, suggesting that development is impacted by challenges and one's belief system when dealing with the world and one's experience. "The experience" is therefore a crucial part of this research. The framework is applicable to research and leadership in this context based on the experiential nature of the topic. Its explorative feature also fits into the personal development perspective that the researchers want to explore. The theory gives the scope to delve into various challenging scenarios and encourages individuals to reflect, thus providing opportunity to apply insights and knowledge to practical leadership contexts. The cyclical nature of the theory highlights the importance of continuous learning, integration of experience and reflection.

Kolb's views correspond with the constructivists in that he includes concrete experience as part of the learning process and requires "a student" to test knowledge by engaging the environment (Dewey, 2018). Dewey's advocacy around "utility education" and the practical usefulness of learning establishes a connection between these two theorists and reinforces ELT as a fitting selection for this research.

Constructivism and Leadership

Constructivism is the theory where learners construct their own understanding and knowledge of the world through experiencing things and reflecting on those experiences. When one is exposed to a new experience, the individual has to re-solve it with past ideas and experiences. The theory therefore is ideal for a study on leadership as it gives a central role to individuals in the construction of their learning and development. Constructivism therefore encourages interrogation, exploration, and assessment of knowledge. In the teaching and learning process, the constructivist view of learning is seen as a social collaborative activity (Rice & Wilson, 1999). It involves encouraging students to use active techniques to build and share more knowledge.

The researchers, upon examination of the respondents, adopted this framework as a fundamental tenet of this study. Constructivism has benefits for the student in particular. The process is active rather than passive which makes the student the creator of knowledge; this will bring joy to the learning process and in so doing, learning occurs. From the leadership perspective this is an exciting and refreshing outlook as it facilitates adaptive leadership. The constructivist leader understands the pace and nature of knowledge which allows for quick adaptation and adjustment - thus better serving a team or organisation. Education is at its optimal when it con-centrates on thinking and understanding rather than on memorization. Constructivist learning is transferable; student leaders therefore are able to manipulate knowledge and extrapolate relevant areas for application. The theory supports social and com-munication skills by constructing an environment that underscores collaboration and exchange of ideas (Dewey, 2018).

Social Cognitive Career Theory

The Social Cognitive Career Theory (SCCT) is a career development construct theory based on Albert Bandura Social Cognitive Theory. The theory values acquisition of knowledge through lived experiences, reinforcement and observation. These elements coupled with the environment help students to synthesise and develop a sense of self, which should ultimately lead to better life choices and a fulfilling vocation. The theory speaks to six focal areas namely "observational learning, cognitive processes, reciprocal determinism, self-efficacy, modelling and reinforcement". The theory's view on career development compliments constructivist theories based on the emphasis on individual experiences, social influences and environmental contexts. SCCT will also help the researchers to locate and qualify the value of the professional experiences of the respondents which is critical to the discourse in this study (Brown et al, 1996).

Methodology

The researchers therefore embarked on an explanatory qualitative assessment, which provided them with the opportunity to uncover the main reasons or explanations associated with the success of The Guild's contribution to individuals becoming leaders (Casper, 2023). To facilitate this, the researchers engaged in both interviews and focus group discussions to collect the qualitative data. For the interviews, past students were engaged to share their perceptions and the impact that the Guild of Students had on their personal and professional development. Students who were also a part of the current Guild of Students were also interviewed to demonstrate the impact of the Guild on their personal and professional development. Focus groups were conducted with university stakeholders to better understand the various leadership programmes that The University of the West Indies introduced as a part of its leadership curriculum for the Guild of Students. The study used a phenomenological methodological approach in assessing the experiences of these students and assess these various factors with regards to their personal development. To achieve this, the researchers began by understanding the subjective experience of individuals by their lived reality as a student. The individuals were also allowed to share through their interviews, perceptions, and meanings attached to various phenomena. The phenomenological approach also allowed the university stakeholders to explore the meanings and provide a holistic perspective of the leadership initiative through the Guild of Students and the impact it would have on students as a guild member and the university output rate after leaving the Guild of Students (Bouzioti, 2023).

Triangulation of both interviews and focus group discussions allowed the researchers to capture the nuances, complexities, and contextual factors that shape individuals' experiences, leading to a deeper understanding of the phenomenon under study and will help in the development of practices and policies based on recommendations shared. The researchers also asked the past guild representatives to provide a story of their lived experiences while they were on campus. This helped the researchers to better determine the themes for the findings. The researchers also started the conversation by bracketing their experience as previous members of the Guild, while also sensing, analysing and describing the leadership experience and contributing to the development it has had in their various careers.

Glaser and Strauss constant comparative method was used as the main way of analysing both the interviews and focus group discussions. As the researchers examined the three (3) stages within the coding process - open, axial and selective coding. (Glaser, & Strauss, 1967). The theories identified were pulled by looking at the theoretical perspectives and comparing them with the stories that were shared, this was also facilitated with the use of the NVIVO platform. The sample focussed on twelve (12) past Guild of Students leaders from all campuses and included past guild representatives from various Caribbean countries. The focus groups had three (3) groups of different UWI stakeholders who were involved with the development, training and execution of the leadership curriculum. Additionally, focus groups were also conducted with current UWI students to examine the availability, application and credibility of the current leadership programmes available. The groups also offered recommendations. These sessions were all conducted via Zoom. The interview sessions lasted for an hour and the focus groups for one and a half hours.

Discussion of Findings

In this section of the paper, a discussion of the findings from the inquiry is presented as it relates to the themes and research objectives of the study. The interviews and focus groups produced a wealth of qualitative data that were utilised and analysed in order to demonstrate to whom these activities speak - both the personal and professional experiences. This is designed to enhance leadership skills by involving students in various governance and organisational activities on campus.

The Guild Leadership Programme at The University of the West Indies (UWI), plays a significant role in its participants' personal and professional development. From the findings, we can see how the programme is designed to enhance leadership skills through the involvement of students in various governance and organisational activities on campus. The researchers will accentuate the view that both past and current members of the Guild Councils expressed, regarding their appreciation to the leadership programme for the building of their self-confidence and communication skills. They also noted that they learned how to balance academic responsibilities with their leadership roles, thus enhancing their time management and organisational skills. Among the other benefits gained from the Guild leadership programmes are - improvement in critical thinking, improvement in problem-solving skills as well as their decision making skills. Professionally, the following skills were highlighted: project management, the ability to network, and the ability to be better leaders while developing their teamwork. This professional development has also assisted with their careers choice. The Guild has provided a comprehensive development experience that prepares them for future success in various fields

WHAT ARE THE MAIN FACTORS THAT HAVE CONTRIBUTED TO YOUR PERSONAL DEVELOPMENT WHILE ON THE GUILD OF STUDENTS?

Three themes emerged from this research question which points to strong developmental value from The Guild; they were balancing time and obligation; critical thinking and event execution and developing identity and confidence. These areas are discussed in depth in the paragraphs below.

Balancing time and obligations

Time management is a critical component of leadership, if one is to be effective in the field (Pidgeon, 2017). The interview highlighted the fact that the guild's tenure spans nine months which includes the summer months; this poses significant challenges for the councilors who have a relatively short window of time to execute plans and projects. The issue of time and the obligation of the office requires balance as stated by one of the interviewees.

> "The summer months are really for planning, but after that there is a short period in time when we have to get activities together which can be really hard when you have schoolwork and life to deal with" (Interview A, 2023)

Poor time management can have a debilitating effect on leadership which then can lead to poor decision making, performance dissonance and even fatigue (Itri & Lawson, 2016). The focus group session spoke to this issue:

"They pointed out that the Guild, despite best efforts oftentimes under performs because of student leaders having to juggle portfolios and life which affect their plans and execution of duties" (Stakeholder focus group discussion, 2023).

Effective time management as a leadership tool has the potential to transform the leadership experience for persons on The Guild as it will allow these student leaders the opportunity to manage their tasks effectively. The effective use of these tools according Samad (2012) provides an opportunity for student leaders to reflect and bring their own coping mechanisms to the job. The feedback from respondents indicated that past guild members had to figure time management out as part of their developmental experience. Samad also goes further to show the nexus between leadership mindset and organisational performance. The experience factor also links to Kolb and constructivist theorists who see the environment as an ideal opportunity for engagement and learning (Dewey, 2018). The Guild from the discussion therefore presents an opportunity for both growth and development of its members.

Critical thinking and event execution

Another theme that emerged from the data was critical thinking and event execution. The respondents felt that a critical approach to programmes and activities was important for efficiency on the Guild.

"You have to think seriously and deeply about your plans and activities because most times you are competing with halls, faculties and even the Guild itself" (Interview 2, 2023).

Critical thinking produces higher quality solutions which benefits both the individual and organisation (Kellet, 2014). This view is further extended by Costa (2008) who posits that individuals who acquire critical thinking skills become more productive in the workforce and society at large.

The central location of student leaders in the research reinforces the constructivist narrative of adaptive leadership and the ability of the subject to interrogate, explore, and develop. The focus group also supported this:

"They were of the view that the Guild encourages its members to troubleshoot and resolve key issues given the dynamic nature of student activities and the university itself" (Stakeholder focus group discussion, 2023)

As an institution of higher learning The UWI is a stakeholder in the drive to foster critical thinking. The institution identifies critical and creative thinking as distinctive characteristics of its ideal graduate (UWI, 2024). It also identifies key areas such as the generation of alternative ideas and problem solving which is connected to the information in the study.

Developing identity and confidence

From the interview it was highlighted that the Guild was ideal for character building. The respondents contended that the pressure of the portfolio coupled with the exposure to administrative and political actors caused a change in perspective and confidence. This kind of movement is in line with Josselson's theory of identity. Identity achievement in Josselson's model is a critical stage in one's development where the individual weighs the parental values against social and emergent ones with an aim to develop their own personal perspectives on life (Josselson, 1972). This is in tandem with Kolb's experiential theory that speaks to how knowledge develops from transformational experiences.

The focus group stated:

"The exposure at the guild level to senior administrators, politicians and key business players allowed for different approaches about how to present self and how to have conversations and make a case for things" (stakeholder focus group discussion, 2023)

The opportunity to meet influential persons from various fields has a profound effect on identity development and confidence as this is the source of emergent values as referred to by Josselson (1997). These individuals from various fields provide the kind of challenging atmosphere that student leaders must navigate and in so doing discover different versions of themselves. This is the "self" that Korejan & Shahbazi (2016) talk about in their expectations of transformational leaders in contemporary societies.

The factors contributing to personal development varied on The Guild, ranging from time management to identity development. The experiences recorded highlighted the importance of transformational and adaptive leadership. The values exposed while in service on The Guild formed a foundation for the personal and professional lives of these past student leaders. The expectation according to literature is that student leaders will take these transformational experiences into the world of work and the society beyond.

WHAT ARE THE MAIN OPPORTUNITIES THAT YOU ACCESSED WHILE ON THE GUILD AND HOW HAS THAT HELPED WITH REGARDS TO YOUR PROFESSIONAL DEVELOPMENT?

A key component that was identified as a benefit from being on the Guild of Students is that it presents several positive opportunities, which helped these individuals to conceptualise their professional development in advance (Northouse, 2015). This advancement included a greater appreciation to develop their leadership skill sets, the ability to network and being able to be more transformative in their programmes for their personal and professional lives. Some of the areas identified by respondents included the opportunity to network, development in confidence and personal growth. Three individuals also pointed to the fact that it had helped them with their experiential learning and had provided them with the opportunity to have greater reach with persons in the Caribbean and globally. They also shared that the programme has helped with the development of the philanthropy component especially through the community engagement portion.

Figure 1. The Contribution of the Guild to Professional Development

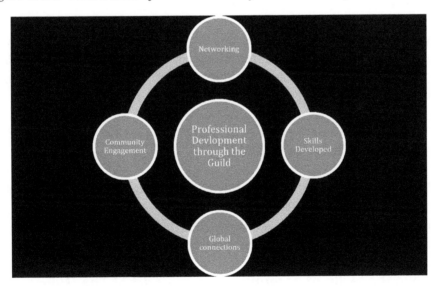

Better networking

From the interviews, it was shared that being on The Guild has provided students with the opportunities to liaise with various leaders (national and international) at the business and political level. Baltodano et al, (2012) also emphasised the point that the leadership development programme that is offered focuses on building the profession of its students through various professions, business, and industry. (Baltodano et al, 2012). The point was also reiterated by one interviewee who shared that:

"through the guild I was able to network and land my first job. The persons were so impressed with the way I spoke on behalf of students and they offered me a job right after I finished my degree." (Interview C, 2023)

The focus group session also highlighted the point that:

"One of the areas that they observed is the ability for students to network, for example they highlighted the point of students negotiating during the UWI carnival and their ability to secure and maintain funds for the event" (Focus Group 1, 2023)

As demonstrated, the leadership programme has armed past guild members with the opportunity to network and has provided them with opportunities to better their career choices. It was also shared that this activity has also helped them in their personal and professional lives.

"Being on the Guild has built me personally and I am forever grateful for that opportunity" (Interview D, 2023)

Fredricks, et al. (2003) also emphasises the point by sharing that these leadership programmes also offer team-building activities, and networking events, and spoke about the ability to connect with like-minded individuals, exchange ideas, and build meaningful relationships within and beyond the professional sphere.

Improve the skills of persons who are a part of The Guild

The Guild has also allowed for a number of persons to develop various skill sets and learn more through the activities hosted by the entity. It was shared that:

"Participating in the Guild has provided framework for developing essential leadership skills" (Interview A, 2023)

"Being on The Guild has also assisted with me being able to develop a budget, developing work plan, and agenda" as these were all skill sets I was not exposed to based on my major" (Interview B, 2023)

The focus groups also noted that:

"... The leadership training programmes that were being offered through workshops and seminars, also covered topics such as how better to communicate, how to manage conflict, what are the key areas that you need to consider when making a decision and how better to plan strategically, ... ". (Stakeholder focus group discussion 2023)

The involvement of leadership training programmes is key to helping students better develop their leadership capabilities in a more structured way. It also provides them with the opportunity to develop soft skills that they will learn within their classroom, while this is the case it has been found that unfortunately, there are a limited number of studies conducted in this area at the higher education level (Cansoy, 2017).

Establish connections with persons within the Caribbean and Globally

The University of the West Indies Guild of Students extends itself to all four campuses and creates an opportunity for students to interact with other guild councillors from those campuses, which has also helped with establishing friendship, and contribute to their networking.

"I now have friends from different Caribbean islands and when I travel I have the opportunity to stay with a friend that I would not have made if I wasn't on the Guild..." (Interview A, 2023)
"Some of my colleagues from other counties are actually persons who were in the St Augustine guild and it is interesting when we have meetings and we share and laugh about our guild experience..." (Interview F, 2023)

Various leadership programmes have created spaces where students are given the opportunity to create global friendships and have a cross-cultural understanding. This was facilitated by their interaction with participating in international initiatives. Students can broaden their perspectives and develop cultural competence especially from a number of these leadership programmes (Cansoy, 2017).

Greater Community Engagement

The Leadership programme also creates a space for the students to be given the opportunity to participate in various community engagement projects (Astin, 2000). The UWI also encourages students from The Guild to participate in the UWI community engagement initiatives (The UWI Quality Leadership Programme and The UWI Mentorship Programme), which speaks to service learning that was offered out of the Office of Student Services and Development.

> *"Students were given the opportunity to identify a community and to plan an outreach programme where they were told to develop a proposal and a budget that university would provide a small amount of money to fund during implementation.... and they were also a part of the UWI Student Awards Ceremony"* (Stakeholder focus group, 2023)

Several guild councillors also reflected and shared their opinions.

> *"I remember that we painted the Mona Commons Basic School. It felt so good when the work was completed and we distributed books to the children. It is from there I have always been giving back"* (Interview B, 2023)
> *"I was also a part of painting the school grounds for children at the National Water Commission basic school...."* (Interview F, 2023)

Most higher education institutions have various service leadership programmes that focus more on an involvement of community service projects and outreach activities - this they have found give students the opportunity to make an impact in their communities which in turn fosters a sense of civic responsibility and social consciousness (Astin, 2000).

WHAT ARE THE MAIN CHALLENGES WHILE ON THE GUILD AND HOW HAS THAT HELPED WITH REGARDS TO YOUR PROFESSIONAL DEVELOPMENT?

There were several challenges identified by the respondents in the study. But these challenges also brought value to the personal and professional lives of these individuals. Three themes emerged from the coding namely: financial limitations and resourcefulness, managing conflict and activism despite apathy.

Financial limitations and Resourcefulness

The interview revealed that financial limitation was one of the issues student leaders had to contend with and despite that, be resourceful. The researchers from observation did not sense this as a particularly negative experience for the respondents spoke with calm, clear, confident voices and quickly pivoted to the topic of resourcefulness. One interviewee stated:

> "Sometimes cash flow throughout the year will hamper some of your programmes. It is the same thing now in the corporate world where you have to be creative in times of scarcity" (Interview D, 2023)

This was also endorsed by the focus group respondents:

> "Even when you present a budget at retreat, you still have to revise it, because the school [UWI] has little to no money; but as a Guild we make it work" (Stakeholder focus group discussion, 2023)

The recurring theme of creativity despite challenges is an important issue to identify in the students' experiences. According to Rice and Wilson (1999), this kind of adaptive leadership is a social collaborative effort where students are using active techniques to build and share knowledge. This kind of effort forms an environment of resourcefulness which in turn enhances creativity and performance (Semeda et al, 2016). These respondents were able to transfer the limitations experienced on The Guild into resourcefulness that transcended the school setting. The adaptiveness of these student leaders who have become titans of industries is the ideals described by constructivists.

Managing conflict

The research underlined the contentious nature of leadership, especially in an organisation like the Guild of Students which is heavily influenced by politics and individual agendas. The Guild, based on several articles in the two major daily newspapers in Jamaica (The Daily Gleaner and The Observer) is associated with national politics and in fact several of the student leaders on The Guild have gone on to serve in representational politics nationally and internationally. The interplay of ideologies therefore makes for a contentious environment. Based on how conflict is managed it can frustrate the working environment or stimulate peer to peer relationship and decision making; this is referred to as constructive conflict management (Tjosvold et al, 2019).

One focus group had this to say:

> "The Guild can be a very divided place due to people having different agendas, but it is for the person to know themselves and what they stand for to excel in the environment. The Guild is basically a smaller sample of the society ..." (Stakeholder focus group discussion, 2023)

It is the position of scholars such as Holmes & Marra (2019) that good leaders manage conflict by choosing strategies that will lead to the desired outcome. Dewey's argument of utility education is relevant here as it brings into sharp focus the engagement and experiences that these student leaders had and how this shaped their worldview as individuals and professionals (Dewey, 2018).

Activism in spite of apathy

Another theme that emerged from the study was that of student representation and the difficulty to ascertain buy-in from the student body. One interviewee said:

> "My time on The Guild was rewarding, but at the same time disappointing because of the lack of interest from my constituents. No matter what initiative it was, the same persons turned up, but I learnt to represent all the same and later in life that same stick-to-it-tiveness paid off in my promotion" (Interview F, 2023).

Activism also has the potential to reactivate voices in society which can renew societal action (Zompetti, 2006). One interviewee recalled his time on the guild and how such reactivation took place:

> "We marched to Spain [Spanish Town] at the time when gang violence was at its peak and the students followed. Our students can be re-energized" (Interview D, 2023).

It was the view of one respondent (Interview F, 2023) that the experience of activism paid off despite the challenges of representation which is the core tenant of constructivist theories. The real value of this research is the experience that students bring to the table and how having encountered alternative ideas they can assemble and transfer them in meaningful ways (Dewey, 2018).

Transformational leadership is about developing people and those around them. Our interaction with the respondents demonstrated how challenges, if met with the right mindset and environment can transform people and ideas into far more enriching experiences that will translate into the labour market and life in general. This aligns with the literature which opines that the world needs leaders with the skills to manage the complex nature of contemporary societies (Korejan & Shahbazi, 2016). These two scholars further state that this kind of skill set elevates society and its productivity. Leadership programmes in universities therefore have an impact on communities and the world at large.

WHAT FACTORS WOULD YOU CONSIDER ENCOURAGING MORE PERSONS TO PARTICIPATE IN THE GUILD OF STUDENTS AND ITS LEADERSHIP PROGRAMME?

The leadership programme is considered beneficial in higher education. However, we find that not all students find participating in leadership programmes an attractive venture (Dopson, 2018). In Jamaica, the consensus is that most students are not concerned about selecting political leaders along with guild officials and many students will share that this is something that they are not interested in trying. A key component for higher institutions is to try to create a space where more students will want to become better leaders or will aspire to lead (Dopson, 2018). To achieve this, there are several factors that could be put in place to encourage more students to find this initiative a good co-curricular activity by highlighting the benefits of being a part of the Guild of Students. Therefore, it is necessary to create a space that is more tailored and inclusive giving them the opportunity to note that their voices are being heard. Along with faculty members who will provide mentorship and create rewards both academically and financially to encourage more students to consider this an important initiative.

Figure 2. Encourage Student Leadership

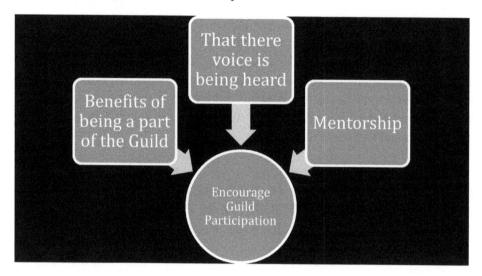

Relevance and Benefits of being a part of the Guild of Students

Some students shared that *"Being on the Guild does not translate to much and I don't want to get distracted from my academics"* (Focus group with students 2023)

While this is the general sentiment shared by students, we have to spend additional time sharing with them the major benefits of being a part of the Guild of Students; which includes an enhancement in student resume and a greater increase in the competitiveness of the job market (Komives, 2013). All the former guild representatives who participated in the study have secured several important jobs in various sectors of the Jamaican and other Caribbean economies. This was also shared as an opportunity by a number of the participants who said that being on the Guild allowed them to network with peers, faculty members, alumni and other professionals. The Guild also provides a space for students to reflect and gain a better understanding of their strengths and weaknesses and they are able to demonstrate this skill through various activities and support learning through community interventions (Searle, 2011)

"We try our best to invest in people and offer various leadership interventions, this can encourage our students and also build them as they move ahead. (Stakeholder focus group discussion 2023)

With all these benefits, it is important that this information is communicated and allowed for students to make the linkages with experimental learning and how this learning contributes to developing students' soft skills within higher education; and also demonstrate how participation can enhance their skills, expand their networks, and increase their competitiveness in the job market or graduate school applications (Searle, 2011).

> *"We ensure that all students attend UWI have an equal opportunity to be representative on the Guild of Students"* (Stakeholder focus group discussion 2023) *"Most students who resided on halls of residence shared that they are aware of the guild's positions being offered" .... "while commuting students shared that they weren't aware"* (Focus group with students, 2023)

Higher institutions take on a very inclusive approach ensuring that all students are given the opportunity to participate in their leadership programmes. Factors such as gender, socio economic conditions, political will, age, academic majors are not excluded (Komives, 2013). The Office of Student Services and Development encourages students to participate in the various programmes offered.

Ensuring that student "voice" is being heard

While higher institutions try to be very inclusive, a key component that underscores higher education institutions is that students feel that their voices are being heard within the decision-making process both at the policy level and on items that reflect both their academic and financial needs (Kezar, 2006).

> *" While I was on The Guild I felt like my voice was heard as I remember UWI reduced by a particular percentage the number it had planned to raise the school fees by"* (Interview C, 2023)
> *"I know that our president was able to work out an agreement with administration for persons who were benefiting from student loan to do their exams"* (Focus group with students 2023)

Both quotations highlight the linkages of students creating platforms and mechanisms through which students demonstrated how they have utilised their voices in expressing their perspectives, concerns, and ideas. The stakeholder focus group *"identified the ability of students sharing their voices and allowing the university to have a better understanding of the issues of students"* (Stakeholder Focus group 2023)

Moreover, involving students in decision-making fosters a sense of ownership and empowerment, promoting a more inclusive and student-centred academic environment. This therefore can create a governance structure that is transparent, accountable, and responsive - ultimately leading to positive institutional change and improved student outcomes (Kezar, 2006).

Create a mentorship for students

While the university creates an environment for students to understand the leadership, intervention programmes and encourages students to participate in the Guild. We observed from all the interviews and focus group discussions that there is a constant need for providing students with some level of mentorship. This mentorship from faculty, staff, or alumni mentors, student leaders, provide guidance, support, and encouragement throughout their leadership roles and academic journey (Eagan et al., 2017).

> *"I was mentored when I was a guild counsellor. There was always someone I could ask a question to understand how the university manage its operations"* (Interview C, 2023)

This mentorship provides the students with understanding how the university and other institutions operate and help them to better navigate various challenges (Eagan et al., 2017). In some higher institutions, it is seen as a way of encouraging students to connect with the campus community and enhance retention and satisfaction while being a student leader (Pleschova et al, 2015).

By creating these principles, The University of the West Indies can encourage more students who want to be active in the Guild of Students while creating and fostering a culture of leadership development on campus.

Recommendations

It was the consensus of the respondents that student leaders at the Guild level be exposed to more leadership training. The suggestions varied from a train-the-trainer series to more leadership coaching and capacity building activities. Peer to peer training in the higher education context has huge pedagogical benefits such as the development of collaborative and communicative skill sets (Stigmar, 2016). This social constructivist-based approach will offer student leaders the freedom to bring their own knowledge to the fore and to take ownership of the learning experience (Wilson, 1999).

The research also unearthed a call for a year-long course exploring critical areas such as self, ethics and activism. A programme like this would be highly value based and simulated which would also encourage the student leaders to be more intentional about community engagement. The respondents in the research spoke of the community engagement aspect of the guild and how it impacted their worldview. These kinds of values highlighted are in tandem with constructivist learning purported by Rice & Wilson (1999).

Time management and the nature of the guild calendar also featured prominently in the discussion with respondents. It was felt that student leaders were not being prepared properly for the weight of the guild responsibilities. The concern that student leaders were more interested in benefits than the act of service reinforced the idea of sensitization. According to behaviour change theorists such as Dewey (2018) sensitization fits into the frame of diverse learning that transformational leaders need in mainstream society.

Academic support was another concern. The demands on time and duties relating to leadership require a structured and personalised form of academic support. While the institution offers academic support and appreciative advising, the Guild Councillors by virtue of their responsibilities require a more customised designed support model. This kind of support is provided to athletes in some universities, to first generation students in others and in some cases to those with special needs. The point is that there is already precedent for programmes such as these.

CONCLUSION

From the study, it was observed that the implementation of the leadership programme possesses a huge contribution to the development of students and has contributed to their working experience. The participants shared that the programme assisted them with improving a number of skills, including but not limited to effective communication and critical thinking. This point was also shared by some of the industry leaders. A former guild member who is now a politician, noted that being a part of the Guild of Students and participating in the various leadership programmes, allowed for better analysis and critique of the various social, economic, and environmental challenges that persons are now facing in the Caribbean. The respondent also noted that it has helped with seeing these challenges through a developmental lens and has assisted with approach and constituents' communication.

The issue of networking was also shared. The Guild fostered relationships with the five (5) UWI campuses as well as with other regional universities. This engagement was mainly through various meetings and shared social activities. The participants agreed that the leadership programme provided the opportunity for mentorship and job placements. However, while the programme is seen as being beneficial, it also created a challenge for some of the students who experienced difficulty with respect to balancing their leadership training with their academic rigour, especially with the traditional disciplines. It was recommended that student leaders be given a structured and personalised form of academic support. Guild councillors by virtue of their responsibilities require a more customised support model.

The research based on the feedback of respondents who are now in the world of work revealed the value added of the leadership programme. The elements of transformation as cited by Dewey (2018) were evident in the data. The transformative work of these individuals in various industries also supported the literature and scholars such as Samad (2012) and Wilson (1999).

REFERENCES

Astin, A. W., Vogelgesang, L. J., Ikeda, E. K., & Yee, J. A. (2000). *How service learning affects students*. Higher Education Research Institute, University of California.

Baltodano, J., Carlson, S., Jackson, L., & Mitchell, W. (2012). Networking to Leadership in Higher Education: National and State-Based Programs and Networks for Developing Women. *Advances in Developing Human Resources*, 14(1), 62–78. DOI: 10.1177/1523422311428926

Bob, A. (2010). *Managing Your Aspirations: Developing Personal Enterprise in the Global Workplace*. McGraw-Hill.

Bouzioti, D. (2023). Introducing the Phenomenological Model of Performance Practice (PMPP): Phenomenological Research Design and the Lived Experience in Performance. *International Journal of Qualitative Methods*, 22, 16094069231211142. Advance online publication. DOI: 10.1177/16094069231211142

Brown, S. D., & Lent, R. W. (1996). A Social Cognitive Framework for Career Choice Counseling. *The Career Development Quarterly*, 44(4), 354–366. DOI: 10.1002/j.2161-0045.1996.tb00451.x

Cansoy, R. (2017). The Effectiveness of Leadership Skills Development Program for University Students. *Tarih Kültür ve Sanat Arastirmalari Dergisi*, 3(3), 65–87. DOI: 10.7596/taksad.v6i3.899

Casper, M.-O., & Artese, G. F. (2023). *Situated cognition research : methodological foundations*. Springer. March 13 2024 DOI: 10.1007/978-3-031-39744-8

Costa, A. (2008). The thought-filled curriculum. ascd._https://www.ascd.org/el/articles/the-thought-filled-curriculum. Accessed on March 28, 2024

Dewey, J. (2018). *Democracy and Education: With a Critical Introduction by Patricia H. Hinchey*. Myers Education Press. (Original work published 1916)

Dictionary, C. E. dictionary.cambridge.org. Archived from the original on 2017-06-25. Retrieved 2020-12-10.

Dopson, S., Ferlie, E., Mcgivern, G., Fischer, M., Mitra, M., Ledger, J., & Behrens, S. (2018). Leadership Development in Higher Education: A Literature Review and Implications for Programme Redesign. *Higher Education Quarterly*, 73(2), 218–234. Advance online publication. DOI: 10.1111/hequ.12194

Eagan, M. K., Hurtado, S., Chang, M. J., Garcia, G. A., Herrera, F. A., & Garibay, J. C. (2017). Making a difference in science education: The impact of undergraduate research programs. *American Educational Research Journal*, 54(1), 27–73. PMID: 25190821

Fredricks, S. (2003). Creating and Maintaining Networks Among Leaders: An Exploratory Case Study of Two Leadership Training Programs. *Journal of Leadership & Organizational Studies*, 10(1), 45–54. Advance online publication. DOI: 10.1177/107179190301000104

Glaser, B. G., & Strauss, A. L. (1967). *The discovery of grounded theory; strategies for qualitative research*. Aldine.

Goff, D. G. (2003). What Do We Know About Good Community College Leaders: A Study in Leadership Trait Theory and Behavioral Leadership Theory.

Hilliard, A. (2010). Student leadership at the university. *Journal of College Teaching and Learning*, 7(2), ●●●. DOI: 10.19030/tlc.v7i2.93

Holmes, J., & Marra, M. (2004, January). Leadership and managing conflict meetings. *Pragmatics*, 14(4), 439–462. DOI: 10.1075/prag.14.4.02hol

Itri, J., & Lawson, L. (2016, July). Ineffective leadership. *Journal of the American College of Radiology*, 13(7), 849–885. DOI: 10.1016/j.jacr.2016.02.008 PMID: 27026578

Josselson, R. (1972). Identity formation in college women. Unpublished doctoral dissertation, University of Michigan.

Kallet, M. (2014). *Think smarter: critical thinking to improve problem-solving and decision-making skills*. Wiley Publishers.

Kezar, A. J., & Kinzie, J. (2006). Examining the ways institutions create student engagement: The role of mission. *Journal of College Student Development*, 47(2), 149–172. DOI: 10.1353/csd.2006.0018

Kolb, D. (2015). *Experiential learning: experience as a source of learning and development* (2nd ed.). Pearson Education Inc.

Komives, S. R., Lucas, N., & McMahon, T. R. (2013). *Exploring leadership: For college students who want to make a difference*. John Wiley & Sons.

Korejan, M.M. & Shahbazi, H. (2016). An analysis of the transformational leadership theory. Journal of Fundamental and applied Sciences. Vol. 8 No. 3 (2016): Special Issue. DOI: 10.4314/jfas.v8i3s.192

Pidgeon, K. (2017). The key for success: leadership core competences. Journal of Trauma Nursing. 24(6):p 338-341, November/December 2017. I *DOI:* DOI: 10.1097/ JTN.0000000000000322

Pleschova, G., & McAlpine, L. (2015). Enhancing university teaching and learning through mentoring: A systematic review of the literature. *International Journal of Mentoring and Coaching in Education*, 4(2), 107–125. DOI: 10.1108/IJMCE-06-2014-0020

Rice, M., & Wilson, E. (1999). How Technology Aids Constructivism in the Social Studies Classroom. [Helen Dwight Reid Educational Foundation, USA.]. *Social Studies*, 90(1), 28–33. DOI: 10.1080/00377999909602388

Samad, S. (2012). The Influence of Innovation and Transformational Leadership on Organizational Performance Procedia - Social and Behavioral Sciences. Volume 57, Pages 486-493. https://doi.org/DOI: 10.1016/j.sbspro.2012.09.1215l

Searle, T. P., & Barbuto, J. E.Jr. (2011). *Leadership: Enhancing the lessons of experience.* McGraw-Hill Higher Education.

Speck, M., & Knipe, C. (2005). *Why can't we get it right? Designing high-quality professional development for standards-based schools* (2nd ed.). Corwin Press.

Stigmar, M. (2016). Peer to peer teaching in higher education: a critical literature review. Pages 124-136 I Published online: 10 May 2016

Tjosvold, D., Wong, A., Chen, N. (2019). Managing conflict for effective leadership and organizations. Business and Management. https://doi.org/ crefore/9780190224851.013.240DOI: 10.1093/a

Zompetti, J.P. (2006). The role of advocacy in civil society. Volume 20, pages 167-183

Chapter 11
A Study on Powers of Higher Education Leadership and Solutions for Challenges

A. Dinesh

https://orcid.org/0009-0003-1760-9146

Department of Communication, Siva Sivani Institute of Management, Hyderabad, India

Shantanu Shandilya

Department of Languages, Vellore Institute of Technology, India

Dhara Vinod Parmar

Department of Design and Merchandising, Parul Institute of Design, Parul University, Waghodia, India

P. Sundharesalingam

Department of MBA, Kongu Engineering College, Perundurai, India

Somu Chinnusamy

Research and Development, RSP Science Hub, Coimbatore, India

ABSTRACT

Higher education leadership is confronted with numerous challenges in the contemporary landscape, requiring innovative solutions to ensure institutional effectiveness and student success. This paper explores the multifaceted nature of directing leadership in higher education, examining challenges such as financial pressures, demographic shifts, technological advancements, and the imperative for diversity

DOI: 10.4018/979-8-3693-9215-7.ch011

and inclusion. Solutions encompass strategic approaches to financial sustainability, embracing technological change, promoting diversity and equity, enhancing student success and well-being, and fostering collaborative partnerships. By addressing these challenges and implementing proactive solutions, leaders can navigate the complexities of higher education effectively, driving institutional growth, innovation, and positive outcomes for students, faculty, and stakeholders.

INTRODUCTION

Leadership in higher education is crucial for achieving academic excellence, student success, and societal impact. However, this field is complex and requires a deep understanding of the complexities and challenges faced by leaders. The key challenges include the interplay of academic vision, administrative acumen, and stakeholder engagement. Leaders must navigate a diverse range of stakeholders, including faculty, students, staff, alumni, governing boards, and community partners(Prabhuswamy et al., 2024).

Balancing these interests while advancing the institution's mission requires adept leadership skills and a deep understanding of the higher education ecosystem. Leaders in higher education face challenges in adapting to technological advancements, changing student demographics, and evolving pedagogical approaches(Channuwong et al., 2023). They must foster a culture of innovation and experimentation to harness the transformative potential of emerging technologies and pedagogical practices.

Additionally, they must address issues of diversity, equity, and inclusion, aiming to dismantle systemic barriers, promote diversity in hiring and admissions, and cultivate inclusive campus environments where all members feel valued and supported. Effective leadership in this context is crucial for achieving meaningful representation of underrepresented groups(Zimmer & Matthews, 2022).

Leaders in higher education face challenges in financial sustainability due to shrinking public funding, rising tuition costs, and competition for limited resources. They must balance short-term financial needs with long-term sustainability goals. They must also navigate complex regulatory frameworks and accreditation standards, ensuring compliance while fostering institutional autonomy and academic freedom. Adept leadership is crucial in upholding ethical standards and accountability principles in higher education governance. Effective leadership development is crucial for institutional resilience and vitality in higher education(McNair et al., 2022).

Investing in programs, mentorship initiatives, and succession planning is essential for cultivating skilled leaders capable of navigating complexities. Fostering a culture of lifelong learning and professional growth empowers leaders at all levels to drive positive change and innovation. This book explores innovative solutions and best practices for navigating leadership in higher education, examining real-world case studies, expert insights, and practical strategies. It equips current and aspiring leaders with the knowledge and tools needed to lead effectively in the dynamic landscape(Leithwood et al., 2021a).

Higher education is crucial for societal progress, innovation, social mobility, and economic prosperity. However, it faces numerous challenges, complicating its pursuit of excellence and hindering its transformative potential. The global higher education landscape is constantly evolving, with rapid technological advancements, demographic shifts, and economic paradigms demanding adaptability and agility. Leaders must navigate these forces while maintaining academic standards and fulfilling their institutions' missions(Shen et al., 2020).

This introduction explores the multifaceted landscape of higher education, identifying key challenges and proposing innovative solutions to propel the sector forward. Higher education faces a significant challenge in ensuring access and equity for all students, especially those from underrepresented and marginalized communities. Addressing these inequities requires addressing systemic barriers, expanding outreach initiatives, and enhancing support services. Rising tuition fees and student debt burdens also pose a significant obstacle to accessibility and affordability. Academic leaders must balance fiscal sustainability with ensuring equitable access to education for all, addressing the delicate balance between these factors(Cook-Sather, 2020).

The teaching and learning landscape is undergoing a significant transformation due to technological innovations, offering personalized learning opportunities. However, integrating these innovations into traditional models presents challenges in faculty training, curriculum design, and technological infrastructure. Higher education institutions are also under pressure to demonstrate accountability and value to stakeholders, with accreditation standards, regulatory requirements, and transparency demanding robust assessment and improvement systems(King, 2019).

Leadership is crucial for institutional success, navigating complexity, fostering innovation, and inspiring change. Higher education leaders need skills like strategic visioning, consensus-building, and effective communication to navigate turbulent waters. However, developing and nurturing effective leaders in academia is challenging. Succession planning, leadership development, and talent management strategies are often overlooked. Investing in leadership development initiatives is essential for cultivating a pipeline of skilled leaders to address future challenges(Nicolazzo et al., 2019).

The following chapters will explore challenges in higher education, utilizing insights from scholars, practitioners, and thought leaders. They aim to equip academic leaders with innovative solutions, best practices, and real-world case studies to navigate the complexities and lead their institutions to new heights of excellence and impact. Directing leadership in higher education plays a crucial role in shaping the future of institutions and their ability to respond to the dynamic challenges of the modern academic landscape. As colleges and universities face increasing pressure to adapt to technological advancements, demographic shifts, and evolving societal expectations, the role of leaders in guiding these institutions through change becomes increasingly vital. This chapter delves into the concept of directing leadership, its significance in the context of higher education, and the multifaceted challenges that leaders encounter(J. J. Kim et al., 2023; Shaturaev & Bekimbetova, 2021).

Directing leadership is characterized by its focus on providing clear guidance and strategic direction to achieve institutional goals. Unlike other leadership styles that may emphasize collaborative or participative approaches, directing leadership often involves setting explicit objectives, making decisive decisions, and ensuring that all aspects of the institution align with its strategic vision. In the context of higher education, this approach is particularly relevant given the complex and often bureaucratic nature of academic institutions, where strong leadership is required to navigate competing priorities and drive meaningful progress(Kurilovas, 2020; Oke & Fernandes, 2020).

One of the central challenges in higher education is the need to balance multiple, sometimes conflicting, demands. Institutions must address the needs of students, faculty, and staff while also meeting the expectations of accrediting bodies, government agencies, and the public. This balancing act is further complicated by the rapid pace of technological change and the increasing demand for innovative teaching and learning methods. Leaders must not only manage these pressures but also create a culture that supports ongoing development and adaptation(Santos et al., 2019).

The demographic diversity of the student body presents another significant challenge. As higher education becomes more inclusive, leaders are tasked with fostering an environment that supports students from varied backgrounds, including those from marginalized communities. This includes addressing issues related to equity and inclusion, ensuring that all students have access to the resources and opportunities they need to succeed(Pineda-Báez et al., 2019). The rise of DEI (Diversity, Equity, and Inclusion) initiatives underscores the importance of creating an inclusive academic environment where every individual feels valued and supported.

Moreover, financial constraints and resource limitations add another layer of complexity. Many higher education institutions are grappling with budget cuts, declining enrollment, and increasing operational costs. Leaders must devise innovative strategies to manage these financial pressures while maintaining the quality of education and support services. Effective resource management, along with strategic fundraising and partnership development, becomes essential in sustaining institutional viability(Dhanya et al., 2023; Ingle et al., 2023). Technological advancements offer both opportunities and challenges. The integration of digital tools and online learning platforms has transformed the educational landscape, providing new avenues for teaching and learning. However, these changes also require significant adjustments in infrastructure, training, and support systems. Leaders must navigate these technological shifts effectively to harness their potential while addressing the associated challenges.

Hence, directing leadership in higher education involves a complex interplay of strategic vision, resource management, and cultural sensitivity. Leaders must adeptly navigate a landscape marked by rapid change, diverse needs, and financial constraints. This chapter will explore these challenges in detail, offering insights into effective leadership practices and strategies for overcoming the obstacles that institutions face. By examining successful case studies and providing actionable recommendations, the chapter aims to contribute to a deeper understanding of how directing leadership can drive positive change and enhance institutional effectiveness in higher education.

Background

Directing leadership in higher education involves guiding institutions through complex challenges while striving to achieve their mission and vision. This leadership style is pivotal in navigating the rapidly evolving landscape of academia, characterized by increasing diversity, technological advancements, and shifting educational demands. Leaders in higher education face unique obstacles, including balancing administrative responsibilities with academic priorities, addressing the needs of a diverse student body, and managing limited resources. Additionally, the integration of new technologies and evolving pedagogical approaches presents both opportunities and challenges. Effective directing leadership is essential for fostering an environment of growth, innovation, and inclusivity(Prabhuswamy et al., 2024; Singh Madan et al., 2024). Understanding these challenges and developing practical solutions is crucial for enhancing institutional effectiveness and achieving strategic goals. This study aims to explore these issues, offering insights into successful leadership practices and providing actionable recommendations for overcoming the inherent challenges in higher education settings.

Objectives

- Understand the diverse array of challenges facing leaders in higher education, including financial constraints, demographic shifts, technological disruptions, and the imperative for diversity and inclusion.
- Explore innovative and strategic solutions to address the identified challenges, including approaches to financial sustainability, leveraging technological

advancements, promoting diversity and equity, enhancing student success and well-being, and fostering collaborative partnerships.

- Recognize the importance of promoting diversity, equity, and inclusion in higher education leadership, and understand the benefits of creating inclusive campus environments that celebrate diversity and support underrepresented groups.
- Study strategies and initiatives aimed at promoting student success and well-being, including academic support services, career counseling, mentorship programs, and holistic student support approaches.
- Embrace technological change and digital transformation in higher education leadership, understanding the potential of emerging technologies to enhance teaching and learning, improve operational efficiency, and support institutional goals.

LEADERSHIP COMPLEXITIES

Understanding Leadership Dynamics

Leadership within any context, especially in higher education, is a multifaceted and dynamic process shaped by various intricate dynamics. At its core, leadership involves the effective mobilization of resources, guiding individuals or groups toward common goals, and navigating complex organizational landscapes. However, beneath this surface lies a rich tapestry of interrelated factors that significantly influence leadership effectiveness. One of the fundamental dynamics in leadership is the distribution and negotiation of power. Within academic institutions, power dynamics can be complex, with authority dispersed among faculty, administrators, governing bodies, and other stakeholders. Understanding and navigating these power dynamics are essential for leaders to garner support, make decisions, and implement change effectively. Moreover, leaders must be mindful of how power imbalances can impact relationships and decision-making processes, striving to foster a culture of shared leadership and collaboration(Baptiste, 2019; Nicolazzo et al., 2019).

Interpersonal relationships also play a pivotal role in leadership effectiveness. Building trust, fostering open communication, and cultivating positive working relationships are essential for creating a supportive and productive organizational climate. Leaders must invest time and effort in nurturing these relationships, recognizing the importance of empathy, authenticity, and emotional intelligence in building rapport and inspiring loyalty among team members. Decision-making processes represent another critical aspect of leadership dynamics. In academia, where stakeholders may have divergent interests and priorities, decision-making can be particularly challenging. Leaders must employ strategies to engage stakeholders, solicit input, and weigh diverse perspectives before making informed decisions(Cheong et al., 2019; Shen et al., 2020). Moreover, leaders must be willing to embrace ambiguity and uncertainty, recognizing that not all decisions will yield clear-cut outcomes and that adaptability is essential in navigating complex environments(Das et al., 2024a). The figure 1 depicts the various challenges and complexities associated with leadership.

Leadership in higher education is influenced by contextual factors like institutional culture, external pressures, and societal trends. Effective leaders must be aware of these nuances, navigating budget constraints, responding to regulatory changes, and addressing emerging social issues, to navigate their institutions' trajectories effectively. Understanding leadership dynamics involves a comprehensive understanding of power dynamics, interpersonal relationships, decision-making processes, and contextual factors. Leaders can navigate these complexities with confidence and agility, creating environments conducive to innovation, collaboration, and sustained success in higher education through self-awareness, emotional intelligence, and organizational understanding(Cordie et al., 2020; Lumby, 2019).

Figure 1. Leadership Complexities

Navigating Organizational Culture

Leaders play a crucial role in shaping organizational culture, addressing resistance to change and fostering innovation. They set the tone, articulate vision and values, empower employees, and create supportive structures, fostering an environment where creativity thrives and continuous improvement is embraced(Cordie et al., 2020; Steinert et al., 2019).

Setting the Tone: Leaders play a pivotal role in shaping organizational culture by setting the tone through their actions, decisions, and communication style. They embody the values and principles they wish to instill within the organization, serving as role models for employees to emulate.

Articulating Vision and Values: Effective leaders articulate a compelling vision and core values that guide organizational behavior and decision-making. By clearly communicating the organization's purpose and direction, leaders align employees' efforts and foster a shared sense of purpose.

Addressing Resistance to Change: Leaders recognize that resistance to change is a natural response to uncertainty and the disruption of established norms. They employ strategies such as transparent communication, stakeholder engagement, and providing support and resources to mitigate resistance and promote buy-in. Leaders foster a culture of psychological safety where employees feel comfortable expressing concerns and contributing ideas for improvement.

Leading by Example: Leaders lead by example, demonstrating openness to change, adaptability, and a willingness to challenge the status quo. They encourage experimentation and risk-taking, rewarding innovation and learning from failure rather than punishing mistakes.

Empowering Employees: Leaders empower employees by delegating authority, promoting autonomy, and creating opportunities for collaboration and cross-functional teamwork. They foster a culture of trust and accountability, where employees feel empowered to take ownership of their work and contribute to organizational goals.

Celebrating Success and Learning from Failure: Leaders celebrate successes and milestones, recognizing and rewarding individuals and teams for their contributions to innovation and positive change. They also encourage a growth mindset, viewing failures as learning opportunities and promoting a culture of continuous improvement and experimentation.

Creating Supportive Structures and Processes: Leaders establish supportive structures and processes that facilitate innovation, such as dedicated time and resources for research and development, innovation labs, and cross-functional task forces. They remove bureaucratic barriers and encourage a flexible and agile approach to problem-solving and decision-making.

Promoting Diversity and Inclusion: Leaders recognize the importance of diversity and inclusion in fostering innovation and creativity. They champion diversity initiatives, promote inclusive leadership behaviors, and create opportunities for diverse voices to be heard and valued within the organization.

Measuring and Monitoring Progress: Leaders establish metrics and key performance indicators to track progress toward fostering a culture of innovation and change. They regularly assess organizational culture, solicit feedback from employees, and adjust strategies as needed to ensure alignment with desired outcomes.

Leadership in Times of Crisis:

Leaders face unique challenges during crises, requiring swift action to navigate uncertainty and mitigate impact on their organizations(Agrawal et al., 2023; Durairaj et al., 2023a).

- **Decisive Decision-Making:** Crisis situations demand decisive decision-making from leaders, often with incomplete information and under immense pressure. Leaders must assess the situation rapidly, prioritize actions, and communicate decisions clearly and transparently to stakeholders. Establishing a crisis management team and implementing clear protocols for decision-making can help streamline the response process.
- **Effective Communication:** Transparent and timely communication is essential for maintaining trust and confidence during a crisis. Leaders must provide regular updates to employees, customers, and other stakeholders, addressing concerns, sharing relevant information, and outlining the organization's response plan. Utilizing multiple communication channels, such as emails, virtual town halls, and social media, ensures broad dissemination of critical information.
- **Prioritizing Employee Well-Being:** Leaders must prioritize the well-being of their employees, recognizing that crises can take a toll on mental health and morale. Implementing measures such as flexible work arrangements, employee assistance programs, and regular check-ins can support employees' emotional and psychological needs. Demonstrating empathy and compassion toward employees fosters a sense of solidarity and resilience within the organization.
- **Adaptability and Agility:** Crises are inherently unpredictable, requiring leaders to remain adaptable and agile in their response strategies. Leaders must be prepared to pivot quickly as circumstances evolve, adjusting priorities, reallocating resources, and revising plans as needed. Fostering a culture of innovation and experimentation allows organizations to adapt more effectively to changing circumstances and identify creative solutions to emerging challenges.
- **Building Resilience and Continuity:** Leaders must focus on building organizational resilience to withstand and recover from crises effectively. This in-

volves developing robust contingency plans, diversifying supply chains, and investing in technology infrastructure to support remote work and business continuity. Additionally, leaders should conduct post-crisis debriefs to identify lessons learned and implement improvements to enhance preparedness for future challenges.

Effective crisis management necessitates leaders to make decisive decisions, communicate transparently, prioritize employee well-being, adapt, and build resilience to navigate crises, maintain team morale, and ensure long-term organizational success.

LEADERSHIP DEVELOPMENT

Assessment and Feedback

Leadership development programs involve assessing and providing feedback to enhance professional growth and effectiveness, using various methods. The figure 2 depicts the process of leadership development(Cheong et al., 2019; Shen et al., 2020). Assessing leadership skills and providing constructive feedback are crucial for professional growth and effectiveness. Organizations can empower leaders through 360-degree feedback, behavioral assessments, performance reviews, developmental assignments, coaching, and mentoring, resulting in improved performance and organizational success.

- **360-Degree Feedback:** 360-degree feedback involves soliciting input from multiple sources, including supervisors, peers, direct reports, and other stakeholders, to provide a comprehensive assessment of an individual's leadership skills. This approach offers a holistic view of leadership effectiveness, capturing diverse perspectives and identifying areas for improvement. Feedback can be collected through surveys or structured interviews, with an emphasis on providing actionable insights and fostering self-awareness.
- **Behavioral Assessments:** Behavioral assessments, such as personality assessments or leadership style inventories, can provide valuable insights into an individual's leadership strengths and areas for development. These assessments measure specific traits, behaviors, and preferences associated with effective leadership, helping individuals identify their natural leadership tendencies and areas for growth. Results from behavioral assessments can inform targeted development plans and interventions tailored to individual needs.

- **Performance Reviews:** Performance reviews offer a formal mechanism for assessing leadership skills and providing feedback on job performance. Supervisors can evaluate leaders based on predefined competencies, goals, and key performance indicators, providing specific examples and observations to support their assessments. Performance reviews should be conducted regularly, allowing for ongoing feedback and dialogue between leaders and their supervisors.
- **Developmental Assignments:** Developmental assignments provide hands-on opportunities for leaders to apply and refine their skills in real-world settings. Leaders may be assigned stretch projects, cross-functional team roles, or leadership roles in volunteer or community initiatives to broaden their experience and build their capabilities. Feedback from mentors, colleagues, and project stakeholders can inform leaders' development progress and highlight areas for further growth.
- **Coaching and Mentoring:** Coaching and mentoring relationships offer personalized support and guidance to leaders seeking to enhance their skills and capabilities. Coaches and mentors provide feedback, encouragement, and accountability, helping leaders set goals, develop action plans, and navigate challenges effectively. One-on-one coaching sessions and mentoring conversations provide opportunities for leaders to receive targeted feedback and support tailored to their unique needs and aspirations.

Figure 2. Leadership Development Process

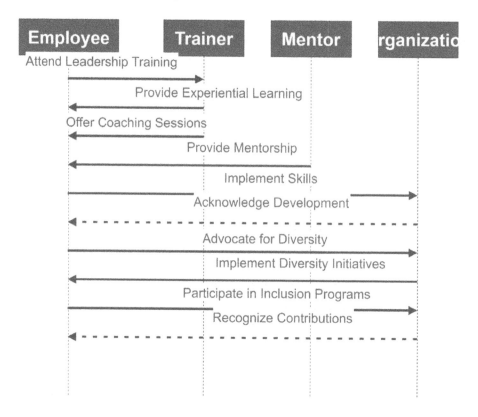

Training and Skill Development:

Leadership training and skill development are essential for developing competencies and capabilities in today's complex environment, and various approaches can be employed(Nicolazzo et al., 2019). Effective leadership training and skill development involve various methods like experiential learning, coaching, mentorship programs, formal training, and action learning projects. These methods, when combined with tailored initiatives, enable leaders to develop confidence, resilience, and impact in their leadership roles.

- **Experiential Learning:** Experiential learning involves hands-on, practical experiences that allow leaders to apply their skills and knowledge in real-world situations. Activities such as simulations, case studies, role-playing exercises, and outdoor challenges provide opportunities for leaders to practice decision-making, problem-solving, and interpersonal skills in a safe and supportive environment. Experiential learning fosters active engagement, reflection, and feedback, accelerating the learning process and promoting transferable skills that can be applied in diverse contexts.

- **Coaching:** Coaching is a personalized development approach that provides leaders with one-on-one support and guidance from a skilled coach. Coaches help leaders set goals, identify strengths and areas for development, and create action plans to achieve their objectives. Through regular coaching sessions, leaders receive feedback, encouragement, and accountability, enabling them to enhance their self-awareness, self-management, and interpersonal effectiveness.
- **Mentorship Programs:** Mentorship programmes pair less experienced leaders (mentees) with more experienced leaders (mentors) to facilitate learning, growth, and career development. Mentors serve as role models, advisors, and sponsors, providing mentees with guidance, support, and opportunities for networking and career advancement. Mentorship relationships often involve ongoing dialogue, skill-building activities, and exposure to new perspectives and experiences, enriching mentees' leadership development journeys.
- **Formal Training Programs:** Formal training programmes offer structured learning experiences designed to develop specific leadership competencies and capabilities. These programmes may include workshops, seminars, webinars, and online courses covering topics such as communication, decision-making, conflict resolution, and strategic thinking. Formal training programmes often incorporate a blend of instructional methods, including lectures, discussions, case studies, and interactive exercises, to accommodate diverse learning styles and preferences.
- **Action Learning Projects:** Action learning projects involve tackling real-world challenges or opportunities within the organization while simultaneously developing leadership skills. Leaders work in teams to identify, analyze, and solve complex problems, applying leadership principles and techniques learned during training. Action learning projects provide a valuable opportunity for leaders to practise collaboration, innovation, and change management while making tangible contributions to the organization's success.

Promoting Diversity and Inclusion in Leadership

Diversity and inclusion in leadership are crucial for organizational success, innovation, and sustainability. They are essential in leadership development initiatives and strategies for promoting diversity at all organizational levels(Cordie et al., 2020; M. Kim & Beehr, 2020).

a) **Driving Innovation and Creativity:** Diversity of thought, background, and perspective fuels innovation and creativity within organizations. Leaders from diverse backgrounds bring unique insights and experiences to the table, leading to more robust decision-making processes and innovative solutions to complex problems.

b) **Enhancing Organizational Performance:** Diverse leadership teams are more effective at driving organizational performance and achieving business objectives. Research has shown that companies with diverse leadership teams outperform their less diverse counterparts in terms of financial performance, employee engagement, and customer satisfaction.

c) **Reflecting Stakeholder Diversity:** In today's globalized world, organizations serve diverse stakeholders, including customers, clients, employees, and communities. Leadership teams that reflect the diversity of their stakeholders are better equipped to understand their needs, preferences, and perspectives, leading to more responsive and inclusive decision-making.

d) **Attracting and Retaining Talent:** A commitment to diversity and inclusion in leadership can enhance an organization's employer brand and attractiveness to top talent. Millennials and Gen Z employees, in particular, prioritize diversity and inclusion when evaluating potential employers, and diverse leadership teams signal a commitment to creating an inclusive workplace culture where all employees can thrive.

e) **Mitigating Bias and Stereotypes:** Diverse leadership teams help mitigate unconscious bias and stereotypes that may influence decision-making processes. By bringing together individuals from different backgrounds and experiences, organizations can challenge assumptions, broaden perspectives, and foster a culture of inclusion where all voices are valued and heard.

Strategies for Promoting Diversity and Inclusion in Leadership

Promoting diversity and inclusion in leadership is a moral and strategic advantage for organizations. It drives innovation, enhances performance, and attracts top talent. By prioritizing diversity in leadership development and implementing strategies at all levels, organizations can create inclusive cultures where all individuals can succeed and thrive(M. Kim & Beehr, 2021; Leithwood et al., 2021b).

a) **Diverse Recruitment and Hiring Practices:** Implement proactive strategies to attract diverse candidates for leadership positions, including targeted outreach, partnerships with diverse professional organizations, and inclusive job postings.

b) **Leadership Development Programs:** Design leadership development programs that prioritize diversity and inclusion, providing opportunities for underrepresented groups to access training, mentorship, and networking opportunities.
c) **Implicit Bias Training:** Offer training and education on implicit bias and stereotype threat to help leaders recognize and mitigate unconscious biases in decision-making processes.
d) **Accountability and Measurement:** Establish metrics and accountability mechanisms to track progress on diversity and inclusion goals, holding leaders accountable for creating inclusive environments and fostering diverse leadership pipelines.
e) **Inclusive Leadership Behaviors:** Promote inclusive leadership behaviors, such as active listening, empathy, allyship, and cultural competence, among all leaders within the organization.
f) **Transparent Communication:** Communicate openly and transparently about the organization's commitment to diversity and inclusion, highlighting the business case, values, and expectations for leadership accountability.

RECRUITMENT SOLUTIONS

Talent Acquisition Strategies

Organizations must employ effective talent acquisition strategies, including employer branding, recruitment marketing, and technology for efficient hiring processes, to remain competitive in today's dynamic marketplace. Best practices in each area are discussed. Figure 3 illustrates various leadership recruitment solutions(Hernández-de-Menéndez et al., 2022; Ziakkas et al., 2023).

Employer Branding: Employer branding encompasses the reputation, values, and culture of an organization as an employer.

Best practices for employer branding include:

a) Clearly defining and communicating the organization's mission, vision, and values to prospective candidates.
b) Showcasing employee testimonials, success stories, and company culture through various channels, such as social media, career websites, and employer review sites like Glassdoor.
c) Highlighting unique perks, benefits, and career development opportunities that differentiate the organization as an employer of choice.

d) Consistently monitoring and managing the employer brand to ensure alignment with the organization's values and desired employer image.

Recruitment Marketing: Recruitment marketing involves using marketing techniques to attract and engage potential candidates.

Best practices for recruitment marketing include:

a) Developing targeted messaging and content tailored to specific candidate personas and demographics.
b) Utilizing multiple channels, such as social media, job boards, industry events, and employee referrals, to reach a diverse pool of candidates.
c) Implementing inbound marketing strategies, such as content marketing and search engine optimization (SEO), to attract passive candidates and build a talent pipeline.
d) Analyzing data and metrics to measure the effectiveness of recruitment marketing efforts and refine strategies based on performance.

Leveraging Technology: Technology plays a critical role in streamlining and optimizing the hiring process, from sourcing candidates to onboarding(Kalaiselvi et al., 2024; Prabhuswamy et al., 2024). Best practices for leveraging technology in talent acquisition include:

a) Implementing applicant tracking systems (ATS) to manage the recruitment process efficiently, track candidate progress, and streamline communication with applicants.
b) Utilizing artificial intelligence (AI) and machine learning algorithms to automate repetitive tasks, such as resume screening, candidate matching, and interview scheduling, freeing up recruiters' time for more strategic activities.
c) Embracing video interviewing platforms and virtual assessment tools to conduct remote interviews and evaluations, especially in distributed or global talent markets.
d) Enhancing the candidate experience through mobile-friendly application processes, personalized communication, and self-service portals for accessing information and updates.

Integrating best practices into talent acquisition strategies can attract top talent, strengthen employer brand, and build a high-performing workforce. Continuous monitoring, evaluation, and optimization are crucial to align with market dynamics and candidate preferences.

Figure 3. Various leadership Recruitment Solutions

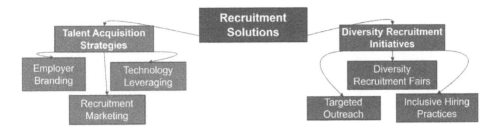

Diversity Recruitment Initiatives

Promoting diversity and inclusion in recruitment is crucial for organizations to build high-performing teams and foster innovation. By actively seeking and engaging diverse talent, organizations can tap into a wider range of perspectives, experiences, and skills, leading to better decision-making, improved employee engagement, and enhanced business outcomes(Leithwood et al., 2021b; McNair et al., 2022). Promoting diversity and inclusion in recruitment requires a comprehensive strategy that includes targeted outreach, participation in diversity fairs, inclusive job postings, diverse candidate sourcing, structured interview processes, and diversity training for hiring managers. This approach attracts, hires, and retains a diverse workforce, drives innovation, and contributes to organizational success.

a. **Targeted Outreach:** Targeted outreach involves proactively identifying and engaging with diverse candidate pools through strategic partnerships, networking events, and community outreach initiatives. Organizations can collaborate with diversity-focused professional associations, affinity groups, and minority-serving organizations to expand their reach and connect with underrepresented talent. Engaging in targeted outreach efforts allows organizations to build relationships with diverse communities, raise awareness of job opportunities, and cultivate a pipeline of qualified candidates from diverse backgrounds.

b. **Diversity Recruitment Fairs:** Diversity recruitment fairs provide platforms for organizations to showcase their commitment to diversity and connect with diverse candidates seeking employment opportunities. Participating in diversity recruitment fairs allows organizations to engage with a diverse audience of job seekers in a face-to-face setting, fostering meaningful interactions and building rapport. Organizations can also host their own diversity recruitment events, such as job fairs, networking mixers, and informational sessions, to showcase their culture, values, and career opportunities to diverse candidates.

c. **Inclusive Job Postings:** Crafting inclusive job postings is essential for attracting a diverse pool of candidates and signalling the organization's commitment to diversity and inclusion. Best practices for inclusive job postings include using gender-neutral language, avoiding biased language or stereotypes, and clearly articulating the organization's commitment to diversity and inclusion. Organizations can also highlight their diversity initiatives, employee resource groups, and inclusive policies and benefits to attract candidates who value diversity and seek inclusive work environments.

d. **Diverse Candidate Sourcing:** Leveraging diverse candidate sourcing channels, such as specialized job boards, diversity-focused recruiting agencies, and alumni networks, can help organizations identify and connect with diverse talent. Organizations can also implement blind resume screening processes or anonymized application platforms to reduce unconscious bias in the initial screening stages and ensure fair consideration of all candidates.

e. **Structured Interview Processes:** Implementing structured interview processes and standardized evaluation criteria helps mitigate bias and ensure fair and equitable treatment of candidates. Training interviewers on unconscious bias awareness and inclusive interviewing techniques, such as asking behavior-based questions and assessing candidates against objective criteria, can help promote fairness and objectivity in the selection process.

f. **Diversity Training for Hiring Managers:** Providing diversity training and education for hiring managers and recruitment teams is essential for fostering awareness, empathy, and cultural competence in the recruitment process. Training programs can cover topics such as unconscious bias, stereotype threat, inclusive language, and mitigating bias in decision-making, empowering hiring managers to make more informed and equitable hiring decisions.

Onboarding and Retention

The article emphasizes the importance of effective onboarding processes and retention strategies in fostering long-term success and engagement of new hires within an organization. By providing a structured and supportive experience and implementing proactive retention strategies, organizations can improve employee satisfaction, productivity, and retention rates(Cordie et al., 2020; Zimmer & Matthews, 2022).

i. **Creating a Positive First Impression:** The onboarding process represents new hires' first impression of the organization and plays a significant role in shaping their perceptions and attitudes toward their roles and the company. A well-designed onboarding program helps new hires feel welcomed, valued, and integrated into the organization from day one, fostering a sense of belonging and commitment.

ii. **Accelerating Time to Productivity:** Effective onboarding processes aim to accelerate new hires' time to productivity by providing them with the information, resources, and support they need to quickly ramp up in their roles. Clear expectations, role clarity, and access to training and development opportunities enable new hires to become productive contributors more efficiently, reducing time-to-competency and enhancing job satisfaction.

iii. **Facilitating Social Integration:** Onboarding is not just about learning job-related tasks; it's also about social integration and building relationships with colleagues and supervisors. Social activities, team-building exercises, and networking opportunities during the onboarding process help new hires establish connections, build rapport, and navigate the organization's culture and dynamics.

iv. **Providing Ongoing Support and Feedback:** Effective onboarding extends beyond the initial orientation period and includes ongoing support, feedback, and mentorship to help new hires succeed in their roles. Regular check-ins, performance reviews, and coaching sessions enable managers to provide constructive feedback, address any concerns or challenges, and support new hires' professional development and growth.

v. **Retention Strategies:** Retention strategies are proactive measures aimed at reducing employee turnover and retaining top talent within the organization(Prabhuswamy et al., 2024; Saravanan et al., 2024). Main retention strategies include:

- Offering competitive compensation and benefits packages to attract and retain top talent.
- Providing opportunities for career advancement, skill development, and ongoing learning and growth.
- Creating a positive work environment that values diversity, inclusion, and work-life balance.
- Recognizing and rewarding employees for their contributions and achievements.
- Conducting exit interviews and employee satisfaction surveys to gather feedback and identify areas for improvement.

Effective onboarding processes and retention strategies are crucial for long-term success, engagement, and retention of new hires. By providing a positive experience, facilitating social integration, accelerating productivity, and implementing proactive retention strategies, organizations can enhance employee satisfaction, productivity, and retention rates.

REPRESENTATION BARRIERS

Identifying Representation Gaps:

Underrepresentation of women, minorities, and other marginalized groups in leadership roles is a significant issue affecting organizations, societies, and individuals. Despite progress in diversity and inclusion, representation gaps persist, posing challenges and limitations for these groups(Zawacki-Richter et al., 2019).

- **Barriers to Entry:** Women, minorities, and other marginalized groups often face systemic barriers to entry into leadership roles, including bias, discrimination, and structural inequalities. Implicit bias in hiring and promotion processes, lack of access to mentorship and sponsorship opportunities, and stereotypical perceptions of leadership capabilities can hinder individuals' career advancement and limit their opportunities to assume leadership positions.
- **Lack of Role Models and Representation:** The lack of visible representation of women, minorities, and other marginalized groups in leadership roles can perpetuate stereotypes and reinforce perceptions of who belongs in positions of power and authority. Without role models and mentors who share their backgrounds and experiences, individuals from underrepresented groups may struggle to envision themselves as leaders and may face additional pressure to conform to dominant cultural norms and expectations.
- **Limited Access to Networks and Opportunities:** Networking and access to influential networks are crucial for career advancement and accessing leadership opportunities. Individuals from underrepresented groups may face barriers to building and accessing professional networks, as existing networks may be homogeneous and exclusionary, limiting their visibility, access to resources, and opportunities for advancement.
- **Impacts on Organizational Performance:** The underrepresentation of women, minorities, and other marginalized groups in leadership roles can have detrimental effects on organizational performance, innovation, and decision-making. Diverse leadership teams are better equipped to understand

and respond to the needs and preferences of diverse stakeholders, leading to more informed decision-making, greater creativity, and enhanced problem-solving capabilities.

- **Addressing Bias and Discrimination:** Organizations must take proactive measures to address bias and discrimination in recruitment, hiring, and promotion processes. Implementing diversity and inclusion training, unconscious bias awareness programs, and inclusive leadership development initiatives can help mitigate bias and create more equitable opportunities for advancement.

- **Creating Inclusive Organizational Cultures:** Fostering inclusive organizational cultures where diversity is valued, celebrated, and integrated into all aspects of operations is essential for attracting, retaining, and advancing talent from diverse backgrounds. Organizations can promote inclusion by providing diversity training, establishing diversity and inclusion councils or affinity groups, and implementing policies and practices that promote equitable treatment and opportunities for all employees.

Underrepresentation of women, minorities, and other marginalized groups in leadership roles is a significant issue that affects individuals, organizations, and society. Addressing systemic barriers, promoting diversity, and creating leadership development opportunities can help close representation gaps and build more equitable leadership structures. Figure 4 demonstrates the process of identifying representation gaps and breaking down barriers.

Figure 4. Identifying Representation Gaps and Breaking Down Barriers

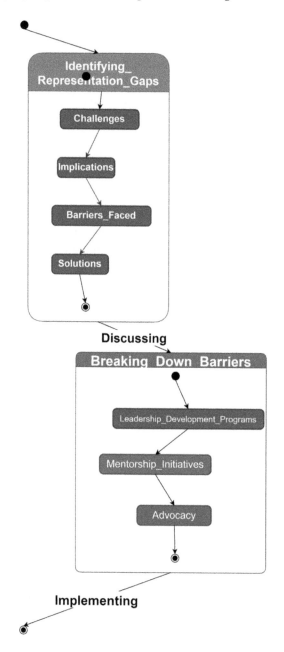

Breaking Down Barriers:

It discusses strategies for overcoming representation barriers and promoting diversity in leadership, emphasizing the need for a comprehensive approach that addresses systemic inequalities, biases, and structural barriers(Cook-Sather, 2020; Cordie et al., 2020).

a) **Leadership Development Programs:** Implementing targeted leadership development programs for underrepresented groups is essential for providing them with the skills, resources, and support needed to advance into leadership roles. These programs may include specialized training, workshops, mentoring, and networking opportunities tailored to the unique needs and experiences of participants. By investing in the development and advancement of diverse talent, organizations can cultivate a pipeline of future leaders who reflect the diversity of their workforce and communities.

b) **Mentorship Initiatives:** Mentorship programs pair emerging leaders from underrepresented backgrounds with experienced mentors who can provide guidance, support, and career advice. Mentors can offer insights into navigating organizational politics, building networks, and overcoming challenges commonly faced by individuals from marginalized groups. Mentorship initiatives help foster a sense of belonging, build confidence, and expand access to opportunities for career advancement and leadership development.

c) **Advocacy for Inclusive Policies:** Advocating for inclusive policies and practices within the organization is crucial for creating a supportive and equitable environment for all employees. This may include advocating for policies such as flexible work arrangements, parental leave policies, diversity training, and anti-discrimination measures. Organizations can also establish diversity and inclusion councils or task forces to promote awareness, drive change, and hold leadership accountable for advancing diversity and inclusion initiatives.

d) **Diverse Representation in Leadership:** Actively promoting diverse representation in leadership roles sends a powerful message about the organization's commitment to diversity and inclusion. Organizations can implement strategies to increase representation of women, minorities, and other underrepresented groups in leadership positions, such as setting diversity targets, implementing diverse slates for hiring and promotion, and providing leadership opportunities based on merit and potential.

e) **Creating Safe Spaces for Dialogue:** Creating safe spaces for dialogue and discussion about diversity, equity, and inclusion is essential for fostering understanding, empathy, and collaboration across diverse perspectives. Employee resource groups, diversity training workshops, and facilitated discussions can provide opportunities for employees to share their experiences, address biases, and work together to identify solutions for promoting diversity and inclusion in the workplace.

f) **Continuous Evaluation and Improvement:** Organizations must continuously evaluate and refine their diversity and inclusion initiatives to ensure they are effective and responsive to the evolving needs of their workforce. This may involve collecting and analyzing data on diversity metrics, conducting employee engagement surveys, and soliciting feedback from employees on their experiences and perceptions of inclusion.

Promoting diversity in leadership requires a comprehensive approach that addresses systemic inequalities, biases, and structural barriers. Strategies include leadership development programs, mentorship initiatives, advocacy for inclusive policies, diverse representation, dialogue spaces, and continuous evaluation and improvement. These efforts foster a culture of diversity, equity, and inclusion, allowing all individuals to thrive and succeed.

Measuring Progress

The article emphasizes the importance of tracking and measuring progress in addressing representation barriers to evaluate the effectiveness of diversity and inclusion initiatives, identify areas for improvement, and hold organizations accountable for their commitments to diversity, equity, and inclusion(Cheong et al., 2019; King, 2019; Lumby, 2019).

- **Representation Metrics:** Representation metrics quantify the demographic composition of the workforce, particularly in leadership and decision-making positions. Important metrics include the percentage of women, minorities, and other underrepresented groups in leadership roles, as well as their representation in hiring, promotion, and retention rates. Tracking representation metrics allows organizations to assess the diversity of their workforce and leadership pipeline and identify disparities or areas of underrepresentation that need to be addressed.

- **Employee Engagement and Satisfaction Surveys:** Employee engagement and satisfaction surveys provide insights into employees' experiences, perceptions, and attitudes toward diversity and inclusion in the workplace. Surveys may include questions about employees' sense of belonging, opportunities for advancement, perceptions of fairness and equity, and experiences of discrimination or bias. Analyzing survey data helps organizations understand the impact of diversity and inclusion initiatives on employee morale, engagement, and retention.

- **Promotion and Advancement Rates:** Tracking promotion and advancement rates by demographic group allows organizations to assess whether opportunities for career progression are equitable and accessible to all employees. Analyzing promotion rates by gender, race, ethnicity, and other demographic factors helps identify potential barriers or biases in the promotion process and inform targeted interventions to address disparities.

- **Employee Turnover and Retention Rates:** Monitoring employee turnover and retention rates by demographic group provides insights into the effectiveness of retention strategies and the inclusiveness of the organizational culture. High turnover rates among specific demographic groups may indicate dissatisfaction or disengagement resulting from inequitable treatment, bias, or lack of opportunities for advancement.

- **Diversity Training Participation and Impact:** Tracking participation rates and evaluating the impact of diversity training and education programs helps organizations assess employees' awareness, knowledge, and attitudes toward diversity and inclusion. Surveys or assessments administered before and after training programs can measure changes in employees' understanding of diversity issues, attitudes toward inclusion, and intentions to promote diversity in the workplace.

- **Supplier Diversity and Community Engagement:** Assessing supplier diversity initiatives and community engagement efforts helps organizations evaluate their impact on economic opportunities for diverse businesses and communities. Metrics may include the percentage of contracts awarded to minority-owned or women-owned businesses, philanthropic investments in underserved communities, and partnerships with diversity-focused organizations and initiatives.

To effectively address representation barriers, organizations should use a comprehensive approach that includes metrics such as employee engagement, promotion and advancement rates, turnover and retention rates, diversity training participation, and supplier diversity and community engagement. This will help assess the effectiveness of diversity and inclusion initiatives, identify areas for improvement, and drive meaningful change towards more equitable workplaces.

HIGHER EDUCATION GAP

Addressing Access Disparities

Access to higher education remains a critical issue globally, with disparities existing along socioeconomic lines, educational inequities, and systemic barriers that disproportionately affect marginalized communities. Socioeconomic factors, such as income level and parental education, play a significant role in determining access to higher education. High tuition costs, limited financial aid, and lack of access to resources for test preparation and college application support can pose significant barriers for students from low-income families. Educational inequities, including disparities in K-12 school funding, quality of instruction, and access to advanced coursework and extracurricular opportunities, further exacerbate access disparities(Saravanan et al., 2024; Sharma et al., 2024a). Students from under-resourced schools and communities often lack the academic preparation and support needed to succeed in higher education. Systemic barriers, such as discrimination, racism, and cultural biases embedded within educational institutions, create additional challenges for marginalized communities, including Black, Indigenous, and People of Color (BIPOC), LGBTQ+ individuals, first-generation college students, and individuals with disabilities(Cordie et al., 2020; Lumby, 2019).

These systemic barriers manifest in admissions processes, financial aid policies, and campus climates that perpetuate inequalities and limit opportunities for historically marginalized groups. Addressing access disparities in higher education requires multifaceted solutions that address structural inequities, increase financial aid and support services for low-income students, improve K-12 education quality and equity, and dismantle systemic barriers to inclusion and belonging within higher education institutions(Cordie et al., 2020; Farrukh et al., 2019). Implementing equity, diversity, and inclusion initiatives and focusing on supporting underrepresented and marginalized students can enhance accessibility and inclusivity in higher education for all individuals. The figure 5 depicts the significant disparity in the quality of higher education.

Figure 5. Higher Education Gap

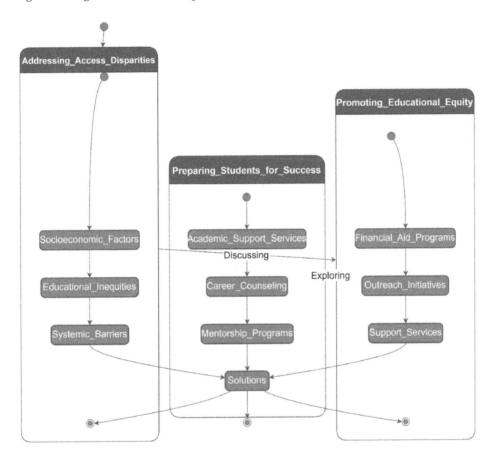

Promoting Educational Equity

Educational equity is crucial for a fair society, ensuring all students have access to necessary resources and support. Addressing the higher education gap requires multiple levels of effort, including targeted initiatives and policies to address systemic barriers and support underrepresented students. This article explores various initiatives and policies aimed at promoting educational equity(Lumby, 2019).

- **Financial Aid Programs:** Financial aid programs, including need-based scholarships, grants, and tuition assistance programs, play a crucial role in increasing access to higher education for low-income students. Initiatives such as Pell Grants, state-funded scholarship programs, and institutional aid

packages help offset the cost of tuition and fees, making college more afford-
able and accessible for students from underprivileged backgrounds.

- **Outreach Initiatives:** Outreach initiatives aim to reach students from underrepresented and underserved communities early in their educational journey,
  providing information, resources, and support to help them navigate the college application and enrollment process. Programs such as college readiness
  workshops, campus tours, and college fairs bring college representatives directly to high schools and communities, demystifying the college experience
  and empowering students to envision themselves as future college graduates.
- **Support Services:** Support services for underrepresented students provide
  crucial academic, social, and emotional support to help them thrive in higher
  education. Initiatives such as mentoring programs, academic tutoring, counseling services, and peer support groups offer personalized assistance and
  guidance to students from diverse backgrounds, helping them overcome academic challenges and navigate the college environment successfully.
- **Diversity, Equity, and Inclusion Initiatives:** Diversity, equity, and inclusion (DEI) initiatives within higher education institutions aim to create inclusive campus environments where all students feel valued, supported, and
  empowered to succeed. These initiatives may include cultural competency
  training for faculty and staff, multicultural programming and events, and the
  establishment of diversity-focused student organizations and affinity groups.
- **Policy Reform:** Policy reforms at the federal, state, and institutional levels
  are needed to address systemic inequities and promote educational equity.
  Policies that prioritize equitable funding for K-12 education, address disparities in school resources and facilities, and support college affordability and
  accessibility are essential for closing the higher education gap and ensuring
  equitable opportunities for all students.

To promote educational equity and close the higher education gap, coordinated
efforts across financial aid programs, outreach initiatives, support services, diversity,
equity, inclusion initiatives, and policy reforms are needed. These investments can
create more inclusive pathways for students from underrepresented backgrounds,
leading to a more diverse, equitable, and prosperous society.

Preparing Students for Success

This concept emphasizes the importance of providing students with the necessary resources and support to succeed in higher education, such as academic
support services, career counseling, and mentorship programs, to foster academic

achievement, personal growth, and long-term career success.(Channuwong et al., 2023; Seider et al., 2020):

- **Academic Support Services:** Academic support services, such as tutoring centers, writing labs, and supplemental instruction programs, provide students with additional assistance and resources to enhance their academic skills and performance. These services offer individualized support tailored to students' specific needs, helping them strengthen their study habits, improve their understanding of course material, and overcome academic challenges(Prabhuswamy et al., 2024; Venkatasubramanian et al., 2024).
- **Career Counseling:** Career counseling services assist students in exploring their interests, skills, and career goals, as well as identifying potential career pathways and opportunities. Career counselors provide guidance on academic program selection, internship and job search strategies, resume writing, interview preparation, and career development planning, helping students make informed decisions about their future.
- **Mentorship Programs:** Mentorship programs pair students with experienced mentors who provide guidance, advice, and support throughout their academic journey and beyond. Mentors offer insights into navigating the college experience, balancing academic and personal responsibilities, and planning for post-graduation success, serving as role models and sources of encouragement for mentees.
- **Personalized Support and Advising:** Personalized support and advising from faculty, staff, and peer mentors help students navigate the complexities of higher education and address individual challenges and concerns. Academic advisors assist students in developing personalized academic plans, selecting courses, and monitoring progress toward degree completion, ensuring that students stay on track to achieve their academic goals.
- **Holistic Student Support:** Holistic student support approaches recognize that academic success is intertwined with students' physical, emotional, and social well-being. Comprehensive support services may include access to counseling and mental health resources, financial aid and assistance programs, housing and food security initiatives, and student engagement opportunities, addressing the diverse needs of students and promoting holistic development.

Providing students with necessary resources and support is crucial for academic excellence, personal growth, and career readiness in higher education. These include academic support services, career counseling, mentorship programs, personalized advising, and holistic student support initiatives. These resources empower students to overcome challenges, achieve academic and career goals, and reach their full potential. Investing in these systems fosters a supportive, inclusive learning environment for all students.

FUTURE DEVELOPMENTS ACTIVITIES

Future leadership in higher education will likely involve key activities and initiatives to tackle challenges and find solutions in this dynamic sector(Das et al., 2024b; Durairaj et al., 2023b; Sharma et al., 2024b).

a. **Adapting to Technological Advancements:** Embracing emerging technologies such as artificial intelligence, machine learning, and data analytics to enhance decision-making processes, improve operational efficiency, and personalize learning experiences for students. Implementing digital transformation initiatives to modernize administrative processes, streamline communication channels, and optimize resource allocation within higher education institutions.

b. **Promoting Diversity, Equity, and Inclusion:** Developing and implementing comprehensive DEI strategies to foster a more inclusive and equitable campus environment. Prioritizing recruitment and retention efforts aimed at increasing representation of underrepresented groups in leadership positions, faculty roles, and student populations.

c. **Addressing Financial Sustainability:** Developing innovative funding models and revenue streams to address budgetary constraints and ensure long-term financial sustainability in the face of changing economic landscapes and funding challenges. Exploring alternative financing options, such as public-private partnerships, philanthropic investments, and income-sharing agreements, to diversify revenue sources and support institutional growth and development(Singh Madan et al., 2024; Venkatasubramanian et al., 2024).

d. **Enhancing Student Success and Well-being:** Implementing holistic student success initiatives that prioritize students' academic, personal, and career development needs. Expanding access to mental health resources, wellness programs, and support services to address the growing demand for mental health support and promote student well-being.

e. **Fostering Collaborative Partnerships:** Cultivating strategic partnerships and collaborations with industry stakeholders, government agencies, community organizations, and other higher education institutions to address shared challenges and leverage collective expertise and resources. Engaging in cross-sector initiatives focused on workforce development, research collaboration, community engagement, and economic development to drive innovation and create impact at local, regional, and global levels.

f. **Empowering Adaptive Leadership:** Developing adaptive leadership competencies and skills among current and future higher education leaders to navigate uncertainty, complexity, and change effectively. Providing leadership development opportunities, coaching, and mentorship programs to equip leaders with the knowledge, tools, and resilience needed to lead with agility and creativity in a rapidly evolving higher education landscape.

Future leadership in higher education will prioritize technological advancements, diversity, financial sustainability, student success, collaboration, and adaptive leadership to prepare institutions for future challenges and opportunities, ensuring their readiness for the future.

CONCLUSIONS

The chapter discusses the evolving landscape of higher education, offering leaders both opportunities and challenges. It highlights the multifaceted nature of directing leadership, the key challenges faced, and innovative solutions to address them. The main conclusions drawn from the discussion are summarized.

Higher education leadership is a complex task that involves navigating diverse stakeholders, competing priorities, and rapidly changing external factors. Leaders face financial pressures, demographic shifts, technological advancements, and increasing accountability demands. These challenges strain resources, create tensions, and require difficult decisions to ensure institutional sustainability and student success. A nuanced and adaptive approach is required to navigate these multifaceted challenges. Promoting diversity and inclusion in higher education is crucial for creating a more equitable environment. Leaders should increase representation of underrepresented groups in leadership roles, faculty positions, and student populations. A campus culture that values diversity is also important. Adapting to technological advancements is vital for staying competitive and meeting evolving needs. Leaders should invest in digital infrastructure, data analytics, and innovative teaching technologies to enhance student engagement and support institutional goals.

Higher education leaders must prioritize financial sustainability and student success and well-being. To address declining public funding, rising costs, and economic uncertainties, they must explore innovative funding models, diversify revenue streams, and invest strategically. They must also prioritize initiatives supporting academic, personal, and career development, providing access to resources and support services that address the holistic needs of students. Leaders in higher education must foster strategic partnerships with industry stakeholders, government agencies, community organizations, and other institutions to address complex challenges and drive innovation, leveraging collective expertise and resources for meaningful impact.

Leadership in higher education necessitates a multifaceted approach that tackles complex challenges while embracing innovative solutions. This includes prioritizing diversity, embracing technological change, ensuring financial sustainability, promoting student success, and fostering collaborative partnerships. This approach positions institutions for success and positively impacts the evolving higher education landscape.

KEY TERMS

- **SEO**: Search Engine Optimization
- **ATS**: Applicant Tracking System
- **AI**: Artificial Intelligence
- **DEI**: Diversity, Equity, and Inclusion

REFERENCES

Agrawal, A. V., Pitchai, R., Senthamaraikannan, C., Balaji, N. A., Sajithra, S., & Boopathi, S. (2023). Digital Education System During the COVID-19 Pandemic. In *Using Assistive Technology for Inclusive Learning in K-12 Classrooms* (pp. 104–126). IGI Global. DOI: 10.4018/978-1-6684-6424-3.ch005

Baptiste, M. (2019). No Teacher Left Behind: The Impact of Principal Leadership Styles on Teacher Job Satisfaction and Student Success. *Journal of International Education and Leadership*, 9(1), n1.

Channuwong, S., Snongtaweeporn, T., Harnphanich, B., Benjawatanapon, W., Katangchol, S., Vongsurakrai, S., Chantarotron, N., Trerutpicharn, S., Damrongsiri, T., & Kongyoungyune, R. (2023). Creative leadership affecting organizational performance according to the Balanced Scorecard: A case study of Public Limited Companies in Bangkok, Thailand. *Journal of Namibian Studies: History Politics Culture*, 33, 4034–4057.

Cheong, M., Yammarino, F. J., Dionne, S. D., Spain, S. M., & Tsai, C.-Y. (2019). A review of the effectiveness of empowering leadership. *The Leadership Quarterly*, 30(1), 34–58. DOI: 10.1016/j.leaqua.2018.08.005

Cook-Sather, A. (2020). Student voice across contexts: Fostering student agency in today's schools. *Theory into Practice*, 59(2), 182–191. DOI: 10.1080/00405841.2019.1705091

Cordie, L. A., Brecke, T., Lin, X., & Wooten, M. C. (2020). Co-Teaching in Higher Education: Mentoring as Faculty Development. *International Journal on Teaching and Learning in Higher Education*, 32(1), 149–158.

Das, S., Lekhya, G., Shreya, K., Shekinah, K. L., Babu, K. K., & Boopathi, S. (2024a). Fostering Sustainability Education Through Cross-Disciplinary Collaborations and Research Partnerships: Interdisciplinary Synergy. In *Facilitating Global Collaboration and Knowledge Sharing in Higher Education With Generative AI* (pp. 60–88). IGI Global.

Das, S., Lekhya, G., Shreya, K., Shekinah, K. L., Babu, K. K., & Boopathi, S. (2024b). Fostering Sustainability Education Through Cross-Disciplinary Collaborations and Research Partnerships: Interdisciplinary Synergy. In *Facilitating Global Collaboration and Knowledge Sharing in Higher Education With Generative AI* (pp. 60–88). IGI Global.

Dhanya, D., Kumar, S. S., Thilagavathy, A., Prasad, D., & Boopathi, S. (2023). Data Analytics and Artificial Intelligence in the Circular Economy: Case Studies. In *Intelligent Engineering Applications and Applied Sciences for Sustainability* (pp. 40–58). IGI Global.

Durairaj, M., Jayakumar, S., Karpagavalli, V., Maheswari, B. U., & Boopathi, S. (2023a). Utilization of Digital Tools in the Indian Higher Education System During Health Crises. In *Multidisciplinary Approaches to Organizational Governance During Health Crises* (pp. 1–21). IGI Global. DOI: 10.4018/978-1-7998-9213-7.ch001

Durairaj, M., Jayakumar, S., Karpagavalli, V., Maheswari, B. U., & Boopathi, S. (2023b). Utilization of Digital Tools in the Indian Higher Education System During Health Crises. In *Multidisciplinary Approaches to Organizational Governance During Health Crises* (pp. 1–21). IGI Global. DOI: 10.4018/978-1-7998-9213-7.ch001

Farrukh, M., Lee, J. W. C., & Shahzad, I. A. (2019). Intrapreneurial behavior in higher education institutes of Pakistan: The role of leadership styles and psychological empowerment. *Journal of Applied Research in Higher Education*, 11(2), 273–294. DOI: 10.1108/JARHE-05-2018-0084

Hernández-de-Menéndez, M., Morales-Menendez, R., Escobar, C. A., & Ramírez Mendoza, R. A. (2022). Learning analytics: State of the art. [IJIDeM]. *International Journal on Interactive Design and Manufacturing*, 16(3), 1209–1230. DOI: 10.1007/s12008-022-00930-0

Ingle, R. B., Swathi, S., Mahendran, G., Senthil, T., Muralidharan, N., & Boopathi, S. (2023). Sustainability and Optimization of Green and Lean Manufacturing Processes Using Machine Learning Techniques. In *Circular Economy Implementation for Sustainability in the Built Environment* (pp. 261–285). IGI Global. DOI: 10.4018/978-1-6684-8238-4.ch012

Kalaiselvi, D., Ramaratnam, M. S., Kokila, S., Sarkar, R., Anandakumar, S., & Boopathi, S. (2024). Future Developments of Higher Education on Social Psychology: Innovation and Changes. In *Advances in Human and Social Aspects of Technology* (pp. 146–169). IGI Global. DOI: 10.4018/979-8-3693-2569-8.ch008

Kim, J. J., Waldman, D. A., Balthazard, P. A., & Ames, J. B. (2023). Leader self-projection and collective role performance: A consideration of visionary leadership. *The Leadership Quarterly*, 34(2), 101623. DOI: 10.1016/j.leaqua.2022.101623

Kim, M., & Beehr, T. A. (2020). Empowering leadership: Leading people to be present through affective organizational commitment? *International Journal of Human Resource Management*, 31(16), 2017–2044. DOI: 10.1080/09585192.2018.1424017

Kim, M., & Beehr, T. A. (2021). The power of empowering leadership: Allowing and encouraging followers to take charge of their own jobs. *International Journal of Human Resource Management*, 32(9), 1865–1898. DOI: 10.1080/09585192.2019.1657166

King, F. (2019). Professional learning: Empowering teachers? []. Taylor & Francis.]. *Professional Development in Education*, 45(2), 169–172. DOI: 10.1080/19415257.2019.1580849

Kurilovas, E. (2020). On data-driven decision-making for quality education. *Computers in Human Behavior*, 107, 105774. DOI: 10.1016/j.chb.2018.11.003

Leithwood, K., Jantzi, D., & Steinbach, R. (2021a). Leadership and other conditions which foster organizational learning in schools. In *Organizational learning in schools* (pp. 67–90). Taylor & Francis. DOI: 10.1201/9781003077459-5

Leithwood, K., Jantzi, D., & Steinbach, R. (2021b). Leadership and other conditions which foster organizational learning in schools. In *Organizational learning in schools* (pp. 67–90). Taylor & Francis. DOI: 10.1201/9781003077459-5

Lumby, J. (2019). Leadership and power in higher education. *Studies in Higher Education*, 44(9), 1619–1629. DOI: 10.1080/03075079.2018.1458221

McNair, T. B., Albertine, S., McDonald, N., Major, T.Jr., & Cooper, M. A. (2022). *Becoming a student-ready college: A new culture of leadership for student success.* John Wiley & Sons.

Nicolazzo, Z., Pitcher, E. N., Renn, K. A., & Woodford, M. (2019). An exploration of trans* kinship as a strategy for student success. In *What's Transgressive about Trans* Studies in Education Now?* (pp. 95–109). Routledge. DOI: 10.4324/9781351034029-6

Oke, A., & Fernandes, F. A. P. (2020). Innovations in teaching and learning: Exploring the perceptions of the education sector on the 4th industrial revolution (4IR). *Journal of Open Innovation*, 6(2), 31. DOI: 10.3390/joitmc6020031

Pineda-Báez, C., Bauman, C., & Andrews, D. (2019). Empowering teacher leadership: A cross-country study. *International Journal of Leadership in Education*.

Prabhuswamy, M., Tripathi, R., Vijayakumar, M., Thulasimani, T., Sundharesalingam, P., & Sampath, B. (2024). A Study on the Complex Nature of Higher Education Leadership: An Innovative Approach. In *Challenges of Globalization and Inclusivity in Academic Research* (pp. 202–223). IGI Global. DOI: 10.4018/979-8-3693-1371-8.ch013

Santos, J., Figueiredo, A. S., & Vieira, M. (2019). Innovative pedagogical practices in higher education: An integrative literature review. *Nurse Education Today*, 72, 12–17. DOI: 10.1016/j.nedt.2018.10.003 PMID: 30384082

Saravanan, S., Chandrasekar, J., Satheesh Kumar, S., Patel, P., Maria Shanthi, J., & Boopathi, S. (2024). The Impact of NBA Implementation Across Engineering Disciplines: Innovative Approaches. In *Advances in Higher Education and Professional Development* (pp. 229–252). IGI Global. DOI: 10.4018/979-8-3693-1666-5.ch010

Seider, S., Clark, S., & Graves, D. (2020). The development of critical consciousness and its relation to academic achievement in adolescents of color. *Child Development*, 91(2), e451–e474. DOI: 10.1111/cdev.13262 PMID: 31140588

Sharma, D. M., Ramana, K. V., Jothilakshmi, R., Verma, R., Maheswari, B. U., & Boopathi, S. (2024a). Integrating Generative AI Into K-12 Curriculums and Pedagogies in India: Opportunities and Challenges. *Facilitating Global Collaboration and Knowledge Sharing in Higher Education With Generative AI*, 133–161.

Sharma, D. M., Ramana, K. V., Jothilakshmi, R., Verma, R., Maheswari, B. U., & Boopathi, S. (2024b). Integrating Generative AI Into K-12 Curriculums and Pedagogies in India: Opportunities and Challenges. *Facilitating Global Collaboration and Knowledge Sharing in Higher Education With Generative AI*, 133–161.

Shaturaev, J., & Bekimbetova, G. (2021). *The difference between educational management and educational leadership and the importance of educational responsibility*. InterConf.

Shen, J., Wu, H., Reeves, P., Zheng, Y., Ryan, L., & Anderson, D. (2020). The association between teacher leadership and student achievement: A meta-analysis. *Educational Research Review*, 31, 100357. DOI: 10.1016/j.edurev.2020.100357

Singh Madan, B., Najma, U., Pande Rana, D., & Kumar, P. K. J., S., S., & Boopathi, S. (2024). Empowering Leadership in Higher Education: Driving Student Performance, Faculty Development, and Institutional Progress. In *Advances in Educational Technologies and Instructional Design* (pp. 191–221). IGI Global. DOI: 10.4018/979-8-3693-0583-6.ch009

Steinert, Y., O'Sullivan, P. S., & Irby, D. M. (2019). Strengthening teachers' professional identities through faculty development. *Academic Medicine*, 94(7), 963–968. DOI: 10.1097/ACM.0000000000002695 PMID: 30844931

Venkatasubramanian, V., Chitra, M., Sudha, R., Singh, V. P., Jefferson, K., & Boopathi, S. (2024). Examining the Impacts of Course Outcome Analysis in Indian Higher Education: Enhancing Educational Quality. In *Challenges of Globalization and Inclusivity in Academic Research* (pp. 124–145). IGI Global.

Zawacki-Richter, O., Marín, V. I., Bond, M., & Gouverneur, F. (2019). Systematic review of research on artificial intelligence applications in higher education–where are the educators? *International Journal of Educational Technology in Higher Education*, 16(1), 1–27. DOI: 10.1186/s41239-019-0171-0

Ziakkas, D., Sarikaya, I., & Natakusuma, H. C. (2023). EBT-CBTA in Aviation Training: The Turkish Airlines Case Study. *International Conference on Human-Computer Interaction*, 188–199. DOI: 10.1007/978-3-031-35389-5_14

Zimmer, W. K., & Matthews, S. D. (2022). A virtual coaching model of professional development to increase teachers' digital learning competencies. *Teaching and Teacher Education*, 109, 103544. DOI: 10.1016/j.tate.2021.103544

Compilation of References

Abd Latiff, Z. I., Sidik, N., Zin, N. A. M., & Zainuddin, A. (2022). Implementation of Electrical Engineering Laboratory Course for Diploma Studies in Electrical Engineering during [*Pandemic Phase.*]. *COVID*, 19.

Aboramadan, M., Dahleez, K. A., & Hamad, M. H. (2020). Servant leadership and academics outcomes in higher education: The role of job satisfaction. *The International Journal of Organizational Analysis*, 29(3), 562–584. DOI: 10.1108/ijoa-11-2019-1923

Acosta, D., & Freier, L. F. (2023). Expanding the Reflexive Turn in Migration Studies: Refugee Protection, Regularization, and Naturalization in Latin America. *Journal of Immigrant & Refugee Studies*, 21(4), 597–610. DOI: 10.1080/15562948.2022.2146246

Adams, J. S. (1963). Toward an understanding of inequity. *Journal of Abnormal and Social Psychology*, 67(5), 422–436. https://ia800704.us.archive.org/view_archive.php?archive=/24/items/wikipedia-scholarly-sources-corpus/10.1037%252Fh0034974.zip&file=10.1037%252Fh0040968.pdf. DOI: 10.1037/h0040968 PMID: 14081885

Adhikari, A., Saha, B., & Sen, S. (2023). Nel Noddings' Theory of Care and its Ethical Components. *International Research Journal of Education and Technology*, 5(8), 198-206.

Agboola, B. M., & Adeyemi, J. K. (2013). Projecting enrolment for effective academic staff planning in Nigerian universities. *Educational Planning*, 21(1), 6-17. https://isep.info/wp[REMOVED HYPERLINK FIELD]content/uploads/2015/12/21-1_1ProjectingEnrollment.pdf

Agboola, B. M. (2024). Total Quality Management (TQM) Approach to Administration of Higher Education Institutions: Implications for Leadership Effectiveness in Jamaica. In Afzal, S. M., Uzoechi, N., & Yahaya, A. (Eds.), *Edited book on Promoting Crisis Management and Creative Problem-Solving Skills in Educational Leadership. Publisher*. IGI Global.

Agrawal, A. V., Pitchai, R., Senthamaraikannan, C., Balaji, N. A., Sajithra, S., & Boopathi, S. (2023). Digital Education System During the COVID-19 Pandemic. In *Using Assistive Technology for Inclusive Learning in K-12 Classrooms* (pp. 104–126). IGI Global. DOI: 10.4018/978-1-6684-6424-3.ch005

Aithal, P. S., & Aithal, S. (2023). How to increase emotional infrastructure of higher education institutions. [IJMTS]. *International Journal of Management, Technology, and Social Sciences*, 8(3), 356–394. DOI: 10.47992/IJMTS.2581.6012.0307

Akanji, B., Mordi, C., Ituma, A., Adisa, T. A., & Ajonbadi, H. (2020). The influence of organisational culture on leadership style in higher education institutions. *Personnel Review*, 49(3), 709–732. DOI: 10.1108/PR-08-2018-0280

Al-Abrrow, H., Fayez, A. S., Abdullah, H., Khaw, K. W., Alnoor, A., & Rexhepi, G. (2023). Effect of open-mindedness and humble behavior on innovation: Mediator role of learning. *International Journal of Emerging Markets*, 18(9), 3065–3084. DOI: 10.1108/IJOEM-08-2020-0888

Alden, S. (n.d). Co-production: Research and practice review full report. https://www .sheffield.ac.uk>... Alsaedi, F. (2022) The important role of collective leadership in the face of change: Literature review. *Open Journal of Leadership*, 11, 1-12. DOI: 10.4236/ojl.2022.111001

Alexander, G., & Glasgow, J. (1981). UNICEF regional primary school project: Report on teacher training and curriculum development activities, 1978–1980. *Caribbean Journal of Education*, 8(1), 75–101.

Al-Husseini, S., El Beltagi, I., & Moizer, J. (2021). Transformational leadership and innovation: The mediating role of knowledge sharing amongst higher education faculty. *International Journal of Leadership in Education*, 24(5), 670–693. DOI: 10.1080/13603124.2019.1588381

Ali, A. H., Kineber, A. F., Elyamany, A., Ibrahim, A. H., & Daoud, A. O. (2023). Modelling the role of modular construction's critical success factors in the overall sustainable success of Egyptian housing projects. *Journal of Building Engineering*, 71, 106467. DOI: 10.1016/j.jobe.2023.106467

Aljumah, A. (2023). The impact of extrinsic and intrinsic motivation on job satisfaction: The mediating role of transactional leadership. *Cogent Business & Management*, 10(3), 2270813. DOI: 10.1080/23311975.2023.2270813

Alo, E. A., & Dada, D. A. (2020). Employees' Turnover Intention: A Survey of Academic Staff of Selected Private Universities in Ondo State, Nigeria. *International Journal of Scientific and Research Publications*, 10(2), 263–268. DOI: 10.29322/IJSRP.10.02.2020.p98377

American Association of Physics Teachers (AAPT). (n.d.). STEM Leadership Framework. Retrieved from https://www.aapt.org/aboutaapt/organization/contactus.cfm

Amutuhaire, T. (2010). Terms of service and job retention among academic staff at Makerere University. Master of Arts in Higher Education Studies Thesis, Makerere University, Kampala.

Anderson, L. A., & Anderson, D. (2010). *The change leader's roadmap: How to navigate your organization's transformation* (Vol. 384). John Wiley & Sons.

Anderson, V., Rabello, R., Wass, R., Golding, C., Rangi, A., Eteuati, E., Bristowe, Z., & Waller, A. (2020). Good teaching as care in higher education. *Higher Education*, 79(1), 1–19. DOI: 10.1007/s10734-019-00392-6

Anft, M. (2013). The STEM crisis: Reality or myth. *The Chronicle of Higher Education*, 58(12), 1–14.

Antonopoulou, H., Halkiopoulos, C., Barlou, O., & Beligiannis, G. N. (2020). Leadership types and digital leadership in higher education: Behavioural data analysis from University of Patras in Greece. *International Journal of Learning. Teaching and Educational Research*, 19(4), 110–129.

Apella, I., & Gonzalo, Z. (2022). Technological change and labour market trends in Latin America and the Caribbean: A task content approach. *CEPAL Review*, 2022(136), 63–85. DOI: 10.18356/16840348-2022-136-4

Apostolou, P. P., & Avgerinou, M. D. (2021). The coding maestros project: Blending steam and non-steam subjects through computational thinking. In *Handbook of research on K-12 blended and virtual learning through the i²Flex classroom model* (pp. 504–518). IGI Global. DOI: 10.4018/978-1-7998-7760-8.ch029

Arday, J. (2018). Understanding mental health: What are the issues for black and ethnic minority students at university? *Social Sciences (Basel, Switzerland)*, 7(10), 196. DOI: 10.3390/socsci7100196

Ärleskog, C., Vackerberg, N., & Andersson, A. (2021). Balancing power in co-production: Introducing a reflection model. https://doi.org/.DOI: 10.1057/s41599-02-00790-1

Artess, J., Mellors-Bourne, R., & Hooley, T. (2017). Employability: A review of the literature 2012-2016. https://www.advance-he.ac.uk/knowledge-hub/employability -review-literature-2012-2016

Asghar, M. Z., Barbera, E., Rasool, S. F., Seitamaa-Hakkarainen, P., & Mohelská, H. (2023). Adoption of social media-based knowledge-sharing behaviour and authentic leadership development: Evidence from the educational sector of Pakistan during COVID-19. *Journal of Knowledge Management*, 27(1), 59–83. DOI: 10.1108/ JKM-11-2021-0892

Ash, A. N., Hill, R., Risdon, S., & Jun, A. (2020). Anti-racism in higher education: A model for change. *Race and Pedagogy Journal: Teaching and Learning for Justice*, 4(3), 2.

Aslam, A. (2020). The hotly debated topic of human capital and economic growth: Why institutions may matter? *Quality & Quantity*, 54(4), 1351–1362. DOI: 10.1007/ s11135-020-00989-5

Astin, A. W. (1997). How "good" is your institution's retention rate? *Research in Higher Education*, 38(6), 647–658. DOI: 10.1023/A:1024903702810

Astin, A. W., Vogelgesang, L. J., Ikeda, E. K., & Yee, J. A. (2000). *How service learning affects students*. Higher Education Research Institute, University of California.

ation quarterly, 52(2), 221-258.

Avis, M. (2009). The problem of brand definition. www. duplication.net.au/---/ ANZMAC200

Awan, F. H., Dunnan, L., Jamil, K., & Gul, R. F. (2023). Stimulating environmental performance via green human resource management, green transformational leadership, and green innovation: A mediation-moderation model. *Environmental Science and Pollution Research International*, 30(2), 2958–2976. DOI: 10.1007/ s11356-022-22424-y PMID: 35939187

Azmi, A. N. (2024). *Relationships Between Lecturers' Caring Leadership And Pre-Service Teachers' Thinking Styles And Attitudes Towards Teaching Profession At Teacher Education Institutes In Kuala Lumpur*[Unpublished Doctoral Thesis]. University of Malaya

Baashar, Y., Alkawsi, G., Mustafa, A., Alkahtani, A. A., Alsariera, Y. A., Ali, A. Q., Hashim, W., & Tiong, S. K. (2022). Toward predicting student's academic performance using artificial neural networks (ANNs). *Applied Sciences (Basel, Switzerland)*, 12(3), 1289. DOI: 10.3390/app12031289

Babu, B. S., Kamalakannan, J., Meenatchi, N., Karthik, S., & Boopathi, S. (2022). Economic impacts and reliability evaluation of battery by adopting Electric Vehicle. *IEEE Explore*, 1–6.

Bagga, S. K., Gera, S., & Haque, S. N. (2023). The mediating role of organizational culture: Transformational leadership and change management in virtual teams. *Asia Pacific Management Review*, 28(2), 120–131.

Bagheri, A., Newman, A., & Eva, N. (2022). Entrepreneurial leadership of CEOs and employees' innovative behavior in high-technology new ventures. *Journal of Small Business Management*, 60(4), 805–827. DOI: 10.1080/00472778.2020.1737094

Bagheri, S., Zarshenas, L., Rakhshan, M., Sharif, F., Sarani, E. M., Shirazi, Z. H., & Sitzman, K. (2023). Impact of Watson's human caring-based health promotion program on caregivers of individuals with schizophrenia. *BMC Health Services Research*, 23(1), 711. DOI: 10.1186/s12913-023-09725-9 PMID: 37386572

Baker, S., & Burke, R. (2023). What Is Care? In *Questioning Care in Higher Education: Resisting Definitions as Radical* (pp. 21–58). Springer International Publishing. DOI: 10.1007/978-3-031-41829-7_2

Balti, M., & Karoui Zouaoui, S. (2023). Employee and manager's emotional intelligence and individual adaptive performance: The role of servant leadership climate. *Journal of Management Development*, 43(1), 13–34. DOI: 10.1108/JMD-04-2021-0117

Baltodano, J., Carlson, S., Jackson, L., & Mitchell, W. (2012). Networking to Leadership in Higher Education: National and State-Based Programs and Networks for Developing Women. *Advances in Developing Human Resources*, 14(1), 62–78. DOI: 10.1177/1523422311428926

Bandola-Gill, J., Arthur, M., & Ivor Leng, R. (2023). What is co-production? Conceptualising and understanding co-production of knowledge and policy across different theoretical perspectives. *Evidence & Policy*, 19(2), 275–298. DOI: 10.1332/174426421X16420955772641

Baptiste, M. (2019). No Teacher Left Behind: The Impact of Principal Leadership Styles on Teacher Job Satisfaction and Student Success. *Journal of International Education and Leadership*, 9(1), n1.

Barbera, S. A., Berkshire, S. D., Boronat, C. B., & Kennedy, M. H. (2020). Review of Undergraduate Student Retention and Graduation Since 2010: Patterns, Predictions, and Recommendations for 2020. *Journal of College Student Retention*, 22(2), 227–250. DOI: 10.1177/1521025117738233

Barboza, L., & Teixeira, E. S. (2020). Effect of data science teaching for non-stem students: A systematic literature review. *ICSEA*, 2020, 128.

Barbuto, J. E., & Wheeler, D. W. (2006). Scale development and construct clarification of servant leadership. *Group & Organization Management*, 31(3), 300–326. DOI: 10.1177/1059601106287091

Baron, J. (2019). Actively open-minded thinking in politics. *Cognition*, 188, 8–18. DOI: 10.1016/j.cognition.2018.10.004 PMID: 30366602

Bartlett, T. (2021). The antiracist college. *The Chronicle of Higher Education*, ●●●, 2021.

Bashayreh, A. M., Assaf, N., & Qudah, M. (2016). Prevailing organizational culture and effect on academic staff satisfaction in the Malaysian higher education institutes. *International Journal of Statistics and Systems*, 11(1), 89–102. https://www.ripublication.com/ijss16/ijssv11n1_09.pdff

Bass, B. M., & Riggio, R. E. (2006). *Transformational Leadership* (2nd ed.). Lawrence Erlbaum Associates. DOI: 10.4324/9781410617095

Bean, J. P. (1980). Dropouts and Turnover: The Synthesis and Test of a Causal Model of Student Attrition. *Research in Higher Education*, 12(2), 155–187. DOI: 10.1007/BF00976194

Becker, G. S. (2009). *Human Capital*. University of Chicago Press.

Beckles, H., & Richards-Kennedy, S. (2021). Accelerating the Future into the Present: Reimagining Higher Education in the Caribbean in Land, A. Corcoran & D-C. Lancu (Eds.). *The Promise of Higher Education.*https://link.springer.com/chapter/10.1007/978-3-030[REMOVED HYPERLINK FIELD]67245-4_54

Beerkens, M., & van der Hoek, M. (2022). Academic leaders and leadership in the changing higher education landscape. In *Research Handbook on Academic Careers and Managing Academics* (pp. 121–136). Edward Elgar Publishing. DOI: 10.4337/9781839102639.00017

Bellei, C., Morawietz, L., Valenzuela, J. P., & Vanni, X. (2020). Effective schools 10 years on: Factors and processes enabling the sustainability of school effectiveness. *School Effectiveness and School Improvement*, 31(2), 266–288. DOI: 10.1080/09243453.2019.1652191

Bensimon, E. M. (2018). Reclaiming Racial Justice in Equity. *Change*, 50(3-4), 95–98. DOI: 10.1080/00091383.2018.1509623

Bensimon, E. M., & Neumann, A. (2017). *Diversity's Promise for Higher Education: Making it Work*. Johns Hopkins University Press.

Bergman, Z., Bergman, M., Fernandes, K., Grossrieder, D., & Schneider, L. (2018, November 28). The contribution of UNESCO chairs toward achieving the UN Sustainable

Besterfield-Sacre, M., Gerchak, J., Lyons, M. R., Shuman, L. J., & Wolfe, H. (2004). Scoring concept maps: An integrated rubric for assessing engineering education. *Journal of Engineering Education*, 93(2), 105–115. DOI: 10.1002/j.2168-9830.2004.tb00795.x

Bhat, A., Ahmad, F., Jain, D., Hussain, A., & Ahmad, S. (2023). Numerical Techniques for Calculating Attainment of Course Outcome and Programme Outcome under NEP-2020: Numerical technique for CO and PO under NEP-2020. *International Journal of Information Technology. Research and Applications*, 2(2), 65–72.

Bhat, R., Kamath, C. R., Mathias, K. A., & Mulimani, P. (2022). Practical Implementation of Outcome-Based Education Practices in the Indian Engineering Institutes–Approach An Objective Based Investigation. *Journal of Engineering Education Transformations*, 36(1). Advance online publication. DOI: 10.16920/jeet/2022/v36i1/22133

Black, I., & Veloutsou, C. (2017). Working consumers: Co-creation of brand identity, consumer identity and brand community identity. *Journal of Business Research*, 70, 416–429. DOI: 10.1016/j.jbusres.2016.07.012

Black, W. R., & Simon, M. D. (2014). Leadership for all students: Planning for more inclusive school practices. *The International Journal of Educational Leadership Preparation*, 9(2), 153–172.

Bloemhard, M. (2016). On contemporary leadership and branded organisations. (Doctoral dissertation, Antioch University). https://etd.ohiolink.edu/!etd.send_file?

Bob, A. (2010). *Managing Your Aspirations: Developing Personal Enterprise in the Global Workplace*. McGraw-Hill.

Bocconi, S., Chioccariello, A., Dettori, G., Ferrari, A., Engelhardt, K., Robson, R., & Underwood, J. (2020). Computational thinking in K-9 education. A review. *Computers in Human Behavior*, 102, 56–67.

Bodolica, V., & Spraggon, M. (2021). Incubating innovation in university settings: Building entrepreneurial mindsets in the future generation of innovative emerging market leaders. *Education + Training*, 63(4), 613–631. DOI: 10.1108/ET-06-2020-0145

Boisselle, L. N. (2016). Decolonizing science and science education in a postcolonial space (Trinidad, a developing Caribbean nation, illustrates). *SAGE Open*, 6(1), 2158244016635257. DOI: 10.1177/2158244016635257

Bolden, R., Petrov, G., & Gosling, J. (2008). Distributed leadership in higher education: Rhetoric and reality. Educational Management Administration & Leadership. https://doi.org/ Bolman, L. G., & Deal, T. E. (2017). *Reframing organizations: Artistry, choice, and leadership*. John Wiley & Sons. DOI: 10.1177/1741143208100301

Bombard, Y., Baker, G. R., Orlando, E., Fancott, C., Bhatia, P., Casalino, S., Onate, K., Denis, J-L., & Pomey, M-P. (2018). Engaging patients to improve quality of care: A systematic review. *Implementation Science*, 13(1), 1–22. 42.

Bonet, G., & Walters, B. R. (2016). High impact practices: Student engagement and retention. *College Student Journal*, 50(2), 224–235.

BOOST. (2022). Building out our STEM Teacher-A well needed boost for the education sector. *The Jamaica Gleaner*. Retrieved on March 14, 2024 from https://jamaica-gleaner.com/article/news/20220622/building-out-our-stem-teachers-well-needed-boost-education-sector

Borah, P. S., Iqbal, S., & Akhtar, S. (2022). Linking social media usage and SME's sustainable performance: The role of digital leadership and innovation capabilities. *Technology in Society*, 68, 101900. DOI: 10.1016/j.techsoc.2022.101900

Borden, V. M. (2005). Using alumni research to align program improvement with institutional accountability. *New Directions for Institutional Research*, 2005(126), 61–72. DOI: 10.1002/ir.148

Bouzioti, D. (2023). Introducing the Phenomenological Model of Performance Practice (PMPP): Phenomenological Research Design and the Lived Experience in Performance. *International Journal of Qualitative Methods*, 22, 16094069231211142. Advance online publication. DOI: 10.1177/16094069231211142

Bower, B. L., & Wolverton, M. (2023). *Answering the call: African American women in higher education leadership*. Taylor & Francis. DOI: 10.4324/9781003443001

Bowers, S. W., Williams Jr, T. O., & Ernst, J. V. (2020). Profile of an elementary STEM educator.

Bowman, N. A. (2013). How much diversity is enough? The curvilinear relationship between college diversity interactions and first-year student outcomes. *Research in Higher Education*, 54(8), 874–894. DOI: 10.1007/s11162-013-9300-0

Brandsen, T., & Honingh, M. (2015). Distinguishing different types of co-production: A conceptual analysis based on the classical definitions. *Public Administration Review*, 75(3), 427–435. DOI: 10.1111/puar.12465

Brathwaite, W. E. (1978). *In-service strategies for improving teacher abilities in science education*. In the proceedings of the regional primary science conference, (pp. 156-160). University of the West Indies, Cave Hill, Barbados: Caribbean Regional Science Project.

Breaux, G., Danridge, J., & Pearson, P. D. (2002). Scott Elementary School: Homegrown school improvement in the flesh. In Taylor, B. M., & Pearson, P. D. (Eds.), *Teaching reading: Effective schools, accomplished teachers* (pp. 217–236). Lawrence Erlbaum.

Breese, P., Burman, W. J., Goldberg, S., & Weis, S. E. (2007). Education level, primary language, and comprehension of the informed consent process. *Journal of Empirical Research on Human Research Ethics; JERHRE*, 2(4), 69–79. DOI: 10.1525/jer.2007.2.4.69

Breiner, J. M., Harkness, S. S., Johnson, C. C., & Koehler, C. M. (2012). What is STEM? A discussion about conceptions of STEM in education and partnerships. *School Science and Mathematics*, 112(1), 3–11. DOI: 10.1111/j.1949-8594.2011.00109.x

Bright, C. (2019). Coproduction and working with experts by experience. https://www. cordisbright.co.uk.A.

Brissett, N. O. M. (2018). Education for Social Transformation (EST) in the Caribbean: A Postcolonial Perspective. Mathematics (2227-7390), 6(12), 197. DOI: 10.3390/educsci8040197

Brissett, N. (2021). *A critical appraisal of education in the Caribbean and its evolution from colonial origins to twenty-first century responses*. Oxford Research Encyclopedia of Education., DOI: 10.1093/acrefore/9780190264093.013.1650

Britt, S. L., Ammerman, D. A., Barrett, S. F., & Jones, S. (2017). Student Loans, Financial Stress, and College Student Retention. *Journal of Student Financial Aid*, 47(1), 3. DOI: 10.55504/0884-9153.1605

Brown, S. D., & Lent, R. W. (1996). A Social Cognitive Framework for Career Choice Counseling. *The Career Development Quarterly*, 44(4), 354–366. DOI: 10.1002/j.2161-0045.1996.tb00451.x

Bryman, A. (2007). Effective leadership in higher education: A literature review. *Studies in Higher Education*, 32(6), 693–710. DOI: 10.1080/03075070701685114

Bryson, J. M. (2018). *Strategic planning for public and nonprofit organizations: A guide to strengthening and sustaining organizational achievement.* John Wiley & Sons.

Buchanan, R., Mills, T., & Mooney, E. (2022). Working across time and space: Developing a framework for teacher leadership throughout a teaching career. In *Leadership for Professional Learning* (pp. 65–77). Routledge. DOI: 10.4324/9781003357384-5

Bugaj, T. J., Blohm, M., Schmid, C., Koehl, N., Huber, J., Huhn, D., Herzog, W., Krautter, M., & Nikendei, C. (2019). Peer-assisted learning (PAL): Skills lab tutors' experiences and motivation. *BMC Medical Education*, 19, 353. DOI: 10.1186/s12909-019-1760-2

Burke, B. M., & Ceo-DiFrancesco, D. (2022). Recruitment and retention of world language teacher education majors: Perspectives of teacher candidates and alumni to remedy a global shortage. *Foreign Language Annals*, 55(2), 333–360. DOI: 10.1111/flan.12613

Bussu, S., & Galanti, M. T. (2018). Facilitating co-production: The role of leadership in co-production initiatives in the UK. *Policy and Society*, 37(3), 347–367. DOI: 10.1080/14494035.2018.1414355

Byrd, K. L., & MacDonald, G. (2005). Defining college readiness from the inside out: First-generation college student perspectives. *Community College Review*, 33(1), 22–37. DOI: 10.1177/009155210503300102

Calhoun, J. C. (1996). The student learning imperative: Implications for student affairs. *Journal of College Student Development*, 37(2), 188–122.

Camara, W. (2013). Defining and measuring college and career readiness: A validation framework. *Educational Measurement: Issues and Practice*, 32(4), 16–27. DOI: 10.1111/emip.12016

Campbell-Whatley, G. D., Wang, C., Toms, O., & Williams, N. (2015). Factors affecting campus climate: Creating a welcoming environment. *New Waves-Educational Research and Development Journal*, 18(2), 40–52.

Cansoy, R. (2017). The Effectiveness of Leadership Skills Development Program for University Students. *Tarih Kültür ve Sanat Arastirmalari Dergisi*, 3(3), 65–87. DOI: 10.7596/taksad.v6i3.899

Cardichon, J., Darling-Hammond, L., Yang, M., Scott, C., Shields, P. M., & Burns, D. (2020). *Inequitable Opportunity to Learn: Student Access to Certified and Experienced Teachers.* Learning Policy Institute.

Carr, P. L., Raj, A., Kaplan, S. E., Terrin, N., Breeze, J. L., & Freund, K. M. (2018). Gender Differences in Academic Medicine: Retention, Rank, and Leadership Comparisons from the National Faculty Survey. *Academic Medicine*, 93(11), 1694–1699. https://pubmed.ncbi.nlm.nih.gov/29384751/. DOI: 10.1097/ACM.0000000000002146 PMID: 29384751

Casper, M.-O., & Artese, G. F. (2023). *Situated cognition research : methodological foundations*. Springer. March 13 2024 DOI: 10.1007/978-3-031-39744-8

Cellina, F., Castri, R., Simão, J. V., & Granato, P. (2020). Co-creating app-based policy measures for mobility behavior change: A trigger for novel governance practices at the urban level. *Sustainable Cities and Society*, 53, 101911. DOI: 10.1016/j.scs.2019.101911

Cels, S., De Jong, J., & Nauta, F. (2012). *Agents of change: Strategy and tactics for social innovation*. Rowman & Littlefield.

Center for Organizational Development and Leadership. (CODL, 2023). Strategic Planning in Higher Education: A Guide for Leaders, 1-12. Publisher: the Department of University Relations, the State University of New Jersey, Rutgers. https://www2.cortland.edu/offices/institutional-research-and-assessment/planning-and-assessment-support/file-uploads/RutgersPlanning.pdf

Cerit, Y. (2009). The Effects of Servant Leadership Behaviours of School Principals on Teachers' Job Satisfaction. *Educational Management Administration & Leadership*, 37(5), 600–623. DOI: 10.1177/1741143209339650

Cetin, M., & Kinik, F. S. F. (2016). Effects of Leadership on Student Success through the Balanced Leadership Framework. *Universal Journal of Educational Research*, 4(4), 675–682. DOI: 10.13189/ujer.2016.040403

Chan, C. K. Y., & Lee, K. K. (2023). The AI generation gap: Are Gen Z students more interested in adopting generative AI such as ChatGPT in teaching and learning than their Gen X and millennial generation teachers? *Smart Learning Environments*, 10(1), 60. DOI: 10.1186/s40561-023-00269-3

Chankseliani, M., Qoraboyev, I., & Gimranova, D. (2021). Higher education contributing to local, national, and global development: New empirical and conceptual insights. *Higher Education*, 81(1), 109–127. DOI: 10.1007/s10734-020-00565-8 PMID: 33173242

Channuwong, S., Snongtaweeporn, T., Harnphanich, B., Benjawatanapon, W., Katangchol, S., Vongsurakrai, S., Chantarotron, N., Trerutpicharn, S., Damrongsiri, T., & Kongyoungyune, R. (2023). Creative leadership affecting organizational performance according to the Balanced Scorecard: A case study of Public Limited Companies in Bangkok, Thailand. *Journal of Namibian Studies: History Politics Culture*, 33, 4034–4057.

Cheng, L., Ritzhaupt, A. D., & Antonenko, P. (2019). Effects of the flipped classroom instructional strategy on students' learning outcomes: A meta-analysis. *Educational Technology Research and Development*, 67(4), 793–824. DOI: 10.1007/s11423-018-9633-7

Chen, P., Yang, D., Metwally, A. H. S., Lavonen, J., & Wang, X. (2023). Fostering computational thinking through unplugged activities: A systematic literature review and meta-analysis. *International Journal of STEM Education*, 10(1), 47. DOI: 10.1186/s40594-023-00434-7

Chen, S., Zhu, Y., Guo, L., & Liu, W. (2023). The impact of leader gratitude expressions on followers' behaviours: Increasing gratitude and increases proactivity. *Journal of Leadership & Organizational Studies*, 30(2), 187–204. DOI: 10.1177/15480518231151575

Cheong, M., Yammarino, F. J., Dionne, S. D., Spain, S. M., & Tsai, C.-Y. (2019). A review of the effectiveness of empowering leadership. *The Leadership Quarterly*, 30(1), 34–58. DOI: 10.1016/j.leaqua.2018.08.005

Chevannes, B. (2005). Legislation of tertiary education in the Caribbean.

Chiniara, M., & Bentein, K. (2017). The servant leadership advantage: When perceiving low differentiation in leader-member relationship quality influences team cohesion, team task performance, and service OCB. *The Leadership Quarterly*, 29(3), 333–345. DOI: 10.1016/j.leaqua.2017.05.002

Chirikov, I. (2016). *How global competition is changing universities: Three theoretical perspectives. Research & Occasional Paper Series*. Center for Studies of Higher Education, University of California., https://escholarship.org/content/qt50g3t797/qt50g3t797_noSplash_c538a92a248d853a236c 6d2147b0bbde.pdf?t=ohtfhs

Chisholm, L., Holttum, S., & Springham, N. (2018). Processes in an experience-based co-design project with family carers in community mental health. *SAGE Open*, 8(4), 2158244018809220. DOI: 10.1177/2158244018809220

Choi, H. (2021). Effect of chief executive officer's sustainable leadership styles on organization members' psychological well-being and organizational citizenship behavior. *Sustainability*, 13(24), 13676. DOI: 10.3390/su132413676

Choudhary, M., & Paharia, P. (2018). Role of leadership in quality education in public and private higher education institutions: A comparative study. *GYANODAYA: The Journal of Progressive Education*, 11(1), 17. Advance online publication. DOI: 10.5958/2229-4422.2018.00004.X

Chughtai, A. A. (2016). Servant leadership and follower outcomes: Mediating effects of organizational identification and psychological safety. *The Journal of Psychology*, 150(7), 11–15. DOI: 10.1080/00223980.2016.1170657

Clements, D. H., Sarama, J., Baroody, A. J., Kutaka, T. S., Chernyavskiy, P., Joswick, C., & Joseph, E. (2021). Comparing the efficacy of early arithmetic instruction based on a learning trajectory and teaching-to-a-target. *Journal of Educational Psychology*, 113(7), 1323–1337. DOI: 10.1037/edu0000633

Coates, H., & Matthews, K. E. (2018). Frontier perspectives and insights into higher education student success. *Higher Education Research & Development*, 37(5), 903–907. DOI: 10.1080/07294360.2018.1474539

Coleman, M., & Lumby, J. (2007). Leadership and diversity: Challenging theory and practice in education. *Leadership and Diversity*, 1-160.

Colket, L., Carswell, A., & Light, T. P. (2021). *Becoming*. Dio Press Incorporated.

Collar, M. (2013). Collective Leadership. https://www.shrm.org>news>col....
Cumming, T. M., Bugge, A. S-J., Kriss, K., McArthur, I., Watson, K., & Jiang, Z. (2023). Diversified: Promoting co-production in course design and delivery. *Front. Educ.* 8:1329810. DOI: 10.3389/feduc.2023.1329810

Colos, L. (2023: February, 03) How HR Policies and Procedures Can Help Improve Employee Retention. Pitchgrade publication. https://pitchgrade.com/blog/hr-policies -procedures-improve-employee-retention

Conley, D. T. (2007). Redefining college readiness. Educational Policy Improvement Center. https://eric.ed.gov/?id=ED539251

Conrad, A. (December 22, 2020). 4 Strategic Planning Tools and Models for 2021 and Beyond. https://www.softwareadvice.com/resources/strategic-planning-tools/

Cook-Sather, A. (2020). Student voice across contexts: Fostering student agency in today's schools. *Theory into Practice*, 59(2), 182–191. DOI: 10.1080/00405841.2019.1705091

Corbett, F., & Spinello, E. (2020). Connectivism and leadership: Harnessing a learning theory for the digital age to redefine leadership in the twenty-first century. *Heliyon*, 6(1), e03250. DOI: 10.1016/j.heliyon.2020.e03250 PMID: 31993523

Cordie, L. A., Brecke, T., Lin, X., & Wooten, M. C. (2020). Co-Teaching in Higher Education: Mentoring as Faculty Development. *International Journal on Teaching and Learning in Higher Education*, 32(1), 149–158.

Cordova Jr, N., Kilag, O. K., Andrin, G., Tañiza, F. N., Groenewald, E., & Abella, J. (2024). Leadership Strategies for Numeracy Development in Educational Settings. *Excellencia: International Multi-disciplinary Journal of Education (2994-9521)*, 2(1), 58-68.

Costa, A. (2008). The thought-filled curriculum. ascd._https://www.ascd.org/el/articles/the-thought-filled-curriculum. Accessed on March 28, 2024

Costa, A. L., & Garmston, R. J. (2002). *Cognitive coaching: A foundation for Renaissance Schools* (2nd ed.). Christopher-Gordon Publishers.

Council, N. R., Engineering, N. A. O., & Education, C. O. I. S. (2014, February 28). *STEM Integration in K-12 Education*. National Academies Press.

Council, N. R., Education, D. O. B. A. S. S. A., Education, B. O. S., & Standards, C. O. A. C. F. F. N. K. S. E. (2012). *A Framework for K-12 Science Education*. National Academies Press.

Cox, S. E. *"Perceptions and Influences Behind Teaching Practices: Do Teachers Teach as They Were Taught?"* (2014). Theses and Dissertations. 5301. https://scholarsarchive.byu.edu/etd/5301

Craig, A. J., & Ward, C. V. (2008). Retention of Community College Students: Related Student and Institutional Characteristics. *Journal of College Student Retention*, 9(4), 505–517. DOI: 10.2190/CS.9.4.f

Crane, B. (2022). Leadership mindsets: Why new managers fail and what to do about it. *Business Horizons*, 65(4), 447–455. DOI: 10.1016/j.bushor.2021.05.005

Crawford, J., Cowling, M., & Allen, K. A. (2023). Leadership is needed for ethical ChatGPT: Character, assessment, and learning using artificial intelligence (AI). *Journal of University Teaching & Learning Practice, 20*(3), 02.

Creswell, J. W. (2014). *Research Design: Qualitative, Quantitative, and Mixed Methods Approaches* (4th ed.). Sage.

Creswell, J. W., & Creswell, J. D. (2018). Mixed methods procedures. In *Research design: Qualitative, quantitative, and mixed methods approaches* (5th ed., pp. 213–246). SAGE Publications, Inc.

Cripps, K. (2023). University Sustainability Career Information Events for Future Leaders. In *Events Management for the Infant and Youth Market* (pp. 55–65). Emerald Publishing Limited. DOI: 10.1108/978-1-80455-690-020231009

Cruickshank, V. (2017). The Influence of School Leadership on Student Outcomes. *Open Journal of Social Sciences*, 5(9), 115–123. DOI: 10.4236/jss.2017.59009

Cullen, J., Joyce, J., Hassall, T., & Broadbent, M. (2003). Quality in higher education: From monitoring to management. *Quality Assurance in Education*, 11(1), 5–14. DOI: 10.1108/09684880310462038

Cutumisu, M., Adams, C., & Lu, C. (2019). A scoping review of empirical research on recent computational thinking assessments. *Journal of Science Education and Technology*, 28(6), 651–676. DOI: 10.1007/s10956-019-09799-3

Czerkawski, B. C., & Lyman, E. W.III. (2015). Exploring issues about computational thinking in higher education. *TechTrends*, 59(2), 57–65. DOI: 10.1007/s11528-015-0840-3

D'Ascoli, S., & Piro, J. (2022). Educational servant-leaders and personal growth. *Journal of School Leadership*, 33(1), 26–49. DOI: 10.1177/10526846221134001

Dadvand, B., van Driel, J., Speldewinde, C., & Dawborn-Gundlach, M. (2024). Career change teachers in hard-to-staff schools: Should I stay or leave? *Australian Educational Researcher*, 51(2), 481–496. DOI: 10.1007/s13384-023-00609-9 PMID: 36817651

Daft, R., & Lengel, R. (1983). Information Richness. A New Approach to Managerial Behavior and Organization Design. *Research in Organizational Behavior*. Advance online publication. DOI: 10.21236/ADA128980

Dami, Z. A., Imron, A., & Supriyanto, A. (2022). Servant leadership and job satisfaction: The mediating role of trust and leader-member exchange. *Frontiers in Education*, 7. Advance online publication. DOI: 10.3389/feduc.2022.1036668

Dantley, M. E., & Tillman, L. C. (2006). Social justice and moral transformative leadership. *Leadership for social justice: Making revolutions in education*, 16-30.

Darling-Hammond, L., Hyler, M. E., & Gardner, M. (2017). *Effective Teacher Professional Development*. Learning Policy Institute.

Darling-Hammond, L., Saunders, R., Podolsky, A., Kini, T., Espinoza, D., Hyler, M., & Carver-Thomas, D. (2019). *Best practices to recruit and retain well-prepared teachers in all classrooms*. Learning Policy Institute.

Das, S., Lekhya, G., Shreya, K., Shekinah, K. L., Babu, K. K., & Boopathi, S. (2024). Fostering Sustainability Education Through Cross-Disciplinary Collaborations and Research Partnerships: Interdisciplinary Synergy. In *Facilitating Global Collaboration and Knowledge Sharing in Higher Education With Generative AI* (pp. 60–88). IGI Global.

Das, S., Lekhya, G., Shreya, K., Shekinah, K. L., Babu, K. K., & Boopathi, S. (2024a). Fostering Sustainability Education Through Cross-Disciplinary Collaborations and Research Partnerships: Interdisciplinary Synergy. In *Facilitating Global Collaboration and Knowledge Sharing in Higher Education With Generative AI* (pp. 60–88). IGI Global.

Das, S., Lekhya, G., Shreya, K., Shekinah, K. L., Babu, K. K., & Boopathi, S. (2024b). Fostering Sustainability Education Through Cross-Disciplinary Collaborations and Research Partnerships: Interdisciplinary Synergy. In *Facilitating Global Collaboration and Knowledge Sharing in Higher Education With Generative AI* (pp. 60–88). IGI Global.

David, J. Forrest (1999). Employer Attitude. The Foundation of Employee Retention http://www.keepemployees.com/WhitePapers/attitude.pdf

Davidaviciene, V., & Al Majzoub, K. (2022). The effect of cultural intelligence, conflict, and transformational leadership on decision-making processes in virtual teams. *Social Sciences (Basel, Switzerland)*, 11(2), 64. DOI: 10.3390/socsci11020064

Day, C., Gu, Q., & Sammons, P. (2016). The impact of leadership on student outcomes: How successful school leaders use transformational and instructional strategies to make a difference. Educational administration quarterly, 52(2), 221-258

de Bruijn, E., Billett, S., & Onstenk, J. (Eds.). (2017). *Enhancing teaching and learning in the Dutch vocational education system*. Professional and Practice-Based Learning., DOI: 10.1007/978-3-319-50734-7

De Lisle, J. (Ed.). External examinations beyond national borders: Trinidad and Tobago and the Caribbean Examination Council. In B. Vlaardingerbroek & N. Taylor (Eds.), Secondary School External Examination Systems: Reliability, Robustness and Resilience (pp. 265-290). New York: Cambria Press, 2009.

De Santo, A., Farah, J. C., Martínez, M. L., Moro, A., Bergram, K., Purohit, A. K., Felber, P., Gillet, D., & Holzer, A. (2022). Promoting computational thinking skills in non-computer-science students: Gamifying computational notebooks to increase student engagement. *IEEE Transactions on Learning Technologies*, 15(3), 392–405. DOI: 10.1109/TLT.2022.3180588

Delener, N. (2013). Leadership excellence in higher education: Present and future. *Journal of Contemporary Issues in Business and Government*, 19(1), 19–33. DOI: 10.7790/cibg.v19i1.6

DeMatthews, D. E., Knight, D. S., & Shin, J. (2022). The principal-teacher churn: Understanding the relationship between leadership turnover and teacher attrition. *Educational Administration Quarterly*, 58(1), 76–109. DOI: 10.1177/0013161X211051974

DeMatthews, D., Billingsley, B., McLeskey, J., & Sharma, U. (2020). Principal leadership for students with disabilities in effective inclusive schools. *Journal of Educational Administration*, 58(5), 539–554.

Deming, D., & Noray, K. (2019). STEM careers and the changing skill requirements of work. In *National Bureau of Economic Research, Inc.* EconPapers. Retrieved January 5, 2024, from https://econpapers.repec.org/paper/nbrnberwo/25065.htm

Denis, J.-L., Langley, A., & Sergi, V. (2012). Leadership in the plural. *The Academy of Management Annals*, 6(1), 211–283. DOI: 10.5465/19416520.2012.667612

Dennis, J. (2022, August 30). Jamaica teacher migration: Treating the symptoms and not the causes. *The Jamaica Observer*. https://www.jamaicaobserver.com/2022/08/30/jamaica-teacher-migration-treating-the-symptoms-and-not-the-causes/

Development Goals. (●●●)... *Sustainability*, 10(12), 4471. DOI: 10.3390/su10124471

Devonish, D. (2021). The role of professional organizations in education: The COVID-19 response in Jamaica by science teachers. *Revista Conexiones: Una Experiencia Más Allá Del Aula, 13*(2), 42–55. https://www.mep.go.cr/sites/defaultfiles/2revistaconexion es2021_a4.pdf

Devonish, D. D. (2016). The cognitive coaching approach: A professional Development model for science educators and for students' academic achievement. (Unpublished doctoral dissertation). Northern Caribbean University, Manchester, Jamaica

Devonish, D. D., Lawrence, P. S., & Zamore, C. (2018). A case study on the challenges of implementing diverse instructional strategies into the science lesson post university. *Journal of Arts Science and Technology.*, 11(1), 55–71.

Dewey, J. (2018). *Democracy and Education: With a Critical Introduction by Patricia H. Hinchey*. Myers Education Press. (Original work published 1916)

Dexter, S., & Richardson, J. W. (2020). What does technology integration research tell us about the leadership of technology? *Journal of Research on Technology in Education*, 52(1), 17–36. DOI: 10.1080/15391523.2019.1668316

Dhanya, D., Kumar, S. S., Thilagavathy, A., Prasad, D., & Boopathi, S. (2023). Data Analytics and Artificial Intelligence in the Circular Economy: Case Studies. In *Intelligent Engineering Applications and Applied Sciences for Sustainability* (pp. 40–58). IGI Global.

Dictionary, C. E. dictionary.cambridge.org. Archived from the original on 2017-06-25. Retrieved 2020-12-10.

Dietlin, O. R., Loomis, J. S., & Preffer, J. (2019). Pedagogy of authenticity in the online learning environment: An interdisciplinary overview. In Kyei-Blankson, L., Blankson, J., & Ntuli, E. (Eds.), *Care and Culturally Responsive Pedagogy in Online Settings* (pp. 214–229)., DOI: 10.4018/978-1-5225-7802-4.ch011

Dopson, S., Ferlie, E., Mcgivern, G., Fischer, M., Mitra, M., Ledger, J., & Behrens, S. (2018). Leadership Development in Higher Education: A Literature Review and Implications for Programme Redesign. *Higher Education Quarterly*, 73(2), 218–234. Advance online publication. DOI: 10.1111/hequ.12194

Douglass, J. A., Roebken, H., & Thomson, G. (2020). The immigrant university: Assessing the dynamics of race, major and socioeconomic characteristics at the University of California. Center for Studies in Higher Education. https://cshe .berkeley.edu/publications/immigrant-university-assessing-dynamics-race-major -and-socioeconomic-characteristics

Drath, W. H., McCauley, C. D., Palus, C. J., Van Velsor, E., O'Connor, P. M. G., & McGuire, J. B. (2008). Direction, alignment, commitment: Toward a more integrative ontology of leadership. *The Leadership Quarterly*, 19(6), 635–653. DOI: 10.1016/j.leaqua.2008.09.003

Dreer, B. (2024). Teachers' well-being and job satisfaction: The important role of positive emotions in the workplace. *Educational Studies*, 50(1), 61–77. DOI: 10.1080/03055698.2021.1940872

Du Plessis, A. E. (2018). The lived experience of out-of-field STEM teachers: A quandary for strategizing quality teaching in STEM? *Research in Science Education*, 50(4), 1465–1499. DOI: 10.1007/s11165-018-9740-9

Duan, X., Du, X., & Yu, K. (2018). School culture and school effectiveness: The mediating effect of teachers' job satisfaction. *International Journal of Learning. Teaching and Educational Research*, 17(5), 15–25. DOI: 10.26803/ijlter.17.5.2

Dugan, J. P. (2024). *Leadership theory: Cultivating critical perspectives*. John Wiley & Sons.

Durairaj, M., Jayakumar, S., Karpagavalli, V., Maheswari, B. U., & Boopathi, S. (2023). Utilization of Digital Tools in the Indian Higher Education System During Health Crises. In *Multidisciplinary Approaches to Organizational Governance During Health Crises* (pp. 1–21). IGI Global. DOI: 10.4018/978-1-7998-9213-7.ch001

Dwijayani, N. M. (2019). Development of circle learning media to improve student learning outcomes. *Journal of Physics: Conference Series*, 1321(2), 022099. DOI: 10.1088/1742-6596/1321/2/022099

Eagan, M. K., Hurtado, S., Chang, M. J., Garcia, G. A., Herrera, F. A., & Garibay, J. C. (2017). Making a difference in science education: The impact of undergraduate research programs. *American Educational Research Journal*, 54(1), 27–73. PMID: 25190821

Ehrhart, M. G. (2004). Leadership and procedural justice climate as antecedents of unit-level organizational citizenship behavior. *Personnel Psychology*, 57(1), 61–94. DOI: 10.1111/ j.1744-6570.2004.tb02484.x

Ekanem, E. E., & Uchendu, C. C. (2012). University academic staff service delivery quality and vision 2020 attainment in Nigeria. *Journal of National Library and Information Practitioners CRS*, 3(2), 13–143.

El Nagdi, M., Leammukda, F., & Roehrig, G. (2018). Developing identities of STEM teachers at emerging STEM schools. *International Journal of STEM Education*, 5(1), 36. Advance online publication. DOI: 10.1186/s40594-018-0136-1 PMID: 30631726

El-Amin, A. (2022). *Improving Organizational Commitment to Diversity, Equity, Inclusion, and Belonging*. Social Justice Research Methods for Doctoral Research., DOI: 10.4018/978-1-7998-8479-8.ch010

Eldegwy, A., Elsharnouby, T. H., & Kortam, W. (2018). How sociable is your university brand? An empirical investigation of university social augmenters' brand equity. *International Journal of Educational Management*, 32(5), 912–930. DOI: 10.1108/IJEM-12-2017-0346

Eva, N., Robin, M., Sendjaya, S., Van Dierendonck, D., & Liden, R. C. (2019). Servant leadership: A systematic review and call for future research. *The Leadership Quarterly*, 30(1), 111–132. DOI: 10.1016/j.leaqua.2018.07.004

Farah, J. C., Moro, A., Bergram, K., Purohit, A. K., Gillet, D., & Holzer, A. (2020). Bringing computational thinking to non-STEM undergraduates through an integrated notebook application. In *15th European Conference on Technology Enhanced Learning*.

Farrell, C. C., Penuel, W. R., Allen, A., Anderson, E. R., Bohannon, A. X., Coburn, C. E., & Brown, S. L. (2022). Learning at the boundaries of research and practice: A framework for understanding research–practice partnerships. *Educational Researcher*, 51(3), 197–208. DOI: 10.3102/0013189X211069073

Farrukh, M., Lee, J. W. C., & Shahzad, I. A. (2019). Intrapreneurial behavior in higher education institutes of Pakistan: The role of leadership styles and psychological empowerment. *Journal of Applied Research in Higher Education*, 11(2), 273–294. DOI: 10.1108/JARHE-05-2018-0084

Federal Ministry of Education. (2021). Nigerian University System Statistical Digest 2018 & 2019. https://education.gov.ng/wp-content/uploads/2021/09/2019-NIGERIAN[REMOVED HYPERLINK FIELD]UNIVERSITY-SYSTEM-STATISTICAL-DIGEST.pdf

Federal Republic of Nigeria. (2013). *National Policy on Education* (6th ed.). NERDC Press Lagos.

Fischer, T., & Sitkin, S. B. (2023). Leadership styles: A comprehensive assessment and way forward. *The Academy of Management Annals*, 17(1), 331–372. DOI: 10.5465/annals.2020.0340

Forrest, L. L., & Geraghty, J. R. (2022). Student-Led Initiatives and Advocacy in Academic Medicine: Empowering the leaders of tomorrow. *Academic Medicine*, 97(6), 781–785. DOI: 10.1097/ACM.0000000000004644 PMID: 35234719

Fowler, J., Zachry, M., & McDonald, D. W. (2023). Policy recommendations from an empirical study of an online foster care community. *Child Indicators Research*, 16(5), 2033–2054. DOI: 10.1007/s12187-023-10037-x

Fredricks, S. (2003). Creating and Maintaining Networks Among Leaders: An Exploratory Case Study of Two Leadership Training Programs. *Journal of Leadership & Organizational Studies*, 10(1), 45–54. Advance online publication. DOI: 10.1177/107179190301000104

Freudenthal, E., Ogrey, A. N., Roy, M. K., & Siegel, A. (2010, April). A computational introduction to STEM studies. In *IEEE EDUCON 2010 Conference* (pp. 663-672). IEEE.

Fullan, M. (2007). *Leading in a culture of change*. John Wiley & Sons.

Fullan, M. (2009). Leadership development: The larger context. *Educational Leadership*, 67(2), 45–49.

Fullan, M. (2014). *Teacher development and educational change*. Routledge. DOI: 10.4324/9781315870700

Fullan, M., & Scott, G. (2009). *Turnaround leadership for higher education*. John Wiley & Sons.

Fulton, K., & Britton, T. (2011). STEM Teachers in professional learning communities: From good teachers to great teaching. In *ERIC*. National Commission on Teaching and America's Future. Retrieved March 12, 2024, from https://eric.ed .gov/?id=ED521328

Fumasoli, T., & Hladchenko, M. (2023). Strategic management in higher education: Conceptual insights, lessons learned, emerging challenges. *Tertiary Education and Management*, 29(4), 331–339. DOI: 10.1007/s11233-024-09134-5

Fürstenau, B., Pilz, M., & Gonon, P. (2014). The dual system of vocational education and training in Germany – What can be learnt about education for (other) professions. *International Handbook of Research in Professional and Practice-Based Learning*, 427–460. https://doi.org/DOI: 10.1007/978-94-017-8902-8_16

Gao, R., & Li, B. (2023). Avoiding the scenario of "The farmer and the snake": The dark side of servant leadership and an intervention mechanism. *Journal of Managerial Psychology*, 38(4), 289–302. DOI: 10.1108/JMP-02-2022-0062

Garcia, I., Noguera, I., & Cortada-Pujol, M. (2018). *Students' perspective on participation in a co-design process of learning scenarios. Journal of*. Educational Innovation Partnership and Change., DOI: 10.21100/jeipc.v4i1.760

Gassner, D., & Gofen, A. (2019). Coproduction investments: Street-level management perspective on co-production. *Cogent Business Management*, 6(1), 1617023. DOI: 10.1080/23311975.2019.1617023

Gay, G. (2018). *Culturally Responsive Teaching: Theory, Research, and Practice* (3rd ed.). Teachers College Press.

Gentles, C. H. (2020). Stemming the tide: A critical examination of issues, challenges and solutions to Jamaican teacher migration. In *Exploring Teacher Recruitment and Retention* (pp. 197–209). Routledge. DOI: 10.4324/9780429021824-18

George, L. (2020). Exploring the M in STEM: Post-secondary participation, performance and attrition in mathematics. *Canadian Journal of Science, Mathematics and Technology Education = Revue Canadienne de l'Enseignement des Sciences, des Mathématiques et de la Technologie*, 20(3), 441–461. DOI: 10.1007/s42330-020-00095-6

Georgolopoulos, V., Papaloi, E., & Loukorou, K. (2018). Servant leadership as a predictive factor of teachers' job satisfaction. *European Journal of Education*, 1(2), 15. DOI: 10.26417/ejed.v1i2.p15-28

Ghafar, A. (2020). Convergence between 21st century skills and entrepreneurship education in higher education institutes. *International Journal of Higher Education*, 9(1), 218. DOI: 10.5430/ijhe.v9n1p218

Ghasemy, M., Mohajer, L., Frömbling, L., & Karimi, M. (2021). Faculty members in polytechnics to serve the community and industry: Conceptual skills and creating value for the community—the two main drivers. *SAGE Open*, 11(3), 215824402110475. DOI: 10.1177/21582440211047568

Gift, M. D. M., Senthil, T. S., Hasan, D. S., Alagarraja, K., Jayaseelan, P., & Boopathi, S. (2024). Additive Manufacturing and 3D Printing Innovations: Revolutionizing Industry 5.0. In *Technological Advancements in Data Processing for Next Generation Intelligent Systems* (pp. 255–287). IGI Global. DOI: 10.4018/979-8-3693-0968-1.ch010

Gigliotti, R. A., & Ruben, B. D. (2017). Preparing higher education leaders: A conceptual, strategic, and operational approach. *Journal of Leadership Education*, 16(1), 96–114. DOI: 10.12806/V16/I1/T1

Glaser, B. G., & Strauss, A. L. (1967). *The discovery of grounded theory; strategies for qualitative research*. Aldine.

Goff, D. G. (2003). What Do We Know About Good Community College Leaders: A Study in Leadership Trait Theory and Behavioral Leadership Theory.

Government of Saint Vincent and the Grenadines. (n.d.). Retrieved on March 5, 2024 fromhttps://www.gov.vc/

Goyal, M., Gupta, C., & Gupta, V. (2022a). A meta-analysis approach to measure the impact of project-based learning outcome with program attainment on student learning using fuzzy inference systems. *Heliyon*, 8(8), e10248. DOI: 10.1016/j.heliyon.2022.e10248 PMID: 36042720

Granshaw, B. (2016). STEM education for the twenty-first century: A New Zealand perspective. *Australasian Journal of Technology Education*, 3(1). Advance online publication. DOI: 10.15663/ajte.v3i1.43

Grant, N. (1997). Some Problems of Identity and Education: A comparative examination of multicultural education. *Comparative Education*, 33(1), 9–28. DOI: 10.1080/03050069728613

Grawe, N. D. (2018). *Demographics and the demand for higher education*. JHU Press.

Greenleaf, R. K. (1970). *Center for Applied Studies*.

Greenleaf, R. K. (2002). *Servant leadership: A journey into the nature of legitimate power and greatness*. Paulist Press.

Griffith, S. (2024). The Future of Research in the Caribbean: The Roles and Responsibilities of Caribbean Scholars in Producing Knowledge for the Region. *Caribbean Journal of Education and Development*, 1(1), 51–56. DOI: 10.46425/cjed601018736

Grover, S., & Pea, R. (2013). Computational thinking in K–12: A review of the state of the field. *Educational Researcher*, 42(1), 38–43. DOI: 10.3102/0013189X12463051

Guo, L., & Hau, K. T. (2024). Adolescents want to be teachers? Affecting factors and two-decade trends in 39 educational systems. *International Journal of Educational Research*, 123, 102274. DOI: 10.1016/j.ijer.2023.102274

Guo, Y., & Kroll, B. M. (2014). A review of studies on Rogerian rhetoric and its implications for English writing instruction in East Asian countries. *Theory and Practice in Language Studies*, 4(3), 481–488. DOI: 10.4304/tpls.4.3.481-488

Haider, A., Khan, M. A., & Taj, T. (2020). Impact of servant leadership on teaching effectiveness: A study of public sector universities, KP, Pakistan. *Global Regional Review*, V(I), 509–518. DOI: 10.31703/grr.2020(v-i).54

Haines, S., Krach, M., Pustaka, A., Li, Q., & Richman, L. (2019). The effects of computational thinking professional development on STEM teachers' perceptions and pedagogical practices. *Athens Journal of Sciences*, 6(2), 97–122. DOI: 10.30958/ajs.6-2-2

Hair, J. F., Hult, G. T. M., Ringle, C. M., & Sarstedt, M. (2022). *A primer on partial least squares structural equation modeling (PLS-SEM)* (3rd ed.). Sage.

Hair, J. F., Sarstedt, M., Ringle, C. M., & Gudergan, S. P. (2024). *Advanced issues in partial least squares structural equation modeling (PLS-SEM)* (2nd ed.). Sage.

Hale, F. W. (2023). *What makes racial diversity work in higher education: Academic leaders present successful policies and strategies.* Taylor & Francis. DOI: 10.4324/9781003448662

Hammoudi Halat, D., Soltani, A., Dalli, R., Alsarraj, L., & Malki, A. (2023). Understanding and fostering mental health and well-being among university faculty: A narrative review. *Journal of Clinical Medicine*, 12(13), 4425. DOI: 10.3390/jcm12134425 PMID: 37445459

Hansson, S., & Polk, M. (2017). Evaluation of knowledge co-production for sustainable urban development. In: Part I: experiences from project leaders and participants at Gothenburg local interaction platform 2012–2015. www.mistraurbanfutures.org/sites/mistraurban futures.org/files/hansson-polk-wp-2017-2.pdf

Harper, S. R., & Simmons, I. (2019). *Black students at public colleges and universities: A 50-state report card.* University of Southern California, Race and Equity Center.

Harris, A. (2013a). *Distributed leadership matters: Perspectives, practicalities, and potential.* Corwin Press. DOI: 10.4324/9780203607909

Harris, A. (2013b). Distributed leadership: Friend or foe? *Educational Management Administration & Leadership*, 41(5), 545–554. DOI: 10.1177/1741143213497635

Harris, A., & Jones, M. (2019). Leading professional learning with impact. *School Leadership & Management*, 39(1), 1–4. DOI: 10.1080/13632434.2018.1530892

Hartcher, K., Chapman, S., & Morrison, C. (2023). Applying a band-aid or building a bridge: Ecological factors and divergent approaches to enhancing teacher wellbeing. *Cambridge Journal of Education*, 53(3), 329–356. DOI: 10.1080/0305764X.2022.2155612

Harvey, J. F., Johnson, K. J., Roloff, K. S., & Edmondson, A. C. (2019). From orientation to behavior: The interplay between learning orientation, open-mindedness, and psychological safety in team learning. *Human Relations*, 72(11), 1726–1751. DOI: 10.1177/0018726718817812

Heffernan, A., MacDonald, K., & Longmuir, F. (2022). The emotional intensity of educational leadership: A scoping review. *International Journal of Leadership in Education*, ●●●, 1–23.

Heifetz, R. A., Grashow, A., & Linsky, M. (2009). *The practice of adaptive leadership: Tools and tactics for changing your organization and the world.* Harvard business press.

Hein, V. L. (2020). *Combatting the Drive Deficit: An Exploration of Conative Skill Inclusion in College and Career Readiness Policy* (Doctoral dissertation, DePaul University).

Helm, C., & Huber, S. G. (2022). Predictors of central student learning outcomes in times of COVID-19: Students', parents', and teachers' perspectives during school closure in 2020—A multiple informant relative weight analysis. *Frontiers in Education*, 7, 7. DOI: 10.3389/feduc.2022.743770

Hendrickson, K. A., & Askew, K. (2024). Broadening participation in STEM, caring intelligence as a leadership intelligence: Perspectives of HBCU faculty leaders. *Journal of Applied Research in Higher Education*. Advance online publication. DOI: 10.1108/JARHE-08-2023-0368

Hendrikz, K., & Engelbrecht, A. (2019). The principled leadership scale: An integration of value-based leadership. *SA Journal of Industrial Psychology*, 45. Advance online publication. DOI: 10.4102/sajip.v45i0.1553

Henry, C. (2020). *GSAJ Assisting Technology Focused MSMEs To Grow*. Retrieved January 24, 2024, from https://jis.gov.jm/gsaj-assisting-technology-focused-msmes-to-grow/

Hernández-de-Menéndez, M., Morales-Menendez, R., Escobar, C. A., & Ramírez Mendoza, R. A. (2022). Learning analytics: State of the art. [IJIDeM]. *International Journal on Interactive Design and Manufacturing*, 16(3), 1209–1230. DOI: 10.1007/s12008-022-00930-0

Herrera-Pavo, M. Á. (2021). Collaborative learning for virtual higher education. *Learning, Culture and Social Interaction*, 28, 100437. DOI: 10.1016/j.lcsi.2020.100437

Hersey, P., & Blanchard, K. H. (1969). Life cycle theory of leadership. *Training and Development Journal*.

Hewitt, P. M., Denny, G. S., & Pijanowski, J. C. (2014). Teacher preferences for alternative school site administrative models. *Administrative Issues Journal: Connecting Education, Practice, and Research*, 2(1), 35–47. DOI: 10.5929/2011.2.1.5

Hilliard, A. T. (2010). Student leadership at the university. https://core.ac.uk>pdf.

Hilliard, A. (2010). Student leadership at the university. *Journal of College Teaching and Learning*, 7(2), ●●●. DOI: 10.19030/tlc.v7i2.93

Hillman, N. W., Hicklin Fryar, A., & Crespín-Trujillo, V. (2018). Evaluating the impact of performance funding in Ohio and Tennessee. *American Educational Research Journal*, 55(1), 144–170. DOI: 10.3102/0002831217732951

Holmes, J., & Marra, M. (2004, January). Leadership and managing conflict meetings. *Pragmatics*, 14(4), 439–462. DOI: 10.1075/prag.14.4.02hol

Holmes, M., Rulfs, J., & Orr, J. (2007). Curriculum Development And Integration For K 6 Engineering Education. *2007 Annual Conference & Exposition*, 12–436. DOI: 10.18260/1-2--2812

Holt, D. T., Armenakis, A. A., Feild, H. S., & Harris, S. G. (2007). Readiness for organizational change: The systematic development of a scale. *The Journal of Applied Behavioral Science*, 43(2), 232–255. DOI: 10.1177/0021886306295295

Hoque, K. E., & Raya, Z. T. (2023). Relationship between principals' leadership styles and teachers' behavior. *Behavioral Sciences (Basel, Switzerland)*, 13(2), 111. DOI: 10.3390/bs13020111 PMID: 36829339

Huafang, L. (2019). Communication for co-production: A systematic review and research agenda. *Journal of Chinese Governance*, 1695711. Advance online publication. DOI: 10.1080/23812346.2019

Huang, W., Looi, C. K., & Yeter, I. H. (2022). Comparison of STEM, non-STEM, and mixed-disciplines pre-service teachers' early conceptions about computational thinking.

Huber, S. G., & Muijs, D. (2010). School leadership effectiveness: The growing insight into the importance of school leadership for the quality and development of schools and their pupils. In S. Huber (Ed.), *School Leadership - International Perspectives (Studies in Educational Leadership*, vol. 10). Springer, Dordrecht. https://doi.org/DOI: 10.1007/978-90-481-3501-1_4

Hunter, J. (October 30, 2020). Support for teacher training institutions. *JIS*. Retrieved on February 5, 2024 from https://jis.gov.jm/support-for-teacher-training-institutions/

Hunter, J. (2020). *High Possibility STEM Classrooms*. Routledge.

Huq, A., & Gilbert, D. (2017). All the world's a stage: Transforming entrepreneurship education through design thinking. *Education + Training*, 59(2), 155–170. DOI: 10.1108/ET-12-2015-0111

Hylton, K. (2022). STEM education in Jamaica: A case of practitioners. *International Studies in Educational Administration (Commonwealth Council for Educational Administration & Management, 50*(2), 46.

Iglesias, O., Ind, N., & Alfaro, M. (2013). The organic view of the brand: A brand value co-creation model. *Journal of Brand Management*, 20(8), 670–688. DOI: 10.1057/bm.2013.8

ILO. (2015). Global employment trends for youth: Scaling up investments in decent jobs for youth. https://www.ilo.org/publications/global-employment-trends-youth -2015-scaling-investments-decent-jobs-youth

Imaduddin, I., Putra, H. G., Tukiyo, T., Wahab, A., & Nurulloh, A. (2022). The effect of servant leadership on the quality of education through the characteristics of millennial teachers. Al-Tanzim. *Jurnal Manajemen Pendidikan Islam*, 6(4), 1092–1102. DOI: 10.33650/al-tanzim.v6i4.4069

Ingle, R. B., Swathi, S., Mahendran, G., Senthil, T., Muralidharan, N., & Boopathi, S. (2023). Sustainability and Optimization of Green and Lean Manufacturing Processes Using Machine Learning Techniques. In *Circular Economy Implementation for Sustainability in the Built Environment* (pp. 261–285). IGI Global. DOI: 10.4018/978-1-6684-8238-4.ch012

Innocentina-Marie, O., Bollen, K., Aaldering, H., Robijn, W., & Euwema, M. (2020). Servant leadership, third-party behavior, and emotional exhaustion of followers. *Negotiation and Conflict Management Research*. Advance online publication. DOI: 10.1111/ncmr.12184

International Organization for Migration. (IOM, 2023). How to "solve" migration: A practical guide. IOM UN Migration, Regional Office for Central, North America and the Caribbean. https://rosanjose.iom.int/en/blogs/how-solve-migration-practical -guide

Israel-Fishelson, R., & Hershkovitz, A. (2022). Studying interrelations of computational thinking and creativity: A scoping review (2011–2020). *Computers & Education*, 176, 104353. DOI: 10.1016/j.compedu.2021.104353

Itri, J., & Lawson, L. (2016, July). Ineffective leadership. *Journal of the American College of Radiology*, 13(7), 849–885. DOI: 10.1016/j.jacr.2016.02.008 PMID: 27026578

Iwasaki, Y., Bartlett, J., MacKay, K., Mactavish, J., & Ristock, J. (2005). Social exclusion and resilience as frameworks of stress and coping among selected non-dominant groups. *International Journal of Mental Health Promotion*, 7(3), 4–17. DOI: 10.1080/14623730.2005.9721870

Jackson, D. (2017). Exploring the challenges experienced by international students during work-integrated learning in Australia. *Asia Pacific Journal of Education*, 37(3), 344–359. DOI: 10.1080/02188791.2017.1298515

Jacob, M. Selesho & Naile, I. (2014). Academic staff retention as a human resource factor: University Perspective. *The International Business & Economics Research Journal*, 13(2), 295304.

Jakobsen, M., & Andersen, S. C. (2013). Co-production and equity in public service delivery. *Public Administration Review*, 73(5), 704–713. DOI: 10.1111/puar.12094

JAMPRO. (2021). *Outsourcing*. Retrieved February 24, 2024, from https://dobusinessjamaica.com/wp-content/uploads/2021/11/Sector-E-book-Outsourcing.pdf

Jang, H. S., Valero, J. N., & Jung, K. (2023). Effective leadership in network collaboration: Lessons learned from continuum of care homeless programs. In *Understanding Nonprofit Organizations* (pp. 150–161). Routledge. DOI: 10.4324/9781003387800-18

Jeffs, C., Nelson, N., Grant, K. A., Nowell, L., Paris, B., & Viceer, N. (2023). Feedback for teaching development: Moving from a fixed to growth mindset. *Professional Development in Education*, 49(5), 842–855. DOI: 10.1080/19415257.2021.1876149

Jehn, K. A. (1997). A qualitative analysis of conflict types and dimensions in organizational groups. *Administrative Science Quarterly*, 42(3), 530. DOI: 10.2307/2393737

Jehn, K. A., Greer, L. L., Levine, S. S., & Szulanski, G. (2008). The effects of conflict types, dimensions, and emergent states on group outcomes. *Group Decision and Negotiation*, 17(6), 465–495. DOI: 10.1007/s10726-008-9107-0

Jennings, Z. (2001). Teacher education in selected countries in the Commonwealth Caribbean: The ideal of policy versus the reality of practice. *Comparative Education*, 37(1), 107–134. DOI: 10.1080/03050060020020453

JIS. (2018, May 14). Gov't looking to create integrated higher education system. *JIS*. Retrieved January 5, 2024, from https://moey.gov.jm/govt-looking-to-create-integrated-higher-education-system/

Jit, R., Sharma, C. S., & Kawatra, M. (2016). Servant leadership and conflict resolution: A qualitative study. *International Journal of Conflict Management*, 27(4), 591–612. DOI: 10.1108/ijcma-12-2015-0086

Jit, R., Sharma, C. S., & Kawatra, M. (2017). Healing a broken spirit: Role of servant leadership. *Vikalpa*, 42(2), 80–94. DOI: 10.1177/0256090917703754

John, E. P. S. (Ed.). (2022). *Co-learning in higher education: Community wellbeing, engaged scholarship, and creating futures*. Taylor & Francis. DOI: 10.4324/9781003310112

Johnson, J. F. Jr, & Uline, C. L. (2005). Preparing educational leaders to close achievement gaps. *Theory into Practice*, 44(1), 45–52. DOI: 10.1207/s15430421tip4401_7

Jones, W. A. (2011). Faculty involvement in institutional governance: A literature review. *Journal of the Professoriate*, 6(1), 118–135.

Joo, B., Yoon, S. K., & Galbraith, D. D. (2022). The effects of organizational trust and empowering leadership on group conflict: Psychological safety as a mediator. *Organizational Management Journal*, 20(1), 4–16. DOI: 10.1108/omj-07-2021-1308

Josselson, R. (1972). Identity formation in college women. Unpublished doctoral dissertation, University of Michigan.

Kakavas, P., & Ugolini, F. C. (2019). Computational thinking in primary education: A systematic literature review. *Research on Education and Media*, 11(2), 64–94. DOI: 10.2478/rem-2019-0023

Kalaiselvi, D., Ramaratnam, M. S., Kokila, S., Sarkar, R., Anandakumar, S., & Boopathi, S. (2024). Future Developments of Higher Education on Social Psychology: Innovation and Changes. In *Advances in Human and Social Aspects of Technology* (pp. 146–169). IGI Global. DOI: 10.4018/979-8-3693-2569-8.ch008

Kallet, M. (2014). *Think smarter: critical thinking to improve problem-solving and decision-making skills*. Wiley Publishers.

Kalra, A., Briggs, E., & Schrock, W. (2023). Exploring the synergistic role of ethical leadership and sales control systems on salesperson social media use and sales performance. *Journal of Business Research*, 154, 113344. DOI: 10.1016/j.jbusres.2022.113344

Kalsbeek, D. H. (Ed.). (2013). *Reframing Retention Strategy for Institutional Improvement: New Directions for Higher Education, Number 161*. John Wiley & Sons.

Karsono, B., Suraji, R., & Sastrodiharjo, I. (2022). The Influence of Leadership Spirituality to Improving the Quality of Higher Education in Indonesia. *International Journal of Social Sciences and Humanities Invention*, 9(01), 6832–6841. DOI: 10.18535/ijsshi/v9i02.06

Kartam, N. A. (1998). Integrating design into a civil engineering education. *International Journal of Engineering Education*, 14(2), 130–135.

Karthikeyan, M., Vigilia, J. K. N., Sequeira, S. L., Vidhya Priya, P., Ghamande, M. V., & Boopathi, S. (2024). NBA Implementation Across Engineering Disciplines for Driving Social Changes in India. In *Advances in Human and Social Aspects of Technology* (pp. 240–265). IGI Global. DOI: 10.4018/979-8-3693-2569-8.ch012

Kelchen, R. (2018). *Higher education accountability*. JHU Press. DOI: 10.1353/book.58123

Kelemen, T. K., Matthews, S. H., Matthews, M. J., & Henry, S. E. (2023). Humble leadership: A review and synthesis of leader expressed humility. *Journal of Organizational Behavior*, 44(2), 202–224. DOI: 10.1002/job.2608

Keller, L. L. (2013). *Strategic brand management: Building, measuring and managing brand equity* (4th ed.). Pearson.

Kelley, T. R., & Knowles, J. G. (2016). A conceptual framework for integrated STEM education. *International Journal of STEM Education*, 3(1), 11. Advance online publication. DOI: 10.1186/s40594-016-0046-z

Kelly, H. (2023). *School leaders matter: Preventing burnout, managing stress, and improving wellbeing*. Routledge. DOI: 10.4324/9781003198475

Kennedy, B., Hefferon, M., & Funk, C. (2018). Half of Americans think young people don't pursue STEM because it is too hard. *Pew Research Centre*. Retrieved January 25, 2024, from http://pewrsr.ch/2Dr2RxJ

Kennedy, T. J., & Odell, M. R. L. (2014). Engaging students in STEM Education. *International Council of Associations for Science Education*, 25(3), 246–258. https://eric.ed.gov/?id=EJ1044508

Kenny, R., & Gunter, G. (2015). Building a competency-based STEM curriculum in non-STEM disciplines: A sySTEMic approach. In *The design of learning experience: Creating the future of educational technology* (pp. 181-198). DOI: 10.1007/978-3-319-16504-2_13

Kezar, A., Fries-Britt, S., Kurban, E., McGuire, D., & Wheaton, M. M. (2019). Speaking Truth and Acting with Integrity: Confronting Challenges of Campus Racial Climate (2018). http://hdl.handle.net/10919/90753

Kezar, A. (2018). *How colleges change: Understanding, leading, and enacting change*. Routledge. DOI: 10.4324/9781315121178

Kezar, A. J. (2023). *Rethinking leadership in a complex, multicultural, and global environment: New concepts and models for higher education*. Taylor & Francis. DOI: 10.4324/9781003446842

Kezar, A. J., & Kinzie, J. (2006). Examining the ways institutions create student engagement: The role of mission. *Journal of College Student Development*, 47(2), 149–172. DOI: 10.1353/csd.2006.0018

Kezar, A., & Eckel, P. D. (2002). The effect of institutional culture on change strategies in higher education: Universal principles or culturally responsive concepts? *The Journal of Higher Education*, 73(4), 435–460. DOI: 10.1080/00221546.2002.11777159

Khalifa, M. A., Gooden, M. A., & Davis, J. E. (2016). Culturally Responsive School Leadership: A Synthesis of the Literature. *Review of Educational Research*, 86(4), 1272–1311. DOI: 10.3102/0034654316630383

Khan, A. N. (2023). A diary study of social media and performance in service sector: Transformational leadership as cross-level moderator. *Current Psychology (New Brunswick, N.J.)*, 42(12), 10077–10091. DOI: 10.1007/s12144-021-02310-5

Khan, F. Q., Buhari, S. M., Tsaramirsis, G., & Rasheed, S. (2021). A study of faculty retention factors in educational institutes in context with ABET. *Frontiers in Education*, 6, 678018. https://www.frontiersin.org/articles/10.3389/feduc.2021.678018/full. DOI: 10.3389/feduc.2021.678018

Khan, I. U., Idris, M., & Amin, R. U. (2023). Leadership style and performance in higher education: The role of organizational justice. *International Journal of Leadership in Education*, 26(6), 1111–1125. DOI: 10.1080/13603124.2020.1854868

Khan, M. M., Mubarik, M. S., Islam, T., Rehman, A., Ahmed, S. S., Khan, E., Khattak, M. N., Asghar, Z., Mumtaz, F., & Sohail, F.. (2021). How servant leadership triggers innovative work behavior: Exploring the sequential mediating role of psychological empowerment and job crafting. *European Journal of Innovation Management*, 25(4), 1037–1055. DOI: 10.1108/ejim-09-2020-0367

Khumalo, S. S. (2019). Analyzing abusive school leadership practices through the lens of social justice. *International Journal of Educational Management*, 33(4), 546–555. DOI: 10.1108/IJEM-11-2017-0320

Kilag, O. K. T., Uy, F. T., Abendan, C. F. K., & Malbas, M. H. (2023). Teaching leadership: An examination of best practices for leadership educators. *Science and Education*, 4(7), 430–445.

Kim, J. J., Waldman, D. A., Balthazard, P. A., & Ames, J. B. (2023). Leader self-projection and collective role performance: A consideration of visionary leadership. *The Leadership Quarterly*, 34(2), 101623. DOI: 10.1016/j.leaqua.2022.101623

Kim, K., Bae, E., & Lee, M. (2023). Developing a Model for Sustainable Development in Education Based on Convergence Education. *International Journal of Educational Methodology*, 9(1), 249–259. DOI: 10.12973/ijem.9.1.249

Kim, M., & Beehr, T. A. (2020). Empowering leadership: Leading people to be present through affective organizational commitment? *International Journal of Human Resource Management*, 31(16), 2017–2044. DOI: 10.1080/09585192.2018.1424017

Kim, M., & Beehr, T. A. (2021). The power of empowering leadership: Allowing and encouraging followers to take charge of their own jobs. *International Journal of Human Resource Management*, 32(9), 1865–1898. DOI: 10.1080/09585192.2019.1657166

Ki-Moon, B. (2013). *Secretary-General's Remarks to High-Level Dialogue on International Migration and Development*. United Nations.

King, F. (2019). Professional learning: Empowering teachers? []. Taylor & Francis.]. *Professional Development in Education*, 45(2), 169–172. DOI: 10.1080/19415257.2019.1580849

Kjellström, S., Sarre, S., & Masterson, D. (2024). The complexity of leadership in co-production practices: A guiding framework based on a systematic literature review. *BMC Health Services Research*, 24(1), 219. Advance online publication. DOI: 10.1186/s12913-024-10549-4 PMID: 38368329

Knie, L., Standl, B., & Schwarzer, S. (2022). First experiences of integrating computational thinking into a blended learning in-service training program for STEM teachers. *Computer Applications in Engineering Education*, 30(5), 1423–1439. DOI: 10.1002/cae.22529

Kolb, D. (2015). *Experiential learning: experience as a source of learning and development* (2nd ed.). Pearson Education Inc.

Komives, S. R., & Dugan, J. P. (2010). Contemporary leadership theories. *Political and civic leadership: A reference handbook, 1*, 111-120.

Komives, S. R., Lucas, N., & McMahon, T. R. (2013). *Exploring leadership: For college students who want to make a difference*. John Wiley & Sons.

Komives, S. R., & Wagner, W. (Eds.). (2016). *Leadership for a better world: Understanding the social change model of leadership development*. John Wiley & Sons.

Komunjeru, B., & Roberts, R. (2023). Navigating a culture of evidence: The lived experiences of college of agriculture faculty regarding the academic assessment of students. *Journal of Agricultural Education*, 64(2), 56–70. DOI: 10.5032/jae.v64i2.109

Konkol, P., & Dymek, D. (2023). *Supporting Higher Education 4.0 Challenges and Opportunities* (1st ed.). Routledge.

Konstantinou, C. (2015). *To kalo sxoleio, o ikanos ekpaideutikos kai i katallili agogi os pedagogiki theoria kai praksi* [The effective school, the competent teacher, and the appropriate education as pedagogical theory and practice]. Gutenberg.

Korejan, M.M. & Shahbazi, H. (2016). An analysis of the transformational leadership theory. Journal of Fundamental and applied Sciences. Vol. 8 No. 3 (2016): Special Issue. DOI: 10.4314/jfas.v8i3s.192

Kotter, J. P. (1996). Leading Change, Harvard Business School Press, Boston. *Search in.*

Kraft, M. A., & Lyon, M. A. (2024). *The rise and fall of the teaching profession: Prestige, interest, preparation, and satisfaction over the last half century* (No. w32386). National Bureau of Economic Research.

Krise, R. (2023). Faculty perceptions of how their altruistic and servant teaching behaviors influence student learning. *International Journal of Responsible Leadership and Ethical Decision-Making*, 5(1), 1–14. DOI: 10.4018/ijrledm.317372

Kuh, G. D., Kinzie, J. L., Buckley, J. A., Bridges, B. K., & Hayek, J. C. (2006). *What matters to student success: A review of the literature* (Vol. 8). National Postsecondary Education Cooperative.

Kupriyanova, V., Estermann, T., & Sabic, N. (2018). Efficiency of Universities: Drivers, Enablers and Limitations. In Curaj, A., Deca, L., & Pricopie, R. (Eds.), *European Higher Education Area: The Impact of Past and Future Policies.* Springer., DOI: 10.1007/978-3-319-77407-7_36

Kurilovas, E. (2020). On data-driven decision-making for quality education. *Computers in Human Behavior*, 107, 105774. DOI: 10.1016/j.chb.2018.11.003

Kurup, P. M., Yang, Y., Li, X., & Dong, Y. (2021). Interdisciplinary and integrated STEM. *Encyclopedia*, 1(4), 1192–1199. DOI: 10.3390/encyclopedia1040090

Kutasi, R. (2023). Cultivating a Classroom Culture of Growth: Nurture the Power of a Growth Mindset. *Acta Marisiensis.Philologia*, 5(5), 91–101.

Kyangwe, L., Onyango, D. O., & Alloph, J. M. (2023). Strategies to Enhance Teachers' Job Satisfaction in Secondary Schools in Butiama District, Mara, Tanzania. *East African Journal of Education Studies*, 6(1), 120–132. DOI: 10.37284/eajes.6.1.1078

Labaree, D. F. (2020). *A perfect mess: The unlikely ascendancy of American higher education*. University of Chicago Press.

Lake, R. S., & Mrozinski, M. D. (2011). The conflicted realities of community college mission statements. *Planning for Higher Education*, 39(2), 5–14.

Lanaj, K., Jennings, R. E., Ashford, S. J., & Krishnan, S. (2022). When leader self-care begets other care: Leader role self-compassion and helping at work. *The Journal of Applied Psychology*, 107(9), 1543–1560. DOI: 10.1037/apl0000957 PMID: 34647780

Lane, J. E. (2007). The spider web of oversight: An analysis of external oversight of higher education. *The Journal of Higher Education*, 78(6), 615–644. DOI: 10.1080/00221546.2007.11772074

Lane, M., Moore, A. J., Hooper, L., Menzies, V. J., Cooper, B., Shaw, N., & Rueckert, C. (2019). Dimensions of student success: A framework for defining and evaluating support for learning in higher education. *Higher Education Research & Development*, 38(5), 954–968. DOI: 10.1080/07294360.2019.1615418

Langhof, J. G., & Güldenberg, S. (2020). Servant leadership: A systematic literature review—toward a model of antecedents and outcomes. *German Journal of Human Resource Management*, 34(1), 32–68. DOI: 10.1177/2397002219869903

Larey, D. P., Le Roux, A., & Jacobs, L. (2021). Evoking edupreneurial leadership towards social justice among historically disadvantaged communities. *International Journal of Leadership in Education*, •••, 1–17. DOI: 10.1080/13603124.2021.1882700

Lashley, L. (2019). A reflective analysis of the selection and production of instructional material for curriculum delivery at the primary level in postcolonial Guyana. *SAGE Open*, 9(2), 215824401985844. DOI: 10.1177/2158244019858445

Laub, J. (2010). The servant organization. In van Dierendonck, D., & Patterson, K. (Eds.), *Servant Leadership*. Palgrave Macmillan., DOI: 10.1057/9780230299184_9

Lauder, H., & Mayhew, K. (2020). Higher education and the labour market: An introduction. *Oxford Review of Education*, 46(1), 1–9. DOI: 10.1080/03054985.2019.1699714

Leal Filho, W., Eustachio, J. H. P. P., Caldana, A. C. F., Will, M., Lange Salvia, A., Levay, C., & Andersson Bäck, M. (2022). Caring leader identity between power and powerlessness. *Organization Studies*, 43(6), 953–972. DOI: 10.1177/01708406211006245

Leal Filho, W., Eustachio, J. H. P. P., Caldana, A. C. F., Will, M., Lange Salvia, A., Rampasso, I. S., Anholon, R., Platje, J., & Kovaleva, M. (2020). Sustainability leadership in higher education institutions: An overview of challenges. *Sustainability (Basel)*, 12(9), 3761. DOI: 10.3390/su12093761

Ledger, M., See, B. H., Gorard, S., & Morris, R. (2024). A new approach to understanding the global teacher supply crisis. In *An International Approach to Developing Early Career Researchers* (pp. 160–176). Routledge. DOI: 10.4324/9781003455066-17

Ledlow, G. R., Bosworth, M., & Maryon, T. (2023). *Leadership for health professionals: Theory, skills, and applications*. Jones & Bartlett Learning.

Leithwood, K., Harris, A., & Hopkins, D. (2020). Seven strong claims about successful school leadership revisited. [Crossref.]. *School Leadership & Management*, 40(1), 5–22. DOI: 10.1080/13632434.2019.1596077

Leithwood, K., & Jantzi, D. (2005). Transformational leadership. In Davies, B. (Ed.), *The Essentials of School Leadership* (pp. 31–43). SAGE Publications.

Leithwood, K., Jantzi, D., & Steinbach, R. (2021a). Leadership and other conditions which foster organizational learning in schools. In *Organizational learning in schools* (pp. 67–90). Taylor & Francis. DOI: 10.1201/9781003077459-5

Lemoine, G. J., & Blum, T. C. (2019). Servant leadership, leader gender, and team gender role: Testing a female advantage in a cascading model of performance. *Personnel Psychology*, 74(1), 3–28. DOI: 10.1111/peps.12379

Liao, C. H., Chiang, C. T., Chen, I. C., & Parker, K. R. (2022). Exploring the relationship between computational thinking and learning satisfaction for non-STEM college students. *International Journal of Educational Technology in Higher Education*, 19(1), 43. DOI: 10.1186/s41239-022-00347-5

Liden, R. C., Wayne, S. J., Zhao, H., & Henderson, D. (2008). Servant leadership: Development of a multidimensional measure and multi-level assessment. *The Leadership Quarterly*, 19(2), 161–177. DOI: 10.1016/j.leaqua.2008.01.006

Li, M., Ahmed, A., Syed, O. R., Khalid, N., & Muñoz, J. E.Jr. (2022). Impact of abusive leader behavior on employee job insecurity: A mediating roles of emotional exhaustion and abusive peer behavior. *Frontiers in Psychology*, 13, 947258. DOI: 10.3389/fpsyg.2022.947258 PMID: 36072034

Liu, W., & Huang, C. (2023). The international comparative approach to higher education leadership development: Evaluating the longer-term impacts. *International Journal of Leadership in Education*, 1–15. DOI: 10.1080/13603124.2023.2224773

LiVecchi. A. J. (2017). *The opportunity cost of teaching for secondary STEM instructors*. [Doctoral dissertation, University of Houston]. https://www.proquest.com/docview/2187144226

Livingstone, S., Ólafsson, K., Helsper, E. J., Lupiáñez-Villanueva, F., Veltri, G. A., & Folkvord, F. (2017). Maximizing opportunities and minimizing risks for children online: The role of digital skills in emerging strategies of parental mediation. *Journal of Communication*, 67(1), 82–105. DOI: 10.1111/jcom.12277

Lizzio, A., & Wilson, K. (2009). Student participation in university governance: The role conceptions and sense of efficacy of student representatives on departmental committees. *Studies in Higher Education*, 34(1), 69–84. DOI: 10.1080/03075070802602000

Looi, C. K., Chan, S. W., Huang, W., Seow, P. S. K., & Wu, L. (2020). Preservice teachers' views of computational thinking: STEM teachers vs non-STEM teachers.

Lu, C., Macdonald, R., Odell, B., Kokhan, V., Demmans Epp, C., & Cutumisu, M. (2022). A scoping review of computational thinking assessments in higher education. *Journal of Computing in Higher Education*, 34(2), 416–461. DOI: 10.1007/s12528-021-09305-y

Lumby, J. (2019). Leadership and power in higher education. *Studies in Higher Education*, 44(9), 1619–1629. DOI: 10.1080/03075079.2018.1458221

Lundqvist, D., Wallo, A., Coetzer, A., & Kock, H. (2023). Leadership and learning at work: A systematic literature review of learning-oriented leadership. *Journal of Leadership & Organizational Studies*, 30(2), 205–238. DOI: 10.1177/15480518221133970

Lyon, J. A., & Magana, A. J. (2020). Computational thinking in higher education: A review of the literature. *Computer Applications in Engineering Education*, 28(5), 1174–1189. DOI: 10.1002/cae.22295

Machado, M. D. L., & Taylor, J. S. (2010). The struggle for strategic planning in European higher education: The case of Portugal. *Research in Higher Education*.

Mahrishi, M., & Abbas, A. (2023). Assessment of Knowledge Gaps in Outcome-Based Education (OBE) Among Engineering Faculty Members: An Empirical Study. *2023 IEEE International Conference on Engineering Veracruz (ICEV)*, 1–6. DOI: 10.1109/ICEV59168.2023.10329631

Majali, T. E., Alkaraki, M., Asad, M., Aladwan, N., & Aledeinat, M. (2022). Green transformational leadership, green entrepreneurial orientation and performance of SMEs: The mediating role of green product innovation. *Journal of Open Innovation*, 8(4), 191. DOI: 10.3390/joitmc8040191

Malahy, M. M. (2008). Contested Challenges: universities, globalisation, and human migration. Proceedings of the 4th International Barcelona Conference on Higher Education, 8. *Higher education and citizenship, participation and democracy*. Barcelona: GUNI. http://www.guni-rmies.net

Mamman-Daura, F. (2022). Forced migration in Nigeria is a development issue. *OECD- Development Matters.*https://oecd-development-matters.org/2022/02/02/forced-migration[REMOVED HYPERLINK FIELD]in-nigeria-is-a-development-issue/

Mandinach, E. B., & Gummer, E. S. (2016a). *Data literacy for educators: Making it count in teacher preparation and practice.* Teachers College Press.

Mandinach, E. B., & Gummer, E. S. (2016b). What does it mean for teachers to be data literate: Laying out the skills, knowledge, and dispositions. *Teaching and Teacher Education*, 60, 366–376. DOI: 10.1016/j.tate.2016.07.011

Mandinach, E. B., & Jimerson, J. B. (2016). Teachers learning how to use data: A synthesis of the issues and what is known. *Teaching and Teacher Education*, 60, 452–457. DOI: 10.1016/j.tate.2016.07.009

Mane, S. D. (2015). NBA and NAAC Accreditation of UG Engineering Programmes/Colleges in India: A Review. *International Journal of Scientific Engineering and Applied Science*, 1(6), 2395–3470.

Manogharan, M. W., Thivaharan, T., & Rahman, R. A. (2018). Academic staff retention in private higher education institute – a case study of private colleges in Kuala Lumpur. *International Journal of Higher Education*, 7(3), 52. Advance online publication. DOI: 10.5430/ijhe.v7n3p52

Margot, K. C., & Kettler, T. (2019). Teachers' perception of STEM integration and education: A systematic literature review. *International Journal of STEM Education*, 6(1), 2. Advance online publication. DOI: 10.1186/s40594-018-0151-2

Mark, P., Joseph, R., & Remy, C. (2005). A harmonized policy framework for teacher education in the Caribbean. Trinidad and Tobago: Retrieved from http://webcache.googleusercontent. com/search

Markey, K., Prosen, M., Martin, E., & Repo Jamal, H. (2021). Fostering an ethos of cultural humility development in nurturing inclusiveness and effective intercultural team working. *Journal of Nursing Management*, 29(8), 2724–2728. DOI: 10.1111/jonm.13429

Marshall, D. T., Pressley, T., Neugebauer, N. M., & Shannon, D. M. (2022). Why teachers are leaving and what we can do about it. *Phi Delta Kappan*, 104(1), 6–11. DOI: 10.1177/00317217221123642

Marshall, S. (2016). *A handbook for leaders in higher education: Transforming teaching and learning.* Routledge. DOI: 10.4324/9781315693798

Martin, C. (2024). The impact of the pandemic on leaders: A pathway to healing and self-care. *Nursing Management*, 55(1), 12–19. DOI: 10.1097/nmg.0000000000000081 PMID: 38170884

Martin, J. S., & Marion, R. (2005). Higher education leadership roles in knowledge processing. *The Learning Organization*, 12(2), 140–151. DOI: 10.1108/09696470510583520

Matthews, K. E. (2018). Engaging students as participants and partners: An argument for partnership with students in higher education research on student success. *International Journal of Chinese Education*, 7(1), 42–64. DOI: 10.1163/22125868-12340089

Ma, X., Khattak, A., Ghani, B., & Huo, M. (2023). Perceived overqualification in higher education institutions: Enhancing employee innovative behavior via creative self-confidence and harmonious workplace climate. *Current Psychology (New Brunswick, N.J.)*, 1–12.

Mayne, H., & Dixon, R. A. (2020). The epistemological dilemma: Student teachers shared experiences of Jamaica's National Standards Curriculum (NSC). *Journal of Curriculum and Teaching*, 9(4), 29. DOI: 10.5430/jct.v9n4p29

McComas, W. F., & Burgin, S. (2020). A Critique of "STEM" Education: Revolution-in-the-Making, Passing Fad, or Instructional Imperative? *Science & Education*, 29(4), 805–829. Advance online publication. DOI: 10.1007/s11191-020-00138-2

McCormick, A. C., Kinzie, J., & Gonyea, R. M. (2013). Student engagement: Bridging research and practice to improve the quality of undergraduate education. In *Higher Education: Handbook of Theory and Research* (Vol. 28, pp. 47–92). Springer Netherlands., DOI: 10.1007/978-94-007-5836-0_2

McCullough, L. B., Coverdale, J., & Chervenak, F. A. (2023). Professional virtue of civility and the responsibilities of medical educators and academic leaders. *Journal of Medical Ethics*, 49(10), 674–678. DOI: 10.1136/jme-2022-108735 PMID: 36889908

McGunagle, D., & Zizka, L. (2020). Employability skills for 21st-century STEM students: The employers' perspective. *Higher Education. Skills and Work-Based Learning*, 10(3), 591–606. DOI: 10.1108/HESWBL-10-2019-0148

McKenzie, N. (Sep 29, 2022). Migrant teachers' perspectives. Jamaica Observer, https://www.jamaicaobserver.com/columns/migrant-teachers-perspectives/

McKenzie, V. (2023, September 18). Jamaica needs more engineers to meet its developmental needs – Clarke. *Our Today*. Retrieved March 24, 2024, from https://our.today/jamaica-needs-more-engineers-to-meet-its-developmental-needs-clarke

McNair, D. E., Duree, C. A., & Ebbers, L. (2011). If I knew then what I know now: Using the leadership competencies developed by the American Association of Community Colleges to prepare community college presidents. *Community College Review*, 39(1), 3–25. DOI: 10.1177/0091552110394831

McNair, T. B., Albertine, S., McDonald, N., Major, T.Jr, & Cooper, M. A. (2022). *Becoming a student-ready college: A new culture of leadership for student success.* John Wiley & Sons.

McQuade, K., Harrison, C., & Tarbert, H. (2020). Systematically reviewing servant leadership. *European Business Review*, 33(3), 465–490. DOI: 10.1108/ebr-08-2019-0162

Meltzer, D. (2018). Today's savvy branding mixes traditional and modern strategies. https://www.neur.com>arrti.... Miller, P. (2017a). University branding, but not as we know it. linkedin.com/pulse/university

Metcalf, H., Rolfe, P., Stevens, P., & Weale, M. (2005). *Recruitment and Retention of Academic Staff in Higher Education.* National Institute of Economic and Social Research, Research Report RR658.

Mikkonen, K., Kuivila, H. M., Sjögren, T., Korpi, H., Koskinen, C., Koskinen, M., Koivula, M., Koskimäki, M., Lähteenmäki, M.-L., Saaranen, T., Sormunen, M., Salminen, L., Mäki-Hakola, H., Wallin, O., Holopainen, A., Tuomikoski, A.-M., & Kääriäinen, M. (2022). Social, health care and rehabilitation educators' competence in professional education—Empirical testing of a model. *Health & Social Care in the Community*, 30(1), e75–e85. DOI: 10.1111/hsc.13414 PMID: 34009683

Miller, P. (2017b). Strategy should reflect the university as a whole. linkedin.com/pulse/university.

Miller, E. (2000). *Education For All in the Caribbean in the 1990s: Retrospect and prospect.* UNESCO., Available online https://www.unesco.org/ext/field/carneid/monograph.pdf

Ming, D., & Christian, C. (August 30, 2022) Teacher migration in Jamaica: Exploring the causes, effects, and solutions. Publisher: Leadership Reimagination Enterprise. https://leadershipreimagination.com/uncategorized/teacher-migration-in-jamaica-exploring-the-causes-effects-and-solutions/

Mishra, N., & Aithal, P. (2023). Academic Leadership in Higher Education. [IJPL]. *International Journal of Philosophy and Languages*, 2(2), 85–97.

Mohanty, A., Venkateswaran, N., Ranjit, P., Tripathi, M. A., & Boopathi, S. (2023). Innovative Strategy for Profitable Automobile Industries: Working Capital Management. In *Handbook of Research on Designing Sustainable Supply Chains to Achieve a Circular Economy* (pp. 412–428). IGI Global.

Moharir, M., Agavekar, R., Bhore, P., Kadam, H., & Bewoor, A. (2022). Effective Implementation of Peer Review as an Active Learning Technique to Attain Course Outcome: A Case Study. *Journal of Engineering Education Transformations, 36*(Special Issue 1).

Mohr, S., & Purcell, H. (2020). Sustainable Development of Leadership Strategies in Higher Education. In *Introduction to Sustainable Development Leadership and Strategies in Higher Education* (pp. 55–66). Emerald Publishing Limited. DOI: 10.1108/S2055-364120200000022007

Moldoveanu, M., & Narayandas, D. (2019). The future of leadership development. *Harvard Business Review*, 97(2), 40–48.

Morales, J. C. (2022). Transformational Leadership and Teacher Work Motivation in Private Educational Institutions. *International Journal of Research Publications*, 105(1), 578–614. DOI: 10.47119/IJRP1001051720223687

Morris, A. (2021). Cabinet approves development of national higher-education policy. Jamaica Information Service.https://jis.gov.jm/cabinet-approves-development -of-national-higher[REMOVED HYPERLINK FIELD]education-policy/

Morrison, J. L. (1992). Environmental scanning. *A primer for new institutional researchers*, 86-99.

Muma, M.M., Nzulwa, D.J., Ombui, D.K., Odhiambo, R.O., Wekesa, D.S., Omondi, M., Lumiti, P.A., Ochego, C., & Charles, M. (2019). Influence of recruitment strategies on retention of employees in universities in Kenya.

Mweemba, A. H., McClain, J.Jr, Harris, B., & Newell-McLymont, E. F. (2021). Improving Teaching Practices and Repertoire using the Cognitive Coaching Approach for 21st Century Teachers: A Call for Action. *East African Journal of Education and Social Sciences*, 2(2), 17–33.

Nabatchi, T., Sancino, A., & Sicilia, M. (2017). Varieties of participation in public services: The who, when, and what of co-production. *Public Administration Review*, 77(5), 766–776. DOI: 10.1111/puar.12765

Näsman, Y. (2018). The theory of caritative leadership applied to education. *International Journal of Leadership in Education*, 21(4), 518–529. DOI: 10.1080/13603124.2017.1349183

National Academies of Sciences, Engineering, and Medicine. (2018). *Graduate STEM education for the 21st century*. National Academies Press.

National Research Council. (2011, 2012). Retrieved February 3, 2024 from https://www.nationalacademies.org/

National Security Council. (2021). Collaborative migration management strategy. US White House, Washington. https://www.whitehouse.gov/wp-content/uploads/2021/07/Collaborative-Migration-Management-Strategy.pdf

Needham, C., & Carr, S. (2009). Co-production: An emerging evidence base for adult social care transformation. https://ix.iriss.org.uk>content>Co-prod.... Norsiah, A. (2015). The way forward for customer co-production behaviour. *Procedia-Social and Behavioral Sciences*, 224, 238–245.

Ng'ethe, M., Iravo, M. E., & Namusonge, G. S. (2012). Determinants of Academic Staff Retention in Public Universities in Kenya: Empirical Review Jane. *International Journal of Humanities and Social Science*, 2(13), 205–212. https://www.ijhssnet.com/journals/Vol_2_No_13_July_2012/22.pdf

Nicolazzo, Z., Pitcher, E. N., Renn, K. A., & Woodford, M. (2019). An exploration of trans* kinship as a strategy for student success. In *What's Transgressive about Trans* Studies in Education Now?* (pp. 95–109). Routledge. DOI: 10.4324/9781351034029-6

Noland, A., & Richards, K. (2015). Servant teaching: An exploration of teacher servant leadership on student outcomes. *The Journal of Scholarship of Teaching and Learning*, 15(6), 16–38. DOI: 10.14434/josotl.v15i6.13928

Noor, A., & Ampornstira, F. (2019). Effect of Leadership on Employee Morale in Higher Education. *International Journal of Business and Social Science*, 10(7), 141–144. DOI: 10.30845/ijbss.v10n7p15

Norma, A. Sugden (2010). Teacher workload: and Formula to maximize teacher job performance and well-being. (Unpublished Dissertation) Walden University. https://pdfs.semanticscholar.org/f928/9b4ff7320fece395aa488df2ee5de916b175.pdf?_ga=2. 188060136.119827029.1588006256-311954297.1581345624

Northouse, P. G. (2021). *Leadership: Theory and practice*. Sage publications.

Ntemngwa, C., & Oliver, J. S. (2018). The implementation of Integrated Science Technology, Engineering and Mathematics (STEM) Instruction using robotics in the middle school science classroom. *International Journal of Education in Mathematics, Science and Technology*, 12–40. DOI: 10.18404/ijemst.380617

Nwoko, J. C., Emeto, T. I., Malau-Aduli, A. E., & Malau-Aduli, B. S. (2023). A systematic review of the factors that influence teachers' occupational wellbeing. *International Journal of Environmental Research and Public Health*, 20(12), 6070. DOI: 10.3390/ijerph20126070 PMID: 37372657

Obi, I., Bollen, K., Aaldering, H., & Euwema, M. (2021). Servant and authoritarian leadership, and leaders' third-party conflict behavior in convents. *International Journal of Conflict Management*, 32(5), 769–790. DOI: 10.1108/ijcma-02-2021-0027

Odhiambo, G. (2022). Toxic Leadership in Education: An Understanding of the Dark Side of Leadership. In *Handbook of Research on Educational Leadership and Research Methodology* (pp. 233-255). IGI Global.

Ogunsola, K. O., Sarif, S. M., & Fonatine, R. A. (2020). Islamic performance instrument: An alternative servant leadership tool for sustainable development goals. *International Journal of Islamic Business Ethics*, 5(1), 1. DOI: 10.30659/ijibe.5.1.1-20

Oke, A., & Fernandes, F. A. P. (2020). Innovations in teaching and learning: Exploring the perceptions of the education sector on the 4th industrial revolution (4IR). *Journal of Open Innovation*, 6(2), 31. DOI: 10.3390/joitmc6020031

Okello, N. G., & Lamaro, G. (2015). Perceptions on remunerations and turnover intentions in public universities in Uganda. *International Journal of Developmental Research*, 5(01), 3061–3068. https://hdl.handle.net/20.500.14270/434

Oleksiyenko, A. (2018). Zones of alienation in global higher education: Corporate abuse and leadership failures. *Tertiary Education and Management*, 24, 193–205. DOI: 10.1080/13583883.2018.1439095

Olesen, A., & Hora, M. T. (2013). Teaching the way they were taught? Revisiting the sources of teaching knowledge and the role of prior experience in shaping faculty teaching practices. *Higher Education*. Advance online publication. DOI: 10.1007/s10734-013-9678-9

Orr, D., Luebcke, M., Schmidt, J. P., Ebner, M., Wannemacher, K., Ebner, M., & Dohmen, D. (2020). *Higher education landscape 2030: A trend analysis based on the ahead international horizon scanning*. Springer Nature., DOI: 10.1007/978-3-030-44897-4

Osborne, S. P., & Strokosch, K. (2013). It takes two to tango? Understanding the co-production of public services by integrating the services management and public administration perspectives. *British Journal of Management*, 24(S1), 31–47. DOI: 10.1111/1467-8551.12010

Ospina, S. M., & Foldy, E. G. (2016). Collective Dimensions of Leadership. In Farazmand, A. (Ed.), *Global Encyclopedia of Public Administration*. Public Policy, and Governance., DOI: 10.1007/978-3-319-31816-5_2202-1

Owens, B. P., & Hekman, D. R. (2016). How does leader humility influence team performance? Exploring the mechanisms of contagion and collective promotion focus. *Academy of Management Journal*, 59(3), 1088–1111. DOI: 10.5465/amj.2013.0660

Ozaki, H. (2023). Caring and Education. In *Philosophy of Education in Dialogue between East and West* (pp. 1–13). Routledge. DOI: 10.4324/9781003271024-1

Pacella, D., Fabbricatore, R., D'Enza, A. I., Galluccio, C., & Palumbo, F. (2022). Teaching STEM subjects in non-STEM degrees: An adaptive learning model for teaching statistics. In *Artificial intelligence in STEM education: The paradigmatic shifts in research, education, and technology* (pp. 61–75). CRC Press. DOI: 10.1201/9781003181187-6

Palmer, H., Polk, M., Simon, D., & Hansson, S. (2020). Evaluative and enabling infrastructures: Supporting the ability of urban co-production processes to contribute to societal change. *Urban Transformations*, 2(1), 6. DOI: 10.1186/s42854-020-00010-0

Papazoglou, A., & Koutouzis, M. (2020). Schools as learning organizations in Greece: Measurement and first indications. *European Journal of Education*, 55(1), 43–57. DOI: 10.1111/ejed.12380

Pare, S. K. (2023). Outcome-based Education: Calculating Attainment of Programme Outcome through Course Outcome. *UNIVERSITIES HANDBOOK–34th EDITION (2018), 61*, 60.

Paris, K. A. (2003). Strategic planning in the university. *University of Wisconsin System Board of Regents, USA*. https://www.uwsa.edu/opar/reports/primer-2003.pdf

Parris, D. L., & Peachey, J. W. (2013). A systematic literature review of servant leadership theory in organizational contexts. *Journal of Business Ethics*, 113(3), 377–393. DOI: 10.1007/s10551-012-1322-6

Pasumarthy, R., Mohammed, S., Laxman, V., Krishnamoorthy, V., Durga, S., & Boopathi, S. (2024). Digital Transformation in Developing Economies: Forecasting Trends, Impact, and Challenges in Industry 5.0. In *Convergence of Human Resources Technologies and Industry 5.0* (pp. 47–68). IGI Global. DOI: 10.4018/979-8-3693-1343-5.ch003

Paulsen, M. B., & Smart, J. C. (Eds.). (2001). *The finance of higher education: Theory, research, policy, and practice*. Algora Publishing.

Paunova, M. (2015). The emergence of individual and collective leadership in task groups: A matter of achievement and ascription. *The Leadership Quarterly*, 26(6), 935–957. DOI: 10.1016/j.leaqua.2015.10.002

Peist, E., McMahon, S. D., Davis-Wright, J. O., & Keys, C. B. (2024). Understanding teacher-directed violence and related turnover through a school climate framework. *Psychology in the Schools*, 61(1), 220–236. DOI: 10.1002/pits.23044

Peng, A. C., Gao, R., & Wang, B. (2023). Linking servant leadership to follower emotional exhaustion through impression management. *Journal of Organizational Behavior*, 44(4), 643–659. DOI: 10.1002/job.2682

Pennington, D. (2008). Cross-Disciplinary Collaboration and Learning. *Ecology and Society*, 13(2), 8. DOI: 10.5751/ES-02520-130208

Pestoff, V. (2014). Collective action and the sustainability of co-production. *Public Management Review*, 16(3), 383–401. DOI: 10.1080/14719037.2013.841460

Peterson, R. R. (2020). Over the Caribbean top: Community well-being and over-tourism in small island tourism economies. *International Journal of Community Well-being*, 6(2), 89–126. DOI: 10.1007/s42413-020-00094-3 PMID: 34723109

Petraglia, E., Green, J., Taie, S., Ferg, R., Hubbell, K., Salinas, V., Greene, A., & Lewis, L. (2023). User's Manual for the 2020–21 National Teacher and Principal Survey: Vol. 1–4. *(NCES 2022-061rev through 2022-064rev). U.S. Department of Education.* National Center for Education Statistics., https://nces.ed.gov/pubs2024/2024039SummaryM.pdf

Pidgeon, K. (2017). The key for success: leadership core competences. Journal of Trauma Nursing. 24(6):p 338-341, November/December 2017.I *DOI:* DOI: 10.1097/JTN.0000000000000322

Pineda-Báez, C., Bauman, C., & Andrews, D. (2019). Empowering teacher leadership: A cross-country study. *International Journal of Leadership in Education.*

Pleschova, G., & McAlpine, L. (2015). Enhancing university teaching and learning through mentoring: A systematic review of the literature. *International Journal of Mentoring and Coaching in Education*, 4(2), 107–125. DOI: 10.1108/IJMCE-06-2014-0020

Plowden, K. O., & Young, A. E. (2003). Sociostructural factors influencing health behaviors of urban African-American men. Journal of National Black Nurses' Association: JNBNA, 14(1), 45-51. PMID: 15259998

Poornima, S. N. (2019). Outcome based education, need for the hour-NBA. *Int. J. Adv. Res. Ideas Innov. Technol*, 5(2), 1030–1033.

Powell, W. W. (2010). Understanding attrition and predicting employment durations of former staff in a public social service organization. *Journal of Social Work : JSW*, 10(4), 407–435. DOI: 10.1177/1468017310369606

Prabhuswamy, M., Tripathi, R., Vijayakumar, M., Thulasimani, T., Sundharesalingam, P., & Sampath, B. (2024). A Study on the Complex Nature of Higher Education Leadership: An Innovative Approach. In *Challenges of Globalization and Inclusivity in Academic Research* (pp. 202–223). IGI Global. DOI: 10.4018/979-8-3693-1371-8.ch013

Pradhan, D. (2021). Effectiveness of outcome based education (OBE) toward empowering the students performance in an engineering course. *Journal of Advances in Education and Philosophy*, 5(2), 58–65. DOI: 10.36348/jaep.2021.v05i02.003

Praslova, L. N. (2023: January 10). Today's Most Critical Workplace Challenges Are About Systems. Published by *Havard Business Review*. https://hbr.org/2023/01/todays-most-critical-workplace-challenges-are-about-systems

Pulimood, S. M., Pearson, K., & Bates, D. C. (2016, February). A study on the impact of multidisciplinary collaboration on computational thinking. In *Proceedings of the 47th ACM technical symposium on computing science education* (pp. 30-35). DOI: 10.1145/2839509.2844636

Pullin, A. S., & Stewart, G. B. (2006). Guidelines for systematic review in conservation and environmental management. Conservation biology, 20(6), 1647-1656DOI: 10.1111/j.1523-1739.2006.00485.x PMID: 17181800

Puranik, T. A., Shaik, N., Vankudoth, R., Kolhe, M. R., Yadav, N., & Boopathi, S. (2024). Study on Harmonizing Human-Robot (Drone) Collaboration: Navigating Seamless Interactions in Collaborative Environments. In *Cybersecurity Issues and Challenges in the Drone Industry* (pp. 1–26). IGI Global.

Purwaningtyas, E. K., Arifin, Z., Aghniacakti, A., & Hawabi, A. I. (2023). Characteristics of servant leadership in Islamic educational institutions. In *Proceedings of the First Conference of Psychology and Flourishing Humanity (PFH 2022)* (pp. 286-292). DOI: 10.2991/978-2-38476-032-9_29

Qiu, S., Alizadeh, A., Dooley, L. M., & Zhang, R. (2019). The effects of authentic leadership on trust in leaders, organizational citizenship behavior, and service quality in the Chinese hospitality industry. *Journal of Hospitality and Tourism Management*, 40, 77–87. DOI: 10.1016/j.jhtm.2019.06.004

Quaquebeke, N. V., & Gerpott, F. H. (2023). The now, new, and next of digital leadership: How Artificial Intelligence (AI) will take over and change leadership as we know it. *Journal of Leadership & Organizational Studies*, 30(3), 265–275. DOI: 10.1177/15480518231181731

Quinn, C. M., Reid, J. W., & Gardner, G. E. (2020). S+ T+ M= E as a convergent model for the nature of STEM. *Science & Education*, 29(4), 881–898. DOI: 10.1007/s11191-020-00130-w

Radloff, J., & Guzey, S. (2016). Investigating preservice STEM teacher conceptions of STEM education. *Journal of Science Education and Technology*, 25(5), 759–774. DOI: 10.1007/s10956-016-9633-5

Radnor, Z., Osborne, S. P., Kinder, T., & Mutton, J. (2014). Operationalizing co-production in public services delivery: The contribution of service blueprinting. *Public Management Review*, 16(3), 402–423.

Rae, J. (2023). Connecting for creativity in higher education. *Innovative Higher Education*, 48(1), 127–143. DOI: 10.1007/s10755-022-09609-6

Regal, B., Budjanovcanin, A., van Elk, S., & Ferlie, E. (2023). Organising for co-production: The role of leadership cultures. *Public Management Review*, 2271477. Advance online publication. DOI: 10.1080/14719037

Reynolds, J. (February1, 2014. Ripped to Shreds-JTA says it could trigger legal action. Retrieved on July 30, 2024 from https://jamaica-gleaner.com/gleaner/20140201/lead/lead1.html

Reynolds, D. (2010). *School effectiveness*. A&C Black.

Reynolds, K. (2011). Servant-leadership as gender-integrative leadership. *Journal of Leadership Education*, 10(2), 155–171. DOI: 10.12806/v10/i2/rf8

Rice, M., & Wilson, E. (1999). How Technology Aids Constructivism in the Social Studies Classroom. [Helen Dwight Reid Educational Foundation, USA.]. *Social Studies*, 90(1), 28–33. DOI: 10.1080/00377999909602388

Ringle, C. M., Wende, S., & Becker, J.-M. (2024). *SmartPLS 4. Bönningstedt: SmartPLS*. Retrieved from https://www.smartpls.com

Rissanen, I., & Kuusisto, E. (2023). The role of growth mindset in shaping teachers' intercultural competencies: A study among Finnish teachers. *British Educational Research Journal*, 49(5), 947–967. DOI: 10.1002/berj.3875

Rocco, M. L., & Priest, K. L. (2023). Extending the scope of leadership identity development. *New Directions for Student Leadership*, 2023(178), 107–117. DOI: 10.1002/yd.20559 PMID: 37309859

Ruben, B. D., De Lisi, R., & Gigliotti, R. A. (2023a). *A guide for leaders in higher education: Concepts, competencies, and tools*. Taylor & Francis.

Russell, R. F., & Stone, A. G. (2002). A review of servant leadership attributes: Developing a practical model. *Leadership and Organization Development Journal*, 23(3), 145–157. DOI: 10.1108/01437730210424

Ryu, J., Walls, J., & Seashore Louis, K. (2022). Caring leadership: The role of principals in producing caring school cultures. *Leadership and Policy in Schools*, 21(3), 585–602. DOI: 10.1080/15700763.2020.1811877

Saad, A., & Zainudin, S. (2022). A review of project-based learning (PBL) and computational thinking (CT) in teaching and learning. *Learning and Motivation*, 78, 101802. DOI: 10.1016/j.lmot.2022.101802

Salau, O., Worlu, R., Osinbanjo, A., Adeniji, A., Atolagbe, T., & Salau, J. (2020). Determinants of retention strategies and sustainable performance of academic staff of government-owned universities in Nigeria. *F1000Research*, 1-19. DOI: 10.12688/f1000research.25011.1

Salmon. S. (September 1, 2022). Tourism Workers Receive Training and Certification Through HEART/NSTA Trust. *JIS*. Retrieved on January 30, 2024 from https://jis.gov.jm/tourism-workers-receive-training-and-certification-through-heart-nsta-trust/

Samad, S. (2012). The Influence of Innovation and Transformational Leadership on Organizational Performance Procedia - Social and Behavioral Sciences. Volume 57, Pages 486-493. https://doi.org/DOI: 10.1016/j.sbspro.2012.09.1215l

Sam, C. H. (2021). What are the practices of unethical leaders? Exploring how teachers experience the "dark side" of administrative leadership. *Educational Management Administration & Leadership*, 49(2), 303–320. DOI: 10.1177/1741143219898480

Samuel, M. O., & Chipunza, C. (2013). Higher Learning in South Africa: The Strategies, Complexities and Realities. *Journal of Social Sciences*, 35(2), 97–109. DOI: 10.1080/09718923.2013.11893151

Sands, P., Yadav, A., & Good, J. (2018). Computational thinking in K-12: In-service teacher perceptions of computational thinking. In *Computational thinking in the STEM disciplines: Foundations and research highlights* (pp. 151-164).

Sanghoon, B. (2018). Doing 'convergence education' properly in college. *Happy Education, 5*, 59–61. https://url.kr/7ctzf3

Santamaría, L. J. (2014). Critical change for the greater good: Multicultural perceptions in educational leadership toward social justice and equity. *Educational Administration Quarterly*, 50(3), 347–391. DOI: 10.1177/0013161X13505287

Santos, J., Figueiredo, A. S., & Vieira, M. (2019). Innovative pedagogical practices in higher education: An integrative literature review. *Nurse Education Today*, 72, 12–17. DOI: 10.1016/j.nedt.2018.10.003 PMID: 30384082

Saravanan, S., Chandrasekar, J., Satheesh Kumar, S., Patel, P., Maria Shanthi, J., & Boopathi, S. (2024). The Impact of NBA Implementation Across Engineering Disciplines: Innovative Approaches. In *Advances in Higher Education and Professional Development* (pp. 229–252). IGI Global. DOI: 10.4018/979-8-3693-1666-5.ch010

Sasu, D. D. (2023). Immigration in Nigeria - statistics & facts: Africa Migration flow. Statista. https://www.statista.com/topics/7865/immigration-in-nigeria/

Satam, H., Joshi, K., Mangrolia, U., Waghoo, S., Zaidi, G., Rawool, S., Thakare, R. P., Banday, S., Mishra, A. K., Das, G., & Malonia, S. K. (2023). Next-generation sequencing technology: Current trends and advancements. *Biology (Basel)*, 12(7), 997. DOI: 10.3390/biology12070997 PMID: 37508427

Schaubroeck, J., Lam, S. S. K., & Peng, A. C. (2011). Cognition-based and affect-based trust as mediators of leader behavior influences on team performance. *The Journal of Applied Psychology*, 96(4), 863–871. DOI: 10.1037/a0022625

Schweisfurth, M. (2011). Learner-centred education in developing country contexts: From solution to problem? *International Journal of Educational Development*, 31(5), 425–432. https://www.researchgate.net/publication/232398671_Learner-centred_education_in_developing_country_contexts_From_solution_to_problem. DOI: 10.1016/j.ijedudev.2011.03.005

Searle, T. P., & Barbuto, J. E.Jr. (2011). *Leadership: Enhancing the lessons of experience*. McGraw-Hill Higher Education.

Seider, S., Clark, S., & Graves, D. (2020). The development of critical consciousness and its relation to academic achievement in adolescents of color. *Child Development*, 91(2), e451–e474. DOI: 10.1111/cdev.13262 PMID: 31140588

Sela, R. (2023). What is brand dilution? Preventive strategies. https://wwwronsela.com> brand_di.

Senapati, R., & Singh, S. K. (2023). National Education Policy—2020 and Evaluation Reforms in Higher Education: Envisioning Transformation for 21st Century India. *Special Issue of 'University News,' 61*, 21.

Sendjaya, S., & Pekerti, A. A. (2010). Servant leadership as antecedent of trust in organizations. *Leadership and Organization Development Journal*, 31(7), 643–663. DOI: 10.1108/01437731011079673

Sendjaya, S., Sarros, J. C., & Santora, J. C. (2008). Defining and measuring servant leadership behavior in organizations. *Journal of Management Studies*, 45(2), 402–424. DOI: https://doi.org/10. 1111/j.1467-6486.2007.00761.x

Sengupta, S., & Das, A. K. (2023). Automated Mapping of Course Outcomes to Program Outcomes using Natural Language Processing and Machine Learning. *2023 IEEE 3rd Applied Signal Processing Conference (ASPCON)*, 44–48.

Shah, M., & Kolhekar, M. (2021). A Case-Study on Leveraging the Policies on Outcome-Based Education. *Journal of Engineering Education Transformations*, 35(2), 126–139. DOI: 10.16920/jeet/2021/v35i2/22080

Shahnaz, A., & Qadir, A. S. (2020). Branding the higher education: Identity construction of universities through logos, mottos and slogans. *Journal of Research in Social Sciences*. .DOI: 10.52015/jrss.8i1.67

Shapiro, J. P., & Gross, S. J. (2013). *Ethical educational leadership in turbulent times:(Re) solving moral dilemmas*. Routledge. DOI: 10.4324/9780203809310

Sharma, D. M., Ramana, K. V., Jothilakshmi, R., Verma, R., Maheswari, B. U., & Boopathi, S. (2024). Integrating Generative AI Into K-12 Curriculums and Pedagogies in India: Opportunities and Challenges. *Facilitating Global Collaboration and Knowledge Sharing in Higher Education With Generative AI*, 133–161.

Sharma, D. M., Ramana, K. V., Jothilakshmi, R., Verma, R., Maheswari, B. U., & Boopathi, S. (2024a). Integrating Generative AI Into K-12 Curriculums and Pedagogies in India: Opportunities and Challenges. *Facilitating Global Collaboration and Knowledge Sharing in Higher Education With Generative AI*, 133–161.

Sharma, D. M., Ramana, K. V., Jothilakshmi, R., Verma, R., Maheswari, B. U., & Boopathi, S. (2024b). Integrating Generative AI Into K-12 Curriculums and Pedagogies in India: Opportunities and Challenges. *Facilitating Global Collaboration and Knowledge Sharing in Higher Education With Generative AI*, 133–161.

Sharma, P., & Jain, V. (2022). Role of culture in developing transformative leadership for higher education in emerging economies. In *Re-imagining educational futures in developing countries: Lessons from global health crises* (pp. 243–259). Springer International Publishing. DOI: 10.1007/978-3-030-88234-1_13

Shaturaev, J., & Bekimbetova, G. (2021). *The difference between educational management and educational leadership and the importance of educational responsibility*. InterConf.

Shen, J., Wu, H., Reeves, P., Zheng, Y., Ryan, L., & Anderson, D. (2020). The association between teacher leadership and student achievement: A meta-analysis. *Educational Research Review*, 31, 100357. DOI: 10.1016/j.edurev.2020.100357

Shonk, K. (2024). What is collective leadership? https://www.pon.harvard.edu>daily.

Silveira, I., & Deshmukh, A. (2022). Computational thinking, history and non-formal learning-A well-crafted blend!.

Silver, R., & Martín, M. C. R. d. (2021). Servant leadership and its association with an environment of empathic care: An empirical analysis of the perspectives of mid-level practitioners. *Leadership in Health Services*, 35(1), 116–136. DOI: 10.1108/LHS-06-2021-0052

Sims, C., & Morris, L. R. (2018). Are women business owners authentic servant leaders? *Gender in Management*, 33(5), 405–427. DOI: 10.1108/GM-01-2018-0003

Sims, S., Fletcher-Wood, H., O'Mara-Eves, A., Cottingham, S., Stansfield, C., Van Herwegen, J., & Anders, J. (2021). *What are the characteristics of teacher professional development that increase pupil achievement? A systematic review and meta-analysis*. Education Endowment Foundation.

Singh Madan, B., Najma, U., Pande Rana, D., & Kumar, P. K. J., S., S., & Boopathi, S. (2024). Empowering Leadership in Higher Education: Driving Student Performance, Faculty Development, and Institutional Progress. In *Advances in Educational Technologies and Instructional Design* (pp. 191–221). IGI Global. DOI: 10.4018/979-8-3693-0583-6.ch009

Sipahioğlu, M. (2020). *Yükseköğretimde kurumsal itibar yönetimi*. İksad Yayınevi.

Sives, A., Morgan, W. J., & Simon Appleton, S. (2006). Teacher migration from Jamaica: Assessing the short-term impact. Caribbean Journal of Education, 27(1), 85-111. https://www.researchgate.net/publication/274017514_Teacher_Migration_from_Jamaica_assessing_the_short_term_impact

Small, S. (2023, November 18). Mixed views on sanctions against unlicensed teachers: Committee reviewing JTC bill debates whether principals should also be sanctioned. Jamaica Gleaner. Retrieved on July 30, 2024, from https://jamaica -gleaner.com/article/news/20231118/mixed-views-sanctions-against-unlicensed -teachers#google_vignette

Smith, R. (2023, October 25). *Master of Science in STEM Education.* Shortwood Teachers College. Retrieved January 18, 2024, from https://shortwood.edu.jm/master -of-science-in-stem-education/

Smith, D. G. (2020). *Diversity's promise for higher education: Making it work.* JHU Press. DOI: 10.56021/9781421438405

Smith, W. K. (2014). Dynamic decision making: A model of senior leaders managing strategic paradoxes. *Academy of Management Journal,* 57(6), 1592–1623. DOI: 10.5465/amj.2011.0932

Smylie, M. A., Murphy, J., & Louis, K. S. (2016). Caring school leadership: A multidisciplinary, cross-occupational model. *American Journal of Education,* 123(1), 1–35. DOI: 10.1086/688166

Smyth, E. (2024). "Education." T*he national development plan in 2023: Priorities and capacity* (2024): 66.

Snively, E. (2021). Diversity, Equity, and Inclusion vs. Social Justice Positioning in Higher Education: Identifying communication strategies that serve both the institution and society. https://doi.org/DOI: 10.17615/m4fv-nk38

Social Care Institute for Excellence. (2013). Co-production in social care: What it is and how to do it. www.scie.org.uk

Social Care Institute for Excellence. (2019). Breaking down the barriers to co-production. https://www.yhphnetwork.co.uk>... Tipurić, D. (2022). The enactment of strategic leadership, DOI: 10.1007/978-3-031-03799-3_1

Sondakh, D. E., Kom, S., Pungus, S. R., & Putra, E. Y. (2022). Indonesian undergraduate students' perception of their computational thinking ability. *CogITo Smart Journal,* 8(1), 68–80. DOI: 10.31154/cogito.v8i1.387.68-80

Soyibo, K. (1994). Occupational stress factors and coping strategies among Jamaican high school science teachers. *Research in Science & Technological Education,* 12(2), 187–192. DOI: 10.1080/0263514940120207

Soyibo, K. (1998). An Assessment of Caribbean integrated science textbooks' practical tasks. *Research in Science & Technological Education*, 16(1), 31–41. DOI: 10.1080/0263514980160103

Spears, L. (1998). *Insights on leadership: Service, stewardship, spirit, and servant leadership*. Wiley.

Speck, M., & Knipe, C. (2005). *Why can't we get it right? Designing high-quality professional development for standards-based schools* (2nd ed.). Corwin Press.

Spillane, J. P. (2006). *Distributed Leadership*. Jossey-Bass.

Ssebikindu, L. (2021). Certificate vs. endorsement: what's the difference? *Graduate Programs for Educators*. Retrieved January 18, 2024, from https://www.graduateprogram.org/2021/10/certificate-vs-endorsements-whats-the-difference/

Starratt, R. J. (2005, June). Responsible leadership. In *The educational forum* (Vol. 69, No. 2, pp. 124-133). Taylor & Francis Group. https://doi.org/DOI: 10.1080/00131720508984676

STATIN. (2017). Retrieved on March 8, 2024 from https://statinja.gov.jm/Demo_SocialStats/Education.aspx

Steilen, K., & Stone-Johnson, C. (2023, June). "There wasn'ta guidebook for this": Caring leadership during crisis. [). Frontiers.]. *Frontiers in Education*, 8, 1183134. DOI: 10.3389/feduc.2023.1183134

Steinert, Y., O'Sullivan, P. S., & Irby, D. M. (2019). Strengthening teachers' professional identities through faculty development. *Academic Medicine*, 94(7), 963–968. DOI: 10.1097/ACM.0000000000002695 PMID: 30844931

Sterrett, W., & Richardson, J. W. (2020). Supporting professional development through digital principal leadership. *Journal of Organizational and Educational Leadership*, 5(2), 4.

Stigmar, M. (2016). Peer to peer teaching in higher education: a critical literature review. Pages 124-136 | Published online: 10 May 2016

Stoytcheva, B., Horissian, K., & You, W. (2024). Factors Affecting Theatre Faculty Job Satisfaction: A Thematic Analysis. *Theatre Topics*, 34(1), 19–31. DOI: 10.1353/tt.2024.a920470

Strayhorn, T. L. (2018). *College students' sense of belonging: A key to educational success for all students*. Routledge. DOI: 10.4324/9781315297293

Sudhakar, V., & Tamilselvi, T. (2023). Analysis of Student's Performance in Engineering Courses Based on Outcome Based Education. *J Adv Educ Philos*, 7(9), 372–375. DOI: 10.36348/jaep.2023.v07i09.006

Sweeney, A. E. (2003). An overview of science education in the Caribbean: Research, policy and practice.

Sweeney, A. E., & George, L. (2024). STEM Education in the Caribbean: Challenges, Goals, and Possibilities. *Caribbean Journal of Education and Development*, 1(1), 103–110. DOI: 10.46425/cjed1101019192

Tagare, D. (2023). *Factors that predict K-12 teachers' ability to apply computational thinking skills*. ACM Transactions on Computing Education.

Tang, X., Yin, Y., Lin, Q., Hadad, R., & Zhai, X. (2020). Assessing computational thinking: A systematic review of empirical studies. *Computers & Education*, 148, 103798. DOI: 10.1016/j.compedu.2019.103798

Tariq, M. U. (2024). Multidisciplinary service learning in higher education: Concepts, implementation, and impact. In S. Watson (Ed.), *Applications of service learning in higher education* (pp. 1-19). IGI Global. https://doi.org/DOI: 10.4018/979-8-3693-2133-1.ch001

Tariq, M. U. (2024). Neurodiversity inclusion and belonging strategies in the workplace. In J. Vázquez de Príncipe (Ed.), *Resilience of multicultural and multigenerational leadership and workplace experience* (pp. 182-201). IGI Global. https://doi.org/DOI: 10.4018/979-8-3693-1802-7.ch009

Tariq, H., Abrar, M., & Ahmad, B. (2023). Humility breeds creativity: The moderated mediation model of leader humility and subordinates' creative service performance in hospitality. *International Journal of Contemporary Hospitality Management*, 35(12), 4117–4136. DOI: 10.1108/IJCHM-07-2022-0851

Tariq, M. U. (2024). AI and IoT in flood forecasting and mitigation: A comprehensive approach. In Ouaissa, M., Ouaissa, M., Boulouard, Z., Iwendi, C., & Krichen, M. (Eds.), *AI and IoT for proactive disaster management* (pp. 26–60). IGI Global., DOI: 10.4018/979-8-3693-3896-4.ch003

Tariq, M. U. (2024). AI and the future of talent management: Transforming recruitment and retention with machine learning. In Christiansen, B., Aziz, M., & O'Keeffe, E. (Eds.), *Global practices on effective talent acquisition and retention* (pp. 1–16). IGI Global., DOI: 10.4018/979-8-3693-1938-3.ch001

Tariq, M. U. (2024). Application of blockchain and Internet of Things (IoT) in modern business. In Sinha, M., Bhandari, A., Priya, S., & Kabiraj, S. (Eds.), *Future of customer engagement through marketing intelligence* (pp. 66–94). IGI Global., DOI: 10.4018/979-8-3693-2367-0.ch004

Tariq, M. U. (2024). Challenges of a metaverse shaping the future of entrepreneurship. In Inder, S., Dawra, S., Tennin, K., & Sharma, S. (Eds.), *New business frontiers in the metaverse* (pp. 155–173). IGI Global., DOI: 10.4018/979-8-3693-2422-6.ch011

Tariq, M. U. (2024). Crafting Authentic Narratives for Sustainable Branding. In Rodrigues, P. (Eds.), *Compelling Storytelling Narratives for Sustainable Branding* (pp. 194–229). IGI Global., DOI: 10.4018/979-8-3693-3326-6.ch011

Tariq, M. U. (2024). Emerging trends and innovations in blockchain-digital twin integration for green investments: A case study perspective. In Jafar, S., Rodriguez, R., Kannan, H., Akhtar, S., & Plugmann, P. (Eds.), *Harnessing blockchain-digital twin fusion for sustainable investments* (pp. 148–175). IGI Global., DOI: 10.4018/979-8-3693-1878-2.ch007

Tariq, M. U. (2024). Emotional intelligence in understanding and influencing consumer behavior. In Musiolik, T., Rodriguez, R., & Kannan, H. (Eds.), *AI impacts in digital consumer behavior* (pp. 56–81). IGI Global., DOI: 10.4018/979-8-3693-1918-5.ch003

Tariq, M. U. (2024). Empowering student entrepreneurs: From idea to execution. In Cantafio, G., & Munna, A. (Eds.), *Empowering students and elevating universities with innovation centers* (pp. 83–111). IGI Global., DOI: 10.4018/979-8-3693-1467-8.ch005

Tariq, M. U. (2024). Enhancing cybersecurity protocols in modern healthcare systems: Strategies and best practices. In Garcia, M., & de Almeida, R. (Eds.), *Transformative approaches to patient literacy and healthcare innovation* (pp. 223–241). IGI Global., DOI: 10.4018/979-8-3693-3661-8.ch011

Tariq, M. U. (2024). Equity and inclusion in learning ecosystems. In Al Husseiny, F., & Munna, A. (Eds.), *Preparing students for the future educational paradigm* (pp. 155–176). IGI Global., DOI: 10.4018/979-8-3693-1536-1.ch007

Tariq, M. U. (2024). Fintech startups and cryptocurrency in business: Revolutionizing entrepreneurship. In Kankaew, K., Nakpathom, P., Chnitphattana, A., Pitchayadejanant, K., & Kunnapapdeelert, S. (Eds.), *Applying business intelligence and innovation to entrepreneurship* (pp. 106–124). IGI Global., DOI: 10.4018/979-8-3693-1846-1.ch006

Tariq, M. U. (2024). Leading Smart Technologies and Innovations for E-Business 5.0: Applications and Management Frameworks. In Popkova, E. (Ed.), *Smart Technologies and Innovations in E-Business* (pp. 25–46). IGI Global., DOI: 10.4018/978-1-6684-7840-0.ch002

Tariq, M. U. (2024). Leveraging AI for Entrepreneurial Innovation in Healthcare. In Özsungur, F. (Ed.), *Generating Entrepreneurial Ideas With AI* (pp. 192–216). IGI Global., DOI: 10.4018/979-8-3693-3498-0.ch009

Tariq, M. U. (2024). Leveraging artificial intelligence for a sustainable and climate-neutral economy in Asia. In Ordóñez de Pablos, P., Almunawar, M., & Anshari, M. (Eds.), *Strengthening sustainable digitalization of Asian economy and society* (pp. 1–21). IGI Global., DOI: 10.4018/979-8-3693-1942-0.ch001

Tariq, M. U. (2024). Metaverse in business and commerce. In Kumar, J., Arora, M., & Erkol Bayram, G. (Eds.), *Exploring the use of metaverse in business and education* (pp. 47–72). IGI Global., DOI: 10.4018/979-8-3693-5868-9.ch004

Tariq, M. U. (2024). Multi-Agent Models in Healthcare System Design. In Dall'Acqua, L. (Ed.), *Bioethics of Cognitive Ergonomics and Digital Transition* (pp. 143–170). IGI Global., DOI: 10.4018/979-8-3693-2667-1.ch008

Tariq, M. U. (2024). Revolutionizing health data management with blockchain technology: Enhancing security and efficiency in a digital era. In Garcia, M., & de Almeida, R. (Eds.), *Emerging technologies for health literacy and medical practice* (pp. 153–175). IGI Global., DOI: 10.4018/979-8-3693-1214-8.ch008

Tariq, M. U. (2024). Social Innovations for Improving Healthcare. In Chandan, H. (Ed.), *Social Innovations in Education, Environment, and Healthcare* (pp. 302–317). IGI Global., DOI: 10.4018/979-8-3693-2569-8.ch015

Tariq, M. U. (2024). The role of AI ethics in cost and complexity reduction. In Tennin, K., Ray, S., & Sorg, J. (Eds.), *Cases on AI ethics in business* (pp. 59–78). IGI Global., DOI: 10.4018/979-8-3693-2643-5.ch004

Tariq, M. U. (2024). The role of AI in skilling, upskilling, and reskilling the workforce. In Doshi, R., Dadhich, M., Poddar, S., & Hiran, K. (Eds.), *Integrating generative AI in education to achieve sustainable development goals* (pp. 421–433). IGI Global., DOI: 10.4018/979-8-3693-2440-0.ch023

Tariq, M. U. (2024). The role of emerging technologies in shaping the global digital government landscape. In Guo, Y. (Ed.), *Emerging developments and technologies in digital government* (pp. 160–180). IGI Global., DOI: 10.4018/979-8-3693-2363-2.ch009

Tariq, M. U. (2024). The transformation of healthcare through AI-driven diagnostics. In Sharma, A., Chanderwal, N., Tyagi, S., Upadhyay, P., & Tyagi, A. (Eds.), *Enhancing medical imaging with emerging technologies* (pp. 250–264). IGI Global., DOI: 10.4018/979-8-3693-5261-8.ch015

Tasker-Mitchell, A., & Attoh, P. A. (2019). The mediating effect of faculty trust in principals on the relationship between servant leadership practices and organizational health. *Journal of School Leadership*, 30(4), 297–336. DOI: 10.1177/1052684619884784

Taylor-Powell, E., & Henert, E. (2008). Developing a logic model: Teaching and training guide. *Benefits*, 3(22), 1–118.

Tettey, W. J. (2009). Deficits in academic staff capacity in Africa and challenges of developing and retaining the next generation of academics. *Partnership for higher education in Africa.* https://www.semanticscholar.org/paper/DEFICITS -IN-ACADEMIC-STAFF-CAPACITY-IN-AFRICA-AND-Tettey/acf6a510cb ce13b2f21449623103ccbaf3b38ee7

The Future of Jobs Report. 2023. (2023, April 30). In https://www.weforum.org/ publications/the-future-of-jobs-report-2023/in-full/. World Economic Forum.

The White House Office of Science and Technology Policy. (2022, November). Convergence education: A guide to transdisciplinary STEM learning and teaching. Retrieved February 27, 2024, from https://www.whitehouse.gov/ostp/news-updates/ 2022/11/30/nstc-convergence-education-a-guide-to-transdisciplinary-stem-learning -and-teaching/

Thiruvengadam, S., Baskar, S., Jeyamala, C., & Abirami, A. (2022). Systematic Approach in Assessment of Course Outcomes/Program Outcomes for Undergraduate Engineering Programs–A Case Study. *Journal of Engineering Education Transformations, 35.*

Thorpe, S. (2023). A vision for STEM education at the University of Technology, Jamaica. *In SoutheastCon 2023 (Pp. 793-797)*, 793–797.

Tierney, W. G. (2008). *The Impact of Culture on Organizational Decision-Making: Theory and Practice in Higher Education.* Stylus Publishing, LLC.

Tinto, V. (2012). *Leaving college: Rethinking the causes and cures of student attrition.* University of Chicago press.

Tjosvold, D., Wong, A., Chen, N. (2019). Managing conflict for effective leadership and organizations. Business and Management. https://doi.org/ crefore/9780190224851.013.240DOI: 10.1093/a

Topal, M. R. (2022). The relationship between school principals' servant leadership behaviors and conflict management styles. *SDU International Journal of Educational Studies*, 9(2), 105–136. DOI: 10.33710/sduijes.1200956

Torney-Purta, J., Cabrera, J. C., Roohr, K. C., Liu, O. L., & Rios, J. A. (2015). Assessing civic competency and engagement in higher education: Research background, frameworks, and directions for next-generation assessment. *ETS Research Report Series*, 2015(2), 1–48. DOI: 10.1002/ets2.12081

Torres-Coronas, T., Vidal-Blasco, M. A., & Simón-Olmos, M. J. (2014). Aligning educational outcomes to boost employment and workforce employability. In *Handbook of research on education and technology in a changing society* (pp. 407–417). IGI Global., DOI: 10.4018/978-1-4666-6046-5.ch031

Tsang, M. C., Fryer, M., & Gregorio, G. (2002). *Access, equity and performance: Education in Barbados, Guyana, Jamaica, and Trinidad and Tobago.* Inter-American Development Bank. https://publications.iadb.org/en/access-equity-and-performance-education-barbados-guyana-jamaica-and-trinidad-and-tobago

Tsarava, K., Moeller, K., Román-González, M., Golle, J., Leifheit, L., Butz, M. V., & Ninaus, M. (2022). A cognitive definition of computational thinking in primary education. *Computers & Education*, 179, 104425. DOI: 10.1016/j.compedu.2021.104425

Tsarkos, A. (2023). The effect of servant leadership on Greek public secondary schools acting as learning organizations. *International Journal of Leadership in Education*, ●●●, 1–26. DOI: 10.1080/13603124.2023.2264261

Tsortanidou, X., Daradoumis, T., & Barberá-Gregori, E. (2023). Unplugged computational thinking at K-6 education: Evidence from a multiple-case study in Spain. *Education 3-13, 51*(6), 948-965.

Tuckwiller, E., Fox, H., Ball, K., & St. Louis, J. (2024). More than just a "nod" to care: Expanding Nel Noddings' ethics of care framework to sustain educator resilience. *Leadership and Policy in Schools*, 1–18. DOI: 10.1080/15700763.2024.2311249

Tupper, H., & Ellis, S. (2022). It's time to reimagine employee retention. *Havard Business Review.* https://hbr.org/2022/07/its-time-to-reimagine-employee-retention

Turner, S., & Tsang, Y. (2023). Nature versus nurture: What underpins great leadership? The case for nurture. *Clinical Oncology*, 35(1), 6–9. DOI: 10.1016/j.clon.2022.09.053 PMID: 36270863

Tuurnas, S. (2016). The professional side of co-production. (Academic Dissertation, School of Management, University of Tampere, Finland). https://tampub.uta.fi>bitstream> handle.

Uche, C. M., & Jack, I. F. (2014). Level of female academic staff development and mobility in the University of Port Harcourt. *Research Journal in Organizational Psychology & Educational Studies* 3(3) 152-158. www.emergingresource.orgg

Udi, G. (2010). Determinants of Staff Retention in Service Organisations. A Case of Consumer Insight Ltd. Master's thesis, Jomo Kenyatta University of Agriculture and Technology.

Ullah, S. (2021). Examining the role of grit in the relationship between servant leadership and work performance: An empirical study of the higher education sector of Quetta, Balochistan, Pakistan. *Journal of Development and Social Sciences*, 2(3), 191–201. DOI: 10.47205/jdss.2021(2-III)18

UNESCO. (2019). Migration, displacement, and education: Building bridges, not walls. *Global Education Monitoring Report*. https://unesdoc.unesco.org/ark:/48223/pf0000265866.page=117

UNESCO. (2023). *Global report on teachers: addressing teacher shortages*. United Nations Educational, Scientific and Cultural Organization.

United Nations. (2015). *Transforming our World: The 2030 Agenda for Sustainable Development*. Retrieved June 18, 2023, from https://sdgs.un.org/publications/transforming-our-world-2030-agenda-sustainable-development-17981Vasquez, J. A., Sneider, C., & Comer, M. (2013). STEM Lesson Essentials. Heinemann Educational Books.

University of Connecticut. (2022). Guidelines for the Development of Faculty Workload Assignment Policies. Provost Office Document. https://policy.uconn.edu/wp-content/uploads/sites/243/2022/08/Guidelines-for-the[REMOVED HYPERLINK FIELD]Development-of-Faculty-Workload-Assignment-Policies-Final-8-22-22.pdf# U.S. Department of Education (1990-91). Teacher Supply, Teacher Turnover, and Teacher Qualifications. *National Center for Education Statistics, 1990-91 (NCES 95-744)*.https://nces.ed.gov/pubs95/web/95770.asp# Vedder, R. (2021, January,11). Migrants Flee States With Highly Educated People: Why? Publisher: Forbes, Leadership Education. https://www.forbes.com/sites/richardvedder/2021/01/11/migrants-flee-states-with-highly-educated-people-why/

Uusiautti, S., & Maatta, K. (2013). Enhancing university students'study success through caring leadership. *European Scientific Journal, 9*(19). Twenge, J. M. (2023). *Generations: The Real Differences Between Gen Z, Millennials [Boomers, and Silents—and What They Mean for America's Future*. Simon and Schuster.]. *GEN*, X.

Van der Hoven, A. G., Mahembe, B., & Hamman-Fisher, D. (2021). The influence of servant leadership on psychological empowerment and organizational citizenship on a sample of teachers. *SA Journal of Human Resource Management*, 19(0), a1395. DOI: 10.4102/sajhrm.v19i0.1395

Van Dierendonck, D. (2010). Servant leadership: A review and synthesis. *Journal of Management*, 37(4), 1228–1261. DOI: 10.1177/0149206310380462

Van Dierendonck, D., & Patterson, K. (2015). Compassionate Love as a Cornerstone of Servant Leadership: An Integration of Previous Theorizing and Research. *Journal of Business Ethics*, 128, 119–131. DOI: 10.1007/s10551-014-2085-z

Vanleene, D., Verschuere, B., & Voets, J. (2015). Benefits and risks of co-production: A preliminary literature review. https://core.ac. uk>pdf.

Vasudevan, N. (2020). Development of a common framework for outcome based accreditation and rankings. *Procedia Computer Science*, 172, 270–276. DOI: 10.1016/j.procs.2020.05.043

Venkatasubramanian, V., Chitra, M., Sudha, R., Singh, V. P., Jefferson, K., & Boopathi, S. (2024). Examining the Impacts of Course Outcome Analysis in Indian Higher Education: Enhancing Educational Quality. In *Challenges of Globalization and Inclusivity in Academic Research* (pp. 124–145). IGI Global.

Venkatesh, K., & King, C. S. (2021). Challenges and Issues in Implementation of OBE. *Assessment Tools for Mapping Learning Outcomes With Learning Objectives*, 83–96.

Vermeulen, M., Kreijns, K., & Evers, A. T. (2022). Transformational leadership, leader–member exchange and school learning climate: Impact on teachers' innovative behaviour in the Netherlands. *Educational Management Administration & Leadership*, 50(3), 491–510. DOI: 10.1177/1741143220932582

Verschuere, B., Vanleene, D., Trui Steen, T., & Brandsen, T. (2018). 18 Democratic co-production: Concepts and determinants. https://www.taylorfrancis.com>

Vijaya Lakshmi, V., Mishra, M., Kushwah, J. S., Shajahan, U. S., Mohanasundari, M., & Boopathi, S. (2024). Circular Economy Digital Practices for Ethical Dimensions and Policies for Digital Waste Management. In *Harnessing High-Performance Computing and AI for Environmental Sustainability* (pp. 166–193). IGI Global., DOI: 10.4018/979-8-3693-1794-5.ch008

Vindrola-Padros, C., Eyre, L., Baxter, H., Cramer, H., George, B., Wye, L., Fulop, N. J., Utley, M., Phillips, N., Brindle, P., & Marshall, M. (2019). Addressing the challenges of knowledge co-production in quality improvement: Learning from the implementation of the researcher-in-residence model. *BMJ Quality & Safety*, 28, 67–73. doi:10.1136/bmjqs-2017-007127

Viswanadhan, K., & Rao, N. (2005). Effectiveness of NBA accreditation processes. *National Symposium on Engineering Education (NSEE05)*, 100–108.

Vlahović, I., & Biškupić, I. O. (2023, May). Fostering critical and computational thinking in the field of primary and secondary education in non-STEM subjects by using data sets and applications. In *2023 46th MIPRO ICT and Electronics Convention (MIPRO)* (pp. 672-677). IEEE. DOI: 10.23919/MIPRO57284.2023.10159750

Vnoučková, L. (2012). Monitoring labour mobility as a way to competitiveness. *Journal of Competitiveness*, 4(3), 105–121. https://www.cjournal.cz/files/111.pdf. DOI: 10.7441/joc.2012.03.08

Wahab, N. A., Talib, O., Razali, F., & Kamarudin, N. (2021). The big why of implementing computational thinking in STEM education: A systematic literature review. [MJSSH]. *Malaysian Journal of Social Sciences and Humanities*, 6(3), 272–289.

Walker, B. T., Lee, T. J., & Li, X. (2021). Sustainable development for small island tourism: Developing slow tourism in the Caribbean. *Journal of Travel & Tourism Marketing*, 38(1), 1–15. DOI: 10.1080/10548408.2020.1842289

Walk, M. (2023). Leaders as change executors: The impact of leader attitudes to change and change-specific support on followers. *European Management Journal*, 41(1), 154–163. DOI: 10.1016/j.emj.2022.01.002

Walls, J. (2022). Performativity and caring in education: Toward an ethic of reimagination. *Journal of School Leadership*, 32(3), 289–314. DOI: 10.1177/1052684620972065

Wei, H., Corbett, R. W., Ray, J., & Wei, T. L. (2020). A culture of caring: The essence of healthcare interprofessional collaboration. *Journal of Interprofessional Care*, 34(3), 324–331. DOI: 10.1080/13561820.2019.1641476 PMID: 31390903

Wenger, E. (2011). Communities of practice: A brief introduction. https://www.nsf.gov/pubs/2012/nsf12544/nsf12544.pdf

Wieser, C. (2024). Teacher qualities that make teachers stay in the profession: Addressing teacher shortage in Nordic countries with ethics of care. *Teacher ethics and teaching quality in Scandinavian schools*, 51-65.

Wilcox, C. (2023). Women faculty feel 'pushed' from academia by poor workplace climate. *Science*. Advance online publication. DOI: 10.1126/science.caredit.adl4899

Wilcox, P., Winn, S., & Fyvie-Gauld, M. (2005). 'It was nothing to do with the university, it was just the people': The role of social support in the first-year experience of higher education. *Studies in Higher Education*, 30(6), 707–722. DOI: 10.1080/03075070500340036

Wilkinson, J. (2020). Educational leadership as practice. In *Oxford research encyclopedia of education*. DOI: 10.1093/acrefore/9780190264093.013.613

Williams, D. H., Bellis, E. C., & Wellington, S. W. (1980). Deinstitutionalization and social policy: Historical perspectives and present dilemmas. American Journal of Orthopsychiatry, 50(1), 54.DOI: 10.1111/j.1939-0025.1980.tb03262.x PMID: 6986789

Williams, S. A. S., & Staulters, M. L. (2014). Instructional collaboration with rural educators in Jamaica: Lessons learned from an international interdisciplinary consultation project. *Journal of Educational & Psychological Consultation*, 24(4), 307–329. DOI: 10.1080/10474412.2014.929968

Windschitl, M. (2009, February). Cultivating 21st century skills in science learners: How systems of teacher preparation and professional development will have to evolve. In Presentation given at the National Academies of Science Workshop on 21st Century Skills, Washington, DC (Vol. 15).

Wing, J. M. (2006). Computational thinking. *Communications of the ACM*, 49(3), 33–35. DOI: 10.1145/1118178.1118215

Workforce Planning for Wisconsin State Government. (2005). Employee retention http://workforceplanning.wi.gov/category.asp?linkcatid=15&linkid=18

Worth, J., Tang, S., & Galvis, M. A. (2022). Assessing the Impact of Pay and Financial Incentives in Improving Shortage Subject Teacher Supply. Report. *National Foundation for Educational Research*.

Xie, Y., Fang, M., & Shauman, K. (2015, August 1). STEM Education. *Annual Review of Sociology*, 41(1), 331–357. DOI: 10.1146/annurev-soc-071312-145659 PMID: 26778893

Yang, J., Liu, H., & Gu, J. (2017). A multi-level study of servant leadership on creativity. *Leadership and Organization Development Journal*, 38(5), 610–629. DOI: 10.1108/LODJ-10-2015-0229

Yee Han, P., Joong, N., Ramsawak-Jodha, P., Anderson, S., & Hutton, S. (2020). Understanding the ecologies of education reforms: Comparing the perceptions of secondary teachers and students in Jamaica, Guyana, and Trinidad and Tobago. *Caribbean. Journal of Mixed Methods Research*, 1(1). Advance online publication. DOI: 10.37234/CJMMR

Yenugu, S. (2022). The new National Education Policy (NEP) of India: Will it be a paradigm shift in Indian higher education? *Perspectives: Policy and Practice in Higher Education*, 26(4), 121–129.

York, T. T., Gibson, C., & Rankin, S. (2019). Defining and measuring academic success. *Practical Assessment, Research & Evaluation*, 20(1), 5. DOI: 10.7275/hz5x-tx03

Young, M. D. (2015). The leadership challenge: Supporting the learning of all students. *Leadership and Policy in Schools*, 14(4), 389–410. DOI: 10.1080/15700763.2015.1073330

Zacarias. (2021). Teaching under construction. Challenges in teacher professional development in Central America and the Caribbean. *SUMMA*.

Zarandi, N., Soares, A. M., & Alves, H. (2022). Student roles and behaviors in higher education co-creation – a systematic literature review. *International Journal of Educational Management*, 36(7), 1297–1320. DOI: 10.1108/IJEM-08-2021-0317

Zawacki-Richter, O., Marín, V. I., Bond, M., & Gouverneur, F. (2019). Systematic review of research on artificial intelligence applications in higher education–where are the educators? *International Journal of Educational Technology in Higher Education*, 16(1), 1–27. DOI: 10.1186/s41239-019-0171-0

Zepeda, S. J. (2019). *Professional development: What works*. Routledge.

Zepke, N. (2014). Student engagement research in higher education: Questioning an academic orthodoxy. *Teaching in Higher Education*, 19(6), 697–708. DOI: 10.1080/13562517.2014.901956

Zhang, F., Peng, X., Huang, L., Liu, Y., Xu, J., He, J., Guan, C., Chang, H., & Chen, Y. (2022). A caring leadership model in nursing: A grounded theory approach. *Journal of Nursing Management*, 30(4), 981–992. DOI: 10.1111/jonm.13600 PMID: 35312131

Zhang, J. (2020). The application of human comprehensive development theory and deep learning in innovation education in higher education. *Frontiers in Psychology*, 11. Advance online publication. DOI: 10.3389/fpsyg.2020.01605

Zhang, Z., Gao, Y., & Li, Z. (2020). Consensus reaching for social network group decision making by considering leadership and bounded confidence. *Knowledge-Based Systems*, 204, 106240. DOI: 10.1016/j.knosys.2020.106240

Zhao, C. M., & Kuh, G. D. (2004). Adding value: Learning communities and student engagement. *Research in Higher Education*, 45(2), 115–138. DOI: 10.1023/B:RI-HE.0000015692.88534.de

Zhen, Y., Luo, J.-D., & Chen, H. (2023). Prediction of Academic Performance of Students in Online Live Classroom Interactions—An Analysis Using Natural Language Processing and Deep Learning Methods. *Journal of Social Computing*, 4(1), 12–29. DOI: 10.23919/JSC.2023.0007

Ziakkas, D., Sarikaya, I., & Natakusuma, H. C. (2023). EBT-CBTA in Aviation Training: The Turkish Airlines Case Study. *International Conference on Human-Computer Interaction*, 188–199. DOI: 10.1007/978-3-031-35389-5_14

Zimmer, W. K., & Matthews, S. D. (2022). A virtual coaching model of professional development to increase teachers' digital learning competencies. *Teaching and Teacher Education*, 109, 103544. DOI: 10.1016/j.tate.2021.103544

Zin, M. L. M., Ibrahim, H., Aman-Ullah, A., & Ibrahim, N. (2022). Transformational leadership, job enrichment and recognition as predictors of job satisfaction in non-profit organizations. *Nankai Business Review International*, 14(2), 338–351.

Zompetti, J.P. (2006). The role of advocacy in civil society. Volume 20, pages 167-183

About the Contributors

Debbie Devonish is an Associate Professor at the University of Technology, Jamaica. She is an executive member of the Association of Science Teachers of Jamaica (ASTJ). Her areas of research interest are science pedagogy and curriculum, research methodology, professional development for science teachers, and educational leadership. DDevonish@utech.edu.jm

Sadpha Bennett is an Assistant Chief Education Officer in the Ministry of Education and Youth, Jamaica. He is a science educator and leads the national science programme of the Ministry, with a focus on improving Science and STEM education in Jamaica. Sapha.Bennett@moey.gov.jm

Kavelle Hylton is a certified STEM Educator and Education technology entrepreneur with over thirteen (13) years of experience in STEM education and training. Ms. Hylton is also a former coordinator for the Science and Technology Education Unit at the Scientific Research Council (SRC), an agency of the Ministry of Science Energy, and Technology.

Donna Barrett is the Coordinator of the STEM endorsement at Metro RESA in Atlanta, Georgia. She previously served as the STEM Director in Fulton County Schools, Georgia, and Program Director for the Georgia Intern-Fellowships for Teachers at the Georgia Institute of Technology. donna.barrett@mresa.org

Vikash Singh is a Professor at the Department of Civil Engineering, Integral University, Lucknow, Uttar Pradesh. vikashs@iul.ac.in

Prakash Dhopte is a Professor at the Department of Mechanical Engineering, Jhulelal Institute of Technology, Maharashtra. p.dhopte@jitnagpur.edu.in

Anwar Ahmad is a Professor at the Department of Civil Engineering, Integral University, Lucknow, Uttar Pradesh. anwarahmad@iul.ac.in

Jeyalakshmi, R. is a Professor at the Department of English (S&H), R.M.K. Engineering College, Kavaraipettai, Tamil Nadu. rji.sh@rmkec.ac.in

Sudhakar, M. with a PhD is a lecturer at the Department of Mechanical Engineering, Sri Sai Ram Engineering College, Chennai, Tamil Nadu. sbmech7@gmail.com

Muhammad Usman Tariq PhD is a lecturer at the Abu Dhabi; University of Glasgow. He has more than 16+ years of experience in industry and academia. He has authored more than 200+ research articles, 100+ case studies, 50+ book chapters, and several books other than 4 patents. He has been awarded a Principal Fellowship from Advance HE UK & Chartered Fellowship of CIPD.

Urmila Yadav is a Professor at the Sharda School of Law, Sharda University, Greater Noida, Uttar Pradesh, India. urmila.yadav@sharda.ac.in

Pitchai, R. is a Professor at the Department of Computer Science and Engineering, B V Raju Institute of Technology, Telangana, India. pitchrks1984@gmail.com

Gopal, V. is a Professor at the Department of Mechanical Engineering, KCG College of Technology, Karappakkam, Tamil Nadu, India. gopal@kcgcollege.com

Senthil Kumar, is a Professor Department of Mechanical Engineering, R.M.K College of Engineering and Technology, Puduvoyal, Tamil Nadu, India krskiitm@gmail.com

Mitali Talukdar is affiliated with Amity Business School at Amity University in Kolkata, West Bengal, India

Sampath Boopathi is an accomplished individual PhD lecturer with a strong academic background in the field of engineering with 17 years of academic and research experience. Dr. Boopathi has enriched the engineering community through his teaching, research publication and mentorship roles. boopasangee@gmail.com

Bolapeju Mary Agboola (MNAEAP) is a Senior Lecturer of Educational Planning, Policy, Leadership, and Management at the University of the West Indies (UWI), Mona, and an Associate Professor at the University of Uyo, Nigeria. A Facilitator with the National Open University, Nigeria, and a Fellow of the Institute of Policy Management Development. bolaagboola11@gmail.com

Mete Sipahioglu is an Associate Professor at Samsun University, and he works as a lecturer, researcher, and Coordinator of European Mobilities. His research interests include Teacher Education, Educational Leadership and Policies, and Internationalization of Higher Education Institutions. He is a member and stakeholder advisor for WG3 at ENIS (COST Action 20115). metesipahioglu@gmail.com

Athanasios Tsarkos is from Kos Island, Greece. He currently serves in the Greek Ministry of Education, Religious Affairs, and Sports and has over 20 years of experience teaching in Greek secondary schools. Currently, his research interests focus on the development and application of servant leadership, innovative pedagogies, and the enhancement of organizational learning and wisdom in school settings.

Mandu Umoren is a PhD holder and a lecturer at the Department of Curriculum Studies, Educational Management and Planning, University of Uyo, Nigeria. Her research interests are in the areas of institutional branding, innovative education management, and creative roles of service users. manduumoren@uniuyo.edu.ng

Ahmad Najmuddin bin Azmi is a PhD candidate in the Faculty of Education at the University of Malaya, studying teacher training and education sciences. He is an administrative officer at one of the institutes of teacher education in Kuala Lumpur. He won the Best Paper award at the International Conference on Education 2021 held by the University of Malaya and the National Chung Cheng University, Taiwan. ahmadnajmuddinazmi@gmail.com

Roger Bent is an MPhil student in Educational Administration at the University of the West Indies, where he also works as a Student Services, Students Affairs, Programme Management, Education, and Media and Development Manager. roger.bent02@uwimona.edu.jm

Shinique Walters is a lecturer in the Department of Government, Faculty of Social Sciences at The University of the West Indies, Mona Campus. Her areas of interest include Community Development, Project Management, Institutional Research, Monitoring and Evaluation, and Gender Studies. Shinique is also a Research Fellow at the Centre for Leadership and Government. shiniq21@hotmail .com

Dinesh, A. is a Professor at the Department of Communication, Siva Sivani Institute of Management, Hyderabad Telangana, India. dineshthehuman@gmail.com

Shantanu Shandilya is a Professor at the Department of Languages, Vellore Institute of Technology, Vellore (shantanu.shandilya@vit.ac.in) Tamil Nadu, India. Orchid ID: 0009-0000-0110-4811

Dhara Vinod Parmar is a Professor at the Department of Design and Merchandising, Parul Institute of Design, Parul University, Waghodia, Gujarat, India dharaatmail@gmail.com; Orchid ID: 0000- 0002-4800-4807

Sundharesalingam, P. is a Professor at the Department of MBA, Kongu Engineering College, Perundurai, Erode (sundharesalingam@gmail.com) Tamil Nadu 638060, India. Orchid ID: 0000-0002-8301-7881

Somu Chinnusamy is a PhD holder at the Research and Development, RSP Science Hub, Coimbatore Tamil Nadu 637103, India. igibook3@gmail.com; https://orcid.org/0000-0002-9918-7412

Index

Milton Keynes UK
Ingram Content Group UK Ltd.
UKHW030904191024
449758UK00007B/49

9 798369 392164